Entrepreneur
MAGAZINE'S

SEVENTH EDITION

Franchise Bible

HOW TO BUY A FRANCHISE OR FRANCHISE YOUR OWN BUSINESS

Erwin J. Keup and Peter E. Keup

EP
Entrepreneur
PRESS®

Publisher: Entrepreneur Press
Cover Design: Andrew Welyczko
Production and Composition: Eliot House Productions

This publication is designed to provide accurate and authoritative information in regard to the subject matter covered. It is sold with the understanding that the publisher is not engaged in rendering legal, accounting, or other professional services. If legal advice or other expert assistance is required, the services of a competent professional person should be sought.

Library of Congress Cataloging-in-Publication Data
Keup, Peter E.
    Franchise bible: how to buy a franchise or franchise your own business/by Peter E. Keup and
        Erwin J. Keup.—7th ed.
            p.   cm.
        Rev. ed. of: Franchise bible : how to buy a franchise or franchise your own business / Erwin J.
    Keup. 6th ed.
    Includes index.
    ISBN-10: 1-59918-448-6 (alk. paper)
    ISBN-13: 978-1-59918-448-7 (alk. paper)
        1. Franchises (Retail trade)—United States. 2. Franchises (Retail trade)—United States—
    Forms. 3. Franchises (Retail trade)—Law and legislation—United States. I. Keup, Erwin J.
    Franchise bible. II. Title.
    HF5429.235.U5K478 2012
    658.8'708—dc23   2012018778

Printed in the United States of America

16 15 14 13 12   10 9 8 7 6 5 4 3 2 1

In loving memory of Erwin James Keup, who served as a counselor, mentor, and friend for those who traveled the franchise pathway to their dream businesses.

Contents

PART I

Buying a Franchise or Small Business

PART II
━━━

Franchising Your Business

PART III

Appendices

Acknowledgments

THIS SEVENTH EDITION OF *FRANCHISE BIBLE* IS THE RESULT OF 51 YEARS of business law practice and the knowledge, experience, and insight that Erwin J. Keup obtained during his lengthy and successful career. It is also the result of collaboration among my family and our friends in the franchise industry.

My dad and I started on this revised edition a few months before he passed away. Since he and I lived on different coasts, he would often ask my siblings to be scribes, note takers, and sounding boards for ideas and changes for the new edition. He and I also called upon my brother, Craig Keup, to provide legal research and ideas for the new volume. Without these strong family ties, this book would not have been possible. So, I would like to thank my mom, my seven siblings, and the rest of my large, caring family for their patience and support.

I am also thankful to Rick Grossmann and Michael Katz for their contributions to the book. Rick is a franchise developer and consultant who assists both franchisees and franchisors in building successful business enterprises. He and his group provided essential input for this edition, including drafting new chapters (5 and 12) on marketing. Michael is a franchise attorney with a wealth of legal and business experience. He provided the "ark" that is the sample franchise disclosure document and franchise agreement (Appendixes A and B) to keep readers afloat on the flood of franchise information in the book. Rick and Michael are sage franchise advisors, and should you wish to enlist their assistance in your business venture, their contact information is provided in Appendix H.

Thank you all,
—Peter Erwin Keup

In This Seventh Edition

THIS SEVENTH EDITION OF *FRANCHISE BIBLE* PROVIDES VALUABLE information and tools for those seeking to buy a franchise and for those seeking to expand their business by establishing a franchise system. Along with detailed explanations of franchise laws and regulations, the seventh edition includes:

- ▶ A new sample franchise disclosure document and new sample franchise agreement to help guide readers through the franchising process;
- ▶ Tips for marketing a franchise business with current marketing tools such as social media and websites;
- ▶ A copy of current Federal Trade Commission (FTC) franchising guidelines, including all of the content requirements for franchise disclosure documents;
- ▶ An updated directory of state and federal agencies to assist readers in obtaining state-specific franchise information;
- ▶ Checklists and questionnaires to assist potential franchisees (those seeking to buy a franchise) on how to:
  - Determine whether buying a franchise is the right decision;

– Evaluate franchise opportunities;
– Select a franchise or small business; and
– Understand the terms of franchise transactions.

▶ Checklists and questionnaires to assist potential franchisors (those seeking to expand their business by establishing a franchise system) on how to:

– Set up the infrastructure for expanding a business;
– Create a legally compliant franchise disclosure document;
– Develop a franchise agreement that will support a good franchisor-franchisee relationship; and
– Select franchisees who will build upon the business infrastructure.

Preface

BEFORE YOU ENTER INTO ANY BUSINESS VENTURE, IT IS CRITICAL TO understand your options. If you are looking to start a small business, your options include buying a franchise, buying an existing business that is not a franchise, and starting a business from scratch. If you are looking to expand your business you have options as well. For example, you can franchise your business, open additional business locations, or enter into other product distribution arrangements.

This book provides fundamental information on the option of franchising and insight into what makes a franchise operation successful. Whether you are interested in franchising your business or buying a franchise, *Franchise Bible, Seventh Edition*, will be a valuable resource for you in your research and investigation for a new business opportunity.

To begin, what is franchising? Franchising, in business language, is a method of marketing through which successful business owners (potential franchisors) expand the retail distribution of their goods or services by contracting with independent, third parties. These third parties (potential franchisees) agree to operate the retail sales or service outlets featuring the franchisor's original trademarked goods or services and implementing marketing methods at their capital costs. In exchange for this opportunity to share in the net proceeds from the sale of trademarked goods or services, the franchisees pay an initial fee and ongoing royalties to the franchisor. Franchising is not a method of generating income solely through the sale of franchises. The franchise itself is not what makes a franchisor wealthy; it is the marketability and efficient distribution of a particular product or service.

Why use franchising? Franchising can be effective and successful in a range of business sectors. The most common industries for franchising include: fast food, service, restaurants, building and construction, business services, retail, automotive, maintenance, and lodging. Further, franchising offers many unique benefits that apply across various business environments, including:

► Group advertising;

► Bulk purchasing power;

► Independent business owners at each location guided by the experience of a successful business enterprise;

► The ability to sell products and services to markets that company-owned outlets have difficulty serving because of higher operational costs and lower motivation of employees in company-owned outlets;

► The benefit of recognized and proven service marks, trademarks, proprietary information, patents, and/or designs;

► Being a part of a uniform operation, which means all franchises will share the same interior and exterior physical appearance, the same product, and the same service and product quality; and

► Central operational support in areas such as financing, accounting, employee training, and operational procedures.

Due to these and other advantages and economic conditions, franchising has become a major part of the United States economy. Collectively, there are about 735,000 franchise businesses across the nation. Further, according to the *Franchise Business Economic Outlook: 2012*, prepared by HIS Global Insight for the International Franchise Association Education Foundation ("2012 Economic Outlook"), franchises provide about 7.9 million jobs and account for about $745 billion of the U.S. economy and 3 percent of the U.S. gross domestic product (GDP).

As with most economic sectors, franchising slowed during the recent recession. In 2009, the number of franchise establishments decreased by 3.5 percent, employment in the franchise industry decreased by 2.8 percent, and franchise economic output decreased by 2.8 percent. In 2010, the number of franchise establishments and franchise employment remained relatively flat, while franchise economic output increased by 3.6 percent. 2011 showed signs of a turnaround as both the economic output and number of employees for franchises increased and, with an improving economic outlook and encouraging tax and investment incentives, the franchise sector appears poised for expansion and growth. The 2012 Economic Outlook estimates annual growth at 1.9 percent for franchise establishments, 2.1 percent for franchise employment, and 5 percent for franchise economic output. Thus, by building upon the foundation of small businesses and local ownership, franchising will likely provide an important avenue for economic stimulation, both on a personal and national level. *Franchise Bible* provides a practical guide into this important business pathway.

Franchise Bible is organized into two sections. Part I is concerned with individuals who are interested in going into business by buying a franchise or existing small business. Part II of the text addresses business owners who have started a business, made it successful, and now wish to expand through franchising. To gain a full understanding of how a franchise operation works, it is important to understand the operation from both sides. So, whether you are a successful business owner desiring to expand your market through franchising or an individual desiring to go into business for yourself, you should read both parts of this book thoroughly.

By reading this book, the business owner intending to franchise his or her business will gain insight into what a franchisee should look for when evaluating a franchise agreement and disclosure documents. Likewise, the person seeking to buy a franchise can find valuable information in this book regarding the desired methods of operation that a good franchisor should utilize. If a prospective franchisee has some idea of what constitutes a well-run franchise system, he or she can make an informed choice. By the same token, many successful franchisors started out as franchisees, developing franchises and subsequently selling them, using their knowledge in franchising new business entities in a role-reversal situation.

To help you in your quest for more information on franchising, *Franchise Bible* also features several sample franchise documents and other franchising resources. Part III contains eight appendixes, each with its own unique content. Be sure to review these appendixes and refer to them while reading Parts I and II.

The prospect of owning a franchise or franchising your business is very exciting and challenging. Let *Franchise Bible* take some of the worry out by informing you more about the laws, documents, and responsibilities of being a franchisor or franchisee.

PART I

Buying a Franchise or Small Business

CHAPTER 1

Buying a Franchise

ARE YOU CURRENTLY WORKING FOR SOMEONE BUT LONGING TO BE your own boss and to own your own business? Are you retired and looking for a way to get back into a new line of work? Are you a recent college graduate who wants to get into your own business? Whatever your situation, if you are looking for new business ownership opportunities, then the first part of *Franchise Bible*—Chapters 1 to 5—is definitely for you. This section of the book is intended for the person who wants to buy either a franchise or an existing business that is not a franchise. It is not intended to help you start a business from scratch.

When looking for new business opportunities, buying a franchise or existing business may be the way for you to go. But how do you select your own business? As a new business purchaser, you must first select a particular field of business you like and then decide whether or not that endeavor is suitable to your past experience and talents. Once you have done so, you can pursue a more established course of action.

When starting a business, you have three options. First, you can start your business from scratch, using your own name, knowledge, and background. Second, you can buy an existing business—own the business outright and operate it without any controls from a third party. Third, you can purchase a form of license to sell a product or service utilizing the name, good will, marketing techniques, and operating procedures from a franchisor.

This initial chapter is mostly concerned with purchasing a franchise, while Chapter 2, "Understanding Franchise Documents" discusses the details regarding a franchise disclosure document and franchise agreement. If you are also interested in learning about purchasing an existing business that is not a franchise, Chapter 3, "Buying a Local Business," discusses some of the activity involved there. Chapter 4, "Buying a Local Franchise Operation," deals with purchasing a franchise from a local franchisee and evaluating potential franchisors and sellers.

Once you have given adequate consideration to the advantages and disadvantages of buying outright or franchising and have carefully weighed your conclusions along these lines with your conclusions about other forms of business, you can then decide how best to invest your savings and fulfill your dream of being your own boss. According to statistics provided by the U.S. Department of Commerce, the chances of success in a franchise operation are generally recognized as greater than those of a business started from scratch or even purchasing an existing business. You must also realize, however, that the autonomy in operating a franchise is not necessarily less than in operating a business you start from scratch or a business you purchase.

In addition, any prospective business owner should remember that the risk of failure exists in purchasing any business, be it a franchise or a local business venture. One important item to keep in mind in any business purchase is the ground rules set forth in the purchase agreement. These ground rules are often a determining factor in the success or failure of any purchased entity. It is not so much that the purchase agreement must contain legal loopholes or escape clauses that allow a buyer to regain his or her compensation if the business should fail—which is often not the case when a franchise is purchased—but the terms must be workable for both parties. To be workable and successful, the terms should include that the initial and ongoing fees and obligations provide a reasonable profit to the franchisor or seller and are also affordable to the buyer.

To begin this discussion on purchasing a franchise, you first need to understand the two definitions of franchising. Franchising can be defined from two different perspectives—the business owner's perspective and the legal perspective as defined in statutes and guidelines.

Business Owner's Definition of Franchising

The business owner's definition is the most important definition to both the franchisor and franchisee, because if the franchise entity does not succeed, the legal requirements are a moot point. The business owner's definition of franchising is as follows:

Franchising is a method of market expansion utilized by a successful business entity wanting to expand its distribution of services or products through retail entities owned by independent operators using the trademarks or service marks, marketing techniques, and controls of the expanding business entity in return for the payment of fees and royalties from the retail outlet.

Essentially, the franchisee is a substitute for the franchisor's company-owned office in the retail distribution of the franchisor's services or products. The success or failure of one party to this unique relationship generally determines the success or failure of the other party. If the franchisor and franchisee keep this business relationship definition in mind, the self-centered attitudes that can sometimes arise under the legal definition can be avoided.

The Legal Definition of Franchising

The legal definition of a franchise differs among the several states that have passed franchise registration statutes and the Federal Trade Commission (FTC). California was the first state to pass a franchising law, and its definition is similar to the definition of franchise used by the other states that have franchise registration statutes. The California definition, taken from California Business and Professions Code, Section 20001, defines "franchise" as follows:

Franchise means a contract or agreement, express or implied, whether oral or written, between two or more persons by which:

- *A franchisee is granted the right to engage in the business of offering, selling, or distributing goods or services under a marketing plan or system prescribed in substantial part by a franchisor; and*

- *The operation of the franchisee's business pursuant to that plan or system as substantially associated with the franchisor's trademark, service mark, trade name, logotype, advertising, or other commercial symbol designating the franchisor or its affiliates; and*

- *The franchisee is required to pay, directly or indirectly, a franchise fee.*

The previously cited business definition of *franchise* meets the elements of the legal definition; however, the attitudes of the franchisor and franchisee in looking upon the franchise as the "marketing arm" or the "independent company-owned office substitute" of the franchisor set the franchising concept in the proper business perspective.

Thus, a potential franchisee should not purchase a franchise from any franchisor that he or she would not consider a reputable and honest business owner and a franchisor should not sell a franchise to any person he or she would not consider a top choice for a lifetime manager of a company-owned office. By the same token, a franchisor should give you the same care and support as he or she would give to his or her top managers if it were company-owned outlets.

Why Buy a Franchise?

With so many options available and all the potential pitfalls possible in buying a business or franchise, you may be wondering why you should invest your time and money in a franchise opportunity. To help you get an idea of some of the advantages you would enjoy as a franchisee, review the list below. As a franchisee, you will enjoy:

▶ Group advertising resources not typically available to small independent business owners;

▶ Bulk purchasing power;

▶ Owning your own business and making day-to-day decisions yourself, guided by the experience of a successful business enterprise;

▶ The ability to sell products and services to markets that company-owned outlets have difficulty serving because of higher operational costs and lower motivation of employees in company-owned outlets;

▶ The benefit of recognized and proven service marks, trademarks, proprietary information, patents, and/or designs;

▶ Training from successful business operators;

▶ A lower risk of failure and/or loss of investments than if you were to start your own business from scratch;

▶ Being a part of a uniform operation, which means all franchises will share the same interior and exterior physical appearance, the same product, and the same service and product quality;

▶ Operational support from the franchisor, both before and after launching your business venture, in areas such as financing, accounting, employee training, and operational procedures; and

▶ An opportunity to enhance your management abilities and for self-directed entrepreneurship within an established business scheme that you could not experience in most employment situations.

In addition, you may wonder how to ensure that you make the best decision possible. Investing in your own business takes guts and the willingness to make important decisions. As a result, you will need to carefully research the statistics regarding new business startups versus the purchase of an existing business from a non-franchisor.

Once you have done this, compare these statistics with research on franchised endeavors. What you find may be useful in helping you make a sound business decision and helping you understand why franchising may be more beneficial for you. Here are some helpful facts of franchising:

▶ The U.S. Department of Commerce, in an early edition of *Franchising in the Economy*, cited statistics showing that franchising had increased phenomenally over the years and it was a significant part of the present U.S. marketing system. Franchising offers tremendous opportunities to individuals and companies seeking wider distribution of their products and services. The U.S. Department of Commerce also pointed out that retail sales from franchise establishments accounted for over one-third of all U.S. retail sales.

▶ According to studies on the economic impact of franchises, the direct impact of franchise businesses produces over 3 percent of nonfarm private output in the United States, and when the total contribution of franchise businesses was considered (which includes the goods and services used or purchased by franchise businesses and their employees), franchise businesses accounted for approximately 9 percent of nonfarm private output in the United States.

▶ Government research over the years has indicated that the success rate for franchise-owned endeavors is significantly better than the rate for non-franchise-owned small businesses.

In short, the good news is that franchising is a significant part of the national economy and presents a statistically better chance for success than other business options. The bad news is that not every franchise is a surefire way to multiply your savings and provide you with an enjoyable occupation.

Buyer Beware

More and more buyers are seeking franchises from relatively unknown franchisors with little-known brand names and service marks. At the same time, an increasing number of people—particularly those who have not been in business before—are also interested in purchasing small businesses from independent business owners operating in a geographically limited neighborhood area. This scenario usually takes the form of older sellers who purportedly wish to dispose of their business as they reach retirement age. Since spending your savings on a business is one of the most important decisions of your life, if not the most important decision, always heed the classic advice, "Buyer beware."

In the late 1950s and 1960s, all kinds of charlatans jumped on the bandwagon and franchised nearly everything imaginable, on a global scale. A buyer didn't always know what he or she was getting into. Typical of our society, help eventually came from legislative enactments that swung the pendulum the other way, at least as far as paperwork is concerned. As a result, franchising today is a much more exacting and time-consuming process because of required procedures and restrictions. But all this activity has resulted in more protection for the franchise buyer.

Franchising and the Law

Under the franchise laws currently in effect, the FTC and all 50 states require a franchise disclosure statement, although registration states retain the right to impose stricter provisions if they so desire, including registration. In all instances, the federal and state statutes do not provide a means of deciding whether or not a franchise is of any value or even whether or not the information submitted by the franchisor is true or not. The statutes merely require the franchisor to make certain representations and reveal certain information that, if untrue, would subject the franchisor to civil and criminal lawsuits.

The bottom line is that no legislation will ever eliminate crime and no legislation will ever eliminate the naiveté of some potential business owners who are obsessed with seeing only the good parts of a transaction and none of the bad. As a prospective franchisee, you must be aware of the con artists that are hard at work trying to present the best possible image of their particular opportunity and who call their business endeavors "partnerships" or "licenses."

This does not mean, however, that all partnerships or license agreements are franchises or fraudulent schemes. Because licensing and franchising have become almost synonymous, the con artists seem to consider arrangements called "partnerships" as convenient labels for circumventing the disclosure requirements of federal and state law. These types of partnerships usually offer the use of the same business name and style, but the seller is a partner whose interest is eventually purchased by the business-seeking entrepreneur. The major drawback to this type of arrangement is that the selling partner does not have the capital and does not wish to reveal information about him or herself. This would not be the case if the seller were a franchisor. In addition, before the new business-seeking entrepreneur purchases the partnership, the business is usually subject to the control of the selling "partner."

In conclusion, beware of any offer that purportedly gives you a going business under a trade name and has you start out as a partner and end up eventually as a sole owner, along with other individuals who also purchased a partnership interest in other areas and became owners, using the same name as yours.

Are You Franchise Material?

Now that you have a better understanding of franchising and its legal background, you need to consider if you are cut out to be a franchise owner and operator. To do this, you need to take a hard look at yourself and evaluate how you would handle the responsibilities and operations of a franchise. Obviously, you want to do this before you make what could be the biggest investment of your life.

Most people have the notion that in franchising a lot of money can be made with a minimum of effort. This is a serious misconception. The franchisee who works the hardest profits the most from a franchise business. Initially at least, you must be able to make sacrifices. You must lay a strong foundation even for the most successful franchise operation. Be prepared to put in long hours of hard work and, above all, to occasionally be disappointed by your employees to a certain extent. The extent of this disappointment is directly related to how good you are at selecting and supervising people. The next consideration is how organized you are. Last, but not least, an important factor is the state of your health.

One thing is certain: If the franchisor is merely interested in your money and does not evaluate you under certain standard criteria geared to determine your potential to succeed, there is something wrong with the franchisor. However, before you even see a franchisor, evaluate yourself.

Ask yourself such questions as:

- ▶ Will your franchise be taking a considerable amount of your time away from your family? If so, how do you feel about that?
- ▶ Is your family enthusiastic about the franchise? Will you enjoy working with them if they will be employees?
- ▶ Do you enjoy working with others?
- ▶ Do you have the background or character traits necessary to succeed in owning a business?
- ▶ Do you have the necessary capital resources? Can you make the financial sacrifices?
- ▶ Are you emotionally prepared for working long, hard hours?

Don't be afraid to ask friends and acquaintances for their opinions on your abilities along these lines. Don't rely on just one opinion; get several. If you find that you are still interested in buying a franchise, evaluate your strengths and weaknesses as a potential franchisee. To help you in such an evaluation, you can use the "Checklist for Evaluating Your Suitability as a Franchisee or Small Business Buyer," in Figure 1.1. on page 10.

Conclusion

Once you have determined that you want to buy a franchise and you are prepared for the franchising challenge, you need to become more familiar with the franchise transaction and protect yourself by investigating each opportunity very carefully and thoroughly. Chapter 2, "Understanding Franchise Documents," is designed to help you in this endeavor by describing what is involved in a franchise disclosure document and a franchise agreement.

Figure 1.1 **Checklist for Evaluating Your Suitability as a Franchisee or Small Business Buyer**

Carefully consider these questions before buying your own franchise or small business.

FINANCIAL

YES   NO

❑   ❑   Have you and your spouse and knowledgeable family members discussed the idea of going into business for yourselves?

❑   ❑   Are you in complete agreement?

❑   ❑   Do you have the financial resources required to buy a franchise or small business? If not, where are you going to get the capital?

❑   ❑   Are you and your spouse ready to make the necessary sacrifices in the way of money and time in order to operate a franchise or small business?

❑   ❑   Will the possible loss of company benefits, including retirement plans, be outweighed by the potential monetary and self-pride rewards that would come from owning your own business?

❑   ❑   Have you made a thorough, written balance sheet of your assets and liabilities, as well as liquid cash resources?

❑   ❑   Will your savings provide you with a cushion for at least one year after you have paid for the franchise or small business, allowing a one-year period of time to break even?

❑   ❑   Do you have additional sources of financing, including friends or relatives who might be able to loan you money in the event that your initial financing proves inadequate?

❑   ❑   Do you realize that most new businesses, including franchises, generally do not break even for at least one year after opening?

❑   ❑   Will one of you remain employed at your current occupation while the franchise or small business is in its initial, pre-profit stage?

Figure 1.1 **Checklist for Evaluating Your Suitability as a Franchisee or Small Business Buyer, cont.**

PERSONAL

YES NO

❏ ❏ Are you and your spouse physically able to handle the emotional and physical strain caused by the long hours and tedious administrative chores involved in operating a franchise or small business?

❏ ❏ Will your family members, particularly small children, suffer from your absence for several years while you build up your business?

❏ ❏ Are you prepared to give up some independence of action in exchange for the advantages the franchise offers you?

❏ ❏ Have you really examined the type of franchise or business you desire and truthfully concluded that you would enjoy running it for several years or until retirement?

❏ ❏ Have you and your spouse had recent physicals?

❏ ❏ Is the present state of your health and that of your spouse good?

❏ ❏ Do you and your spouse enjoy working with others?

❏ ❏ Do you have the ability and experience to work smoothly and profitably with your franchisor, your employees, and your customers?

❏ ❏ Have you asked your friends and relatives for their candid opinions as to your emotional, mental, and physical suitability to running your own business?

❏ ❏ Do you have a capable, willing heir to take over the business if you become disabled?

❏ ❏ If the franchise or new business is not near your present home, do you realize that it would not be beneficial to sell your home and buy one closer until the new venture is successful?

BUSINESS

YES NO

❏ ❏ Do you and your spouse have past experience in business that will qualify you for the particular type of franchise or business you desire?

❏ ❏ Is it possible for either you or your spouse to become employed in the type of business you seek to buy before any purchase?

❏ ❏ Have you conducted independent research on the industry you are contemplating entering?

Figure 1.1 **Checklist for Evaluating Your Suitability as a Franchisee or Small Business Buyer, cont.**

❑ ❑ If you have made your choice of franchises, have you researched the background and experience of your prospective franchisor?

❑ ❑ Does the product or service you propose to sell have a market in your prospective territory at the prices you will have to charge?

❑ ❑ Will there be a market for your product or service five years from now?

❑ ❑ What competition exists in your prospective territory already?

❑ ❑ Is the competition from franchise businesses?

❑ ❑ Is the competition from non-franchise businesses?

OTHER CONSIDERATIONS

YES NO

❑ ❑ Do you know an experienced, business-oriented franchise attorney who can evaluate the franchise contract you are considering?

❑ ❑ Do you know an experienced, business-minded accountant?

❑ ❑ Have you prepared a business plan for the franchise or business of your choice?

CHAPTER 2

Understanding Franchise Documents

WHEN YOU BECOME INTERESTED ENOUGH IN A FRANCHISE opportunity to start gathering information and begin discussions with a prospective franchisor, you will need to be more familiar with two important documents—the franchise disclosure document and the franchise agreement or contract. By learning more about both of these documents and the details they require, you will be better prepared to investigate potential franchise opportunities. This chapter discusses both of these documents in detail and offers tips and strategies on what is involved with each.

The Franchise Disclosure Document

As mentioned in Chapter 1, the Federal Trade Commission (FTC) implemented a rule that required franchisors to present would-be franchisees with a disclosure statement, also known as a franchise disclosure document or FDD, which contains certain information regarding a franchise. The purpose of the FDD is to provide the prospective franchisee with enough information to make an informed decision about investing in a particular franchise.

Under FTC rules, franchisors in all 50 states are required to provide each prospective franchisee with a FDD. Further, in 14 states franchisors must register their FDDs with the state or notify the state that they will be offering franchises before entering into any franchise agreements. The FDD is also used in those states that do not have franchise registration laws. Some of these states with no franchise registration laws have what are called "business opportunity laws," which can also apply to franchise offerings. Franchise laws cover those business agreements that meet the following three conditions:

▶ The buyer pays money for the business;

▶ The buyer uses the trademark of the franchisor so the business appears to be a part of an organization; and

▶ The buyer is subject to marketing directives or controls or both, set forth by the seller/franchisor.

Business opportunity laws cover those businesses that are similar in some aspects to those covered by franchise laws, with the key exception being that business opportunities do not use a trademark as part of the deal between the buyer and the seller. To cover both types of businesses, some states have both franchise laws and business opportunity laws; you need to find out if your state is one of them.

You should have an experienced franchise attorney make sure that you and your franchisor comply with the applicable franchise or business opportunity laws. Because of the complexity, don't attempt to go it alone. For specific information on state franchise and business opportunity laws, turn to Appendix E, "State Franchise Information Guidelines."

FTC rules provide that the FDD must be provided to the prospective franchisee *14 calendar days* before a prospective franchisee may sign any binding agreement or pay any consideration for the franchise. This 14-day "cooling period" allows the franchise purchaser time to reflect on the information provided in the FDD and on the serious business decision he or she is about to make. A sample of what an FDD looks like is in Appendix A, and the FTC guidelines on FDD content are reproduced in Appendix G.

If you are looking to buy a franchise, examine the FDD very carefully, even if you have obtained information on your own regarding a particular franchisor and his or her franchise offering. After receiving the FDD, if possible, try to personally do a field investigation of all the franchises offered in the field of your choice, and compare franchisors doing business in the same area. To do a field investigation, check with current franchisees regarding the following:

▶ Ask about their experiences with their franchisor and whether the franchisor has carried out the representations made in the disclosure document and the franchise agreement;

▶ Find out whether or not the franchisor keeps his or her promises;

▶ Try to discern the attitude of the current franchisees regarding the major people in the franchisor's hierarchy of personnel;

▶ Find out whether the franchisees feel that their franchise opening costs were more than what the franchisor estimated they would be;

▶ Determine if the franchisor provided the franchisees with adequate training or left them on their own.

Remember: Competitors of a franchisor will generally be more than happy to give you all the "dirt" about that franchisor. The same is true of current franchisees. If they have a gripe against their franchisor, they will be the first to tell you in no uncertain terms. To help in gathering more detailed information when talking to franchisees, see Figure 2.1 on page 23 for a "Checklist for Interviewing Existing Franchisees."

Once you have completed your field investigation, you will be better informed when examining the FDD. The procedures discussed in the following paragraphs will help you better examine the document. Remember: If you don't get a FDD from a franchisor, there is something wrong; for example, the franchisor may have violated an act enforceable by the FTC, a state agency, or both. The FTC guidelines emphasize that FDDs are to be clear and understandable.

All required information in the FDD must be stated clearly, legibly, and concisely in a single document using "plain English." Further, the FDD must be provided in a format that "permits each prospective franchisee to store, download, print, or otherwise maintain the document for future reference."

If a FDD is not delivered on time or if it contains a false, incomplete, inaccurate, or misleading statement, the franchisor may be in violation of federal or state law and you can report this violation to the Federal Trade Commission in Washington, DC. If your state has a registration law, you can also contact the state authority that regulates franchising in your state.

The FDD's Cover Page

FTC rules require that a FDD include a cover page that, among other things, briefly identifies the business that is being franchised and summarizes important information about the franchisor and the franchise opportunity that is being offered, such as the total investment needed to begin operation of a franchise. Specifically, the cover page must have the title "FRANCHISE DISCLOSURE DOCUMENT" and include:

1. The franchisor's business and contact information, including email address and website url if applicable;
2. A sample of the primary business trademark for the franchise system;
3. A brief description of the franchise business;

4. Required statements regarding the total investment a franchisee will need to start a franchise operation, the importance of reading the disclosure document and franchise agreement carefully, FTC resources for prospective franchisees, potential applicability of state laws, and issuance date for the FDD.

While the FTC rules provide that the cover page may include additional disclosures and information, such as the availability of the FDD in different formats (e.g., PDF or other electronic format), the information listed above must be included in the FDD cover page.

Table of Contents

The second part of the FDD is a table of contents in a standard form. The table of contents must contain 23 numbered paragraph headings for each of the 23 sections that are described below, as well as a list of exhibits by letter. The exhibits include the franchise agreement, any other agreements signed by the franchisee, the franchisor's financials, and in many cases a directory of state administrators and agencies. (See the table of contents in the sample FDD in Appendix A.)

After the table of contents in the FDD, there are 23 items that must be addressed. To guide you through the items, here is what you should see in a FDD if it complies with FTC rules:

Item 1. The Franchisor, and any Parents, Predecessors, and Affiliates

An FDD will give you the franchisor's background and identify any parent company, predecessors, and affiliates. A predecessor is defined as "a person from whom the franchisor acquired directly or indirectly the major portion of its assets." (The proposed rule adds to the definition "from whom the franchisor obtained a license to use the trademark or trade secret in the franchise operation.") An affiliate is defined as "a person controlled by, controlling, or under common control with the franchisor."

Examine the section on the franchisor and its parents, predecessors, and affiliates closely. Read about the background of the business and the business experiences of its principal officers. If possible, run a credit check on the company and its previous officers. In addition, any information you can obtain regarding the record of the previous businesses—including other franchise businesses—with which the principals were associated, is of paramount importance. This information can also help you make some type of forecast about the possibility of your own success. To assist you in obtaining background information, you can use the "Checklist of Information to Secure from a Franchisor" (see Figure 2.2 on page 37) at the end of this chapter.

Item 2. Business Experience

This section of the FDD gives you some personal information, covering the past five years, on the franchisor's directors, trustees, general partners, officers, and any other individuals who will have management responsibility relating to the offered franchises. "Officer" is defined as "any individual with significant management responsibility for marketing and/or servicing of franchises, such as the chief executive and chief operating officers and the financial, franchise marketing, training, and service officers." It also includes *de facto* officers who perform such duties but whose titles do not reflect the nature of the jobs. If you can check out their backgrounds—both their business experience and the views of their former acquaintances or competitors—you will improve your chances of succeeding with your new endeavor. In addition, you should make every attempt to get to know these people as much as you can. Ask to see the head person before you put your money down. Remember, this person will be a vital part of your story of success, since his or her endeavors will directly affect you.

Check out any affiliates listed in the FDD to make sure that relatives or friends of the franchisor are not supplying all vital items or services. If the suppliers are all family and friends, this may drastically change the profitability of your franchise because they may be charging inflated, noncompetitive prices.

Item 3. Litigation

Pay particular attention to this section of the FDD. Stay away from any prospective franchisor who is under some current effective injunction or restrictive order, particularly one that could result in a drastic change in the franchise operation, such as termination of the franchise. In addition, determine whether or not the franchisor or any of the franchisor's key employees have been convicted of crimes or have a record of unfavorable determinations handed down by courts or government agencies. The FDD must disclose the litigation history of the franchisor *and* the litigation history of a parent or affiliate who guarantees the performance of the franchisor's performance.

If the FDD mentions any such investigations, convictions, or proceedings, view these as warning signs and rethink whether or not you want to purchase the franchise. If you still wish to purchase it, at least check out the proceedings as documented in the courts or government agencies and determine what has taken place in regard to this litigation.

Always remember that the franchisor's side is only one side of the story. Beware if this section reveals any lawsuits against the franchisor by former or existing franchisees. If so, call or write the court clerks where the cases are being litigated to find out the names of the attorneys representing the plaintiffs; then contact the attorneys and their clients.

If the litigation is local, secure the information by visiting the courthouse and talking with the attorney of record. Contact the plaintiffs and ask them why they are dissatisfied with the franchisor and why they are suing or have sued.

Item 4. Bankruptcy

This section must disclose any bankruptcy in the last 10 years that involved the franchisor and any parent, predecessor, affiliate, officer, or general partner of the franchisor, or any other individual who will have management responsibility relating to the sale or operation of the franchise. Carefully check over the section of the offering circular that refers to prior bankruptcies. It is not uncommon to find that franchise founders have started franchises in different business areas and failed in each of them. Each endeavor may be subject to a bankruptcy, but the founder may walk away with a million dollars that is not subject to the proceedings involving his or her corporate entity.

Many great people have incurred numerous failures in their lives before reaching a pinnacle of success. Abraham Lincoln, who failed in the operation of a general store and in his first election, is just one of many such examples. However, as a general rule, people who have failed in the past are likely to fail in the future.

Item 5. Initial Fees

Generally, you will be required to pay a certain amount of money down in order to purchase the franchise. This is commonly referred to as "the initial franchise fee" or "front money." In addition, you may be required to pay other types of money up front for certain services. This section of the FDD should contain valuable information on the range of minimum to maximum fees that the franchisor charges up front. The basis for these ranges should also be stated in this section.

Examine the basis for initial franchise fees very carefully. Use the information to project how much money you will have to spend. It is very important that you determine from this section precisely what you will receive in the way of services, inventory, and other benefits in return for your front money.

Once again, you should contact the franchisor's most valued personnel and ask them questions regarding the benefits you will receive for this front money. If there are current franchisees, contact as many of them as you can to find out if they were satisfied with the benefits they received upon paying this front money.

A franchisor should realistically consider what it would cost to open the franchise and the wealth of the typical type of franchisee who will purchase the franchise. Franchisors need to consider these factors rather than what other franchisors in the same industry charge. If the franchisor breaks even on the sale of each franchise, he or she can still succeed with reasonable royalties and profits from goods and services sold to the "captive franchisee."

Inexperienced franchisors can create franchises that are destined to fail or that will be unmarketable because they choose high figures out of the sky. Before you purchase the franchise, ask the franchisor how the initial franchise fee is determined. If the franchisor can justify the initial franchise fee charges as necessary for the franchisor to break even, and these charges are reasonable, then you can be more secure that the franchisor knows how to make a successful franchise offering. A high initial franchise fee does not necessarily mean the franchise is a better investment or even a good one. Moreover, a low initial franchise fee is not necessarily an indication of a bad investment. Some of the most successful franchise operations have had low initial franchise fees. You need to consider the business sector in which the franchise will be operating, why the fees are being charged, and what you are getting for your money.

In your research, expect to find a wide range of initial fees and royalty payments; however, there should be a uniformity of initial franchise fees within a particular industry. Be sure you are able to determine this average fee for your industry.

Item 6. Other Fees

This section of the FDD advises you in tabular form of any other fees that you will have to pay in addition to your front money, including ongoing royalties, service fees, training fees, renewal fees, advertising fees, and other similar, one-time or ongoing charges that are payable to the franchisor or its affiliates. Check to see if the franchisor will refund these fees if you decide to back out after signing the franchise agreement. Again, it is vital that you determine these amounts and project how they will affect your operations. A good accountant is a very valuable asset when purchasing a franchise.

Also remember that if you are required to pay a royalty on gross sales, this percentage will be substantially greater in terms of the impact on your net revenues. For example, 10 percent of gross sales could represent a cash payment of 50 percent or more of your net profit after expenses, depending on your overhead expense.

Item 7. Estimated Initial Investment

This section of the FDD presents, in tabular form, the franchisor's monetary estimate of what it will cost you to begin operations, including the initial franchise fee, equipment, inventory, rent, working capital, and other miscellaneous costs. These expenses include both pre-opening expenses and those incurred during the initial phase, which is at least three months or a reasonable period for the industry. The franchisor should adjust the estimates for each state where the franchise is being offered. The information outlined in this section is extremely useful when trying to estimate how much of your money will go into the initial phase of the business, and how fast.

Again, if at all possible, contact current franchisees and see if these cost projections appear fairly accurate according to their experiences with the franchisor. If there are no current franchisees available, review these listed costs with local contractors and vendors. Also remember that if these figures are materially misrepresented, it may be a violation of the law that you may wish to report at a future date.

This also would be an appropriate time for you to determine whether or not you can start your own business financially. Check out the bottom line—that is, will you have enough cash to support yourself and still meet your business obligations during the launching stages of the franchise, which could span a year or more?

Item 8. Restrictions on Sources of Products and Services

If the FDD states that franchisees must purchase or lease from designated sources, let this be a warning sign for you to investigate the franchise further. If you are tied into purchasing a particular product or leasing your business premises from the franchisor or his or her affiliates, you may be incurring expensive costs as a result of such tie-ins. Find out if these leases or purchase contracts are competitive with unaffiliated entrepreneurs, both in costs and in benefits received. FTC rules require "specifics" in explaining the legal obligations and restrictions imposed on the purchaser of a franchise. A franchisor could set fees low enough to be very attractive, then require franchisees to contract for goods and services only with the franchisor. The costs could make the franchise a very expensive venture. Therefore, if at all possible, check with current franchisees to see how they feel about any purchase restrictions and whether or not they are receiving their money's worth. Franchisors who spend an extensive amount of time selling or leasing products, equipment, and buildings will generally spread themselves so thin that the chance of the franchise succeeding is slim. In most cases, it is a full-time operation for a franchisor to license, train, promote, and operate a franchise business, without being involved in allied businesses selling equipment, inventory, and facilities to the franchisees.

However, if franchisors can lower their royalty fee by getting a portion of the profit they need from selling ingredients or services to their franchisees at a reasonable cost, then both parties benefit. You are likely to be happier paying for tangible products you use in the business than for intangible values, such as a royalty payment. See Appendix G for further details on what is to be disclosed with respect to product and service restrictions.

Item 9. Franchisee's Obligations

This section of the disclosure document includes a table listing your obligations as a franchisee, with references to the sections of your franchise agreement that contain the obligations. The purpose of the table is to identify your principal obligations under the franchise agreement and other agreements. The table should help you find more detailed information about your obligations in these agreements and in other items of the FDD.

Read over the provisions of the agreements referred to in this section very carefully, since they constitute your contractual obligations of the franchise agreement; breaching these obligagtions may be grounds for terminating your franchise. Make sure that you are capable of complying with the obligations listed here.

If the franchisor has current franchisees, contact them and get their opinions about the obligations listed in this section. Ask them if they have encountered any difficulties complying with the obligations.

Also, be sure to study the quality of the franchisor's product or service and compare it with competitors' products and services. If you find that the franchisor's product or service suffers in comparison, forget about purchasing the franchise.

Item 10. Financing

With variable interest rates, it may be necessary for you to secure financing through the franchisor or else face the prospect of being unable to purchase the franchise. If it is a requirement to finance through the franchisor, a trip to local lending institutions is in order to determine whether or not you will be securing a loan on comparable conditions. Show a copy of the financial arrangements portion of the disclosure document to your local banker and ask for the banker's opinion of such terms and conditions. Again, a credit check on the franchisor would be ideal. If possible, contact current franchisees to see what you can find out from them about their experiences with financing from the franchisor. Common sense is a requirement for all potential franchisees when investing hard-earned money in a franchise.

Item 11. Franchisor's Assistance, Advertising, Computer Systems, and Training

You are not only initially paying for the right to use a trademark or service mark; you are probably also paying both a cash advance and a percentage of your future profits for other benefits to be provided to you by the franchisor. Determine whether or not you are getting your money's worth. When reviewing this part of the FDD, ask yourself:

▶ Does the franchisor state that he or she will furnish a standard plan of specifications vital to the operation of the business or could you come up with specifications of your own if you started your own business?

▶ Does the franchisor provide you with starting inventory and training? If he or she provides training, how, when, and where does the training occur?

▶ Is a training manual provided? How detailed is the manual?

▶ What ongoing support does the franchisor provide you once the franchise is operating?

Make a list of the support items you believe the franchisor needs to provide for you to succeed in the business the franchisor is selling. The would-be franchisor should reverse this thinking and list the items of support that are necessary in order to ensure you have every possibility of succeeding. Once the list is completed, it should be included as obligations in the franchise agreement. Determine from research in the business reference section of the public library and/or internet resources just what training and experience you would need in order to successfully pursue this concern on your own. Answer the following questions:

▶ Does the franchisor offer these types of services?

▶ Does the franchisor offer them on a continuing basis?

▶ Is the franchisor obligated to offer these benefits in the FDD and the franchise agreement?

▶ Does the franchisor merely offer them, even though he or she is not obligated to do so? (Remember: obligations can be enforced in court, while nonobligatory statements cannot.)

▶ Do the services offered fulfill the franchisee's needs?

Once again, contacting current franchisees or potential franchisees of a competitor/franchisor can give you a good idea of what to look for in the way of training and advice from a franchisor. Always remember: Every franchisee went through the same things that you are going through. A telephone call to a franchisee of the franchise operation you are interested in, or to a competitor's franchisee, might give you an opportunity to meet the owner and discuss matters. Perhaps an offer of lunch would help ensure his or her cooperation.

Item 12. Territory

Exclusive areas are extremely important to the franchisee, so you need to carefully review this section of the circular. "Exclusive area" generally means that you will not have any competition in a specified area, at least as far as location of another franchise is concerned. The FTC rules require that the franchisor provide detailed information regarding exclusive territories and the conditions upon which the territories are granted. Before purchasing a franchise, you should understand your territory, whether it will be exclusive or non-exclusive, the territorial restrictions for you and other franchisees, and what competition you may face, from other franchisees and other businesses, in your territory.

It is important to be aware that exclusive areas may not always be granted by the franchisor. Exclusive areas can cause problems for the franchisor. For instance, it could be a possible antitrust violation for the franchisor if competition is unduly impeded, or territorial restrictions could result in costly litigation if territory provisions have to be enforced by the franchisor.

In addition, the franchise system itself is concerned, because it realizes each franchisee must pursue his or her business efforts to the maximum. Therefore, if one franchisee fails to develop his or her area, it behooves the system to place another franchisee in competition in that area; this ensures that the particular franchise potential is fully achieved.

Most franchisors fear that a franchisee will not develop his or her territory, which is one reason why many franchisors will not grant exclusive areas. As an alternative, some franchise agreements provide that the initial franchisee must meet current minimums or lose the franchise or share the territory with another franchisee. Make sure that territories have specific formulas for determining the size of the territory, in order to have an adequate customer base to provide a reasonable profit to a franchisee in each territory. Also be sure to research the impact on your sales with such a condition.

It is very unlikely that a franchisor will deliberately try to destroy an area by selling two franchises in a territory that would provide a suitable profit for only one. In many cases, you will find that you do not have an exclusive area. If not, find out whether or not the franchisor will offer you a right of first refusal so you can purchase any additional franchises that may be offered in the future adjacent to your specified territory or location. This way, you can expand in a given area without fear that someone else is operating in your territory, reaping a part of your profits. One benefit for you, as a prospective franchisee, is a condition set forth by the franchisor that he or she will not open a company-owned office or another franchise in your territory under the same, similar, or different trademark. Some franchisors, however, may retain the right to sell a franchised trademark product or similar product in your territory through supermarkets or other retail outlets. This might hurt your sales.

You should give careful consideration to termination or loss-of-area-exclusivity clauses imposed by the franchisor for failing to meet a minimum sales volume. Your franchise could be withdrawn if you do not meet these minimum sales volume quotas.

If the franchise you are considering imposes such minimum restrictions, you should examine them carefully to see if they are realistic. If possible, consult with current franchisees to see what their experience has been at meeting such minimums. In addition, if your state has a franchise investment act that requires the filing of disclosure documents as a public record, contact the state and review the early filings to determine who the initial franchisees were. Perhaps one of these initial franchisees is no longer in business.

If you can locate a former franchisee of the particular franchise operation you are interested in, you might be able to secure a substantial amount of information from an excellent source. Listen to this person's impressions of the franchisor. If there are many former franchisees, consider this a red flag as to the merits of purchasing a franchise from this particular franchisor. This section of the disclosure document can help you tell whether or not the franchisor favors company-owned offices rather than franchised offices. In many cases, the franchisor-owned offices may be a result of the reclamation of franchises that failed. A high record of failure by previous franchisees is another red flag in your search.

Item 13. Trademarks

One of the prime benefits you are paying for when you purchase a franchise is a well-known trade name, trademark, service mark, service name, or logotype. The FDD must identify each principal trademark to be licensed to the franchisee and state the franchisee's rights if the franchisee is required to modify or discontinue use of a mark under any circumstances.

Preferably, you want to be a licensee of a trademark or service mark that is registered in the Principal Register of the U.S. Patent Office. A registered trademark or service mark of this nature gives the franchisor certain legal presumptions as to ownership and the right to use these marks throughout the United States, which can be very valuable to your franchise. Check with the U.S. Patent and Trademark Office in Washington, DC, and find out if a certificate of registration has actually been granted to the franchisor. A trademark registered in the Supplemental Register does not have these presumptive legal rights. A statement to this effect must be in Item 13 of the disclosure document.

Another consideration is the length of time that the franchisor has held such certificate of registration. An indication that the mark has been applied for but is still pending does not mean that the franchisor has or will attain the registered right to a particular name. Furthermore, the initials "TM" after the trademarks merely indicate that the franchisor uses a particular name as a trademark, not that he or she has a U.S. registration certificate. The key to utilizing a trademark or service mark is to federally register it so you can use the trademark or service mark and advertise it with the symbol ® indicating it is a U.S. registered mark. Registration of a trademark is only one element to consider. Here are some other questions to address:

▶ Are the trademarks and trade names well known in the market area in which you intend to operate?

▶ Are they well known throughout the United States?

▶ Is the trademark or service mark so identified with the franchisor that it will attract customers to the franchise operations?

▶ Do you have full use of every trademark or service mark registered to the franchisor?

Consider, as well, whether or not the franchisor is obligated to protect the trademark and pursue those who violate it. It behooves not only the franchisor but also his or her entire franchise system to extensively police the use of the trademark or service mark and immediately stop infringers through litigation, no matter how expensive the litigation may be.

Item 14. Patents, Copyrights, and Proprietary Information

The section on patents and copyrights is important to you only if patents are material to the franchise. If so, obtain copies of the patents from the U.S. Patent Office and have your patent attorney review them for depth of coverage and length of time remaining on the patent. Examine if there are any possible limitations of the right of the franchisor to use the patent or any dissolution of the patent through licenses to others, particularly potential competitors. Carefully examine any claims of proprietary right and confidential information designated by the franchisor.

Item 15. Obligation to Participate in the Actual Operation of the Franchise Business

This section discloses whether the franchisee must personally participate in the operation of the franchise. If there is no such requirement, this section must state whether the franchisor recommends such participation, whether the manager must complete the franchisor's training program and/or own an equity interest in the franchisee entity, and any limitations that the franchise must place on its manager.

In the opinion of many franchise professionals, the successful franchisee is the one who manages his or her own business or at least spends considerable time supervising the management of the business. The smart franchisor, in many cases, will insist that the franchisee be active in the operation of the business or at least retain qualified managers who will be active. In general, the franchisor must approve these managers. Franchisees can be obligated to train managers, preferably at their own expense. But usually, franchisors will obligate themselves to train a manager at the franchisee's expense. Be sure you can determine the frequency of the training sessions.

Item 16. Restrictions on What the Franchisee May Sell

If you wish to conduct a more extensive business while operating the franchise, this section of the disclosure document will be important for you to review. It is also important if you are limited to selling services or products that alone would not give you the required return on your capital. Again, ask either current franchisees of the franchisor or current franchisees of a competing franchise or other franchisor about their experiences.

There have been instances when franchisees were limited to one service only. In one case, for example, a franchisee who was limited to offering only a tune-up service for automobiles believed that it would be more profitable if allied services, such as oil changes, were also permitted. The question to ask yourself is whether or not such restrictions on your product sales will permit you to make a reasonable profit.

Item 17. Renewal, Termination, Transfer, and Dispute Resolution

This particular section of the FDD, which is in tabular form, is of major importance to your future success, since it dictates the length of time for which you will receive a return on your investment. For many, the best franchises are those that will exist in the name of the franchisees and their heirs or their purchasers for as long as the franchisees, their heirs, successors, or purchasers perform the contracted duties as specified in the agreement. In other words, the ideal franchise agreement allows the franchisee and anyone who purchases the franchise to automatically renew the franchise agreement as long as the agreement has not been breached. A franchise agreement requiring you to spend 10 years of your time, money, and effort only to lose the franchise at the end of 10 years is not a good one.

Under FTC rules, the franchisor must explain just what "renewal" means for the system and, if applicable, a statement that the franchisee may be asked to sign a different contract with materially different terms and conditions. Watch out for clauses that require you to make substantial repairs and/or decorations as a contingency to a renewal. Such clauses should be reasonable and have some formula so that all of the expenses do not have to be incurred in one year. The clauses should set some type of standard so any changes in decor and refurbishing are related to staying competitive within the industry.

An ideal franchise is one you can pass on to your heirs or sell to others subject to the approval of the franchisor and possibly at a reasonable transfer fee. If a franchisor does not allow such transfers or renewals and you still wish to purchase the franchise, consider what provisions, if any, you can make for the franchisor to purchase the franchise back and the amount of consideration for such a deal.

If your state has franchise laws regulating franchise renewals and terminations, consult your attorney to see if the FDD's renewal and termination clauses comply with them. See Appendix E for more information on individual state franchise laws.

A good franchise package should definitely allow you to change legal forms of business organization—for example, from a sole proprietorship to a partnership or from a sole proprietorship or partnership to a corporation—at no extra fee or a minimum fee. Scrutinize very carefully the reasons a franchisor gives for causes of termination when examining this portion of the disclosure document.

Section 17 also reveals whether or not the franchise business can be offered for sale. If the franchisor has the right of first refusal, that right should not be at the franchisor's discretion when the business is being sold to a blood relative. The more rights you receive regarding the continuation of the franchise, as well as its transfer and sale, the better the franchise package you are getting from both practical and legal standpoints.

If the franchise agreement limits your choice of forum to arbitration rather than a court of law or your choice of the law to be applied is an out-of-state jurisdiction, consult an attorney regarding how that affects your rights. The cover page of the FDD should also alert you to these restrictions as possible risks.

Item 18. Public Figures

This section requires the franchisor to disclose whether it uses a famous person to endorse the franchise. If so, it must disclose the compensation paid or promised to the person, the person's involvement in management or control of the franchisor, and the amount of the person's investment in the franchisor. If the franchisor is paying a public figure to endorse the franchise, find out whether or not you can use the person in personal appearances or in advertising without prior written approval of the franchisor, how frequently you can do so, and the cost of such use, if any.

Item 19. Financial Performance Representations

In most cases, the franchisor will not provide actual, average, projected, or forecasted financial sales profits or earnings because of federal and state laws requiring written substantiation of such projections. In addition, there are so many variables involved that it is very difficult to forecast projected earnings in a particular area, especially with a franchise operation that is relatively new. However, if the franchisor does provide such information, you should show it to your accountant for evaluation. This information should also be evaluated against any information that may be supplied by competitive franchisors.

Once again, contacting current franchisees of the franchisor could provide you with considerable information as to the veracity of any projections. Even a franchisee of a competitor could give you some insight into the reliability of such projections. If it is not possible for you to contact a franchisee of either the franchisor or a competitor, a suitable alternative would be to contact someone who is not a franchisee but operates a similar business in the same geographical area. This applies to your efforts to ferret out any of the information described above. There is nothing like relying on experience when deciding whether or not to buy a business.

When the franchisor does not make any financial performance representations, the FDD will include a statement to that effect. It will also state that no employee or representative is authorized by the franchisor to make such representations.

However, the franchisor may provide actual records of an existing outlet, assuming this is the case, as this information is actual historical data and not a representation of potential performance for a new outlet. The FDD will also provide information on who to contact if you receive any other financial performance information or projections of your future income.

Item 20. Outlets and Franchise Information

This section of the disclosure document provides, in tabular form, information regarding existing outlets in the franchise system. It covers outlet transfers—and the status of franchised and company-owned outlets—for the last three fiscal years, as well as projected openings for the next fiscal year. It must also provide information regarding any reporting changes, any confidentiality clauses signed by franchisees during the last three fiscal years ("gag clauses"), and information about certain trademark franchisee associations.

In addition to accessing information about existing outlets, you can also determine whether or not a substantial number of failures have occurred within the franchised operation you are investigating. You can also project just how large the system probably will be in a few years, according to the estimates of the franchisor.

Generally, the more franchisees, the greater the franchisor's chances for success in future sales of franchises; however, don't take this at face value. Check with the franchisees themselves. It is also a general rule that the more franchisees, the more you will pay for a franchise. This is particularly true in situations where the franchisor does not have many company-owned offices. Theoretically, a higher number of franchisees indicates a more extensive distribution of the product and a better public image for the franchise.

Item 21. Financial Statements

The FDD will contain an exhibit with audited financial statements. Take the financial statements to your accountant if you do not have the training to properly evaluate them. Remember: The financial condition of the franchisor not only will affect his or her ability to run a financially successful operation in the future, but it will also determine whether or not he or she will go under, leaving you holding the bag. Most good franchisors have their own successful "pilot plant" company-owned offices, which are the basis of their franchise systems.

Most franchisors use a separate corporate entity for selling their franchises. However, if your particular franchisor doesn't, you then have an opportunity to find out whether or not these company-owned ventures actually made any income for a period of up to three years. If the franchisor can't make a go of the business, how do you expect to do so?

Financial statements are the financial track record of the franchisor. Examine, analyze, and digest this material. Feel free to ask questions of the main representatives of the franchisor concerning these financial statements. In fact, it is a good idea to take your accountant along to such meetings. Retain the services of an experienced accountant and an experienced attorney; both should be familiar with the day-to-day business operations of a franchise and specialize in franchise arrangements.

The franchisor is also required in section 21 to provide a separate, audited financial statement for a company controlling 80 percent or more of the franchisor. An affiliate's audited financial statement may be used in lieu of the franchisor's financial statement if the affiliate guarantees performance.

Item 22: Contracts

This section requires the franchisor to attach to the FDD a copy of all form contracts the franchisees will sign, including the franchise agreement, leases, options, and purchase agreements.

Item 23: Receipt

In this final section, the franchisor is required to include as the last page of the FDD a form for the prospective franchisee to sign to acknowledge receipt of the FDD.

Aligning Statements in the Disclosure Document with the Franchise Agreements

Attached to the FDD, as required in Item 22, you will find a copy of the current franchise agreement or contract and possibly other ancillary agreements issued by your franchisor. Carefully examine these agreements and compare them with the statements that are made in the FDD. Make sure that the statements coincide and there is nothing missing from the agreement or contract and nothing additional that is not in the FDD as previously discussed. See Appendix B for a sample franchise agreement. The rest of this chapter discusses those areas of the agreement you should be aware of, in addition to those that have been discussed in this section.

The Franchise Agreement

In the trade, the franchise agreement or contract is sometimes referred to as "money in the bank" because a good agreement that protects the best interests of the franchisee and franchisor will be a major factor in ensuring future revenues from the franchise business for both parties. Every franchise agreement provides certain basic provisions and conditions. They may be numbered differently, be placed in different locations—or even have different subtitles–but they are basically the same in nature. This section discusses some additional provisions to look for in the agreement and some suggestions of how to handle them.

Generally, franchisors will not agree to negotiate any terms of their agreement, particularly those terms that are material to them. Before the passage of state franchise registration laws, this was not the case. Today, any substantial changes in the agreement require a change in the FDD, so many franchisors may be reluctant to make material changes, particularly if they must first obtain approval from a state franchise regulator. However, there is no harm in asking.

The rules differ from state to state. For instance:

► California allows a restricted type of negotiation. The franchisor must provide a notice of negotiated sales with the California Commissioner of Corporations within 15 business days after the sale and must amend his or her registered FDD in order to disclose the terms of the particular item negotiated before making another sale. The latter disclosure must be made if the negotiated sale occurred within 12 months of the offering being made.

► Illinois allows a one-time-only negotiation without a formal amendment.

► Indiana requires a temporary amendment for negotiating franchises only.

► North Dakota and South Dakota seem to favor negotiated franchise agreements and appear not to require an after-amendment referring to the negotiations. This should be checked out periodically with the state authorities.

► Virginia requires the franchisor to negotiate.

► Minnesota requires an amendment prior to selling the franchise.

► New York doesn't permit negotiation prior to filing.

However, these regulations and rules change as often as the weather, so a franchisor should check with the particular state authority before beginning any negotiations, each time the occasion arises.

Use of Trademarks

As previously indicated, one of the prime benefits you receive when you purchase a franchise is the use of a well-known and registered trademark or service mark. Examine the portion of the agreement that is titled "License" or "Trademark" and make sure you are getting your money's worth. Consider the following:

▶ Is the trademark well known?

▶ Has it been in use for a substantial amount of time?

▶ Does the franchisor have an unrestricted right to use and license such trademark or service mark?

▶ Are there other trademarks, service marks, or logos you are entitled to use?

▶ Will the franchisor enforce the trademark registration to the exclusion of infringers?

Location of the Franchise

Another factor influencing the success of almost any business is location. Franchising is no exception. You will need to ask yourself these questions when reviewing this section of a franchise agreement:

▶ Do you have an exclusive right to operate a facility within a franchised area? If not, do you have the right of first refusal to open other locations within the area?

▶ Is the franchisor required to advise you on site selection? If not, are you qualified to select your own site?

▶ Will the franchisor assist you by providing information and statistics concerning a suitable location?

▶ How close is the nearest franchise outlet (whether owned by a franchisee or the franchisor) to the site proposed for you?

▶ How close are your competitors?

▶ If you are unable to renew your lease at its expiration, will the franchisor make every reasonable effort to relocate you in another premise in the same location?

▶ Who will pay for relocation, the franchisor or you?

Term of the Franchise

Regarding the term of your potential franchise, consider these questions:

- Do you have the franchise as long as you live?
- Is your franchise subject to an option to purchase by the franchisor before it expires? If it is, are you to be paid an amount equal to market value or a certain multiple of earnings or must you take a lower book value?
- If the franchise is for a stated term, do you have a right to renew? If you have a right to renew, is there a renewal fee? What is the renewal fee? Is it reasonable?

Front Money and Royalties

The answers to the following questions are very pertinent to your decision whether to invest in the franchise offered for sale. Some of these concerns are touched upon in other sections of this book as well.

- Is there any front money (initial fee) that you must pay? If so, can you afford the front money?
- What do you receive in the way of services, inventory, and other fringes for the front money?
- When is the front money payable? Will the franchisor finance the front money? Have you calculated your debt service obligations on the total amount borrowed in your projected pro forma financial statements?
- Do you have to pay a royalty? If so, is it based on net income or gross sales? If based on gross sales, what is the effective percentage on your net income before taxes? After taxes? How often do you have to pay the royalty?
- What records of your earnings must you submit to the franchisor?
- Are the amounts of the front money and the royalty consistent with the working capital that you have available?
- What type of investment would you have to provide if you started your own business in competition with the existing franchisees of the franchisor?

Leases

The portion of the franchise agreement that pertains to leases is another important area to review. Here are some sample questions you may want to ask yourself:

- Are you required to lease the location from the franchisor? If so, is the lease reasonable in its term and the monthly payment to the franchisor? Have you checked with landlords in the area to determine if the rent is reasonable, comparable with what they would charge?
- Is this a "net lease"? That is, do you have to pay—in addition to rent—utilities, parking lot improvement costs, and wage increases based on the standard-of-

living clause, and increases in property taxes? If so, have you checked out the actual or probable amount of these additional costs?

▶ Must you lease fixtures, signs, or equipment from the franchisor? If so, are the prices reasonable? Have you compared costs of fixtures, signs, and equipment offered by suppliers other than the franchisor?

▶ Are you required to buy a certain amount of inventory? Is the cost of the inventory comparable with the cost of an inventory purchased from a third party?

▶ Are you required to follow certain customs and standards? Are these customs and standards consistent with the good management of the business and the quality of the products?

Obligations and Duties of the Franchisor

Ask yourself the following questions regarding the franchisor's responsibilities to you:

▶ Will you receive adequate training from the franchisor? If so, when, where, and for how long?

▶ Do you have to pay for such training? Is such training offered at a convenient location not requiring extensive travel expenses?

▶ Are you entitled to continuous training throughout the term of your franchise?

▶ Will you be provided with an operations manual? (See Chapter 11, "Preparing the Operations Manual.")

▶ Will the franchisor give you some idea of the extent of the manual's coverage before you sign the contract?

▶ Will the franchisor provide you with advertising at his or her expense? If not, must you submit any advertising copy to the franchisor to approve in advance?

▶ Are you required to pay an additional fee for advertising? If so, is the franchisor bound to place such an advertising fee in a special account in your name and utilize it for local advertising?

▶ What are the franchisor's obligations to you after you are in operation? Are they worth the royalty you will be paying?

Obligations and Duties of the Franchisee

Be sure to ask about your responsibilities as a franchisee.

▶ Are your obligations and duties under the contract reasonable?
▶ Do other franchisees have the same obligations and duties?
▶ Are the obligations necessary to help ensure service or product uniformity and quality?

- ▶ Are you required to participate in the franchisor's training?
- ▶ Are other franchisees required to participate in initial and ongoing training by the franchisor?
- ▶ Are you obligated to actively participate in the franchise? If not, are you obligated to have a manager approved by the franchisor?
- ▶ Is there any provision regarding the days that your franchise must be kept open?
- ▶ Are there provisions that help ensure that all franchised entities will be clean and kept in an attractive manner?
- ▶ Are you subjected to revisions in the contract at various times or when you transfer the contract by sale to others?
- ▶ Are you required to keep adequate records and books?
- ▶ What records must you submit to the franchisor and how often?
- ▶ What are the penalties for not submitting such records?

Transfer of Agreement and Termination

Regarding the transfer of the franchise agreement or termination of the franchise, consider the following questions:

- ▶ Can you transfer the license to your heirs or to a corporation formed by you for that purpose? If so, must you pay a fee? Is such a fee reasonable?
- ▶ If you die and you are operating as a sole proprietorship or a partnership, will your personal representative be able to carry on the business?
- ▶ Are you required to give a right of first refusal to the franchisor? If the franchisor has a right of first refusal, is the formula for payment of your interest adequate? Will it include a price for goodwill?
- ▶ If the franchisor has a right of first refusal, is the purchase price payable in a lump sum rather than spread out in installments?
- ▶ When can the franchisor terminate the franchise? Can this be done only with good cause? If so, are the causes listed in the franchise agreement reasonable?
- ▶ If the franchisor can terminate for breach of contract, has he or she specified which terms of the agreement are considered material terms, the breach of which will automatically constitute termination?
- ▶ What are your rights upon termination? What are the penalties? Can you terminate this venture without cause prior to its term without any liability? Can you compete after termination?
- ▶ Are there applicable laws regulating the termination of franchises or distributorships in your state?

Arbitration and Court Jurisdiction

Review the agreement to see if there is a provision relating to the arbitration of disputes. Generally, arbitration is much less costly and certainly quicker than court. It is also ideal if the arbitration can be held in the state where you are located. The downside to arbitration is that it normally does not allow for discovery procedure and is binding and final.

You would benefit greatly from the insertion of a paragraph stating that the laws of the state in which the franchise is operated prevail. Usually, the franchisor will attempt to have controlling law in the state where he or she is located, thus causing you a great deal of hardship and expense if legal action takes place away from your franchise area.

Attorney Fees

In addition, review the agreement to see if there is a clause providing that, in the event of litigation of a dispute under the franchise agreement, the winning party shall be entitled to an award for his or her attorney fees. This clause often encourages both parties to litigate, each feeling he or she will be victorious and reimbursed for his or her fees by the loser. However, each party is obligated to pay his or her respective attorney fees as litigation progresses. At the conclusion of the trial, the judge can award whatever he or she deems as reasonable attorney fees, no matter the amount of the actual bill, and the losing party may well be bankrupt at the time of the final award.

Searching for a Franchise

To help you get more information on franchises in general, you can use the resources and publications in Appendix H.

You will also find that most franchise offerings are advertised in either the business opportunity section of *The Wall Street Journal* on Thursdays or the Sunday classified section of your local newspaper. When you answer such ads, the franchisor will probably respond by sending you a brochure and a franchisee business application and net worth form (refer to Figure 13.1 on page 128 for a sample of this form). Once the franchisor determines that you have the financial wherewithal, the FDD will be sent and franchise salespersons will come knocking.

Another way of discovering franchise opportunities is to attend franchise trade shows. Some of the best franchise trade shows are those sponsored by the International Franchise Association (IFA). See Appendix H for IFA information. IFA trade shows take place in major U.S. cities every year.

Conclusion

With the help of some of the resources listed above and your own investigation and research, you will have a good start on prospecting for and purchasing a franchise. To help you investigate and research, review the "Checklist of Information to Secure from a Franchisor" in Figure 2.2. If you are evaluating more than one franchise, make enough copies of this checklist so you can use a form for each franchise offering.

Figure 2.1 **Checklist for Interviewing Existing Franchisees**

Use this questionnaire when trying to investigate franchise opportunities by interviewing existing franchisees.

FINANCIAL

YES NO

❏ ❏ Are you satisfied with the franchisor?

❏ ❏ Is your franchise profitable?

❏ ❏ Have you made the profit you expected to make?

❏ ❏ Are your actual costs those stated in the FDD?

❏ ❏ Is the product or service you sell of good quality?

❏ ❏ Is delivery of goods from the franchisor adequate?

❏ ❏ How long did it take you to break even?

❏ ❏ Was the training provided to you by the franchisor adequate?

❏ ❏ What is your assessment of the training provided?

❏ ❏ Is your franchisor fair and easy to work with?

❏ ❏ Does your franchisor listen to your concerns?

❏ ❏ Have you had any disputes with your franchisor? If so, please specify.

❏ ❏ If you have had disputes, were you able to settle them?

❏ ❏ How was settlement accomplished?

❏ ❏ Do you know of any trouble the franchisor has had with other franchisees? If so, what was the nature of the problem?

❏ ❏ Do you know of any trouble the franchisor has had with the government?

❏ ❏ Do you know of any trouble the franchisor has had with local authorities?

❏ ❏ Do you know of any trouble the franchisor has had with competitors?

❏ ❏ Are you satisfied with the marketing and promotional assistance the franchisor has provided?

❏ ❏ Have the operations manuals provided by the franchisor helped you?

❏ ❏ What do you think of the manuals?

❏ ❏ Are the manuals changed frequently? If so, why?

❏ ❏ Other comments you would like to make.

Figure 2.2 **Checklist of Information to Secure from a Franchisor**

Use this checklist when doing your own investigation and information gathering.

YES   NO

❏   ❏   Is the franchisor a one-person company? or

❏   ❏   Is the franchisor a corporation with an experienced management that is well trained?

❏   ❏   Is the franchisor offering you an exclusive territory for the length of the franchise? or

❏   ❏   Can the franchisor sell a second or third franchise in your market area?

❏   ❏   Do you have the right of first refusal to adjacent areas?

❏   ❏   Will the franchisor sublet space to you? or

❏   ❏   Will he or she assist you in finding a location for your franchise operation?

❏   ❏   Does the franchisor provide financing? If so, what are the terms?

❏   ❏   Does the franchisor require any fees—other than those described in the FDD—from the franchisee? If so, what are they?

❏   ❏   Has the franchisor given you information regarding actual, average, or forecasted sales?

❏   ❏   Has the franchisor given you information regarding actual, average, or forecasted profits?

❏   ❏   Has the franchisor given you information regarding actual, average, or forecasted earnings?

❏   ❏   Will the franchisor provide you with the success rates of existing franchisees?

❏   ❏   Will the franchisor provide you with their names and locations?

❏   ❏   Are there any restrictions on what items you may sell? If so, what are they?

❏   ❏   Does your prospective franchisor allow variances in the contracts of some of his or her other franchisees? What is the nature of the variances?

❏   ❏   In the event you sell your franchise back to your franchisor under the right of first refusal, will you be compensated for the goodwill you have built into the business?

❏   ❏   Does the franchisor have any federally registered trademarks, service marks, trade names, logotypes, and/or symbols?

❏   ❏   Are you, as a franchisee, entitled to use them without reservation? or

❏   ❏   Are there restrictions, exceptions, or conditions? If so, what are they?

❏   ❏   Does the franchisor have existing patents and copyrights on equipment you will use or items you will sell?

❏   ❏   Does the franchisor have endorsement agreements with any public figures for advertising purposes? If so, what are the terms?

Figure 2.2. **Checklist of Information to Secure from a Franchisor, cont.**

❑　❑　Has the franchisor investigated you carefully enough to assure himself or herself that you can successfully operate the franchise at a profit both to him or her and to you?

❑　❑　Has the franchisor complied with FTC guidelines and state disclosure laws?

❑　❑　Does the franchisor have a reputation for honesty and fair dealing among the local firms holding his or her franchise?

OTHER QUESTIONS

- How many years has the firm offering you a franchise been in operation?
- Describe the franchise area offered to you.
- What is the total investment the franchisor requires from the franchisee?
- How does the franchisor use the initial franchise fees?
- What is the extent of the training the franchisor will provide for you?
- What are your obligations for purchasing or leasing goods or services from the franchisor or other designated sources?
- What are your obligations in relation to purchasing or leasing goods or services in accordance with the franchisor's specifications?
- What are the terms of your agreement regarding termination, modification, and renewal conditions of the franchise agreement?
- Under what circumstances can you terminate the franchise agreement?
- If you decide to cancel the franchise agreement, what will it cost you?
- What are the background experience and achievement records of key personnel (their "track records")?
- How successful is the franchise operation? (Use reports or magazine articles to supplement information the franchisor gives you.)
- What is the franchisor's experience in relation to past litigation or prior bankruptcies?
- What is the quality of the financial statements the franchisor provides you?
- Exactly what can the franchisor do for you that you cannot do for yourself?

CHAPTER 3

Buying a Local Business

I F YOU ARE CONSIDERING PURCHASING A LOCAL BUSINESS RATHER than a franchise, you will find the factors you need to consider are similar to those for purchasing a franchise; however, you will also find some dissimilarity. For instance, the local business owner is not going to supply you with a disclosure document or prospectus detailing his or her background and that of the business you are buying. Consequently, you will have to secure this information yourself. To do this, you can have a qualified attorney prepare an agreement that would, in essence, make the seller warrant and represent certain necessary facets of the business which, if untrue, would allow you to bring an action for fraud or rescission or both. Thus, many of the provisions discussed in Chapter 2 can be incorporated into these warranties and representations.

This chapter focuses on some of the factors you need to consider when purchasing a local business. Review each discussion carefully to get a better idea of what types of actions and responsibilities you will have as a prospective business purchaser.

Purchase Agreements

Many people are under the impression that escrow instructions are the only contracts they need when purchasing a business. This is not true. The escrow agreement is merely an instructional type of agreement wherein both parties advise the escrow agent of what he or she must do to complete the closing, such as which payments are in order and which documents must be received and exchanged. This is not a true sales agreement.

A true sales agreement should require the seller to put in writing and warrant every essential part of the business that will make it a success or failure. This includes warranting that the financials are true and correct, that there are no hidden income tax claims or litigation, that the business has made a certain amount of money and will continue to make a certain amount of money (if that information can be obtained from the seller), and that there are no pending lawsuits. There will be many other details you will want to know about as well, but unless you put them in writing and have them warranted by the seller, they will get lost in the shuffle.

Exhibits of purchase agreements should include:

▶ Financial statements;
▶ The type of note that you will sign;
▶ A list of creditors and accounts receivable;
▶ A list of claims and pending litigation; and
▶ A complete list of the outstanding contracts, inventory, fixtures, and equipment you are purchasing, together with their value and the basis of evaluation. (Valuable contracts should be examined to determine if you can assume them.)

The passage of the Clinton Deficit Reduction Act created certain opposing tax advantages between the seller and the buyer of a business on how the purchase price of a business is allocated to various assets being acquired. This tax legislation, which was passed in August 1993, simplified the allocation process by creating a broad new category of amortizable assets, called Section 197 Intangibles. Consequently, intangible assets purchased after August 1993 may now be amortized over a 15-year period by the purchaser. Intangibles include covenants not to compete, know-how, customer lists, goodwill, and going concern value. For the first time ever, a buyer can amortize goodwill and going concern value as Section 197 Intangibles over a 15-year period. See your accountant before signing a purchase agreement that attempts to allocate the purchase price.

Review Financial Statements

The name of the game in any business is the bottom line—profit. The seller should provide you with updated financial statements and warrant and represent that they are true, accurate, and the basis for your purchase. Don't be afraid to run a credit check on your seller or ask his or her creditors and competitors what they know.

Audited financial statements, including a balance sheet and a profit-and-loss statement, are extremely desirable. Unaudited statements prepared by a CPA or an accountant are less desirable and unaudited statements prepared by the seller are much less desirable. In many cases, the seller will contend that an audit would be too expensive. If this is the case, you may want to offer sharing the audit's expense.

You should have all statements reviewed by a qualified, experienced, business accountant. It cannot be emphasized too forcefully that an experienced CPA familiar with business acquisitions should examine not only the current financial statements of the seller, but any projections or forecasts he or she has made. It would be a good idea to attempt to get the seller to set forth in writing his or her sales and earnings projections.

If the financials are not audited, the purchase agreement should contain a clause in which the seller warrants that such financials are true and correct. Any such warranty should indicate that it will survive the closing of the purchase and sale. Having this warranty could certainly save you from disaster and prevent you from buying "a pig in a poke." Sometimes, the best investment is the investment that is not made.

Beware the seller who refuses to give you a financial statement, audited or not.

Bulk Sales Laws

When a business sells all or substantially all of its assets or enters into a major transaction that is not part of its ordinary business activities, the bulk sales law applies. While many states have repealed this law, some states still have a bulk sales law, so you need to find out if yours is one of them.

The bulk sales law is of particular importance to you, because if you purchase a business, this law requires you to perform certain duties to ensure that the seller's creditors' rights are protected.

To comply with this law, both you and the seller have certain responsibilities. The recommended approach is to consult your attorney and escrow agent, if one is involved. In fact, retaining an attorney to research bulk sales law requirements, as well as to help write a purchase agreement, is imperative to protecting yourself from potential pitfalls and liabilities. Preferably, try to find an attorney who specializes in business law.

The Purchase Price

Always remember: The purchase of a business is like an investment in any other type of endeavor—you are seeking a fair and reasonable return on your investment. With interest rates fluctuating, investments in relatively safe endeavors many times can return an annual rate of 5 percent. In other words, in a safe investment, within 20 years, you can obtain a return equal to your original investment. The same is true when you are buying a business. If possible, find out how the seller arrived at the sales price and compare it with the sales price of comparable businesses.

Some business brokers recommend a sales price equal to one year's gross sales, plus the value of the assets on the books. Have your accountant carefully check over the financial statements, including the all-important cash-flow analysis, and have him or her estimate when you should be able to secure back your investment. The better the investment, the faster you will recover your initial investment.

You must ask yourself whether you can afford the down payment and, in many cases, the installment payments that you will be required to make in future years. Will your payments make it difficult to support your family? Will your new business provide enough money to make the current payments and at the same time support your family? A cash-flow analysis will at least give you some idea about the prospects you face along these lines. Check your seller's cash-flow analysis and his or her financial statements and determine how much he or she had left over after expenses. In all probability, you will find that the seller did not have the expenses you have since he or she did not have to pay someone else for the business.

Look not only at the costs of operating the business but also at the contracts that accompany such costs. For example, you should carefully examine the lease to see if it has escalation costs that are not payable now, but will be in the future. In addition, you should make sure that you will have the premises for a sufficient number of years to recoup your investment.

Location of the Business and Lease Agreements

Seriously consider the location of the business you are thinking of buying. Here are some of the questions you may want to raise:

- ▶ Will this location be available for a substantial number of years?
- ▶ Is there any possibility of a major competitor coming to the immediate area? If so, what effect would this have on the business that is for sale?
- ▶ Can the business be relocated without loss of profit? Is the present lease assignable?

You can answer the last question by making a personal visit to the landlord with the understanding that you wish to have the same terms and conditions as those of the seller. Most leases provide that an assignment cannot be made without the consent of the landlord. In many cases, the landlord is given the right to raise the rent if there is a sale.

Not only is it important to examine the lease's contents, assignability, and duration, but it is also imperative to check with the landlord to determine whether or not he or she will abide by such assignment and its existing terms and conditions. See the section in Chapter 2 titled "Leases," beginning on page 32. This section raises additional questions that should be asked by franchise or independent-business buyers.

Market Analysis

As with all businesses, the life or death of a local business depends on its market. Major companies that are generally successful in opening a new location normally conduct a market feasibility study beforehand. There is no reason why you should not make your own market feasibility study.

There is a wealth of information available from the U.S. Department of Commerce regarding Americans' buying patterns in relation to particular businesses, including service- and product-oriented businesses. A trip to your local library can provide you with appropriate statistical information. Business publications such as *The Wall Street Journal* will give you an idea of the American consumer's quickly changing attitudes.

You can also acquire information about a particular business's customers, either by phone or by requesting that the seller make questionnaires available to his or her customers for 30 to 60 days before you purchase the business. You could establish a contingency that the closing be delayed for a certain period of time until you can conduct your own survey.

If the seller will not go for this, your best bet is to tell him or her that you would like a trial period with the business, during which you will contact customers to obtain their viewpoints on the establishment and why they patronize it. If you are buying a small business, you should have permission to contact its customers. To prevent any type of panic, you can do this without indicating that you would be the new owner. With the help of the seller, you can introduce yourself as someone merely seeking to find out for the owner how the business can be improved.

If you are buying a business whose particular trade name is the key to the purchase, make sure your purchase agreement contains a provision stating that:

▶ You can use the name; and
▶ The seller represents and warrants, subject to a fraud action, that such name is his or hers and is not subject to litigation by any third party claiming to have rights to the name.

Competition

You should check the market area thoroughly for current and potential competitors. Most real estate agents will advise you of buildings that might be available to competitors in your line of business. Personally canvass the area for existing or potential competing businesses that may lessen your future profits.

In addition, ask the seller if he or she will include in writing a covenant that ensures he or she will not compete with you in a specific geographical area and for a period of time that is reasonable and enforceable under your state laws. Here again, an experienced attorney is a necessity.

Checking the Seller's Background

It is a good idea for every potential purchaser to study the local county court records to determine whether or not any litigation has been brought against the seller.

You can do this by going to the local courthouse and providing clerks with the last names of the sellers and/or the name under which the business entity has operated. Once any case numbers are secured, you should review the file to determine what the litigation involved. Follow-up conversations with the plaintiffs and their attorneys are also in order. You should then confront the seller to get his or her side of the story regarding these litigated matters. If real property is part of the deal, a title policy should be secured as part of the transaction so you know you are getting clear title to the property.

In all cases where inventory, fixtures, and other items are passing hands, check with the office of the secretary of state or an applicable state or county agency to determine whether or not there are any liens on the items you are purchasing. Specifically, you want to get copies of any and all UCC-1 forms and UCC-3 forms that have been filed. A UCC-1 form is a Uniform Commercial Code form, which is a financing statement that is signed by a debtor indicating that a creditor has a lien on certain enumerated items. A UCC-3 form provides evidence of any assignment, release, or change relating to a UCC-1 form lien. The secretary of state or an applicable state or county agency can provide you with the UCC-1 forms and UCC-3 forms for a small fee. If the seller has not revealed any existing liens, and you discover some, you should confront him or her with the UCC forms, since liens are a cloud on your title to such items. There are some private agencies that, for a fee, will check the secretary of state's files and other appropriate state or county files for you to determine whether there are any liens on the seller's property. This may take considerably less time than if you submitted a request for copies to the secretary of state.

It is also a good idea to check to see if the seller has any outstanding tax liens. You can obtain this information from federal, state, and local tax authorities. The bottom line is that you want to ascertain whether anyone other than the seller can lay claim to property you are purchasing. Obviously, obtaining inventory and other property that is free and clear from outside interests should be the goal.

When checking the background of a seller, you may wish to use the checklist in Figure 3.1 on page 46. This checklist will help you obtain some of the information discussed in this chapter.

Conclusion

To help ensure a good purchase of a local business, there are several tips you can follow:

▶ Determine what the seller is providing you for your money. Does this include a starting inventory, training, promotional advice, customer lists, and other such vital information necessary to your continued success?

▶ Check with competitors and, particularly, with suppliers, to see if the seller has priced up the inventory to you. A high price to which you add your normal markup could price you right out of the retail market. The suppliers can attest to the price that was paid for the inventory and what inventory prices will be in the future.

▶ Try to persuade the seller to allow you to watch him or her operate the business for a suitable period of time. You might be taking one giant step toward ensuring a good purchase.

▶ Encourage the seller to advise you fully as to whether or not his or her own personality has made the difference between success and failure. If it does, make sure you have a similar personality. A successful restaurant that attracts a multitude of people because of the outgoing personality of the owner might become a dismal failure for the purchaser who is much more introverted.

▶ Truly shop for your local business. Investigate several businesses and compare their profit and loss statements. Talk to other small business owners who are in the same line, even if they are not direct competitors, and consider what they have to say. This may cost you a lot of lunches or dinners, but it could prove very beneficial.

▶ Determine whether or not the business will make a profit under your ownership. To help do this, prepare a business plan. Such a plan will also be useful to your bank or investor if you are seeking funding. It also acts as a written confirmation of your long-term business goals.

There are small business development center offices located throughout the country that provide free and/or low-cost counseling on starting, running, and operating a business. This includes information on business plans, finance, and marketing for those wishing to start a business. The SBDC website, where you can search for your local small business development center, is at www.sba.gov/sbdc.

With this brief overview of what factors to consider when buying a local business, you will be better prepared to work with your attorney and accountant when investigating, evaluating, and negotiating the purchase of a small business.

Figure 3.1 **Checklist of Information to Secure from the Seller of an Existing Business**

❑ Obtain information on the background of the business and its owner.

❑ Obtain the seller's financials for the past three years.

❑ Obtain copies of all leases on location and equipment.

❑ Obtain an accurate list of all equipment, fixtures, inventory, and supplies.

❑ Determine the condition of equipment, fixtures, inventory, and supplies—particularly heating and air conditioning.

❑ Obtain copies of all maintenance agreements on equipment.

❑ Ask about potential or actual liability claims against the current business.

❑ Find out if a bulk sale law is applicable.

❑ Run a credit check on the seller.

❑ Question current and past employees on their views of the business.

❑ Check the seller's cash-flow analysis charts.

❑ Determine whether the seller's present prices for his or her products or services are competitive.

❑ Check with suppliers to verify actual prices of inventory and stock items.

❑ Prepare pro forma sales projections in the form of profit-and-loss statements for the next two years.

❑ Make sure the business's past success was not due to the personality of the seller.

❑ Secure a valid not-to-compete covenant from the seller.

❑ Do a market study of the area or hire a qualified person to do this for you.

❑ Find out if any competitors, particularly high discounters, are looking for locations in your area. Make it a practice to contact local real estate and commercial brokers in your area as the source for this important information.

❑ Talk to the seller's customers and find out why they patronize the business and their thoughts on improving the business.

❑ Check with owners of similar businesses for their opinions on the merits of making money in their line.

❑ Check with your bank on the availability of funds to you and the cost.

❑ Find out if the seller's present lease is assignable on the same rental terms.

❑ Check county records for lawsuits and claims against the seller.

❑ Check with the local county or state agency where liens are filed—usually in the secretary of state's office—and determine whether any liens have been filed against the seller with respect to any part of the seller's business.

❑ Check for tax liens.

❑ Find out why the seller is selling his or her business.

CHAPTER 4

Buying a Local Franchise Operation

HAVING READ THE PREVIOUS CHAPTERS, YOU HAVE A BETTER understanding about purchasing a franchise from a franchisor or purchasing a business that is not a franchise from a local business owner. This chapter examines the scenario of purchasing an existing franchise business from a local franchisee.

The big difference between purchasing a franchise from a franchisor and purchasing a franchise from an existing franchisee is that, if it is truly a sale by a franchisee, the franchisee is not bound by restrictions on revealing actual or projected revenue figures. By the same token, the franchisee/seller is also not bound by any legal disclosure requirements, such as those issued by the Federal Trade Commission. Therefore, you should extensively review the previous chapters of this book regarding both purchasing a franchise and purchasing a business from a local business owner and consult the checklists at the end of Chapters 1 through 3 for additional information on what you need to know and research when purchasing a franchise or an existing business.

In essence, ensure that you secure a written purchase agreement in which the franchisee who is selling the franchise produces accurate, truthful financial statements and warrants their veracity. Because the business is also a franchise, familiarize yourself with the terms and conditions of the franchise agreement and with the information in the franchisor's disclosure document.

Reviewing the Disclosure Document

As stated above, in the sale of a franchise that is strictly between the franchisee and the prospective buyer and does not involve the franchisor, the franchisee/seller is not required to provide you with the franchisor's disclosure document. However, since most franchise agreements provide that a franchisee can transfer his or her franchise only with the franchisor's consent and upon the execution of a then-current franchise agreement by the purchaser, it is extremely wise for the franchisor to provide you with a disclosure document that contains the updated franchise agreement. You should thoroughly examine the disclosure document, as indicated in Chapter 2. In addition, you should follow all of the suggestions made in Chapter 3 pertaining to the purchase of a non-franchise business. Additionally, find out whether you must pay for training sessions required by the franchisor or if your training can be obtained from the selling franchisee at no cost to you. This is extremely important to know.

You must realize that your relationship with the selling franchisee is only temporary and short term and that assuming his or her franchise agreement or executing a new franchise agreement means a long-term relationship with the franchisor. Therefore, before you sign any documents or part with any money, familiarize yourself with the franchisor and contact other franchisees to determine answers to the many questions you will have. In addition, find out why the franchisee is selling. In many instances, a franchisee places the business on the market because he or she is unable to make it profitable. This is why it is so important that you find out as much information as you can on the franchise you seek to buy, including the financials, the franchisee's reasons for selling the franchise, and the seller's relationship with and opinion of the franchisor.

Because the franchisee/seller could jeopardize any sale by being too frank about the shortcomings of the franchisor, information from the franchisee/seller is often slanted to avoid any criticism of the franchisor. Other franchisees of the same franchisor will not have this reservation when you approach them regarding the franchisor's performance with the franchisees.

Selling Price of an Existing Franchise

Since this purchase is of an ongoing business as well as a franchise, the transaction is going to be much more costly than buying a new franchise and starting it from scratch. There doesn't seem to be any set formula for determining a fair price for an existing franchise.

Years ago, before inflation, a business would generally sell for three to five times its annual earnings, with all parties assuming that the investment could be recouped in three to five years. In more modern times, businesses generally are sold at one year's net earnings, plus the value of the equipment, fixtures, and inventory on the books. In reality, most businesses sell for a price the seller is willing to accept and the buyer is willing to pay. Anybody buying a business, however, should first consult an accountant or real estate agent familiar with the purchase and sale values of the business in question.

You may want to make arrangements to observe or work in the particular business for several weeks before making any written contractual commitment. However, if there are other prospective purchasers interested in the business, it is unlikely that the franchisee selling the business will entertain such an arrangement.

If the franchise you are thinking about buying is successful, be sure to find out why it has succeeded. If it is a service-oriented business and the sales or technical ability of the franchisee/seller is the primary reason for the business's success, make sure you have some of the same qualities.

The success of the business may stem from competent employees. Therefore, although a franchisee/seller cannot "sell" his or her employees, the purchase agreement could be drafted with a warranty and representation by the seller that he or she will do everything within his or her power to convince the employees to stay on with you. In addition, a restriction that the seller will not compete with you should also be incorporated into a written buy and sell agreement.

In purchasing any existing business, you should make sure there is a long-term assumable lease and the landlord will consent to the transfer. More businesses have been sunk when the purchaser took over a business only to find a few months later that the rent had been doubled or that the lease would shortly expire without any possibility of renewal.

Helpful Tips

Here are some tips for anyone interested in buying an existing franchise or business:

▶ Current federal and state franchise laws offer you what you need the most—information about the seller's franchisor. If you are interested in buying a franchise, utilize this source of information.
▶ If you are interested in buying a local non-franchise business, read over the material in Chapters 1 and 2 to get an idea of the type of information required of franchisors and ask for the same type of information from the owner of the local non-franchise business.

▶ The less information you get from the seller, the greater the risk you may be buying a "lemon."

▶ Remember to personally investigate the deal. Common sense is the key here. Why take a bigger risk than necessary? Check, check, and double check.

▶ Anybody purchasing a business should seek out competent legal counsel versed in the practical business aspects of buying and selling a business.

▶ Use the checklists at the end of Chapters 1, 2, and 3 to evaluate every franchise or business you are seriously considering buying.

▶ Research and review all applicable state and federal franchise laws and any state business opportunity laws. (See Appendix E for information on state laws relating to franchises and businesses.)

Conclusion

The next chapter, Chapter 5, provides information on how franchise opportunities are marketed by franchisors. It also provides information to assist you, the potential franchisee, in evaluating franchisor advertisements, websites, presentations, and other information and materials when considering a franchise opportunity. The chapters that constitute Part II of this book, Chapters 6 through 13, although written for someone who owns a business and is considering franchising it, can also be viewed from the standpoint of someone interested in purchasing a franchise. The chapters in Part II examine the factors that contribute to a good franchise business from a franchisor's viewpoint. The prospective franchisor will soon find that whatever makes the franchisee successful makes the franchisor successful as well. So, potential franchisees can use Part II to see what makes a good franchisor and to evaluate whether specific franchisors have structured their franchise offerings to facilitate franchisee success.

If you are considering buying a franchise, compare the terms of your potential franchise purchase with the information in Part II to determine whether your potential franchisor has done his or her homework. In addition, remember that today's purchaser of an ongoing business may be tomorrow's franchisor.

CHAPTER 5

The Changing Landscape of Franchise Marketing and Recruiting

by Rick Grossmann

THIS CHAPTER DESCRIBES HOW FRANCHISE MARKETING AND RECRUITING has evolved and how you, the potential franchisee, can take an educated approach as you navigate through the discovery and research process with the goal of identifying the best franchise business for you and your family.

In the franchise world, franchisors use the term "recruiting" instead of selling due to the fact that even though franchisees pay for a franchise, they are being chosen vs. being sold something. Franchisors must be selective as they accept new franchise owners into their franchise communities. It is counterproductive to award a franchise to an individual who is not a good fit. The franchisor should award a franchise based on the candidate's compatibility and merit.

Marketing Before the Internet

Singer Sewing Machines introduced franchising as a business expansion model in the late 1800s. The model caught on in the early 1900s, with many business models adopting the successful growth system. Franchising is now the most successful form of business expansion in the world.

In general, franchise businesses have a much higher success rate than non-franchise businesses. These realities have given many franchisors explosive growth by using traditional marketing methods and campaigns to attract franchise buyers.

The traditional methods of marketing franchise opportunities and recruiting franchisees during the pre-internet years looked much like other business models of that time.

The Five Pillars of Marketing Then and Now

Think of marketing as the general term that we use to describe all of the efforts that businesses use to attract buyers. Marketing can be broken down into the following five categories: advertising, sales, direct mail, public relations, and promotions, which we will refer to as "the five pillars of marketing," as visualized in Figure 5.1. These categories, then, are broken down into marketing campaigns.

Figure 5.1 **The Five Pillars of Marketing**

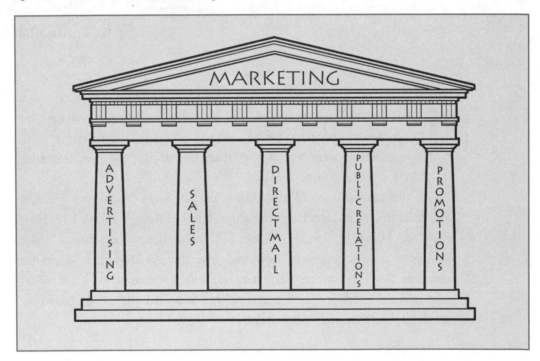

Advertising

Traditional franchise advertising was once focused on TV, radio, and publications such as franchise magazines and catalogs, business magazines, local newspapers, and billboards. The franchise buyer could view ads featuring franchise opportunities for sale; he or she could also read articles and testimonials. The franchisors controlled the content and the messages, which limited the buyer's perception of the business to what the franchisor presented to them.

Today's advertisements are still placed in the traditional form but tend to have a much different call to action. Instead of "Call Now," the ads direct the reader to the franchise website where they can learn more and engage with the franchisor's development department via email. This is less threatening than a phone call. Online advertisements are very popular as well. We will explore this further in the following section.

Television Commercials and Interactive TV

Today you will find more local TV commercials for all subjects including business opportunities and franchises. It has become more affordable for business owners to advertise on television. Interactive TV commercials are also becoming more popular in many markets. These commercials allow you to request information or order a product or service by pressing a button on your remote control. Franchise opportunities that utilize this technology may be showing their commitment to growth by using modern technology.

Sales

Good old-fashioned salesmanship has always been a big part of the franchise-marketing world. Buying and starting a business is typically one of the biggest decisions in a person's life. Franchise buyers tend to do a great deal of research before they choose the best business match. The franchisor's sales department is responsible for educating the prospective franchise owner as they move through the discovery process.

Franchise consultants and brokers have become an extension of the franchisor's sales department. Independent consultants and brokers invest in their own marketing and recruiting efforts to identify prospective franchise buyers. They will then introduce them to franchisors that match their criteria. In many cases, the buyer will experience a more balanced discovery process if they are working with a consultant or broker because they offer their clients more education and resources.

Live events, such as franchise expositions or local franchise seminars, are other sales methods that many franchisors participate in. These events give the franchisor's sales representatives the opportunity to meet with many prospective buyers face-to-face. Franchise buyers can compare a variety of opportunities side-by-side, saving the prospective franchisee a lot of time.

Audio recordings and videos are effective methods for sales communication. Franchisors can also feature their concept overview and testimonials on DVD or on their websites. With these methods, franchisors can showcase their concept professionally, and buyers can "shop" for a franchise at their convenience.

Live web presentations have become a very cost-effective sales presentation tool. Franchisors can host scheduled or impromptu online meetings with interested buyers. The presenter can use various tools such as presentation slides, website content, or other web-based documents or files that can appear on the prospective franchisees' computers as they listen to the presentation.

As you research various franchise opportunities, you will want to make sure that the sales department is doing their job to educate you about the opportunity without pressuring you. With smaller startup franchises you may be dealing direct with the founder of the company. You can learn a great deal about a franchise if they have an effective sales system that utilizes the tools outlined in this section.

Direct Mail

Direct mail has been a very effective marketing and recruiting method for decades. This allows franchisors to stand out from their competitors with a strong message in a post card or sales letter format. Target marketing has become more advanced with the introduction of online mailing list services. These services can identify individuals who fit the criteria the franchisor is looking for based on demographics and buying habits. For instance, you may receive a direct-mail piece from an automotive franchise if you frequent certain automotive websites or subscribe to automotive magazines.

Some franchisors have developed a newsletter program for existing franchisees and even prospective franchise owners. You may be able to sign up on their website to receive their newsletters. This gives you some insight into their company culture and the happenings of the company, and it is a good way to see if you would fit in with their franchise system.

Public Relations

Public relations or PR campaigns can take many forms. PR campaigns are often "good will" efforts that a company makes to show they are involved with their communities. It may be as simple as the company sponsoring a nonprofit organization, or as extravagant as creating a philanthropic movement of its own.

You can learn a lot about a company by the types of PR efforts they participate in. Research the company's PR history to ensure that your values are in line with its philanthropic vision. You may find publicity articles that highlight the company's efforts. You will want to confirm that the company is genuinely supporting certain causes for the good of the cause and not just for the exposure.

Promotions

A promotion is any "out of the ordinary" campaign or event to attract new business or increase awareness of a company. This can be as simple as a special sale or incentive program. You may also see larger efforts such as customer loyalty programs, customer appreciation events, or rewards programs.

In the franchise world, it is common to be invited to attend a franchisor's Discovery or Decision Day event. These events will allow you to meet the franchisor's executive and support team, learn more about their business, and even meet with existing franchise owners.

The Sixth Pillar—The Internet

Even though you will find elements of the original five pillars of marketing within the internet platform, the internet has become unique enough to be considered a stand-alone sixth pillar of marketing. This section will help you identify the best practices for researching franchise opportunities by utilizing technology and the internet.

Not too many years ago, the "Big Boys," or well-known franchisors, had a competitive advantage because they had far more money and resources to market their franchise opportunities. Back then, the marketing and media options were very

Figure 5.2 **Marketing Today Includes a Sixth Pillar—the Internet**

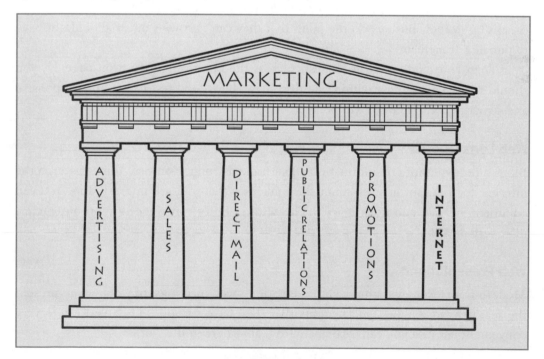

expensive, and new emerging franchisors were priced out of the competition. The internet has leveled the playing field with much lower barriers to entry, giving the advantage to creative companies–not just to those with large bank accounts.

Websites

Franchisor's websites should be professional and educational. A buyer should be able to easily access information about the company's culture, products, and services.

Look for the following when you are evaluating a franchisor's website:

▶ Does the website look professional compared to the competitor's?

▶ Is the site easy to navigate and do you find valuable information about the opportunity?

▶ Does the franchisor address your primary concerns and questions upfront?

▶ Does the franchisor disclose the initial investment, or do they dance around this information?

▶ How does the franchisor treat you now? They should be helping you through the discovery process. If you feel like they are condescending, you should pass.

Email

Email can be tricky, due to spam filters. Once you have identified a few possible franchise opportunities, engage them on all levels to see how they respond. Many franchisors don't respond to their franchise owners or prospective franchise owners. They get caught up in their business to the point that they can't grow. A buyer should not have to pursue a franchisor.

When you send an email request, such as the one in Figure 5.3 on page 57, you should receive a response within one day. It can be a good test to see how responsive and structured a franchisor will be.

Web Logs (Blogs)

Blogs offer a plethora of information about franchise opportunities. You can search the internet for relevant articles about the franchises that you are interested in. You can comment and ask questions as well. This allows you to experience a more interactive discovery process.

Web Presentations

Modern franchisors will offer web presentations, web meetings, or webinars to present the features, advantages, and benefits that they have to offer. This platform is very convenient because you can participate from anywhere in the world.

Figure 5.3 **Sample Inquiry Email to a Franchisor**

SAMPLE EMAIL REQUEST

Mr. Rollins,

Thank you for your quick response to my following questions. I am very interested in this franchise opportunity and look forward to learning more.

1. What is the estimated timeline between signing the franchise agreement and our grand opening?

2. I would like my brother to be a partner. How should we structure this and is this an acceptable model?

3. Should I get in touch with financing companies and commercial real estate brokers now or should I do this after we sign up?

Thank you again,

Larry

Social Media

Today you have more access to influential people via social media, such as Facebook, Twitter, and LinkedIn, and many more (and more to come). First, identify the franchise opportunities you are interested in. Then, go to the franchisors' websites, if available. These sites may provide links to social media sites of the franchise opportunities that you are interested in. Don't be afraid to use social media to engage the franchisor and use this as a research opportunity. Often you can experience a more interactive dialog with the franchisor, their franchisees, and their customers if you use social media and the communication tools on social media sites.

You can join a variety of social media groups that focus on entrepreneurial and franchise topics. Websites such as Facebook and LinkedIn offer groups and discussion forums that focus specifically on franchising and business growth. Join these groups and don't be afraid to ask questions. Engage the franchisors, franchise owners, and individuals considering the purchase of a franchise. You will learn a great deal from the people who assist you in your research.

Social media allows all outsiders and insiders to engage in an ongoing personal conversation about the subject. You can gain a great deal of information by participating in various social media platforms, such as the Twitter string shown in Figure 5.4 on page 59. You can use up to 140 characters (including spaces) per tweet.

As you can see in Figure 5.4, you have the opportunity to engage a community of individuals that share a common interest in the franchise that you are researching. This allows the franchisor to prove themselves by being responsive and informative as well.

Electronic Newsletters (E-Newsletters)

When available, you can sign up for electronic newsletters from franchisors you are interested in. You will glean insights into their company and find out "what makes them tick." Their newsletters should be consistent and educational.

Search Engine Optimization (SEO)

Savvy franchisors are investing in Search Engine Optimization efforts (SEO). They will do the research to identify the search history of the individuals who are attracted to their franchise opportunity. You can type keywords or keyword phrases (groups of keywords) into the search engines to find franchises that align with your interests. An example of this would be to search for "self-serve frozen yogurt franchise." The franchise opportunities that rank high in the organic search results tend to be the companies that have the best SEO programs and can be considered more technology savvy. The organic results appear in order of relevance to your keywords when you perform a web search.

Search Engine Marketing (SEM)

Many franchises are marketed on the internet via Search Engine Marketing. This includes organic results from the search engines that result from effective SEO. SEM also includes "pay" options like pay-per-click or banner advertisements. You will find the pay-per-click listings at the top and side panel of the results pages for most internet search engines.

Texting

Texting is a big communication tool today. Franchisors should be comfortable with communicating via text messaging. Ask upfront if you can communicate via text as this may provide a more efficient and dynamic communication tool for interacting with franchisors and obtaining information. It has been proven that people respond to text messages faster than email or voicemail.

Figure 5.4 **Connecting with a Franchisor on Twitter**

TWEET STRING

@LelaG: Hello to those interested in the Noah's Ark Franchise. I am looking into this. So far it looks good. What do you think of a franchise like this one?

@Hannah_Noah's Ark [franchisor]: Hi @LelaG. Thanks for your interest. We will assist you in your efforts to research our business model. Feel free to call me to discuss.

@SamJoeArt: Very good question @LelaG. Good to see that Noah's Ark is so responsive. I am looking into this franchise, too. What do you think?

@LelaG: Hi @SamJoeArt. I am very excited about Noah's Ark so far. I have spoken to several of their franchise owners and they all have been very positive.

@AFG2011: Are there any available territories in the Dallas area?

@Hannah_Noah's Ark [franchisor]: Hi @AFG2011: We do have one territory in metro Dallas in the north side of the metro area. Could that work for you?

@AFG2011: Thanks Hannah. That could work. I am not to far from that part of the city.

@Hannah_Noah's Ark [franchisor]: Hi @LelaG, @SamJoeArt and @AFG 20011. Join me for a web presentation this Wednesday at 6:30 MT. www.sample.com to register.

@Remix1985: My sister purchased one of these and loves it. She is making great money and enjoys her work every day. She feels like she is giving back. It sounds good to me.

@Remix1985: Can I join the web presentation too?

@Hannah_Noah's Ark [franchisor]: Hi @Remix1985. Sure you can join us. Click on this link to register www.sample.com.

@Sweetface1991: I would like to join in as well if there is still time.

@Hannah_ Noah's Ark [franchisor]: Hi @Sweetface1991. You certainly may join us. Click on this link www.sample.com to register or feel free to call me at 555-555-5555. Thanks.

SAMPLE TEXT MESSAGE

Hello Mr. Rollins. I am meeting with my banker right now and we need the bottom-line build out figures for our Noah's Ark franchise located on Fifth and Main for the loan package.

Hello Larry. I pulled your file and it looks like $257,545 including the landlord's tenant improvement contribution. Let me know if you need anything else. Jim.

Texting can fast track various steps in your discovery and launch process. Discuss this with your contact at the franchisor's headquarters, in advance, so you don't lose valuable time.

Podcasts

You may find podcasts about the franchises that interest you. Podcasts consist of online audio and video messages on the internet. The franchisors have the opportunity to present their franchise opportunity in more detail using this type of media. Sophisticated franchisors may offer more content by utilizing podcasts.

Smart Device Applications

You can now search various smart devices for business opportunities and franchises. If you do so, be sure to investigate the franchisor's history and the depth of their technology.

Future Technologies

Some say that a majority of the technology that we will use 10 years from now has yet to be invented. Business owners must commit to delivering the most cutting-edge products, services, and technology that the world has to offer or risk falling behind. In selecting a franchise opportunity, you may want to consider the technological tools and marketing efficiency of the franchisor as it can be an indicator of an effective franchise operation.

Conclusion

As a franchise buyer, you have more information at your fingertips than any other time in history. Use the tools, tips, and techniques in this chapter to fully investigate the franchise opportunities that you are interested in. Remember that the key to success in the franchise business is a good fit between the franchisor and the franchise owners. Good luck in your new endeavor!

PART II

Franchising Your Business

CHAPTER 6

Franchising Basics

A S A NEW FRANCHISOR, YOU NEED TO REALIZE THAT FRANCHISING IS A method of marketing and therefore entails a business operation in and of itself. Before beginning the franchise process, you will need to know how to:

▶ Structure a workable franchise agreement with franchisees;

▶ Choose and train your franchisees; and

▶ Market not only the product or service the franchisee will sell, but the franchise concept itself to prospective franchisees.

Too often, many new, potential franchisors seek out an attorney who perhaps has worked on only one or two franchise deals at the most rather than a highly experienced franchise attorney to draw up a franchise agreement. This can be problematic because in most cases, these new franchisors are very successful in running their own businesses, but they don't know the first thing about franchising. Consequently, they need knowledgeable guidance but rely on a less experienced source. Many first-time franchisors don't know some of the franchising basics, such as:

▶ What a franchisee is or what to expect from one,

▶ How to provide ongoing support to a franchisee,

▶ How much money is needed to capitalize the franchise venture, or

▶ How much to charge as an initial franchise fee and as an ongoing royalty.

Part II of this book provides you with this type of information so you can set up a franchising operation with some prior knowledge of common mistakes inexperienced franchisors make. With this knowledge you will hopefully avoid making the same mistakes and improve your chances for success. Before deciding if your business can be franchised, you may want to review some of the advantages and disadvantages of doing so.

Advantages of Franchising

When discussing the advantages of franchising for the franchisor, it is inevitable to discuss the advantages available to the franchisee as well. This is because many advantages for one are also considered advantages for the other. So, even though the following list specifies the advantage to the franchisor or the franchisee, most of them are generally held to be advantages for both:

▶ There is potential for rapid expansion with minimum capital expenditures.

▶ Direct managing responsibilities become the franchisee's obligation and allow the franchisor more freedom to do other things.

▶ The franchisee generally has pride of ownership and self-motivation because of his or her capital investment and stake in future profits. (This self-motivation generally results in the franchisee's lowering his or her costs, resulting in higher profit margins for the franchisee and greater consumer markets for the franchisor than normally attainable by company employees.)

▶ A franchisee will generally have a minimum amount of line-management employees and a greater amount of staff advisory employees.

▶ National and local advertising dollars are available for franchisees in far greater amounts than could be generated by the franchisor or franchisee alone.

▶ There is increased buying power, resulting in lower possible purchase prices for goods used by the franchisee.

▶ Research and development facilities are available to the franchisor through reports from franchisees.

▶ The franchisor can have a steady cash flow from royalties.

▶ The franchisor can maintain consistency and quality in its franchises through wise and fair franchise contract provisions.

▶ Some limits of liability extend to the final consumer. (Franchisees generally are not held to be agents of the franchisor in the event of injuries due to the franchisee's negligence, as opposed to liability that extends to a company for injuries suffered in a branch store based on company employee negligence.)

Other advantages a franchisor may enjoy can be directly attributed to the advantages that a franchisee will enjoy. In short, if the franchisee is happy, the franchisor will be happy. For more on franchisee advantages, refer to Chapter 1.

Disadvantages of Franchising

Of course, as is the case with most things in life, there is usually a downside to every decision you make or every venture you pursue. And when it comes to franchising, you need to be aware of some of the disadvantages. This section of the chapter will help you be better informed and more prepared in making your franchising decision.

Decreased Net Receipts

Net receipts from franchisees could be less than net receipts from successful, company-owned operations. In reality, only a few new franchises break even immediately. Most franchises take six months to a year to break even. This is also true of most new company-owned retail outlets. Although the company-owned office retains 100 percent of its net profits, it has obligated itself to an initial capital indebtedness that it would not have if the office were a franchise.

If you are relatively sure that company-owned retail outlets can produce an immediate profit and you have the capital and labor to staff them, you will certainly make much more money with company-owned outlets than if you franchised an equal number of franchises that made the same amount of profit. Your main problem will be to raise the necessary startup capital and secure and retain qualified, hard-working managers and employees while hoping that sales will immediately exceed the substantial startup costs for company-owned outlets. Capital and qualified employees are very hard to get—and the latter are even more difficult to retain.

Independence of Franchisees

As a franchisor, you will be dealing with independent operators rather than with company employees. The key is to treat all franchisees fairly. Franchisees should be subject to only enough control to ensure that your franchised service or product will be marketed to the consumer with the same quality that made you a success.

For example, if the franchisees feel they are overpaying for services they receive from you or that the services are not what were represented to them, they will become disgruntled and eventually may group together, withholding payment of their franchise fees. Most franchisees who withhold payment of fees and sue are those who feel that the franchisor has breached their contracts. And usually, these franchisees have experienced a personality conflict with someone in the franchisor's operation.

Be extremely careful in selecting a franchisee or allowing a franchisee to transfer his or her franchise to someone else. Furthermore, continue to look upon each of your franchisees as an economical substitute for a company manager insofar as assisting and supporting that franchisee.

Many franchisors seem to have the attitude that they now are in the business of making money by selling franchises instead of selling their services or products. Their attention is more attuned to advertising and marketing the franchises rather than marketing the product or service to the consumer.

The primary goal of any franchisor is to sell his or her services or wares. The use of franchisees is a method of attaining this goal.

Difference in Required Business Skills

The business skills you will need for operating a franchisor system are entirely different from those you needed in running your original retail business. Most of the franchisors who fail in the franchising business are those who did not know what they were doing when they first started their franchisor corporation. They were experts at operating an initial retail business and tried to franchise because of their extensive trial-and-error experience in such a business; however, they did not know how to be franchisors.

Overspending

Franchisors tend to spend too much money on show. There seems to be a tremendous temptation for franchisors to immediately "put on the dog." High-rise office buildings, overstaffing, company cars, expensive hotels, elaborate trade show booths, and costly classified advertising are some of the first mistakes many new franchisors make. Franchisors have a tendency to undercapitalize by not budgeting themselves.

No matter what your capital is, be it $20,000, $100,000, or $1,000,000, wisely budget the cost of your office, the marketing of your franchises, the training of your franchisees, and the maintenance and support of your franchise outlets.

Costs Can Be High

In the United States, franchisors are required to have written disclosure documents containing copies of all proposed contracts for signing up franchisees. (See Chapter 2 for more on franchise disclosure documents.) To prepare a disclosure document, you will need to retain the services of an attorney and an accountant. As pointed out in Chapter 11, "Making Your Operation Work," the costs of preparing a disclosure document and audited financial statements sometimes are not in direct proportion with the value given.

Try to get the most for your dollar, but be careful in selecting the attorney and the accountant. Rely heavily upon the references of a particular attorney's or accountant's past clients. Under no circumstances should the costs of setting up the franchise be greater than the costs you would incur if you were to set up company-owned offices with qualified management personnel. When trying to control service costs of attorneys and accountants, complete the questionnaires in both Appendix C and Appendix D. You should complete these questionnaires before your first meeting with an attorney.

In addition to legal and professional fees, the cost of franchising in multiple states is high because of the individual legal costs for disclosure filings in the 14 states that have franchise registration laws that stipulate your legal requirements as a franchisor. In 17 other states, your requirements are governed by business opportunity statutes. (See Appendix E, "State Franchise Information Guidelines," for more on these state statutes.) In the remaining 19 states and Washington, DC, you will need to comply with the Federal Trade Commission's rules on disclosures.

Unfortunately, regulations in registration states differ and a franchise disclosure document in one registration state may not be allowed by another without changes. The same is true in those states having business opportunity laws that require filing. Even the FTC rules require the disclosure documents to differentiate with regard to the individual noncompete, renewal, and termination laws of each of the FTC states, even though these provisions are generally incorporated in one disclosure form.

This cost disadvantage can be minimized if you have a business plan of slow growth that concentrates on one or two states for the first few years and gradually expands to bordering states. By doing this, you will incur attorney fees and filing costs over a period of time rather than all at once. Thoroughly evaluate the particular advantages and disadvantages of franchising as compared with alternatives for expansion before making the franchise decision. Refer to Chapter 7, "Franchising and Alternative Methods of Expansion," for more on alternative expansion methods.

Investors

Make sure that all investors are in complete agreement with all your business plans. Too many cooks spoil the broth. Most investors have no hands-on experience in running a franchise, but will try to reinvent them, and this can eventually bring the franchise down. Further, some insist on company-owned units since their money is at stake only to find out that the costs and liabilities of company-owned offices will soon cause the business that they invested in to incur substantial losses. Thus, the lesson is that you need to choose your investors wisely and beware of undue or misguided influences.

Can Your Business Be Franchised?

If you have a successful business that is susceptible to a regional or national system of marketing and you do not wish to share control or risk the personality conflicts that come with bringing in investors who would become your equals in making business decisions, then franchising may be your best course of action. To help you determine if your business could be franchised, review some of the qualifiers and considerations described below.

Are You Franchisor Material?

Before you evaluate your business as a potential franchise, be sure to evaluate yourself as a potential franchisor. Often, a person who might successfully operate a business that is susceptible to franchising may not be cut out to be a franchisor. Consider your qualities and remember that franchising is more than the business of selling services and/or products to a consumer. In addition, as a franchisor, you will be an educator, trainer, psychologist, minister, and perpetual hand-holder to your franchisees. You will also be a fee collector, extracting an initial fee for the franchisee to begin business and then collecting royalties for the life of the franchise.

You will need to be aware of the franchisee-franchisor relationship and always remember to allow your individual franchisees the flexibility to manage their own businesses and always treat them as independent business owners, not employees. It is important you carefully set forth the guidelines of this independent contractor relationship in the initial contract, the disclosure document, and all further communications to franchisees.

Is There a Market for Your Particular Product or Service?

Do not consider franchising your business unless you have a known, local market for your product or service. Marketability is determined by need, and need is determined by competition.

For example, if you are running a hamburger stand, your chances of finding a market for your franchise and a market for your franchisees are relatively small in today's business community. However, if you have a unique way of running a hamburger stand, it is entirely possible to franchise it. Take the Wendy's operation, for example, which gained steam by introducing the system of in-line preparation of hamburgers as the consumer watches and waits for his or her order. This is in contrast with the traditional method of preparing fast food hamburgers out of view and then setting them on a warming tray until someone places an order. Wendy's catered to consumers who wanted to see their hamburgers made to order right before their eyes.

Demand is the crucial force here. It is just as important as uniqueness. Your unique product or service must be desired not only by the people who wish to buy franchises from you, but also by the people who will buy products or services from the franchisees.

What Market Research Must You Do?

If your product or service is relatively new and not extensively offered by anyone else but has proven to be in demand, your first task is to determine those sections of the country that would most likely buy your products or services, based on needs similar to those of your present customers. For example, a new type of thermal underwear would not go over well with residents of California's Palm Springs area; however, a successful gas-saving device might take hold anywhere in the world.

If your product or service is not relatively new, you can retain market research firms to prepare extensive reports concerning the types of consumers in various regions and their needs and buying power. This could be rather expensive, so an alternative is to do your own research by visiting the reference department of your local library and by searching on the internet. You can study the Yellow Pages of phone books of the various cities in which you would like to offer your product or service to determine if any competition exists in those areas. You can also conduct an internet search and review on-line business directories and business review sites (such as *yelp*) to get information on potential competitors.

You will also want to interview existing franchisors and franchisees for their insights on franchising. People enjoy telling others of their business accomplishments, so this should be a particularly enjoyable aspect of researching the franchising potential of your business.

Government agencies are also very helpful in providing demographic information and market research data. In particular, the U.S. Department of Commerce, Bureau of Economic Analysis (www.bea.gov), and the U.S. Department of Labor, Bureau of Labor Statistics (www.bls.gov) have conducted extensive studies on the regional consumer habits of Americans. Search for "consumer habits" on these government websites and you can obtain useful data for your research.

It is always necessary to do an initial study of the existing demand for the products or services you are thinking of offering through a franchise system. A more extensive study can be conducted by potential franchisees. If you feel an initial market is out there, utilize potential franchisees by encouraging them to make their own market study as a prerequisite to receiving a license from you.

Do You Have a Registrable Trademark?

If you have a product or service that is unique or in demand, you must capture this uniqueness through the use of a trademark (if it is a product) or service mark (if it is a service). The idea is to get the American public to associate your product with a particular trademark.

For many years, purchasers of a certain type of transparent tape would not go into the local stationery store and ask for transparent tape but would instead automatically ask for the trademarked "Scotch" tape. In looking around, you will see that all of the big companies utilize this concept. The producers of cola drinks do not want you to ask for just "a cola," thereby allowing the local dispenser of the product to make the choice for you. The Coca-Cola Company wants you to ask for a Coke and the Pepsi-Cola Company wants you to ask for a Pepsi.

As a result, you will want to apply for a registered trademark or service mark on your product or service as soon as possible. You will most certainly want to do this before the first franchise agreement is negotiated and consummated. Keep in mind that the trademark or service mark must be used in intrastate and interstate commerce before the owner can apply to the U.S. Patent and Trademark Office (USPTO) in Washington, DC, to register it.

Before spending any money to advertise or promote a trademark or service mark, determine that no other entity has already secured the registered rights of that particular trademark or service mark. You can do so for less than $600 by contacting one of many trademark search firms. Even better, Thomson Compumark (www.trademarks. thomsonreuters.com, 800-692-8833) offers a variety of trademark searches including its "U.S. full availability search," which will not only cover registered and pending marks in the USPTO, but also will include state, common law, and domain name coverage so you can determine if someone else may have a prior common-law right to use the mark although that person might not have registered it with the USPTO. It is possible that even with a registration certificate, some entity might have secured a common-law right in a particular area that is superior to your registration date. Be aware that some search firms will provide their services only to attorneys. Since your application for federal trademark or service mark registration will be reviewed and determined by a government attorney, it is advisable to retain a trademark attorney.

If you do not wish to utilize such a search, you can make a preliminary search through the USPTO office pending and registered marks by going to http://www.

uspto.gov and clicking on the trademarks tab. This can be useful but it is not the most reliable type of search because it does not account for all potential sources of coverage. Then, after determining that you probably have a registrable trademark, your next step is to have it registered with the USPTO, and a trademark attorney can do this for you, for between $750 and $1,500.

The filing fees for trademark applications currently range from $275 to $375 depending on the type and form (electronic or paper) of the application. For more information on trademark registration, go to www.uspto.gov, which offers informational videos and documents on the trademark application process.

If the examiner determines that your trademark will not cause confusion with the trademarked goods of others that have registered pending registration with the USPTO, your application will be published in the Federal Register, allowing third parties to object if they disagree with the examiner. If there are no objections, you will receive a certificate of trademark registration approximately three to six months after your application has been published in the Federal Register. Your registered trademark will be in effect for 10 years before it needs to be renewed.

Once you have received your certificate of trademark registration, you should let the world know you have it. Remember that once you have obtained a certificate of registration, you are eligible to seek enforcement of your trademark or service mark against infringers through litigation in federal district courts. In addition, you may register your trademark with state agencies, although this is not necessary if you have a federal registration. Registration laws vary from state to state, but most states require a nominal fee in the range of $20 to $150.

The Final Decision to Franchise

Before you make your final decision to franchise, you need to know the following:

- ▶ You have what it takes to be a franchisor.
- ▶ Your product is unique and in demand, and your business is profitable and promising to prospective franchisees.
- ▶ You have a market for your product or service.
- ▶ Your service or product is associated with a registerable trademark.

In addition, you have probably already decided you do not wish to share your control with any investors in the form of partners or shareholders and you have investigated other business expansion alternatives. (See Chapter 7, "Franchising and Alternative Methods of Expansion".) You should also have a strong idea of what to look for in your future franchisees. (See Chapter 8, "Building a Strong Franchising Foundation" and the section in that chapter on "The Ideal Franchisee" and the discussion of franchisee business application forms in Chapter 13.)

Before you launch your plan to expand by franchising, prepare a thorough business plan so you can realistically look at the financial outlay each new outlet will require to get up and running; then compare that with the revenue you can expect to receive from fees, royalties, and sales of ingredients and services. Some of the costs specific to franchising that you will want to include in your business plan are overhead costs of your franchise operation, such as salaries and benefits for yourself and employees in your head office and trainers and sales staff, as well as normal office expenses like rent, office equipment, car allowances, and travel. Plan in the cost of finding franchisees. This could include buying ads, traveling to franchise shows, preparing brochures and videos, and entertaining. In addition, add a healthy allowance for startup and ongoing legal, accounting, and advertising fees.

Be overly conservative as you project the timing and amount of income you expect to receive from your franchise outlets. You will have determined the mixture of franchise fees, royalties, and product sales that will bring you income from your franchisees. Pad your expectations of how soon these revenues will flow back to you, instead of basing your predictions solely on how your business worked in the past.

Another important factor you should investigate before making your franchise decision is the advantages and disadvantages of each legal form of business organization—sole proprietorship, partnership, or corporation. If you form either a sole proprietorship or a partnership, your operation will be subject to unlimited liability: if the business fails and its debts exceed its assets, the sole proprietor or the partners can be held individually liable for unpaid debts. Because of this liability issue, most franchisors choose a corporate entity, in order to limit their liabilities to the assets of the corporation. To find out more on legal forms of business organization, especially incorporating, consult an attorney and a certified public accountant.

Conclusion

Different factors can affect a business, depending on its location. Before making the final decision to franchise in your state, check the state and local regulations with which your franchise business will have to comply. Refer to Chapter 9, and Appendixes E, F, and G for information on specific state and federal franchise and business opportunity laws and regulations.

CHAPTER 7

Franchising and Alternative Methods of Expansion

M ANY WELL-ORGANIZED COMPANY PROGRAMS THAT ARE SHORT ON expansion capital have turned into efficient, highly profitable networks of franchised outlets. The desired end result of this popular business system called franchising is a highly motivated, cost-cutting, quality-conscious retailer who provides a product or service to the customer. This method of operation can be far more efficient and profitable than a company-owned enterprise, which may be operated by high-priced and/or disinterested company employees.

Franchising, simply put, is a means of expanding a business operation by licensing a third party to engage in a franchise system under a required marketing plan or system using a common trademark, service mark, or trade name, for a fee. Franchising is available to businesses distributing both products and services and to those distributing services only. Today, the latter is by far the most popular category.

This chapter is written for the potential franchisor who has built a profitable business and who craves expansion before the business either becomes stagnant or dies when an aggressive competitor captures the available expansion markets by franchising first. It is also aimed at the potential franchisor who wishes to set up the best operating franchise system at the lowest possible cost. This chapter is set up to help you explore your best expansion options, be it franchising or its alternatives, such as the "as is" alternative, the company-owned outlet alternative, and the agreements of association alternative. As mentioned in the previous chapter, it is valuable to explore all your expansion options before making your final franchise decision. Take the time to review these alternatives and see if any seem applicable to you.

The "As Is" Alternative

The primary alternative to franchising is to let your business continue "as is," without franchising or expanding. This option, however, raises the possibility that your business will be eliminated by a competitor who gains greater brand recognition. It may also restrict you and your business from reaching your full potential. Profits are limited to the amount of gross revenues that can be generated from one location. In many cases, unless a business expands, it risks elimination. In addition, if you choose to continue your company "as is," your advertising budget remains minimal compared with that of a franchisor, whose local, regional, or national advertising fund is fed by a multiple number of franchise entities.

Above all, you must remain on the firing line. In other words, you are still the day-to-day manager and your life is spent hiring, firing, purchasing, and selling on the lower level. As a franchisor, you would direct a sizable operation with franchisees performing many of these duties. Franchising can give a business owner the opportunity to realize his or her full executive ability.

Selling products or services through the internet is an alternative to many businesses, particularly those selling products, instead of expanding by franchising. Of course, the owner bears all the expenses involved in selling direct and receives no franchise fees or royalties, but avoids the possibility of difficult relationships with franchisees.

The Company-Owned Outlet Alternative

The second alternative—formerly considered the only method of expanding a marketing system before the advent of franchising—is opening company-owned outlets. This normally requires a considerable capital investment and handling the difficult problem of securing capable, willing, and hard-working managers for each location.

In addition to the amount of capital necessary to expand your own business through company-owned offices, the amount of time spent in such company expansion is likewise very demanding. Site location, general administration, lease negotiation, and interviewing and hiring managers and employees all require considerable time and money that are not anywhere near the amount required for expansion through franchising. Long-term liability leases you must guarantee individually may hurt your business for many years. Taking on investors may cause you headaches when they start to second-guess your business decisions. In one instance, a good client started a successful franchise program offering a great and needed service only to have a new investor insist on opening only new company-owned units. This quickly resulted in red-ink losses from long-term lease payments, employee benefits, construction costs, and so on.

When opening a company-held retail distribution outlet, you spend money for a considerable time while receiving little, if any, profit in return. In franchising, by comparison, you immediately receive a franchise fee at the outset and then possible royalties if the franchise can generate sufficient sales during the first six months to a year. It is true that you must train the franchisees, but you would also have to train managers and employees of company-owned outlets. It seems that franchising has an advantage, since as the franchisor you do not have to pay the franchisees or their employees any wages or salary while they are being trained.

The Agreements of Association Alternative

A third and perhaps less common alternative to franchising is association through dealerships, licenses, incentive programs, partnerships, and joint ventures. Most dealerships, partnerships, joint ventures, and licenses come about through negotiations between two parties having some adverse interest, resulting in a compromise agreement. In most such cases, to satisfy the whims of both parties, control will be split, even though it should be centered in the hands of one. Often, when one party is supplying only the money, that party will insist upon some control over major decisions, even though he or she may not possess the necessary management abilities. In many cases, when the money provider exercises that control, it results in a decision based on money rather than on what is the most beneficial to the enterprise in the long run. This type of agreement is in contrast to the development of a franchising agreement, in which the franchisor unilaterally prepares his or her contractual arrangements from an objective standpoint, without being pressed into compromises.

Associating with others is even more difficult, since only very loose agreements, exerting practically no marketing control, can be worked out without violating franchise laws. In most such relationships, the entities in a joint venture or a partnership have equal control, which, in many cases, may cause either a stalemate or compromised business decisions. It is difficult to make good business decisions when you have to constantly reach a compromise between two or more people. With a compromise, the best you will have is a partially correct arrangement that could easily result in the loss of a lot of money and loss of market share.

Further, if an entrepreneur expanding through any joint venture or association intends to exert any type of control or even suggests certain marketing methods while receiving compensation for the right of the venture to use his or her particular trademark or service mark, he or she could easily be in danger of civil and criminal penalties for violating various state and federal franchise laws. In other words, if one party has too much control in a joint venture or association, the business arrangement may be treated as a franchise under the law. State and federal franchise laws generally set forth the elements of a franchise as the existence of an agreement wherein one party licenses the other to use a trademark or service mark, exerts some type of control over the person using the trademark or service mark (usually in a form of suggested or required marketing methods), and then receives compensation for such rights.

In essence, many state regulators hold that if it looks like a franchise, it is a franchise. Thus, if you license another to use your trademark or service mark and set him or her up in a business that operates like your other licensees, you are most likely franchising your business. This is especially true if you receive any form of consideration for these rights or require compliance with your marketing plan. In some states, just the suggestion of such marketing procedures is sufficient for government agencies to find a franchise law violation.

A partnership is a limited alternative to franchising, at best. If one partnership composed of one set of partners is the owner of all the retail stores, restaurants, or outlets operating under the partnership trademarks, the state registration authorities and FTC probably will not consider it a franchise. However, if an entrepreneur enters into general partnership agreements with different partners for each additional outlet utilizing the entrepreneur's trademark at each outlet, the arrangements between the entrepreneurial partner and the operating partners are, in essence, a franchise.

If you think about this, you will find that the partner for each store generally will put some money into the partnership, pay the entrepreneurial partner an initial and ongoing fee, salary, or draw for his or her expertise or supervision or both, and operate the outlet under the trademark of the entrepreneur. The same danger of violating franchise laws exists if the entrepreneur sets up different corporate entities and exercises shareholder control of the separate corporations, each operating outlets with different minority shareholders but the same trademark.

The key to a potential violation of the franchise laws is the trademark license agreement that must exist between the corporation holding the trademark registration and the sister corporations. These license agreements might constitute a franchise in the eyes of some state franchise legislation agencies. Such an arrangement should have prior clearances from the appropriate state and federal franchise authorities.

Before using any type of general partnership or majority-controlled, affiliated corporation or sister corporation, consult a competent franchise attorney.

Anyone wishing to expand through company-owned offices, an association, or franchising must look first to available capital and then prepare a business plan that delineates the amount of capital needed to attain the desired level of expansion and the availability of efficient and loyal management personnel.

If expanding through company-owned offices or an association, an entrepreneur also must evaluate the efficiency of his or her own personnel, since he or she most probably will be transferring this personnel to the expansion location. If available capital is limited and/or management personnel for company-owned offices or an association with third parties is insufficient, the entrepreneur should then consider the advantages and disadvantages of franchising as compared with the alternatives just discussed.

Conclusion

Hopefully, this brief discussion of several alternatives to franchising has helped you get a better idea of how you will want to expand your business. If your final decision is to franchise your business, it is then time to begin searching for well-qualified franchisees.

Chapter 8, "Building a Strong Franchising Foundation" discusses some of the issues you will need to explore when recruiting prospective franchisees.

Building a Strong Franchising Foundation

A S A WOULD-BE FRANCHISOR, YOU MUST REALIZE THAT YOUR CURRENT management and operating and marketing techniques probably are insufficient in many ways for a successful franchise operation. For instance, a good computer sales employee is not necessarily a good computer franchise salesperson. A good field manager is not necessarily a good franchise manager, particularly when it comes to supervising multiple, independently operating franchisees. Company managers who have trained company employees informally, one on one, might not be qualified to adequately train a group of potential franchisees who have a significant amount of their savings at stake.

In addition, present advertising media suitable for selling a product or service at the retail level is not necessarily suitable for attracting qualified people with adequate capital interested in purchasing franchises. In short, your previous experience and knowledge of your business may not necessarily be the same experience and knowledge required to successfully operate a franchise business.

To be successful, a potential franchisor must have built his or her own business, no matter what size, on a sound foundation of well-trained personnel, good marketing techniques, and an adequate working capital structure. These foundation blocks are the same for a successful franchise operation as well, but as a franchisor you will need to view them from a different perspective and utilize different skills.

Well-Trained Personnel

Your success really lies in your ability to recognize the business insight necessary to operate a smooth-running, successful franchise. To help you do this, carefully review your current management, marketing, training, advertising, and sales personnel to determine whether or not you should provide franchise management training, engage specialized consultation for present personnel, and/or hire new personnel. The capabilities of current personnel—such as in the case of the very small entity, consisting of the founder and his or her spouse—should be carefully reviewed and, where they are found lacking in franchise experience, they should be properly trained in franchise operating and marketing techniques.

Staffing a well-run franchise operation with knowledgeable, competent personnel can be achieved at a reasonable expense in one of four ways:

- ▶ Educating current personnel;
- ▶ Hiring experienced franchise personnel;
- ▶ Subcontracting for franchise functions; and
- ▶ Retaining an all-purpose franchise consultant.

Educating Current Personnel

First, if current personnel are not only capable of performing franchising duties, but also available for such duties without overextending themselves, franchise-oriented business seminars and literature should be sought out as educational tools. Many such courses are offered by specific professional business symposiums or community colleges and take one or two days. Courses and seminars are usually individual efforts presented by specialists with hands-on experience in their particular franchise fields and should not be confused with the all-purpose franchise consultants discussed later in this section.

Check the business opportunities section of your local Sunday newspaper regularly for listings of upcoming business events and seminars. These listings often contain goldmines of information for new franchisors and their inexperienced staff. The International Franchise Association (IFA) in Washington, DC, can also provide you with a wealth of information regarding franchising:

International Franchise Association
1350 New York Avenue, NW Suite 900

Washington, DC 20005-4709
Phone: 202 628-8000
Fax: 202 628-0812
Web: www.franchise.org
Email: ifa@franchise.org

Hiring Experienced Franchise Personnel

The second method of ensuring adequate personnel familiar with current franchising methods is to hire experienced personnel who have worked for other franchisors. You should review thoroughly not only each applicant's franchise expertise, but also his or her character and knowledge of current franchising laws. An applicant's basic knowledge of franchising could be based on methods now prohibited by franchise laws—methods such as providing actual or projected revenue and sales figures to potential franchisees and/or negotiating material terms of a franchise agreement without proper government approval. Thus, ensure that employee applicants are familiar with not only current franchise marketing techniques, but also the numerous legal restrictions that franchises may face.

Hiring additional experienced franchise personnel can be costly and it may not be necessary if you are a smaller franchisor. In many cases, the smaller franchisor will handle all the administrative, management, and marketing functions of his or her new franchise operation, at least initially. Therefore, if your franchise plan is to start with a small or medium-sized franchise system (maybe limited to one or two states), you may prefer educating current personnel about franchising rather than hiring high-priced new personnel with prior franchise experience.

Subcontracting for Franchise Functions

The third and highly recommended way of educating yourself and your staff on the business aspects of franchising is to subcontract the job to individual franchise specialists in the fields of law, training, advertising, public relations, and marketing. These consultants will evaluate your needs and, instead of providing a complete package, will give you only what you actually need.

The one outside professional that is always necessary is an experienced franchise attorney who understands not only franchise law but the everyday business aspects of franchising. Talk to the attorney's past franchise clients about his or her legal expertise and hands-on knowledge of franchising. Also refer to Chapter 10, "Selecting a Franchise Attorney," for tips on how to choose a good attorney.

When selecting an advertising agency, make sure it is one that specializes in franchising as well as general business. The same holds true with financing and marketing specialists. Carefully check each specialist's references.

Retaining an All-Purpose Franchise Consultant

The fourth method of obtaining franchise business guidance is to retain an "all-purpose" franchise-consultant entity—that is, an entity that provides the franchisor with the entire "franchise package," from legal work to marketing and advertising, all under one roof.

Most such "package" and multi-purpose consultants do not actually sell franchises but offer to train the franchisor's work force. A multi-purpose consultant is one who offers "complete services" to would-be franchisors, including preparing the franchise disclosure documents and other legal documents at costs ranging from $37,500 up to $200,000 or more for a complete package in phases. Such consultants may require their clients to retain their own counsel to review the legal documents and secure any required state registration at additional cost to the clients. Keep in mind that a corporation consultant who would do so without the proper legal qualifications would be practicing law illegally if he or she provides legal advice or representation.

In addition, the all-purpose consultant may provide operations manuals, video training films, and feasibility market and business plan studies that normally can be provided by local specialists in each field at much lower costs, often with a better final product. Never retain any consultant without thoroughly investigating his or her background and contacting his or her references and clients.

Individual franchise consultants who provide various specific services—such as training, marketing, advertising, sales, business planning, or financing—can be more organized, and informed, and less costly and faster than an all-purpose, high-priced consultant. If you go the way of a consulting firm, compare the costs of all-purpose consultants with those of individual specialists in the legal and marketing franchise field. It has been my experience that by farming out specific jobs to a specialist, such as Rick Grossmann (www.enspiren.com), who concentrates on individual areas, you might discover you can receive faster and better franchise guidance at a lower price. Again, the best way to evaluate a consultant or marketing specialist is to thoroughly investigate the person's references, particularly clients who have hired the consultant for assistance in franchising a similar business. It is vital to know about the results, as explained by clients, and the worth of those results compared with the price.

Never retain a consultant just because the consultant was once a franchise executive. First, find out if he or she was a good executive, why he or she left the franchise, and whether or not he or she is a good consultant. There are many former franchise executives who are out of work because of their lack of expertise. Evaluate the consultant's versatility.

In a new and diversified industry, such as computer software and hardware franchising, the experience required might not be compatible with the background of a consultant who had a lifelong career in the restaurant business, for example. A penny-wise but profit-motivated franchisor can retain various specialists as needed for specific functions and end up with less expensive, more suitable, and more extensive franchising services. An experienced, franchise-oriented consultant specializing in advertising will work perfectly with any experienced, franchise-oriented business planning or training consultant or employee. Both should be able to work effectively with an experienced, marketing-oriented attorney, since they will all be somewhat of like minds.

Marketing Techniques

Once you have been licensed to sell franchises as required by registration states or have obtained from your attorney suitable disclosure documents for other states, you must initiate advertising, sales, marketing, and public relations programs geared for launching your franchise operations. Selling your product or service to the final user or consumer of that product or service is drastically different from selling a person on becoming a franchisee.

A small, independent franchise could easily be sold by a one-person franchisor operation where the franchisor has a pool of good, qualified potential franchisees. An example of this would be the franchising of skilled trade services under a common trademark. The market consists of independent operators or skilled tradespeople working for companies engaged in that trade. For such a franchisor, marketing, advertising, and public relations can consist of working through trade papers or trade association meetings.

Even current employees of the franchisor can be a good source of franchisees in a certain situation, depending on the financial status of the employees and the cost of the franchise. A small franchisor capable of using current efficient staff could commence franchising at an initial outlay of amounts as low as $50,000, depending on location and the business to be franchised. This amount encompasses:

▶ The costs of suitable brochures;
▶ An experienced, business-minded franchise attorney; and
▶ The use of the franchisor's existing facilities.

The cost of the existing facilities would be incurred as part of the franchisor's prevailing or existing business being franchised, making the business a "pilot plant" and training facility. However, never capitalize at this low amount unless you have carefully worked out a realistic estimation of your projected income and costs during the initial years of your franchise company.

The Ideal Franchisee

It is a growing trend among some franchisors not to sell a franchise to anyone who has not worked for the franchisor for at least one year. This is a company rule of one of today's leading franchisors, Domino's Pizza. However, if you are not in a position to offer franchises only to persons who have worked for you for at least one year, you must incur the cost of identifying potentially good franchisees and establishing communications with them. In other words, you will need to formulate a profile of the type of franchisee who would have the best chance of succeeding in selling your product or service. The best franchisee is one who:

▶ Is a hard worker;
▶ Follows instructions;
▶ Will enjoy working in that particular type of business;
▶ Has a background suitable to it;
▶ Has adequate financial resources;
▶ Has a family that supports the new venture;
▶ Is able to follow orders; and
▶ Is in good health and of good moral character.

Generally, franchisees who continually wish to change systems or have suggestions for change based purely on theory do not make the best franchisees. The ideal franchisee should have advisory input abilities but not the stubbornness to insist upon changing the franchise system, at least until the franchisee's theories are tested or the franchisee can show, based on experience, that such theories work.

In any potential franchisee, look for the same qualities that made you successful in operating your retail business. There are business consultants who research and identify the profile of ideal franchisees for various industries and companies. It might be a good idea to retain such a consultant if his or her clients have provided good references. In many ways, good common sense and an objective view of what is necessary, as determined by your past experience or your operational personnel, might be the ticket to determining the best profile for the ideal franchisee.

Selecting an Advertising Agency

In situations where it is not a simple matter to attract franchisees, such as through internet advertising, and knowledge of the market for such franchisees is limited, an experienced, franchise-oriented advertising agency should be retained and a market survey initiated. The more difficult it is to attract the first franchisee, the more expensive advertising will be. The more extensive the franchising program is in the number of franchisees sought and the tightness of the timetable of expansion, the greater the necessity for a good, experienced, franchise-oriented advertising agency.

The cost of such an agency's services varies depending on the number of hours of work. Each franchisor is judged individually according to marketing needs and the marketing fee charged by the agency should be set accordingly.

Remember to select an agency or hire an employee with franchise business experience after careful investigation of background and valid references. Marketing products and services to the retail consumer is not the same as marketing a business to potential franchisees.

Most smaller franchisors initially will market their franchises on their own. They usually do this by advertising on the internet and in the classified section of the Thursday edition of *The Wall Street Journal* or the Sunday edition of local metropolitan newspapers. Franchise trade shows, particularly those sponsored by the International Franchise Association, are another good way to recruit franchisees.

Working Capital Considerations

The costs involved in franchising will vary according to geographic areas, expansion time, and availability of potential franchisees, as well as the complexity of the product or service being sold.

A small, one-person operation that has a profitable product or service with controlled lower costs and an ever-increasing market can franchise just as well as a larger competitor, provided the small business offers consistent services or products or both to its franchisees in a manner that will motivate the franchisees to remain in the franchise family. This usually means that the franchisor either performs a service or provides a product to the franchisee that the franchisee cannot obtain elsewhere or offers the product or service to the franchisee at a price lower than any price the franchisee could secure elsewhere or at a quality unavailable anywhere else.

This is necessary at least until the franchisor's trademark attains the recognition that will automatically generate continuing business for the franchisee or until the common franchisee advertising fund grows big enough to enhance the franchisee's business through customer recognition.

As a would-be franchisor, you must have a "glue" or "hold" on the franchisee that will be strong enough to keep the franchisee interested in remaining a licensed franchisee. In addition to providing the franchisee with products at lower prices and of the best available quality, as described above, such additional holds include supporting the franchisee's success. To demonstrate such ongoing support, you can provide continued training sessions, co-op advertising, billing and accounting services, discounted inventory prices from third-party suppliers, and exclusive product distribution.

The amount of working capital you need to start a franchise operation will vary depending on your size, rate of expansion, complexity of training, necessity of site selection and architectural planning, extent of marketing, attractiveness of the franchise, the capital investment required from franchisees, and other factors.

Carefully planned, slow expansion by a franchisor with a small, but efficient franchise-oriented staff or consultants and a product or service attractive to potential franchisees can be capitalized for under $100,000 by utilizing the existing franchise-trained staff.

Do not franchise your business without first developing a well-thought-out business plan. In this plan, you should set forth realistic marketing goals along with expansion plans, advertising programs, capital outlay, and projected costs for a five-year period. Make sure you have sufficient resources available. Don't rely on initial franchise fees and royalties to support you in the first few years of your business.

Realistic financial forecasts and iron-clad budgets, including necessary ongoing support systems for the franchisees, are the keys to successful franchise endeavors.

Conclusion

To build a strong foundation for your franchise operation, ensure that you:

▶ Obtain well-qualified and well-trained personnel to run and operate the business efficiently, as needed;

▶ Carefully develop strategies for marketing your franchise opportunity to potential franchisees; and

▶ Determine the income and cash outlays that will be needed for your first initial years as a franchisor, so you understand the numbers behind the venture.

If you use these resources and information in your franchising investigations and preparations, your franchise opportunity will have a much better chance for success.

CHAPTER 9

Franchise Laws–A Potential Trap for the New Franchisor

As discussed earlier, in Chapter 7, many successful business owners decide to expand their businesses through distributorships, licensees, or joint venture/partnership arrangements to distribute and sell their products or services and, as a result, save themselves a considerable amount of capital investment in building or leasing company-owned outlets. These third-party arrangements—whether they are called distributorships, license agreements, partnerships, or joint ventures—all have one thing in common: They may violate federal and state franchise laws, depending on the nature and terms of the relationship.

These industrious and sincere business owners, in their desire to adopt a successful marketing system and expand their businesses, may very well be entering into a nightmare of litigation and government agency investigations resulting in considerable civil damages and government penalties. In most cases, the business owner is unaware of the impending danger and perhaps has even consulted an attorney not experienced in or aware of the ramifications of federal and state franchise and business opportunity laws.

It is entirely possible that an entrepreneur may purchase, or an uninformed business owner may market, a company that is engaged in franchising without being registered under applicable state law or without following the appropriate directives set forth in federal law.

A typical example of this is the business owner who has developed a new or improved product or service and has experienced a certain degree of success in marketing it. He or she must now decide whether or not to raise and risk additional capital to provide more marketing outlets for the expanding line of products or services, which would include hiring people to conduct his or her business in these new locations. All of this takes a considerable amount of time and money. In most cases, the money is unavailable, interest rates are prohibitive, or it is almost impossible to find additional competent employees to market the product or service properly. The business owner then decides that he or she will teach others to market the product or service and charge them for his or her expertise. The recipients of this training will, of course, want the right to use the name of the business owner, which, in almost all instances, is an integral part of the sales success of the product or service. The business owner, by the same token, will want to exert some type of control or limitations on the use of his or her name by third parties, so that it can be used only under certain controlled circumstances, avoiding any chance of bringing the name into disrepute.

If any of these restrictions are violated, the business owner will want to call off the deal and revoke the right to use the trademark. In addition, in order for the fledgling business to succeed financially, it will be necessary for the business owner to teach the third-party licensee, distributor, or joint venturer methods of marketing the product or service that will bring a degree of success to the third party's operation. This marketing plan or scheme will be such as to correspond to the methods used by the business owner in gaining his or her initial success.

The end result desired by both the third party and the business owner is to maintain an operation engaged in marketing a product or a service that will look to the public as if it is one big organization with a single identity and universal continuity of service. The business owner, of course, is going to want some type of remuneration for training the third party and allowing him or her to become part of what looks like a "big happy family." The consideration is usually in the form of an initial fee to cover the training and, in many cases, a percentage of future gross profits. In some cases it may be the outright sale of a facility and the right to use the name for a one-lump-sum payment. Such an arrangement is clearly a franchise under federal and state franchise law.

The legal reality of the situation—that this is a franchise—is even less apparent to the business owner who is selling a product rather than a service—such as an image-engraving system or coin-stamping equipment—to a third party.

Federal Law

The federal government entered into regulating franchises on October 21, 1979, when the Federal Trade Commission (FTC) published its first original interpretive guides to the agency's trade regulation rule titled "Disclosure Requirements and Prohibitions Concerning Franchising and Business Opportunity Ventures." In essence, the FTC rules, which have been amended over time, are an attempt to remedy the problems of nondisclosure and misrepresentation that arise when people purchase franchises without first obtaining reliable information about them. The rules require franchisors and franchise brokers to furnish prospective franchisees with information about the franchisor, the franchisor's business, and the terms of the franchise agreement in one single document—the basic franchise disclosure document.

Additional information must be furnished if any claims are made about actual or potential earnings. This is referred to as the "earnings claim document." The franchisor must also give the franchisee a copy of the proposed franchise agreement. The disclosures must include important facts in terms of the franchisor-franchisee relationship.

The FTC rule does not require registration, but does require that you provide the potential franchisee with certain written disclosures at your first face-to-face meeting with him or her, and at least 14 calendar days before the franchisee signs any franchise agreement or other binding document or pays any consideration. See Appendix G for more details.

The FTC requires that the franchisor update the disclosure documents within 120 days of the close of the fiscal year. The Franchisor must also prepare revisions within a reasonable time after the close of each quarter, and attach them to or add them into the disclosure document to reflect any material change.

Due to the complexity of creating a disclosure document that meets all levels of legal requirements, it is not safe to attempt to complete this yourself. By following the sample franchise documents in the appendices, you can start to build the framework for your franchise documents that can be reviewed and completed by professionals. Doing this preliminary work will likely help you reduce your attorney fees.

Prior to January 1, 1995, federal law preempted certain state laws where there was overlap in the laws. In other words, if both federal and state law covered an area, federal law controlled. Effective January 1, 1995, the FTC adopted a disclosure format known as the Uniform Franchise Offering Circular (UFOC) that could be used to comply with state registration laws. This eliminated some duplicate disclosure requirements under federal and state statutes. The requirements of the UFOC have been modified, and the document has been renamed the "franchise disclosure document" or "FDD" by an amended FTC rule that became effective on July 1, 2008. See Appendix G for a copy of the amended FTC rule.

A violation of the rules set forth by the FTC for failure to provide the required disclosure document or for misrepresentation will constitute an unfair or deceptive act or practice within the meaning of Section 5 of the Federal Trade Commission Act. It subjects the violator to civil penalty actions brought by the FTC of up to $10,000 in fines per violation per day. The courts have held that the FTC rule does not create a private right of action in wronged franchisees. In other words, the rule is enforced by the FTC and not by lawsuits filed by individuals. However, some franchisees have successfully sought enforcement of disclosure rules using state unfair practice acts.

Under federal law, as the franchisor, you must provide prospective franchisees with a disclosure document that conforms to the law, but you do not have to send a copy to the FTC or register the document with the FTC. In states requiring registration, such as California, you must complete an application for registration that contains, among other things, information regarding the background of the salespersons authorized to sell the franchise and you must pay state registration fees. See Appendix E for more specifics on filing fees in franchise registration states.

State Law

Fourteen states have franchise registration or notice of filing acts: California, Hawaii, Illinois, Indiana, Maryland, Michigan, Minnesota, New York, North Dakota, Rhode Island, South Dakota, Virginia, Washington, and Wisconsin. If you want to sell franchises, these acts require that you file and gain approval of an application that contains information about who you are, submit a copy of your proposed contract, and prepare a proposed franchise disclosure document that is to be given to the franchisee a certain number of days before he or she purchases the franchise or pays any money for it.

The disclosure document required by the applicable state governments typically must contain, among other things, the following information:

- ▶ Background information regarding the franchisor, predecessors, and affiliates;
- ▶ The identity and business experience of key personnel;
- ▶ Pending franchisor litigation;
- ▶ Prior franchisor bankruptcies;
- ▶ Details of franchise fees and other fees;
- ▶ An outline of the franchisee's initial investment;
- ▶ Franchisor's assistance and related obligations of both the franchisor and franchisee;
- ▶ Territory;
- ▶ Trademarks;

▶ Patents, copyrights, and proprietary information;

▶ Obligations of the franchisee to participate in the actual operation of the franchised business;

▶ Restrictions on what the franchisee may sell;

▶ Renewal, termination, transfer, and dispute resolution;

▶ Arrangements with public figures;

▶ Financial performance representations;

▶ Outlets and franchisee information; and

▶ Financial statements of the franchisor.

In addition, a copy of the franchise agreement and an explanation of its more pertinent provisions are also required. Many of these topics are discussed in greater detail in Chapter 2 and illustrated in Appendixes A and B.

In most cases, if you are in a registration state, you will submit your application with the franchise agreement and disclosure document to a state official, who will then determine whether or not it has met the requirements of the state law and advise you accordingly. These state statutes, like the federal statute, require a complete disclosure of certain enumerated items. The states do not determine whether or not the statements in the disclosure document are true or false, but, in the event that a stated item is not true, the state gives the franchisee an additional legal right for damages.

In some cases, a violation may result in administrative or criminal sanctions or both, in addition to the civil remedies afforded to the franchisee. States that have franchise investment laws have statutes that can be used in seeking damages through the courts or arbitration for both loss of profit and return of monies spent in the event that a franchisor violates these laws. This is in addition to remedies for fraud that are available to any victimized business owner.

In addition, the states with franchise registration laws, and the FTC under its rules on franchising, have given government authorities certain powers to seek criminal remedies against franchisors violating the franchise acts and, in some instances, the power to order the franchisor to pay back franchise fees received in violation of the acts.

If you insist upon doing your own disclosure documents—which franchise experts do not recommend—you should familiarize yourself with the laws of the state in which you intend to franchise. At the very least, contact the various state agencies to see whether or not you are required to comply with their laws if you are selling to a franchisee residing in that state or if you want to operate franchises in that state.

In all states with franchise registration laws, if the prospective franchisee is a resident of the state and the franchise is to be operated in that state, the franchise laws of that state will apply. Also remember that you can make no claims regarding existing franchisees' earnings or potential earnings unless you provide an earnings claim document. Those states with franchise registration laws also require an approved earnings claim document.

Conclusion

Before selling your business in any way that will involve third parties—such as distributors, licensees, or partners—be sure to review federal and state franchise laws so you are informed on their requirements. In particular, you want to make sure your legal counsel is aware of these franchise requirements. It is amazing how many business attorneys are unaware of such requirements and legislation.

Ask your attorney if he or she is experienced with FTC rules as well as the acts in your state regulating franchise investment, business opportunities, and seller-assisted marketing plans—in short, franchises and other business ventures that are short of being franchises but are close enough to require a specific type of disclosure form. If your counsel is unfamiliar with these rules and regulations, seek counsel specializing in this area. Even if your counsel is familiar with these laws, request the names of previous clients that he or she has helped franchise and call them for their opinion of his or her knowledge and ability.

For further information on state franchise laws and resources, refer to Appendix E, "State Franchise Information Guidelines."

CHAPTER 10

Selecting a Franchise Attorney

T HROUGHOUT THIS BOOK, YOU ARE ADVISED TO CONSULT A COMPETENT attorney, who preferably specializes in franchise law, to assist you in the franchising arena—be it as a potential franchisor or as a prospective franchisee. The attorney's assistance can range from putting together the required disclosure documents to researching federal and state franchise laws.

Because franchise attorneys have gone through the franchise process before, they can be of particular help to new franchisors who are not familiar with the training, marketing, administrative, and sales functions that are unique to a franchising operation.

Another important area where franchise attorneys can be of assistance is in the marketing of your potential franchise. For many potential franchisees, the disclosure document is the first point-of-sale piece they see. Your disclosure document introduces you, presents your background and those of your predecessors, and outlines all the services, products, and obligations. Having an experienced, business-oriented attorney help you prepare your disclosure document effectively and accurately could prove very valuable, both in terms of marketing and in terms of complying with federal and state franchise laws.

Select an Experienced, Business-Oriented Attorney

A disclosure document must have provisions that are practical, time-proven, business-oriented, workable, and, above all, fair. Because most executives of a prospective franchisor entity, whether large or small, have no prior experience in operating a franchise business and not much, if any, know-how in selling franchises, training franchisees, or opening and servicing franchises, they are of little help to the franchise attorney from a business standpoint. As a result, the situation arises in which the attorney is required to know much more about franchising than his or her client does, in addition to knowing the legal requirements. Therefore, you should find out whether your franchise attorney is more than a legal technician whose only function is to file a legally acceptable document to get you a permit from the state authority to sell franchises.

When you and your experienced, market-oriented attorney begin work on the disclosure document and franchise agreement, you should have already made certain decisions including the franchise fee to be charged, the type of training to be given to the franchisees, the continuing royalty and service fees to be charged and the duties and obligations of both the franchisor and the franchisee. All such business decisions should be made based on time-proven, practical policies that are designed to assist, and not detract from, the overall success of the franchise system.

If you fail to properly prepare yourself for operating a franchise system, including selecting either a business-minded, franchise-oriented attorney or an experienced, business-oriented franchise consultant, you may be launching your new franchise the same way as you started the business you intend to franchise, with absolutely no practical knowledge of how to operate it.

Chances are the attorney you have used in the past will be in the same boat when it comes to franchising the business. You both may have started out as novices in the business start-up world, but through trial and error and working together, you have gained business know-how and developed proven procedures for business success. Now that you have reached the point of expanding your business through franchising, that attorney may not be the one you want to rely on for determining such franchise factors as suitable franchise fees and royalties, setting up and operating a franchise, and the franchise agreement. Trial-and-error methods of operating a franchise company do not succeed, because such companies are operating with other people's money and lives, and on a limited-time basis.

If you have knowledge and experience in opening a franchise or you have guidance from a consultant or a new employee who has actual experience in running a successful franchise company, you or your employee or consultant can tell the attorney what procedural rules are necessary for a workable franchise agreement.

Legal Fees—What to Expect

Attorney fees can vary depending on economic conditions, location, and attorney overhead expenses and experience. However, an experienced attorney in most geographical markets who runs a cost-efficient operation can usually make a fair return on a flat fee rate between $20,000 to $30,000 (depending on the complexity of the business, knowledge of the franchisor, and how much research and information the franchisor has gathered) for preparing and filing a marketable, workable, and well-coordinated disclosure document in the initial state of the franchise.

Attorneys should be able to complete their work within 30 to 60 days, barring any unforeseen circumstances. Legal fees for each additional state (since the disclosure document will have to be amended in certain states) will vary, but should be much less than the fee for the initial state because much of the information for the second document will have already been compiled. Filing fees in registration states range from $250 to $750. You should obtain from the attorney a complete fee quotation for the initial state and for additional states, along with his or her scheduled date of completion. Completion of the franchisor-background questionnaires in Appendices C and D may help you save legal fees and expedite the timetable for completing the franchise disclosure document and franchise agreement. Refer to Chapter 11, "Making Your Franchise Operation Work," for other tips on how to save on attorney fees.

Be very cautious of attorneys who seek hourly fee arrangements with no cap on the total amount. Fees can escalate quickly. Also be cautious of high hourly rates. Higher rates do not necessarily equal better quality. Many attorneys will be able to provide a total estimated fee up front so that you can incorporate the cost into your start -up budget.

Aside from legal costs, remember the cost of a certified audit, which is an initial necessity in certain states and an ultimate necessity in others. Generally, a good franchise attorney will have a client start a new corporation for the purpose of franchising; the audited financials of the new corporation can be nominal—from an estimated $1,000 to $2,000, depending again upon the accountant's location, experience, and his or her cost effectiveness.

Conclusion

As with any professional consultant, you cannot necessarily judge a good franchise attorney by his or her legal fees; you can, however, judge franchise attorneys by what their franchise clients say about them, not only in terms of complying with certain laws and regulations, but also in terms of familiarity with the time-proven and correct methods of operating a franchise in a particular industry. Insist upon references from the attorney and call each reference. Ask each client's opinion of the attorney's legal abilities and his or her ability to draft a disclosure document and franchise agreement that are fair, marketable, and marketing-oriented—all of which are necessary elements of a successful franchise operation.

CHAPTER 11

Making Your Franchise Operation Work

TO MAKE YOUR FRANCHISE OPERATION WORK MORE SMOOTHLY AND TO improve your chances of success, you should do several important activities, including the following:

▶ Assist your franchisees in finding suitable locations for their franchises so they have the best chance for success;

▶ Prepare an operations manual to provide franchisees with guidelines and instructions on how to operate the franchise on a day-to-day basis;

▶ Select a central franchise office that is practical and economical; and

▶ Develop franchise agreement clauses regarding transfer, renewal, and termination of the franchise, so that you can keep your franchise's reputation positive even if a franchisee becomes dissatisfied and leaves your organization.

This chapter discusses all of these activities with the hope that you, as the potential franchisor, will have much of this information and knowledge before dealing with potential franchisees, thus creating a better franchisee-franchisor relationship and, most likely, a more successful franchise operation.

Assisting Franchisees in Selecting a Site

If your franchise involves a restaurant or other business in which location is a key factor in franchise sales, you will want to have someone assist your franchisees in selecting sites. Most franchisors require their franchisees to conduct preliminary research on potential sites. In most cases, real estate brokers or shopping-center managers can provide the demographics and other commercial information pertaining to each potential site.

The primary reason for making your franchisees responsible for site selection is not only to make the franchisee thoroughly familiar with the pros and cons of each potential site location, but also to help alleviate any liability you may face if you are the sole selector of the site and the franchisee subsequently fails. Many franchisees who fail will blame the choice of site location as the primary reason for their failure, even though the failure may be entirely the franchisee's own fault. Therefore, most franchisors require the franchisees to make their own site selection, with the franchisor acting as the final approving authority.

To ensure that the franchisee has picked an appropriate site, however, you should have a qualified broker or other expert evaluate the suitability of the chosen site. This person should be qualified in real estate matters and have some experience in franchising and in the particular business being franchised. In some cases, a new franchisor may act as the site selection appraiser assisting the franchisee; however, most franchisors retain real estate consultants rather than hire full-time personnel, at least in the initial stages. These agents normally are compensated by brokers' fees from the landlord. Again, carefully check out references and accomplishments of the brokers or individuals you hire to help your prospective franchisee find a franchise location.

Costs of Providing Site Selection Assistance

If you and/or the franchisee are knowledgeable regarding the elements necessary for a good site for the business and conduct the site selection yourselves, costs will be minimal. If contacts are made with local real estate brokers who are familiar with your franchisees' needs and territories, costs will also be minimal. Hiring a professional, full-time site selector could be expensive, depending upon your location. In most cases, an employee hired as a site selector will hold other positions in a franchise company, including marketing or training responsibilities. Again, try to keep your costs at a minimum without sacrificing the effectiveness of your organization.

Preparing the Operations Manual

As part of the operational function in a well-developed franchise system, you should prepare and provide an effective operations manual that documents the functions of the franchise business in a written, chronological, step-by-step format, so that the franchisee can easily follow them after completing the initial franchise training program.

You can have an all-purpose consultant prepare your operations manual or, if you are an experienced business owner, you can do it yourself by following the sample "Operations Manual Outline" (in Figure 11.1 on page 103) and merely listing, in chronological order—perhaps by talking into an audio recorder—the steps that complete the operations of your business. This account of basic business practices details the specific elements that made your business unique and successful. If you feel awkward doing this, you can have someone else record and subsequently type up what you have said regarding the basic functions of the business. The operations manual is generally used to establish the framework that you will use for training sessions.

If you feel you do not have the necessary dictation and writing skills to create a training manual and if you do not have a family member or employee who can do so, hire a qualified person to write one. Even individuals who specialize in writing manuals can be hired for fees ranging anywhere from $2,000 to $5,000. If any confidential information is to be contained in the manual, take steps to get a nondisclosure agreement from the person retained to write and/or type the manual and consider obtaining copyrights for the manual.

Contents of an Operations Manual

Each franchisor's operations manual is unique, because in a given industry, each successful franchisor has a quality that distinguishes his or her business from those of his or her competitors. For example, a Wendy's operation featuring orders made up as they are given to the cashier differs from a McDonald's, where food is prepared in advance. Another illustration of this is Subway's method of making sandwiches at the direction of the customer, who deals with the individual preparer instead of ordering through a cashier.

Some franchisors have two operations manuals. One might deal with site selection, the initial opening of the store, bookkeeping, accounting, advertising, and grand-opening procedures. The second manual may address the duties of individual employees and, in the case of a restaurant, preparation of the food. A second manual could also cover such everyday duties as opening and closing procedures, accepting checks, making daily reports, hiring employees, preparing time sheets, receiving and transferring goods, preparing supply lists, and maintaining inventory procedures, security measures, and banking procedures.

Selecting Your Central Office

In many cases, one of the first things new franchisors do is commit themselves and their new franchise to a costly new office showplace. This can be fatal. You must do the same thing for yourself as you do for the franchisee: establish a highly capable, efficient organization at the lowest cost possible. You should have a pilot plant of the operation you are intending to franchise. Often, you can initially work from this location by using a back room and a new telephone number. If this workplace is not feasible because it does not present an attractive appearance, then you can rent, preferably month to month, a location and office furniture in an attractive, but economical building.

In many situations, executive suites that will provide services such as photocopying, faxing, telephone answering, and reception services can be rented by the month at an economical cost. You might want to take this avenue, at least initially, until the franchise business has taken hold.

Budget, budget, budget! Your success or failure can be determined in many instances by how well you plan your initial operation. Thus, plan your franchise operation in the same careful way as you have planned your business and the future business operations of your franchisees.

Reviewing Transfer, Renewal, and Termination Clauses

You must select each of your franchisees carefully. Never sell a franchise to anyone you do not consider completely qualified for the job. The franchisee is also a manager of your business extension, so you should never choose as a franchisee someone you would not hire as a manager. A good selection of franchisees will diminish the chance of franchise failure, especially early transfers and terminations. Treat the franchisee like a member of your team and regard the franchising system as an extension of your marketing arm. It is your services or products that are being sold under your service mark or trademark. You would not hesitate to assist one of your company managers when in trouble or even to remove him or her if it were in the best interest of the company-owned office.

If you look upon the franchisee as a replacement for your company-owned office, your attitude will be positive when concentrating on assisting him or her. Your franchise agreement should allow for transfers, with your consent, which you should not withhold unreasonably. Examples of transfer and termination provisions are contained in the sample franchise agreement in Appendix B.

If a franchisee is dissatisfied, the best procedure is to allow him or her to transfer his operation or for you to buy out the franchisee. Lawsuits are costly and time-consuming and you must report them in the disclosure document. Therefore, a lawsuit could be detrimental to the future sale of franchises, since potential franchisees will be made aware of the dissatisfied franchisees who are suing or have been terminated and these dissatisfied franchisees may give them negative information about you.

Franchise agreements are generally drafted by an attorney with provisions that are applicable in the state where the franchisor and the attorney are located. In many cases, the termination and transfer provisions may be contrary to the laws of other states where the same franchise agreement is being utilized. The cost of tailoring each clause to abide by changing laws in each state can be prohibitive. In addition, new state laws become effective from time to time after the initial franchise agreement has been drafted. Therefore, before any transfer is made, your attorney should check over the particular state law pertaining to transfers or terminations—even if there is a clause in your agreement stating that the laws of the state of the franchisor apply.

State Renewal and Termination Laws

Laws regarding the termination and transfer of franchisees are commonly referred to as "franchise relationship laws." Some of these termination and transfer laws are contained in state franchise investment or disclosure acts. Others are contained in a deceptive franchise act, pyramid scheme act, or retail franchising act and, in Wisconsin, the fair dealership law. For an abbreviated list of such laws, see Appendix E, "State Franchise Information Guidelines."

In the absence of a state statute to the contrary, a fixed-term franchise that does not provide for general renewal will expire upon its expiration date. However, some of the state statutes require good cause for termination. The good-cause requirements in some of these franchise laws may mandate renewal of a fixed-term agreement, even one that clearly states that no renewal is allowed, thereby resulting in the perpetual renewal of the agreement unless the franchisor can prove that the franchisee did something that constituted good cause for termination of the agreement. Some states allow nonrenewal for specified reasons, including failure by the franchisee to agree to the standard terms of the renewal franchise. Other states have specific notice requirements regarding nonrenewal of a franchise agreement. These laws change from time to time and, therefore, it is imperative that any franchisor who does not intend to renew, or has a franchisee who is transferring his or her franchise, consult with an experienced legal counsel for the purpose of checking current law before issuing any communication to the franchisee.

Transfer Fees

Franchise attorneys have a tendency to draft provisions that require substantial transfer fees for the franchisee. Some of these high-figure transfer fee provisions have been attacked as unconscionable in lawsuits. In fact, Iowa and Washington prohibit a transfer fee in excess of an amount necessary to compensate the franchisor for expenses incurred as a result of the transfer. Therefore, it is recommended that transfer and renewal fees be geared more to compensate the franchisor for expenses rather than to make a huge profit. After all, a good franchisee should bring good royalties to the franchisor.

Conclusion

If you take the time to research and compile much of the information pertaining to this chapter's activities before organizing your franchise operation and recruiting potential franchisees, you will be much better off than other prospective franchisors who haven't done their homework.

The more knowledge and tools you have for your franchise business—such as good site location data, resources for your particular business, and a thorough operations manual—the more secure and confident you will appear to potential franchisees. In other words, you will make a better impression on the prospects you talk to when getting your franchise operation going.

In addition to creating a more confident appearance, your research will also make you more aware of the costly mistakes frequently made by new franchisors, such as spending money too extravagantly on new franchise headquarters or making initial or royalty fees so high that new franchisees cannot make a profit. You will be a much wiser franchisor by doing research and investigation on your own and in conjunction with potential franchisees and franchise attorneys.

Figure 11.1 **Sample Operations Manual Outline**

OPERATIONS MANUAL OUTLINE

I. **Introduction**

   A. Welcoming Letter from Chief Operations Officer

   B. Introduction to Manual

   C. Biographical Information on Franchisor's Key Personnel

II. **Pre-Opening Requirements**

   A. Preparation of Chronological Chart by Franchisee, with Franchisor's Assistance, Setting Dates, and Time Periods for:

      1. Selection of the site by franchisee

      2. Approval of the site by franchisor

      3. Approval of the lease by franchisor

      4. Execution of a lease

      5. Commencement of construction within required number of days after execution of the lease

      6. Finalization of construction

   B. Preparation of Pro Forma Financial Statements by Franchisee and His/Her Financial Advisors and Accountants

   C. Checklist of All Necessary Permits and Registration Forms

   D. Review of Franchisor's Specifications Regarding Construction and Decor

   E. List of Equipment, Inventory, and Fixtures

   F. Procurement of Necessary Documents, Items, and Services

      1. Suppliers

      2. Telephone systems

      3. Security systems

      4. Cleaning agencies

      5. Trash removal agency

      6. Pest control service

      7. Map services

      8. Fire extinguishers

      9. Background music installation

      10. Bank services

      11. Appropriate licenses

      12. Sales tax permit

      13. Minimum wage and equal opportunity literature

Figure 11.1 **Sample Operations Manual Outline, cont.**

    14. Cleaning supplies
    15. Hand tools
    16. Office forms

III. **Pre-Opening and Post-Opening Training Procedures**
    A. General Daily-Business Operational Policies
    B. Product or Service to Be Sold
        1. Development of menu or product/service list
        2. Specifications
        3. Purchase lists
    C. Preparation of Personnel to Sell Product or Service
    D. Decor and Dress Code of Restaurant Personnel
    E. Customer Service Procedure Deliveries
    F. Delivery Requirements and Techniques
    G. Preparation of Sales and Financial Reports
        1. Daily business forms
        2. Inventory strategy
        3. Preparation of daily, weekly, and monthly financial statements
    H. Security Procedures
    I. Cash Register Operation
    J. Store Policy on Tipping
    K. In-Store Promotion, Advertising, and Mandatory Direct Mailings
    L. Periodic Amendments to Operation Procedures

IV. **Bookkeeping and Accounting Methods**

V. **Grand Opening Procedures**

VI. **Daily Operational Function**

VII. **Troubleshooting**

VIII. **Conclusion**

CHAPTER 12

Franchise Marketing

by Rick Grossmann

THIS CHAPTER WILL ENABLE YOU AS A FRANCHISOR TO MAKE THE MOST of your franchise marketing and recruiting efforts. You may have the best franchise business model in the world but you can't grow if no one knows about you.

Finding qualified franchise buyers can be the most challenging element of your franchise endeavors. Technology has had a huge impact on the way people research and buy franchises. You can use the concepts in this chapter to implement a comprehensive, multifaceted marketing program to set you apart from your competitors and enjoy consistent growth.

Franchise Historical Timeline

It is surprising to most people that McDonalds was not the first franchise in American history. The first was the Singer Corporation selling sewing machines in the 1800s. By the time McDonalds came around, many businesses had expanded through franchising. These businesses included Arthur Murray, Baskin Robbins, and Orange Julius. In the 1950s, a milk shake machine salesman named Ray Crock connected with the McDonalds brothers who owned a small hamburger stand. He brought the McDonalds franchise to the American population and today it's one of the strongest and most well-known franchises in the world.

Decades of Traditional Marketing

In the late 1960s and early '70s, as franchising began to gain momentum in the U.S. market and a variety of companies became available, franchisors had to determine the most cost-effective way to market their franchises to consistently bring in new franchise buyers. Before technology was the status quo, franchisors found traditional marketing to be most effective. Traditional marketing included direct mail, print advertisements, trade shows, and eventually TV and radio.

Game Changer—The Internet and Beyond

Before the internet, franchisors used traditional marketing methods to attract prospective franchise buyers to in-person meeting events. These events consisted of tradeshows and expos, seminars and presentations, discovery days, and individual meetings. These personal experiences increased the trust level for the franchisors as well as the prospective franchisees. These events were naturally expensive and time consuming, so franchisors welcomed the high-tech and cheaper alternative that the internet offered.

When the internet came along there was a mass exodus from the live events to "virtual events" such as online tradeshows, advertising portals, and franchise clearing houses. These options promised low-cost, 24-hour convenience, stay-at-home benefits, and much more. To most franchisors this made good sense, but they then experienced a loss of the personal experience. It was like asking someone to marry you over the phone or by email. Buying a business is one of the biggest decisions a person will make in life. This "technology backlash" caused many to return to the basics.

The Struggle to Regain the Discovery Process

Franchisors realized that the online experience was good for some things such as convenience and the ability to efficiently communicate and exchange information. On the downside it reduced the amount of personal interaction and commitment between the franchisor and prospective franchisees. The franchisors, despite the reduction in the marketing budget, realized they needed to invest time and money to regain a quality franchise discovery process. They began revisiting some of the traditional marketing methods in combination with the high-tech options that are available to them today. The most successful franchisors have found a balance by using technology to expedite their communication, combined with an in-person experience with their franchisee prospects. Franchisors with a strong website, email follow-up or newsletters, along with an array of personal discovery experiences that offer the franchise buyer convenience, but also demand personal commitment, are often in a better position to successfully enter into a franchisor-franchisee relationship.

Returning to the Basics

As franchisors decided to revitalize some of their preexisting marketing efforts by revisiting the basics of traditional marketing, they brought with them the experiences, successes, and challenges of the technology that had changed marketing so drastically in the last decade. As an example, they may implement a direct-mail campaign that is reinforced by a direct-email campaign, with links in the email to a sweepstakes page or to a "Request Information" page of their website. Or they may use social media sites to announce their presence at a franchise exposition and offer free passes for those who register on their website. Another example would be placing traditional print advertising in franchise industry magazines such as *Entrepreneur*, *Franchise Times*, *Multi-Unit Franchise*, or others, in combination with an e-newsletter announcing their attendance with an electronic form for preregistration. All of these are examples of the combination of traditional marketing along with the more high-tech marketing that has become available in recent years.

Leveling the Playing Field

A beneficial outcome of the introduction of technology to the franchise industry is the reality that the playing field has been leveled for all franchisors in the U.S. and around the world. Not too long ago, franchisors had to have a large marketing budget to enable them to compete in a national or international marketplace. This is one reason why you think of major brands like McDonalds and Subway and other household names when you think about franchising. With the onset of technology, we have seen the smaller franchise brands compete by utilizing creative technology campaigns that have enabled them to gain market share without having huge marketing budgets. In today's market the most creative and innovative franchisors are able to gain the lion's share of the franchise prospects by utilizing the internet, websites, and social media to give them the edge over their competition.

Redefining the Basics of Marketing—The Five Pillars of Marketing

If you think of marketing as a building, the pillars that give marketing structure are advertising, direct mail, sales, promotions, and public relations. Those categories make up the overall umbrella of the term we know as marketing. Most companies don't clearly define these categories and assign resources to each to maximize their overall marketing efforts. The most successful franchisors have been able to break down the five pillars of marketing, assign the appropriate resources, track their return on investment, and continue to fine-tune and adapt as the results vary. There are many specialists and consultants who can assist you in developing an overall marketing and execution plan. See Chapter 5 for a definition of the five pillars of marketing.

Advertising

Advertising is made up of several sub-categories. You may think of advertising as print media only. The truth is, advertising encompasses any media that allows you to purchase space to promote your marketing message. This includes print advertising such as magazines, newspapers, and other printed formats, TV advertisements, radio advertisements, billboards, and now, with the onset of technology, it includes internet advertisements, websites, and more. The franchisors who create innovative advertising campaigns across all platforms realize the best return on investment (ROI).

Direct Mail

Most of us think of direct mail as post cards that we receive in our mailbox. This is still an effective option depending on the strength of the message and the offer. With the onset of technology, other direct mail options are e-newsletters, drip email campaigns (a series of email messages sent to a prospect over a short period of time), and other opt-in alternatives that send information via the internet.

Sales

An effective sales process is a must for every franchise system. It's imperative for every franchisor to have a systematic, step-by-step discovery process for their prospective franchise buyers to follow. This process should be simple to understand, since the prospective franchisee needs to have the information presented to them in such a way that they can absorb it, weigh the pros and cons, and eventually make an educated decision. Methods of sales in the franchise world break down into the following sub categories of:

▶ Person-to-person sales that you might experience at a trade show, discovery day, or other discovery experience that the franchisor participates in.

▶ Phone sales that take place on either an outgoing or incoming basis. It's important as a franchisor to have a designated in-house franchise sales expert who is trained in the entire franchise process so he or she can present the opportunity to the prospective franchisee effectively and can answer questions and handle objections.

▶ Outgoing phone sales, sometimes called telemarketing can also be effective. It is far more challenging today to launch an effective telemarketing campaign due to caller ID, do-not-call lists, and voice mail. The important element of outgoing phone sales is to ensure that you are offering the franchise buyer information that is important to them and that provides them with an incentive to continue the discovery process with you.

▶ Use of technology, which has expanded the sales process. Email, texting, web presentations, and calendar syncing are as much a part of the franchise sales process as any traditional sales tool.

You will find that the best candidates will follow your discovery steps, will seldom miss appointments, and will quickly get back to you when you leave messages. This is a good indicator of their ability to follow a system, and of their enthusiasm and interest in your franchise concept. It also gives you an idea of their potential to be a successful business owner. One powerful tool is to utilize franchise-specific contact relationship management (CRM) software to keep track of your franchise prospects and their progress as they move through your sales pipeline.

Promotions

Traditionally promotions have been used to spark awareness and excitement in a marketing message. You have seen promotions like midnight madness sales, 24-hour sales, sweepstakes, giveaways, special events, customer appreciation dinners, or any kind of special, out-of-the-ordinary promotion that is utilized by various companies to attract new buyers or existing buyers back again. Successful franchisors use a combination of traditional promotions and promotions that utilize new technologies. For instance, they may hold a sweepstakes advertised in traditional media such as print, billboards, radio, and TV while also running the promotion on Facebook, Twitter, and other social media outlets. The internet options have given franchisors a low-investment way to reach masses of prospective buyers, allowing the smaller brand franchises to compete favorably with the bigger brands.

Public Relations

Public relations may be the most underused pillar of marketing. Traditionally, public relations campaigns would consist of press releases, press kits, sponsorships and other goodwill events and campaigns that would usually bring brand awareness through publicity. As the internet increases in popularity, we have found that public relations is still a very viable and important pillar that needs attention. However, the delivery has changed considerably and in some ways made it far easier to launch a successful PR campaign. An example of this may be a press release that in years past would have to be printed, put into a press kit, and mailed to 100 or 200 news and other media outlets hoping that the individuals at those outlets would find it interesting enough to write it into an article or a category of one of their existing articles or stories. It was difficult to have measured success with this technique. Today, successful franchisors enjoy the ability to release their newsworthy articles via blogs and on industry and business startup blog platforms. In most cases this is free and the more creative and informational the articles are, the more traffic they will draw. This method is also measureable since the analytics can be evaluated at the franchisor level and fine-tuned.

As you can see, the five pillars of marketing are alive and well, and probably always will be. These pillars have existed since people began to sell products and services to each other, although the delivery of the marketing message has changed.

Technology: The Sixth Pillar

As we covered in Chapter 5, the internet has become a stand-alone sixth pillar of marketing. This section will reveal the "best practices" of internet marketing for franchisors. Many franchisors are still pretty new at internet marketing; this gives new franchisors with strong internet marketing skills an advantage.

Not too many years ago the "Big Boys," or well-known franchisors, had the advantage because they had far more money and resources to market their franchise opportunities. Back then, the marketing and media options were very expensive so the new emerging franchisors were priced out of the competition. The internet has now leveled the playing field because the barriers of entry are lower, giving creativity, and not big marketing budgets, the advantage.

Consider the following benefits and tips when you develop your internet marketing efforts:

▶ The internet allows an interactive experience. Make sure your websites offer a personal experience to build value and trust. Include audio and video testimonials and introductions to your team. Make sure that you hire a professional to create high-quality recordings.

▶ The internet generation is accustomed to immediate satisfaction. Think how flustered we get when the computer takes 15 whole seconds to open a page! Making sure the information that is most interesting to prospective franchise owners is easily accessible and loads quickly shows your technology competence to tech-savvy buyers.

▶ The internet allows the prospective franchisee access to far more information than does an advertisement or brochure. Your internet marketing should guide them down a discovery path that they can move through at their own pace.

Websites

Website technology has evolved substantially over the last ten years. It is now far less expensive to create and maintain a strong web presence. When websites became a product that everyone needed, thousands joined the ranks of "webmaster." The sad reality is the fact that there is no way for consumers to identify who is a true "master" and who may be a "disaster." Interview several web design companies before making your selection. Also, check with their past clients to see how their sites are doing.

Here are some tips for creating a strong franchise website:

▶ Your site should have simple content and a clear call to action that is on the first page, visible without having to scroll down.

▶ Your site should be built on a Search Engine Optimization (SEO) friendly platform. Some of the older platforms can hurt your SEO rankings.

▶ Your site should be rich with keyword phrases, which are combinations of words that people enter into the search engines to find information. You can analyze the search terms that your prospects are using with a variety of online tools such as Google AdWords Keyword Tool. You may find that "dog grooming franchise" ranks higher than "pet grooming franchise." This enables you to use the more popular term on your site to rank higher for that phrase.

▶ Insert keywords in your titles, headings, and page titles.

▶ Include keywords in your URL (more commonly known as your web address) whenever possible. The URL www.XYZfranchise.com may rank lower than www.XYZautorepairfranchise.com.

▶ Include a web log or "blog" on your website and add new articles every week. Fresh, informative content increases your site's ranking.

▶ Obtain "backlinks" from other websites in your industry. This is explored further in the section on "Blogs" on page 112.

▶ Include social media icons that link directly to your social media pages.

Email

Email has become commonplace in today's world. Email allows you to communicate much faster than traditional mail, or what some call "snail mail" due to the time it takes to deliver. The following are some tips for your email efforts:

▶ Your email addresses should be connected to a dedicated URL. Rick@XYZautore-pairfranchise.com is much better than XYZautorepairfranchise@freeemail.com.

▶ Include a "professional signature." It should contain your picture, logo, contact information, and social media links along with your name.

▶ Include a legal disclosure that specifies that your correspondence does not imply an offer to sell a franchise. Have a competent, experienced franchise attorney provide you with this language.

▶ Be sure to comply with the email rules when sending "email blast" campaigns, including opt-out options and approved recipients.

▶ Always return emails within 24 hours of receipt. Sooner is even better.

▶ Have all company email messages proofread to ensure correct spelling, grammar, and punctuation is used.

▶ Be extra cautious when emailing from a smartphone—the typing is clumsy and the spellcheck is notorious for changing words . Some business people include an apology message for mistakes, but this does not make the best impression.

Blogs

You can think of blogs for your business in two categories. The first is the blog that should be a part of your website(s). You will want keyword-rich articles on your website blog to rank higher on organic searches. The second category is what some call the "blogosphere." There are thousands of great blog sites that already have tons of readership and rank high. You can submit your articles to theses sites and include your website link. This creates a backlink, which increases your organic ranking and directs traffic to your site. Blogs have enabled everyday people the ability to publish their ideas and insights on the web for free. This reality has flooded the internet with content about every imaginable subject. Your company can gain exposure by submitting relevant articles to blogs that prospective franchisees may frequent. Apply the following tips for your blog efforts:

▶ Research your industry niche to find the top blog sites.

▶ Choose a specific keyword phrase for each article. Use it once in the title and once per 100 words. If you use it too many times in the article, it may be overlooked by the search engines; 350 to 450 words is a good length for a blog article.

▶ Insert a link to your franchise website in each article.

▶ Make every article educational and newsworthy.

▶ Change at least 30 percent of the articles if you intend to submit them to more than one blog. The search engines will "de-dupe" or remove duplicate articles from rankings if they are exactly the same. You can buy software that assists you with the re-writing process.

Web Presentations

Technology has made meetings and presentations a snap. Not too many years ago, a meeting would require plane tickets, hotels, travel days, meals, and lost opportunity costs. Web presentations allow the presenter to share presentation slides, web content, audio and video testimonials, live presenter interactivity, and live two-way video.

Franchisors can now invite prospective franchisees to scheduled or impromptu web meetings to present their franchise opportunities. This is almost as effective as an in-person meeting, since you can cover the same information. You can meet with people all over the world from the convenience of your home or office. The following are some tips to consider when you launch your web presentations:

▶ You can sign up for web presentation options for a small monthly fee.

▶ Prepare a professional set of presentation slides and have them proofread. You may want to hire a consultant to develop this for you. This may be your first impression on prospects that are considering a huge investment.

▶ Always have the next step confirmed at the end of your presentation. Schedule the follow-up call, discovery day, or any other step when you are finished.

▶ Use this platform for franchise support and training as well. Connecting with your franchise owners is often the best way to keep you and your team engaged.

Electronic Newsletters (E-newsletters)

Electronic newsletters can be very effective as long as you have an interested readership. You must have impactful and useful content to engage your readers. Newsletters have been used for decades and most have little to no impact on their audience. Ask yourself when you last invested your time to read a newsletter. You must include "game-changing" and compelling ideas. What makes this interesting? In today's world, there is an avalanche of information every day. Consider an interactive e-newsletter with links to actual solutions or informative articles.

Search Engine Optimization (SEO)

Search engine optimization has become a major part of businesses worldwide. SEO can be defined as any online efforts that you make to drive traffic to your websites. Organic search results come from three primary elements of your website, which include fresh content, links, and keywords. You can target the most popular keyword and content based on your prospects' frequent search terms. You may want to hire a competent SEO consultant to help with this effort. They should offer a result guarantee for the keyword or keyword phrases that you choose to target.

Search Engine Marketing (SEM)

Search engine marketing or SEM is any effort to promote your business online. There are many companies that specialize in SEM that can assist you in your efforts. This will include SEO as well as pay options like pay-per-click advertising, banner advertisements, and other internet marketing.

Some of these options can be very targeted based on demographics and the audience's interests. You may notice when you log into your social media sites that the advertisements seem to match your interests. This form of behavioral marketing allows the advertiser to narrow the audience as they set up the campaign. You may even consider using "follow ads" that appear, based on an individuals' interests and online habits, on the sites that the individual frequents.

Social Media

Social media has changed the way people communicate. This platform enables people to create networks with friends, family, and business associates. The people within these networks can then keep track of each other and collectively communicate and have dialogue about anything that comes up, from very deep subjects to nonsense.

Social media has given people more direct access to influential individuals. Now, political figures and celebrities can post their thoughts dynamically as often as they want to their followers or fan base. This creates a more personal experience for many.

As a franchisor, you can have social media components that augment your other internet marketing efforts. Consider the following when you create your social media campaigns:

▶ Hire a professional to help you with this effort unless you are very familiar with social media. You will want to appoint someone within your company to focus on this to ensure consistency. Once you build a group of fans or followers, you must provide good information on a regular basis or you will lose them.

▶ Include great content to keep your audience engaged. Avoid posting "the fact of the day" type of postings just for the sake of posting something.

▶ Allow potential franchisees the ability to ask questions and get to know your company culture.

▶ Monitor the content carefully to make sure that it remains positive and professional.

Many franchisors today are facing the challenges of their franchisees launching their own social media campaigns. Social media can be a great marketing tool for franchise owners if it is closely managed by the franchisor. The downside is the reality that it increases risk to your brand since outside individuals will comment on these platforms and become associated with your company. To promote appropriate social media use, apply the following to your franchisee social media program:

▶ Create a clear set of social media policies that give the franchisees very specific guidelines to adhere to. Include these policies in your operations manual and make sure that everyone understands and conforms accordingly.

▶ Consider hosting corporate-only social media platforms that link to the individual franchisee pages. Allow the franchise owners to post local articles, photos, and other relevant content to give them a local presence. This gives you the highest level of control.

▶ Appoint someone within your company to consistently monitor the content of all social media sites. This individual can also keep the sites current with interesting information. Many "spammers" and "trolls" target social media sites and can post offensive links and content. Be sure to eliminate these individuals from your sites.

▶ You will need more stringent policies and monitoring if you allow your franchise owners to manage their own social media efforts.

▶ Regardless of your final structure, you must be the clear leader for your franchise community when it comes to social media. Do not let it get away from you. It will be far more difficult to implement damage control years down the road than it will be to deal with these issues now.

▶ Include social media and other technology clauses along with your website references in your franchise disclosure document and franchise agreement.

Texting

Today, many of us rely on the instant response that comes from texting. Be prepared to have dynamic texting as a part of your franchise recruiting process. It is proven that people read and respond to text messages far more than email or even phone calls. You will want to offer texting as a communication option for prospective franchisees during the discovery process. You will also want to allow your franchisees texting options for support after they open for business.

Podcasts

This is a series of audio or video messages that can be featured on your website or emails. They are a good way to educate your prospective franchise owners as they move through your discovery process. You can break your franchise sales information into short high-impact audio or video segments. You can also optimize these for the search engines to drive traffic to your websites by posting them on all of the free sites and directing links back to your sites.

Smart Device Applications

Smartphones and tablets have changed the way we "do life." We now have fully functional computers in our pockets. Imagine combining an old-fashioned camera, video camera, desktop computer, global positioning system, music library, library of books, clock, time-management calendar, notebook, weather forecast, calculator, TV, and every game you can imagine in one small package that is smaller than a 1980s calculator.

New smart device applications, commonly referred to as "apps," enter the marketplace daily. You will want to explore the available apps to identify possible options to promote your franchise opportunity. Depending on your business model, you may find the need to create your own app to connect your customers with the services of your franchise owners. Hire a company that has a good track record to create your custom apps.

Television Commercials and Interactive TV

Technology has made television more affordable with cable and network options that allow local commercial customization. TV ads on network television stations were very costly, which made them unaffordable for most small businesses. However, today you can advertise your franchise opportunity by placing commercials in key markets and targeted channels at a fraction of the cost of prior years. In some markets you can add the option for an interactive, immediate response. This option allows viewers to request more information by pressing a button on their remote control immediately, which is when they are most interested in the offer.

Future Technologies

Some say that a majority of the technology that we will be using ten years from now has not even been invented yet. It sounds crazy, but is not hard to imagine when you consider what the first cell phone looked like. If you ever called someone from your car phone and said, "You will never guess where I am calling you from," then you get this.

Commit to staying ahead of your competition when it comes to technology. This can be the deciding factor for many businesses. Listen to your advisors and franchise owners as they experience challenges in the field. Be willing to innovate and push the envelope as technology evolves. Some choose to stick to the good old-fashioned basics and evaporate because they can't keep up. Be the leader!

How Do I Compete?

You may ask yourself this question when you consider the thousands of franchise opportunities available around the world. Some of them are industry giants with huge marketing budgets. This can seem daunting as you consider entering the franchise world as a new, small company. The truth of the matter is there has never been a better time to throw your hat in the ring! The playing field is now level. You don't need a million-dollar marketing budget to be successful. With technology on your side, you can get your message out to the world by being creative and persistent.

Consider the following tips:

▶ *Hire experts—you don't know what you don't know.* An experienced franchise development consultant and franchise attorney will save you tons of money and grief.
▶ *Create a solid marketing plan.* Use this book to outline your marketing and recruiting program to ensure that you are covering all the bases.
▶ *Commit to your plan and execute it* (no matter what).
▶ *When you have success, tell the world.*
▶ *Take the time to build relationships with your franchise owners.* Your first franchisees "buy in" because they trust you and believe in you.
▶ *Include the first franchise owners in the "big picture success story."* Make them part of your owners advisory committee and let them help you solve problems and create new programs.
▶ *Offer funding alternatives.* Become the "rainmaker" by offering financing and investment alternatives to standard bank loans. In today's world, people are buying franchises with creative solutions like self-directed 401(k)s, investor pools, angel investors, and even government programs like the EB5 international investor option.

Conclusion

The American dream has always been based on the reality that we, as U.S. citizens, have the opportunity to achieve successful business enterprise in a free market. We have the privilege to cultivate good ideas, products, systems and methods for delivering products and services and then turn them into businesses.

You wake up at 2:00 A.M. with a groundbreaking epiphany. You sit at the kitchen table with a stack of blank paper and a pen. Your brilliance pours onto the paper, and in short order you have created a business model that has never been done before.

You go online and form a corporation or LLC in minutes. You create a website. You start making money, build a great business and franchise to expand and share your brilliance with others.

America is the birthplace of innovation and franchising. You have the best opportunity right in front of you. Invest in something you can really believe in: yourself and the opportunity of a lifetime!

CHAPTER 13

Final Thoughts on Franchising

I N THIS FINAL CHAPTER, YOU WILL FIND SEVERAL HELPFUL TIPS AND information on franchising your business. Areas include subfranchising, saving on attorney fees, determining capital requirements, and avoiding litigation. By this point, we hope you have gained enough information to understand your responsibilities as a franchisor and perhaps have even begun some of your research and investigation. Take the time here to learn ways to cover all your bases and save money at the same time.

Subfranchising or Area Franchising

Subfranchising, sometimes referred to as area franchising, is a procedure by which a franchisor tries to clone himself or herself. In other words, for a substantial fee, a franchisor sells to a third party, usually a group of investors, the right to use the franchisor's trademarks, trade secrets, and training, administrative, and marketing procedures in designated regions of the United States and the world. Thus, the purchaser of a region will act in the place of the franchisor in that particular region. Usually, the consideration of subfranchising does not come up until a franchisor has successfully franchised in a particular area.

Before embarking upon this venture, however, thoroughly consider the positive and negative aspects of such an arrangement.

The Century 21 system has been a subfranchising pioneer. The cloned subfranchisees did not have to provide a great deal of training to their new franchisees, since, in most cases, they were brokers who knew how to sell real estate. For the most part, they simply changed their coats when they joined the nationwide Century 21 system.

Unlike franchisees, subfranchisees are usually a group of wealthy individuals who are looking for a return on their investment. It is extremely difficult to get one or more investors of a subfranchise to carry on the everyday activities required for a successful subfranchise company. Therefore, this avenue should be reviewed very carefully before any decision is reached. Selling a subfranchise territory is also expensive. The market for subfranchisors is limited to a person or persons with a considerable amount of money—anywhere from a quarter of a million dollars to several million dollars.

Generally, this type of individual is looking for an investment and does not want to be taught the exhaustive, highly difficult job of marketing franchises and following through by providing supportive services to the franchisees. It is much easier to find qualified franchisees than it is to find qualified subfranchisors with huge capital resources. In addition, subfranchisors tend to make changes in the franchise system and often feel they are as competent as the original franchisor or more so, since they usually become more active than the franchisor in the actual operation of the franchise.

In addition, in order to sell subfranchises, a franchisor must prepare a franchise disclosure document and a subfranchise contract detailing the terms and conditions of the arrangement between the franchisor and the subfranchisor, including the splitting of royalties and initial franchise fees, the delegation of someone as a trainer, and more.

Once the subfranchisor has purchased a subfranchise that qualifies in the FTC states, he or she must in turn register his or her own disclosure document before selling franchises in registration states. In nonregistration states, the subfranchisor must still provide prospective franchisees with a disclosure document containing pertinent disclosure items. If you are considering subfranchising as an option, take great care in selecting each subfranchisor and think through all the pros and cons.

Saving on Attorney Fees

Many new franchisors have little personal knowledge of how to run a franchise company; nevertheless, they have definite ideas of what they want to charge as franchise fees, royalties, and advertising fees. They generally base their ideas on what they would like or what others have been doing—that is, seeking franchisees more as a method of making a lot of money rather than as a way to extend their marketing arm by adding franchised retail outlets.

It is an experienced, knowledgeable franchise attorney's job to interview his or her franchisor clients and determine certain biographical information as well as their business desires, particularly those pertaining to royalties and franchise fees, and to reconcile the information so he or she can give a more objective, realistic view of what each new franchisor should do. To help you in your first meeting with your franchise attorney, you will want to complete the two background questionnaires in Appendixes C and D. Both of these questionnaires make you think about what you want contained in the disclosure document and the specific terms you want in the franchise agreement. By completing these questionnaires before your first visit to a franchise attorney, you may be able to convince him or her to lower the bill because of the time you have saved in securing such information.

In addition, if you can supply your attorney at this first meeting with further written documentation of the estimated costs of opening and operating one of your franchises, the number of such franchises that will be sold within the ensuing year, and a complete breakdown of what the franchisee will be required to spend in order to open one of your franchise outlets—including franchise fees, rent, fixtures, equipment, payroll, utilities, insurance, and working capital—you will hasten the preparation of your disclosure document and thus possibly reduce your legal expenses.

Determining Your Capitalization Requirements

One of the first items you, as a potential franchisor, must determine is the amount of money necessary to capitalize your franchise operation. In a registration state, the minimum amount of capital that a franchisor should have is a sufficient amount of liquid cash (current assets) so that he or she can open the number of franchises he or she projects opening in the forthcoming year. However, your capitalization amount should be equal to the amount you have projected to carry you to your break-even point— where income will begin to equal payables. In addition, the higher your capitalization, the easier it will be for you to sell franchises, since your audited financials are part of your disclosure document.

Impounds

If you are in a registration state and the attorney for the state examining your application for franchising determines you do not have sufficient capitalization to open the franchises you plan to open, the applicable state agency may still grant you a permit to sell franchises. To do this, however, you must open an impound account in a bank chartered in that particular state for the direct deposit of all franchise fees. In essence, an impound is a trust account: the franchisor is required to have the franchisee write a check to the designated depository bank, to be held in trust until the franchisee provides a written declaration to the registration state that his or her franchise is open and that the franchisor has performed all of his or her opening obligations under the franchise agreement.

Once this declaration is received, it is filed with the appropriate state registration agency; if the agency approves the declaration, it will prepare an order allowing the franchisor to remove the franchisee's funds from the bank. The franchisor then submits this order to the bank and the bank pays that particular franchise fee to the franchisor.

Unfortunately, there are not too many banks familiar with these trust account procedures and most such escrow accounts are extremely expensive—$1,000 to $2,000 in some cities for each franchisee escrow account. In some instances, your franchise attorney may be able to convince the state authority that you will provide in your franchise agreement that you will not require payment of the initial franchise fee until the franchisee has opened his or her store and advised you that he or she agrees you have fulfilled all your opening obligations under the franchise agreement. Many registration states will allow this type of provision in lieu of impounds.

Franchise Taxes

As a franchisor, you will definitely need to retain the services of a competent accountant who is versed in franchise taxation. Presently, franchise income has generally been held not to be passive income if the franchisor has ongoing responsibilities. In addition, the Internal Revenue Service places certain restrictions on when the franchisor can report income as earned. Generally, the franchisor can report the franchise fee as earned only during the time the franchise is operating. Since you will need annual audited statements, your CPA (required) will advise you of the current tax regulations on these tax matters.

Besides the federal tax regulations on franchise income, many states have franchise tax regulations. To get more information on your tax obligations and reporting requirements, see an experienced accountant or certified public accountant. You don't want any nasty surprises that could cost you money. Be as informed as possible on franchise income taxation.

Franchisee Associations and Advertising Councils

Most registration states have laws that prohibit a franchisor from interfering with the right of franchisees to have their own associations. Franchisees can have an association, but it is in your best interests as a franchisor to form that association and you should be involved in its operations. Generally, a franchisee association will not be formed until seven to 10 franchisees are operating in a given area.

A franchisee association should be an advisory body only, since you, as the franchisor, should still determine the specific procedures to be followed by the franchise system. Many successful franchisors, including McDonald's, have improved their systems by implementing suggestions from franchisees and making changes within the entire system after they have been proven successful at one or two test-franchise operations.

Like franchisee associations, franchisee advertising councils can be effective, too. Each franchisee usually has his or her own idea of what the ideal advertising media should be—and most of the ideas are cost-prohibitive. For instance, almost all franchisees want local, regional, and national television exposure, which is much too costly in most cases and clearly in excess of the advertising fund fees collected from franchisees. It would be better to poll the franchisees from time to time in order to get an idea of which local advertising media they have found effective in their operations.

A good franchise agreement should compel the franchisee to provide written reports of all types, particularly covering sales data, and this information could then be compiled into meaningful results for each franchisee in the system. This is one of the major benefits of the franchise system—the experiences of each franchisee, rather than his or her theories, can be compiled, analyzed, and passed on for the benefit of the entire system.

Cost-Saving Tips for the Disclosure Document

Do not indiscriminately mail or pass out your disclosure document, because this document can be anywhere from 80 to 100 pages long and is costly to reproduce. In addition, circulars shouldn't be easily disassembled, but you should not heavily staple or bind these documents in any way, shape, or form. This is because you will be revising your disclosures quite often, particularly if you have registered in more than one state. You can save yourself the cost of completely replacing your current supply of official disclosure documents by substituting a revised page for the old page. Using a three-ring, loose-leaf binder might be a good idea.

All franchise registration laws and the FTC rule require that the disclosure be modified at least once a year, or at any time a material modification is made, or both. Audited financials, for all practical purposes, must be updated yearly, so you will be amending and filing them annually in the registration states. To save on significant copying costs, screen your potential franchisees by using a customized "Franchisee Business Application and Net Worth Form," such as the sample form in Figure 13.1 on page 128, before sending out any disclosure document.

Steps to Take Before Sending the Disclosure Document

Following a prospective franchisee's initial inquiry, you should send him or her an informational brochure. Brochures can cost anywhere from a few dollars to thousands of dollars to prepare. Depending on your personal taste and budget, it may be preferable to use a simple letter-form brochure stating many of the items that are in the disclosure—but painting a nice picture of the attributes of the particular franchise system.

In California and a few other states where registration is necessary, the brochure, like any advertisement, must be submitted to the appropriate registration authority for prior approval. An ad is generally required to be submitted in duplicate anywhere from three to seven days before publication, with a duty upon the agency to disapprove it within such time or the ad is deemed approved.

In addition to sending a brochure, you should make an attempt to find out if the franchisee is financially qualified to buy a franchise. Therefore, the first document forwarded to the franchisee should be a franchise application seeking the franchisee's background information and net worth. See Figure 13.1 on page 128 for a sample of a "Franchisee Business Application and Net Worth Form." This application should be tailored to your needs and reviewed by your legal counsel.

Receipt

After a prospective franchisee has completed the background application and net worth financial form, use the document to assess his or her suitability to your franchise by checking out every disclosure that you can. If you determine a franchisee to have the necessary qualifications, the next step is to forward your disclosure document to the prospective franchisee or meet with him or her and present the circular. The prospect acknowledges receiving the disclosure by signing a document called a receipt and returning it to you, as the franchisor. At the end of Appendix A, on page 182, is an example of a receipt.

Always prepare two receipt forms, one copy for the prospective franchisee to keep and the other for him or her to sign and return to you. If the franchisee signs one and returns it to you but doesn't retain a copy for his or her own records, he or she may at some time in the future, particularly if the situation involves legal proceedings, contend that he or she didn't receive the disclosure in a timely manner as dictated by the current rule. This initial accusation might be avoided if you provide the franchisee with a copy of his or her acknowledgment receipt at the time it is executed.

It is a good practice to provide the potential franchisee with the required disclosure document before any discussion about it.

If the franchisee is out of state and the franchise is to be operated in your registration state, the disclosure document to be sent to the prospective franchisee would be your in-state disclosure document. However, if the franchise is to be operated in another state, you will be required to register in the other state before offering your franchise.

Deposit and Lease Agreements

After the prospect has reviewed the disclosure and indicated a desire to purchase the franchise, you may have him or her execute a deposit agreement and make a partial franchise fee payment, called a deposit, while he or she evaluates possible franchise locations. Many franchisors prefer to have the franchisee sign the franchise agreement and immediately pay the entire franchise fee. The use of the deposit agreement, when a franchisee does not yet have a location and may be a little reticent, is one way to get your foot in the door. This is a marketing theory based on the premise that once a person pays something down, he or she is more likely to pay the balance and not back out of the deal. A copy of the deposit agreement must be part of the disclosure document.

You should be knowledgeable in lease negotiations or at least able to assist the franchisee in lease negotiations, making sure to inform him or her that final approval of the lease is at your discretion.

The landlord should give the franchisee certain information, such as definite construction completion and opening dates. Many franchisees have leased locations with leases that allowed the landlord to complete construction, for periods up to 18 months or even two years, before the franchisee was allowed to cancel the lease.

The franchisee tenant should have an escape clause so he or she can cancel the lease if the particular building or structure is not completed within the time frame set by the franchisee. Depending on whether there is a seller's or buyer's market, it may be difficult to get a choice location under these conditions. One last warning: Never allow the franchisee and his or her spouse to quit their jobs or sell their house and move until it is absolutely certain that their particular franchise will be opened shortly.

Some franchisors require that franchisees have their landlords execute a lease assignment agreement allowing the franchisor to take over the franchisee's location in the event the franchise agreement is terminated.

Avoiding Litigation and Arbitration

Avoid litigation if at all possible. Not only is litigation expensive—although less so if an arbitration provision is included—but the facts of the litigation or arbitration must be reported in the franchise disclosure document. This includes furnishing the name, address, and phone number of each litigating franchisee. It also makes the marketing of future franchises much more difficult, since prospective franchisees can contact the listed litigating franchisees and, in all probability, will receive negative information about the franchise operation.

Breach of Contract

Some registration states provide that if a franchisor fails to properly register a disclosure document, the franchisee can automatically file an action for rescission and get his or her money back. However, many other states merely make this a possible criminal violation while upholding the validity of the franchise agreement. The general rules of agreement regarding substantial breach would then apply—that is, a franchisee would have the burden to prove to a judge, jury, or arbitrator that the franchisor made a specific written commitment and failed to follow through on that commitment. If this were proved, it would constitute a substantial breach of the franchise agreement. There is a fine line between a "substantial" breach and an "insubstantial" breach, wherein a verdict for rescission would not be granted, but rather a judgment for whatever money damages the franchisee may have proven. In addition, most franchisors, in their franchise agreements, present a minimum amount of written obligations that apply after the franchisee has opened his or her operation.

If you are proven to have committed a fraud—making fraudulent promises that were not true that induced the franchisee to enter into the franchise agreement—he or she may seek to rescind the agreement based on what is called "common-law fraud." It is not the purpose of this book to be a franchise legal manual; therefore, you must take every precaution to make sure your employees, particularly your franchise salespeople, make no representations that are not set forth in the written disclosure document. In addition, actively abide by all after-opening obligations to the franchisee, as provided in the franchise agreement.

Pros and Cons of Arbitration

The positive aspect of arbitration is that you can generally select an arbitrator who has a firm knowledge of franchising from the standpoints of both franchisor and franchisee, as opposed to a judge or jury who know little, if anything, about franchising. The ideal arbitrator is one who has a legal and a franchising background, because arbitrators who are businesspeople tend to give both parties some type of award. Therefore, neither party wins. As a straight legal rule in the judicial system, if a contract is breached or a franchisee has been defrauded, only one party should win and the other party should get nothing. In a major arbitration, three arbitrators may be selected, so as to eliminate the chance of selecting a totally outrageous sole arbitrator who will render a bad decision.

The negative side of arbitration is that it is final and binding and, in most cases, the decision cannot be appealed. However, most court appeals are won by the party that won at the lower level. In addition, court appeals are extremely expensive and time-consuming.

Franchise Fees and Royalties

Many franchisors fail because they expect to immediately profit by charging high initial franchise fees, high royalty fees, and high advertising fees. However, if you look at what is happening in the American market, you will find that discounters who charge lower fees and bank on volume to make profits have overtaken the retail market. Most franchisees cannot handle high initial franchise fees and even higher royalty fees based on their gross sales. So, keep your expenses at a minimum while maintaining a high level of services to the franchisee. The franchisee is the marketing arm of the franchisor; if the franchisor can set up a franchisee by breaking even, he or she has already accomplished a great feat.

Many franchisors who set their fees higher are unable to sell many franchises—and the franchises they sell have such high fees that they soon go out of business. In some states where franchisees have brought lawsuits against franchisors with excessive fees and royalties, the courts have sided with the franchisees! So having 1,000 franchisees paying $50 a month is much more profitable than having 10 franchisees paying $1,000 a month.

Always make detailed projections regarding how much profit you can make with a minimum amount of franchise fees and royalties, taking into consideration the profit you will make from the sale of your products and services to your franchisees. It will be time well spent.

Making the Decision

Now that you are more familiar with franchising in general, you are better prepared to make your final decision. Be sure to consider whether:

- ▶ The advantages of franchising outweigh the disadvantages.
- ▶ Your business has a market and a registrable trademark.
- ▶ Your current personnel or outside consulting personnel familiar with franchising are well qualified and available.
- ▶ You have no problem with selecting sites or preparing the manual.

▶ You have the working capital necessary to start the franchising process.

▶ You have sufficient capital to market your franchise.

▶ You have prepared a realistic business plan and budget for your franchise entity.

▶ You have an attorney who is not only experienced in franchise law but also familiar with the business aspects of franchising and the necessary relationship with the franchisee.

If these statements apply to you, you are ready to move ahead to a new way of conducting business and an exciting way of life.

Figure 13.1 **Franchisee Business Application and Net Worth Form**

FRANCHISEE BUSINESS APPLICATION AND NET WORTH

This information is confidential. We will not contact your present employer without your consent.

Name of Franchise and Franchisor: _____

Name of Applicant Franchisee: _____

Personal Information on Potential Franchisee

Single ❑   Separated ❑   Married ❑   Divorced ❑

Number of minor children: _____ Ages of children: _____

Other dependents: _____

Own/buying home ❑   Rent ❑

Live with parents ❑   Live with spouse ❑   Live with relatives ❑

Home payments $ _____ per month

Rental payments $ _____ per month

If buying, monthly payments $ _____ Paid to: _____

Applicant

Name: _____

Home telephone: _____

Figure 13.1 **Franchisee Business Application and Net Worth Form, cont.**

Business telephone: _____

Home address: _____

City/State/Zip: _____

Social Security number: _____

Birth date (day/month/year): _____

Physical Information

Height: _____   Weight: _____

Physical limitations or health concerns: _____

_____

Educational Record

High school: _____

Last grade completed: 8 9 l0 11 l2 _____

College/university: _____

Major: _____

Degree received: _____ Year: _____

College/university: _____

Major/area of study: _____

Degree received: _____ Year: _____

Employment Record

Current employer: _____

Address: _____

City/State/Zip: _____

Position: _____

Present salary: _____

Figure 13.1 **Franchisee Business Application and Net Worth Form, cont.**

Started (year): _____ to _____

Description of work: _____

_____

Previous employer: _____

Address: _____

City/State/Zip: _____

Position: _____

Salary: _____

Started (year): _____ to _____

Description of work: _____

_____

Employment Record of Applicant's Spouse

Current employer: _____

Address: _____

City/State/Zip: _____

Position: _____

Present salary: _____

Started (year): _____ to _____

Description of work: _____

_____

Previous employer: _____

Address: _____

City/State/Zip: _____

Position: _____

Salary: _____

Figure 13.1 **Franchisee Business Application and Net Worth Form, cont.**

Started (year): _____ to _____

Description of work: _____

_____

Previous Business Owned

Have you ever owned your own franchise or other type of business? If so, give the following details:

Business 1 name: _____How long owned? _____

Address: _____

How many employees? _____

Type of business: _____

Describe how the business changed over the time you owned it. _____

_____

Business 2 name: _____How long owned? _____

Address: _____

How many employees? _____

Type of business: _____

Describe how the business changed over the time you owned it. _____

_____

Financial Information (Note: Additional financial information may be required.)

Net Worth Summary

	Current Assets		**Current Liabilities**
Cash in checking account		Notes payable	
Cash in savings account		Amount owed on real estate	
Total		Total	

Figure 13.1 **Franchisee Business Application and Net Worth Form, cont.**

	Fixed Assets		Long-Term Liabilities
Real estate, home			
Other real estate			
Listed stocks and bonds			
Automobile(s)			
Your own business			
Money due you			
Insurance (cash value)			
Other assets			
(describe)			
Total		Total	
Total Assets		Total Liabilities	

Net Worth (assets less liabilities)	

How much capital can you allocate from the above sources to buy this franchise?

$ _____

What is the cash down payment you can make for a franchise? $ _____

If the required amount is not available, how would the investment be obtained? _____

_____

If you own your home, do you plan to sell it? Yes ❏ No ❏ Equity $ _____

Do you plan to convert any of the above assets into cash? Yes ❏ No ❏

Do you plan to have a partner? Yes ❏ No

If so, will the partner be active? Yes ❏ No ❏

Figure 13.1 **Franchisee Business Application and Net Worth Form, cont.**

Do you plan to have investors? Yes ❑ No ❑   If so, to what extent? _____

_____

Thoroughly explain your answers and any other strategies you have for obtaining the required funds. Use a separate sheet if necessary.

What is the minimum income you need to maintain your family during the first year of business? $ _____

From what sources will it come? _____

_____

References

Business References

Name	Address	Years Known

Character References (other than employers or relatives)

Name	Address	Years Known

Figure 13.1 **Franchisee Business Application and Net Worth Form, cont.**

Former Addresses for the Past Five Years

1. _____

2. _____

3. _____

4. _____

5. _____

Business Goals

In order of priority, list which specific types of business you prefer to become involved with.

1. _____

2. _____

3. _____

4. _____

Are you willing to relocate? Yes ❏ No ❏ If so, state locations in order of priority.

1. _____

2. _____

3. _____

4. _____

When do you want to start your franchise operation? _____

How did you become interested in this particular franchise? _____

_____

What are your realistic personal and professional goals _____

_____

Three years from now? _____

Five years from now? _____

Figure 13.1 **Franchisee Business Application and Net Worth Form, cont.**

10 years from now? _____

State your reasons for believing you will be able to successfully operate one of our franchises. _____

_____

_____

_____

_____

_____

Do there appear to be any disadvantages to owning one of our franchises? If so, please state your concerns. _____

_____

_____

_____

_____

_____

Certification

I certify that the enclosed information as given is complete and correct.

_____   _____
Applicant's Signature   Date

It is understood that the purpose of this questionnaire is to gather general information and is in no way binding upon either the company or the applicant. It is, however, understood that the applicant supplies the information contained herein to the best of his or her knowledge and ability and that the company relies on this fact in assessing the desirability and qualifications of the applicant.

PART III

Appendices

Franchise Disclosure Document

T HIS APPENDIX CONTAINS A SAMPLE DISCLOSURE DOCUMENT THAT conforms to guidelines of the Federal Trade Commission (FTC) amended rule. The 14 registration states may require additional information in their disclosure documents.

Most people, whether seeking to become franchisors or franchisees, initially have no idea what a disclosure document looks like until they contact an attorney. Examine the sample disclosure document, whether you are a potential franchisor or a prospective franchisee, and compare it with the information in Chapter 2.

Pay particular attention to Item 11 of the document, "Franchisor's Obligations." As a franchisee, you will receive important benefits from a good franchise agreement that you could not receive if you started the particular business on your own. For the franchisor, these obligations "glue" the franchisee to the franchise. For example, if the franchisee can purchase inventory at the lowest competitive price from the franchisor, this glues the franchisee to the franchisor for the term of the franchise agreement. The franchisee cannot purchase the inventory at that low price without the franchisor. Other benefits attractive to a franchisee, which serve as glue to the franchisor, may include the exclusive use of a patented process or product, low-cost health plans, secret recipes, or access to national purchasing accounts.

Look for the "glue" when you review the following disclosure document. Using the information you learned from this book, decide for yourself whether the disclosure document you are signing is a good one.

The following franchise disclosure document is fictional and included for illustration purposes only with the consent of its author, Michael Katz, Esq. It represents a disclosure document that conforms to federal guidelines in effect as of February 2012. It is intended to be a reference resource only and should not be used as an exclusive source for developing franchise documents for a specific franchise. You should consult with a franchise attorney to obtain current state and federal requirements before starting any franchise venture.

FRANCHISE DISCLOSURE DOCUMENT

NOAH'S ARK FRANCHISING INC.

AARDVARKS ONLY

Information for Prospective Franchisees

FRANCHISE DISCLOSURE DOCUMENT

NOAH'S ARK FRANCHISING INC.
A Colorado Corporation

AARDVARKS ONLY
123 First Street
Denver, Colorado 80000

(888) 555-1212
_____.com/info@_____. com

Noah's Ark Franchising offers franchisees the right to operate a business that offers to the public pet aardvark care services and products such as grooming and training.

The total investment necessary to begin operation of a Noah's Ark franchise will range from $60,750 to $120,750. This includes $16,750 that must be paid to us.

This disclosure document summarizes certain provisions of your franchise agreement (Franchise Agreement) and other information in plain English. Read this disclosure document and all accompanying agreements carefully. You must receive this disclosure at least 14 calendar days before you sign a binding agreement with, or make any payment to, the franchisor or an affiliate in connection with the proposed franchise sale. **Note, however, that no governmental agency has verified the information contained in this document.**

You may wish to receive your disclosure document in another format that is more convenient for you. To discuss the availability of disclosures in different formats, contact Noah's Ark at Noah@____. com or at 123 First Street Denver, Colorado 80000, (888) 555-1212.

The terms of your contract will govern your franchise relationship. Don't rely on the disclosure document alone to understand your contract. Read your entire contract carefully. Show your contract and this disclosure document to advisors, such as a lawyer and an accountant.

Buying a franchise is a complex investment. The information in this disclosure document can help you make up your mind. More information on franchising, such as "Buying a Franchise: A Consumer Guide," which can help you understand how to use this disclosure document, is available from the Federal Trade Commission. You can contact the FTC at 1-877-FTC-HELP, or by writing to the FTC at 600 Pennsylvania Avenue, NW, Washington, DC, 20580. You can also visit the FTC's home page at www.ftc.gov for additional information. Call your state agency or visit your public library for other sources of information on franchising.

There may also be laws on franchising in your state. Ask your state agencies about them. State authorities are listed at Exhibit A.

Date of Issuance: January 1, 2012

2

STATE COVER PAGE

Your state may have a franchise law that requires a franchisor to register or file with a state franchise administrator before offering or selling in your state. REGISTRATION OF A FRANCHISE BY A STATE DOES NOT MEAN THAT THE STATE RECOMMENDS THE FRANCHISE OR HAS VERIFIED THE INFORMATION IN THIS DISCLOSURE DOCUMENT.

Call the state franchise administrator listed in Exhibit A for information about the franchisor or about franchising in your state.

MANY FRANCHISE AGREEMENTS DO NOT ALLOW YOU TO RENEW UNCONDITIONALLY AFTER THE INITIAL TERM EXPIRES. YOU MAY HAVE TO SIGN A NEW AGREEMENT WITH DIFFERENT TERMS AND CONDITIONS IN ORDER TO CONTINUE TO OPERATE YOUR BUSINESS. BEFORE YOU BUY, CONSIDER WHAT RIGHTS YOU HAVE TO RENEW YOUR FRANCHISE, IF ANY, AND WHAT TERMS YOU MIGHT HAVE TO ACCEPT IN ORDER TO RENEW.

Please consider the following RISK FACTORS before you buy this franchise:

THE FRANCHISE AGREEMENT REQUIRES YOU TO RESOLVE DISPUTES WITH US BY LITIGATION, ARBITRATION, AND MEDIATION ONLY IN A LOCATION THAT IS WITHIN 15 MILES OF OUR THEN-CURRENT HEADQUARTERS (CURRENTLY DENVER, COLORADO). OUT-OF-STATE LITIGATION, ARBITRATION, AND MEDIATION MAY FORCE YOU TO ACCEPT A LESS FAVORABLE SETTLEMENT FOR DISPUTES. IT MAY ALSO COST YOU MORE TO SUE, ARBITRATE, AND MEDIATE WITH US IN OUR THEN-CURRENT HEADQUARTER'S STATE THAN IN YOUR OWN STATE.

THE FRANCHISE AGREEMENT STATES THAT THE LAW OF THE STATE IN WHICH THE FRANCHISOR'S HEADQUARTERS IS LOCATED (CURRENTLY COLORADO), WILL GOVERN THE AGREEMENT, AND THIS LAW MAY NOT PROVIDE THE SAME PROTECTIONS AND BENEFITS AS LOCAL LAW. YOU MAY WANT TO COMPARE THESE LAWS.

THERE MAY BE OTHER RISKS CONCERNING THIS FRANCHISE.

We use now, or may use in the future, the services of one or more franchise brokers or referral sources to assist us in selling our franchise. A franchise broker or referral source represents us, not you. We pay this person a fee for selling our franchise or referring you to us. You should be sure to do your own investigation of the franchise.

The effective date of this Franchise Disclosure Document for your state is listed on the next page.

3

STATE EFFECTIVE DATES

The following states require that the Franchise Disclosure Document be registered or filed with the state, or be exempt from registration: California, Hawaii, Colorado, Indiana, Maryland, Michigan, Minnesota, New York, North Dakota, Rhode Island, South Dakota, Virginia, Washington and Wisconsin

This Franchise Disclosure Document is registered, on file or exempt from registration in the following states having franchise registration and disclosure laws, with the following effective dates:

California	
Florida	
Hawaii	
Indiana	
Kentucky	
Maryland	
Michigan	
Minnesota	
Nebraska	
New York	
Rhode Island	
South Dakota	
Texas	
Utah	
Virginia	
Washington	
Wisconsin	

The effective date of this Disclosure Document for any state that is not included on this list is as shown on the cover of this Disclosure Document.

4

TABLE OF CONTENTS

EXHIBITS

Exhibit A. List of State Agencies/Agents for Service of Process

Exhibit B. Franchise Agreement

Exhibit C. Operations Manual Table of Contents

Exhibit D. List of Franchisees and Franchisees That Have Left the System

Exhibit E. Trademark Specific Franchisee Associations and Independent
Franchisee Associations

Exhibit F. State Specific Addenda

Exhibit G. Financial Statements

Exhibit H. Receipts

5

NOAH'S ARK FRANCHISING INC.
Franchise Disclosure Document

ITEM 1
THE FRANCHISOR, AND ANY PARENTS, PREDECESSORS, AND AFFILIATES

To simplify the language in this Disclosure Document, "we," "us," or "Franchisor" means the Franchisor, Noah's Ark Franchising Inc. The "Franchisee" or "you" means the person or corporation, partnership, or other entity including your owners, stockholders, or partners, who are buying the right to operate under the Franchise Agreement.

The Franchisor

We are a Colorado corporation that was formed on January 1, 2010, and which does business under the name "Noah's Ark Franchising Inc." We maintain our principal office address at 123 First Street Denver, Colorado 80000 (888) 555-1212. We do not conduct business under any other name. You will be licensed to operate under one or more of the following names: "Noah's Ark," "Aardvarks Only," and "Noah's Ark Aardvark Services," and under any other trade names, service marks, logos and the like (Marks) all in accordance with the "Franchise Agreement," which is attached at Exhibit B. We have offered franchises since January 1, 2012.

We do not operate a business of the type being franchised. We have not in the past, and do not now offer franchises in any other line of business. We are not involved in any other business activity.

Our agent for service of process in your state is disclosed in Exhibit A.

Our Parents, Predecessors, and Affiliates

We have no parents or predecessors.

We have 1 affiliate whose name is Ark Pet Services Inc., a Colorado corporation (Affiliate) that was formed on January 1, 2000. It does business as Noah's Ark Pet Services. Its address is the same as ours. It owns one business that is substantially similar to the one that is being offered here, which store has been opened in Colorado since March 1, 2000. It has never offered franchises in this or any other line of business.

The Franchisor's Business

We offer franchisees the right to operate a business that offers pet aardvark care services and products, including grooming and aardvark training. Your business operation will generally be called your "Business."

This Franchise Disclosure Document ("FDD" or "Disclosure Document") and the Franchise Agreement describe the terms and conditions under which we currently offer franchises to new franchisees. As the needs of the market change, we will occasionally offer franchises under different terms and conditions.

6

Competition and Regulations Affecting the Business

You will be competing with other individuals and companies that offer pet aardvark services including established businesses that offer similar services.

You must obtain the business licenses that are required by the locale in which you will be operating your Business. In some jurisdictions you will be required to have a dog boarding, animal grooming, or similar license. You will also be required to conform to any taxation requirements of your locale. The municipality, city, county, or state in which you intend to operate may have special rules, regulations, or laws that affect the operation of your Business and we urge you to make further inquiries about these. You and not we are responsible for determining the scope of such rules, regulations, or laws, and you must adhere to the same to the fullest extent required by the law.

Item 2
BUSINESS EXPERIENCE

Noah's Ark—President

Mr. Ark has been our President since inception and has been the President of our Affiliate since its inception. Mr. Ark is a world-renown expert on aardvark care and has been the President of the World Aardvark Alliance located in St. Louis, Missouri, since 2005.

Item 3
LITIGATION

No litigation is required to be disclosed in this Item.

Item 4
BANKRUPTCY

No bankruptcy information is required to be disclosed in this Item.

Item 5
INITIAL FEES

Initial Franchise Fees

Your initial franchisee fee will be $15,000 (IFF).

Other Fees

If you are awarded the right to operate a Business, you will also be required to purchase from our Affiliate, or us, the "Startup Kit" for $750. The Startup Kit contains your initial inventory of printed materials, including brochures, stationery, advertising materials, and logoed apparel.

We will create your own homepage which will be sponsored on our website, and you will pay us the $1,000.00 Technology Startup Fee.

Unless otherwise stated, all fees are payable in one lump sum, are due at the time you sign the Franchise Agreement, and are non-refundable under any circumstances.

7

Except as described above, you pay our Affiliate or us no other fees or payments for services or goods before your business opens.

Item 6
OTHER FEES

Type of Fee[1]	Amount	Due Date	Remarks
Royalty	7% of the "Gross Revenue" generated by the Business[2]	Paid by you into your account monthly by noon mountain time on the 3rd business day of the month that follows the month for which the Royalty is due. We will collect this by electronic funds transfer.[2]	
Local Advertising Fee	2% of Gross Revenue;	Paid as incurred to your advertising vendors	
National Advertising Fee	1% of Gross Revenue	Payable monthly with the Royalty to us	At the time we have 20 Businesses.
Regional Advertising Cooperative Fee	If Regional Advertising Cooperative is formed, fee will be payable from National Advertising Fee. There currently are no Regional Advertising Cooperatives.	Will be due on the days determined by the Cooperative	We may create a regional advertising cooperative that will include all franchisees within a designated area and will be self-administered by franchisees. (Item 11).
Advanced and Additional Assistance	Our then-current fee, which is now $500 per day, plus travel reimbursement.	14 days before visit	If you require or request advanced or extraordinary services. The then-current fee will be described in the operations manuals ("Manual" or "Manuals").
Initial Training for Replacement Principal Operator or Designated Manager	At our option, we may charge our then-current tuition which now is $500 per day, plus your costs for travel, food, and lodging at our training facility.	14 days before training	This may be charged for each additional Principal Operator or Designated Manager that obtains training.
On-Site Visits	We will charge our then-current fee, which now is $500 per day plus travel, room and board.	10 days before the date of the visit	At our option and after your request. (Item 11)

8

Type of Fee[1]	Amount	Due Date	Remarks
Transfer Fee	50% of the then-current IFF for the type of Business being transferred	At execution of then-current Franchise Agreement	Payable to us if you are permitted to transfer your rights to a third party
Successor Franchise Rights Fee	50% of the then-current IFF for the type of Business being sold	At execution of then-current Franchise Agreement	Successor may be required to sign a contract with terms that are different than found in your current Franchise Agreement.
Technology Maintenance Fee	The then-current fee, which now is $250 per month	Payable monthly with the Royalty to us	
Computer Hardware and Software Maintenance; and Updates	We estimate the cost to update computer hardware to be between $500 and $1,000 and the cost to update computer software at between $100 and $1,000.	As incurred	We will require you to update computer hardware no more often than once every 5 years. Computer software will be updated no more often than once every 3 years. Payable to approved supplier. (Item 11)
Late Fee	$100 late fee plus 1.5% per month for any payment not timely made	Immediately when assessed	Payable only if you fail to make your payments on time.
Maintenance of Business	Will vary	As incurred	This includes upkeep for, the building, the interior and exterior decor, and equipment.
Renovations	Will vary based upon upgrades to décor, design, and equipment	Payable as incurred	You may be required to renovate the Business, no more often than: every 5 years; and at the time you purchase Successor Franchise Rights (and every 5 years thereafter); and, prior to the transfer of Franchised Location to another. Each franchisee should allocate a portion of all Gross Revenue (in an amount decided solely by the franchisee) to meet such renovation requirements. Payable to approved supplier.
Costs and Attorneys Fees	Will vary	As incurred	
Indemnification	Will vary	As incurred	You have to reimburse us if we are held liable for any claims arising from your business.

9

Type of Fee[1]	Amount	Due Date	Remarks
Approval of New Supplier	Our then-current fee (which now is up to $1,000)	As incurred	
Insurance	Will vary	As incurred	Paid to insurance company for liability and other required insurance
Audit Expenses	Cost of audit plus 1.5% per month; plus, if understatement is 2% or greater, our inspection/ audit expenses	As incurred	Incurred if you understate your Gross Revenue or fail to make payments. Paid to us or accountant
Replacement/ Additional Inventory	Will vary	As incurred	Replacement of inventory of consumables, sales literature. Paid to us or approved supplier.
Replacement Tools and equipment	Will vary	As incurred	Will be incurred to replace lost or broken tools and equipment. Paid to approved supplier.
Relocation Fee	Our then-current fee (currently $5,000)	As incurred	Paid to us if we approve the relocation of your Business
Cost of Enforcement	All costs including reasonable attorneys fees	Upon demand	You must reimburse us for all costs in enforcing obligations if we prevail.
Annual Conference	Currently none. Our then-current fee, if any, which we anticipate to be $100 to $500 and your expenses in attending	Expenses are paid as incurred	Currently we don't have an annual conference, but we may have annual conferences in the future. Expenses vary based on travel cost and type of accommodation.

[1]Unless otherwise specified, all fees are imposed by and are paid to us. All fees are non-refundable except as otherwise stated in this FDD.

[2]"Gross Revenue" means the total of all revenues and income from the sale of all products and services from all sources in connection with the Business, whether or not sold at or from the "Franchised Location" (as that term is defined in Item 11), whether received in cash, in services in kind, from barter and/or exchange, on credit (whether or not payment is received), or otherwise. You may deduct from Gross Revenue all sales tax or similar taxes, which by law are chargeable to clients by any taxing authority. You may also deduct from Gross Revenue the amount of any documented refunds. All payments made to us including Royalties will be paid through an automatic electronic bank-to-bank transfer (EFT).

10

Item 7
ESTIMATED INITIAL INVESTMENT

Your Estimated Initial Investment

Type of Expenditure	Amount	Method of Payment	When Due	To Whom Payment is to be Made
IFF[1]	$15,000	Lump sum	At signing of Franchise Agreement[1]	Us
Rent[2]	$1,500 to $4,500	As arranged	As per lease	Landlord
Deposits[2]	$1,500 to $3,000	As arranged	As per lease or agreement	Landlord or utility provider
Leasehold Improvements[2]	$10,000 to $30,000	As arranged	As arranged	Landlord or approved vendors
Startup Kit[3]	$750	Lump sum	At the time you sign the Franchise Agreement	Us or our Affiliate
Furniture, Fixtures, Equipment, Tools, Signage[3]	$10,000 to $30,000	As arranged	As arranged	Approved vendors
Computer Hardware and Software[4]	$500 to $1,000	As arranged	As arranged	Approved vendors
Technology Startup Fee	$1,000	Lump sum	At the time you sign the Franchise Agreement	Us
Training Expenses[5]	$1,000 to $3,000	As arranged	As arranged	Airlines, Hotels, Restaurants
Insurance[6]	$1,000 to $3,000	As arranged	When incurred	Insurer
Professional Services[6]	$3,000 to $7,000	As arranged	When incurred	Architect, contractor, attorney, others
Opening Inventory[7]	$1,000 to $2,000	As arranged	As arranged	Approved vendors
Grand Opening	$500	As arranged	When incurred	Payable to vendors for goods used in the Grand Opening.
Additional Funds–3 Months[8]	$15,000 to $20,000	As arranged	When incurred	Employees, utilities, landlord, suppliers and others
TOTAL[8]	$60,750 to $120,750			

11

Unless otherwise specified, the expenses in this chart are non-refundable.

1 The IFF is for an Exclusive Territory (Item 12).

2 There is no requirement to purchase real estate in connection with ownership of your establishment. A suitable store is normally rented; its size should be in a range of between 500 to 1,000 square feet.

Usually the location will to be remodeled and must be brought up to our current standards, the current zoning requirements, or other standards then in effect. Local, state, or other fees, or taxes could cause extra costs in developing a new location. The location must be accepted by us in writing and construction or improvements must be approved in writing by us. In some cases the landlord may contribute to the build-out expenses, which may reduce your initial investment. These figures are estimates only. Costs will vary widely depending upon your location in the country, the leasing fees, location of the proposed location within your Exclusive Territory, and other factors. Your costs could be significantly greater than are stated here.

The landlord may require you to deliver a security deposit that may be equal to a month or more of rent. A utility provider may require you to make a deposit in order to secure the use of utilities.

These figures represent rent for 3 months.

3 The Startup Kit will be purchased from our Affiliate or us. (Items 5 and 8).

You will be required to have aardvark care equipment including washing stations, grooming tables, kennels, water and food bowls, and other tools. The entire list of items will be identified in the Manuals.

You will also be required to have office equipment such as a table, chairs, and the like. You may already have sufficient furniture or fixtures.

You must display our approved signage both outside and inside the Business, as well as our interior and exterior decor items.

4 You will be required to purchase the computer hardware and software more fully described in Item 11. You may already own computers and software that meet such configuration.

5 You must pay all of your out-of-pocket expenses while attending training at our then-current headquarters. These numbers are estimates only and will depend on the lodging you choose, the method of getting to the training location, and the food you purchase.

6 The amount of insurance includes the initial cost of liability insurance to protect you against claims from customers.

You may also be required to hire an architect and contractor to complete the tenant finish. This also includes fees that you may incur from other professionals, including CPAs and attorneys.

7 These figures include consumables such as shampoo, conditioner, food products, and other retail items.

8 This estimate of additional funds is for the first 3 months of operating capital. The estimate does not include an owner's salary or draw. Your need for these funds will vary by: your geographic location; your business methods and practices; your management skills, experience and business acumen; the effectiveness of your staff; local and national economic conditions; the market for your products and services; your employee wage responsibilities; competition and the sales that you realize during this period. These numbers are approximations only and you may need significantly more initial capital. You may incur other or higher costs or fees. You may also need operating capital when running the Business that is in addition to what is estimated here.

We do not offer financing directly or indirectly for any part of the initial investment. The availability and terms of financing will depend on factors such as the availability of financing generally, your creditworthiness, collateral you may have, and lending policies of financial institutions. This estimate does not include any finance charge, interest

12

or debt service obligation, or your living expenses. In compiling these estimates, we have relied upon the experience of our principals (Item 2) from operating businesses that are similar to the one being offered to you.

You should carefully review these figures with a business advisor before making any decision.

Item 8
RESTRICTIONS ON SOURCES OF PRODUCTS AND SERVICES

Required Purchases

You must adhere to the specifications established by us with respect to furnishing, equipping, establishing, and operating your Business, including all procedures, advertising materials, supplies, inventory, equipment, hardware and software, and insurance. These specifications include standards for appearance, design, quality, performance, and functionality. These specifications are based on our Affiliate's experience in operating a business similar to the one being offered here.

We may communicate our standards and specifications directly to suppliers who wish to supply you with furniture, fixtures, equipment, inventory, and signage. We communicate our standards and specifications to you during training, before you conduct your grand opening advertising, during on-site opening assistance (if any), during periodic visits to your Franchised Location (defined in Item 11), if any, and through the Manual, which may include periodic bulletins.

We may periodically issue new standards and specifications through written notices.

We may modify, add to, and change any specification as to any goods, service, supplies, or the like, at any time, on a regional or national basis, by amendment to the Manuals or by written notice to you. Once you are notified, you must make the change that is specified. We may also add and remove vendors at any time.

Required and Approved Suppliers

You must purchase the Startup Kit from our Affiliate or us (Items 5 and 7).

The replacement inventory of goods and equipment for each Startup Kit will be purchased from us, or a supplier approved by us.

You will also pay us the Technology Startup Fee (Item 7) and our then-current ongoing Technology Maintenance Fee (Item 6).

You will be required to maintain your Business as needed to ensure a clean, safe, and attractive location. To the extent that this requires the purchase of additional goods that can be purchased only from our Affiliate or us, then you must purchase that from us (Item 6). There can be no estimate of these costs as the maintenance may or may not include the purchase of new equipment.

You will be required to renovate your Business every 5 years in order to meet our then-current configuration. Such renovation will also be required at the time that you are awarded Successor Franchise Rights (and at each 5-year period during such Successor Franchise Rights term), and after a transfer. To the extent that this requires you to purchase goods that can be obtained only from our Affiliate or us, you will be required to make such purchases.

Your grand opening advertising must be approved by us (Item 11).

13

You must purchase and maintain in effect, during the term of the Franchise Agreement, the type and amount of insurance and bonds specified in Article 17 of the Franchise Agreement in addition to any other insurance or bonds that may be required by applicable law, any lender, or lessor. Your insurance policies must name us as an additional insured and/or loss payee.

Except as described above, you may purchase all other furniture, fixtures, equipment, or materials from any approved source. A list of approved products and suppliers from whom other products may be purchased is published in our Manuals or in policy and procedures statements or provided to you by other written communication, and such list may be amended by us.

Our principals own an interest in our Affiliate from whom you may now, or in the future, be required to purchase goods or services, and you may be required to purchase goods from us. Except as described here, our principals own no interest in any other supplier.

Approval of Alternative Suppliers

In some cases you may wish to purchase a required good or service from a supplier that has not been previously approved by us. We will charge our then-current fee for this service (Item 6). We do not maintain written criteria for approving suppliers and thus these criteria are not available to you or your proposed supplier. To obtain our approval, you must submit such information as we may reasonably require in order to evaluate the prospective supplier. We will evaluate the submitted information and will provide written notice of our decision to you within 30 days. We may grant or deny approval for any reason or for no reason at all. Other than as stated here, we have no other process for approving suppliers.

Approval of alternative suppliers may be revoked by us if we determine in good faith that the goods or services they are supplying no longer meet the quality standards that are in effect at that time. We will notify you if we revoke our approval of any suppliers and you must immediately stop purchasing disapproved goods or services or purchases from a disapproved supplier.

Revenue from Franchisee Purchases

As this is a new franchise, we have not yet received revenue or material consideration as a result of required purchases or leases, though we will do so in the future.

We or our Affiliate may receive revenue and material considerations as a result of required purchases. As this is a new franchise, there are no figures that represent the percentage of revenue that our Affiliate or we generate as a result of these sales.

Our Affiliate may in the future make payments to us as a result of your purchases from them.

The cost of purchases and the leasing of goods and equipment obtained in accordance with our specifications will represent about 85% of your total purchases and leases of goods and services in establishing the Business and approximately 50% of your total purchases during operation of the Business. The total cost of items purchased through our Affiliate or us will represent 1% to 2% of your total purchases to establish the Business and approximately 1% of your total purchases during the operation of the business.

We do not now, but may in the future, receive rebates and material benefits from vendors with whom you are to do business. We do reserve the right to receive rebates and material benefits at any

14

time in the future. If we do receive additional or new rebate revenue, we may or may not share it with the franchisees.

Cooperatives

Though there is none at this time, we may in the future develop a regional purchasing or distribution cooperative in your area. The purpose of the purchasing or distribution cooperative will be to obtain all goods and services at a more competitive price. Upon the creation of the same, you must participate in the program. Any item carried by the cooperative will be of the same quality as then required by us by any other franchisees.

Negotiated Prices

We have not yet negotiated prices with suppliers for the benefit of the franchisees. We may, in the future, negotiate such prices for the benefit of all franchisees and our Affiliate.

Material Benefits

We neither provide nor withhold material benefits to you (including renewal rights or the right to open additional businesses) based on whether you purchase through the sources we designate or approve. However, purchases of unapproved services, the use of unapproved vendors, or supplying clients with unapproved services will be a violation of the Franchise Agreement, and you may be terminated as a result.

Item 9
FRANCHISEE'S OBLIGATIONS

This table lists your principal obligations under the franchise and other agreements. It will help you find more detailed information about your obligations in these agreements and in other Items of this disclosure document.

Obligation	Section in Agreement	Disclosure Document Item
(a) Site selection and acquisition/lease	2	Items 7 and 11
(b) Pre-opening purchases/ leases	2	Items 7 and 8
(c) Site development and other pre-opening requirements	2	Items 6,7,11
(d) Initial and ongoing training	7	Item 11
(e) Opening	2	Item 11
(f) Fees	3	Items 5,6,7
(g) Compliance with standards and policies/ Manuals	8	Items 8, 11, 14 and 16
(h) Trademarks and proprietary information	6	Items 13 and 14

15

Obligation	Section in Agreement	Disclosure Document Item
(i) Restrictions on products/services offered	8	Items 8, 11 and 16
(j) Warranty and Customer service requirements	8	Item 16
(k) Territorial development and sales quotas	None	Item 12
(l) Ongoing product/service purchases	8	Item 8
(m) Maintenance, appearance, and remodeling requirements	2	Item 11
(n) Insurance	17	Items 7,8
(o) Advertising	3	Items 6,7,11
(p) Indemnification	14	Item 6
(q) Owner's participation/ management/staffing	8	Items 11 and 15
(r) Records/reports	3	Item 11
(s) Inspections/audits	3	Item 6
(t) Transfer	9	Item 17
(u) Renewal	4	Item 17
(v) Post-termination obligations	11	Item 17
(w) Non-competition covenants	15	Item 17
(x) Dispute resolution	16	Item 17

Item 10
FINANCING

Our Affiliate and we: offer no financing arrangements, directly or indirectly to you; do not guarantee your notes, lease, or any other obligation; and do not receive any direct or indirect payments or other consideration from any person for the placement of any financing that you may need.

Item 11
FRANCHISOR'S ASSISTANCE, ADVERTISING, COMPUTER SYSTEMS, AND TRAINING

Except as stated below, Noah's Ark Franchising Inc., is not required to provide you with any assistance.

Pre-Opening Assistance

Before you open your business we will:

    a. Assist you in selecting a "Franchised Location" (the methods used to select and approve sites are described later in this Item 11 below) by providing site selection criteria (Franchise Agreement, Sections 2.2 and 5).

16

b. Review your lease (Franchise Agreement, Sections 2.3 and 5).

c. Once your Franchised Location is approved, we will designate your "Exclusive Territory" (Franchise Agreement, Sections 2.4 and 5).

d. Furnish mandatory design specifications, layout criteria, and specifications for furniture, fixtures, and equipment for the store (Franchise Agreement, Sections 2.5 and 5).

e. Furnish the Startup Kit (Franchise Agreement, Sections 2.8 and 5).

f. Offer training as more specifically set forth below in this Item 11 (Franchise Agreement, Article 7).

g. If requested by you and at your cost, we may agree to send a representative to the Business to ensure that improvements are completed to our specifications (Franchise Agreement, Section 2).

h. At our option, the day before opening and for 2 days thereafter, we may send a representative to the Business to help with opening and initial operations (Franchise Agreement, Sections 2.5 and 5).

i. Lend you one copy of the Manuals (Franchise Agreement, Section 5).

Post-Opening Assistance

During the operation of your Business, we will:

a. Modify, update, or change the System, including, but not limited to, the adoption and use of new or modified list of authorized and approved suppliers, trade names, trademarks, service marks, or copyrighted materials, new products, a new and evolving menu of services, and new techniques (Franchise Agreement, Article 5).

b. Provide you with access to local advertising materials (Franchise Agreement, Articles 3 and 5).

c. Help you coordinate your Grand Opening (Franchise Agreement, Article 3).

d. Provide feedback from the polling of your computers, including a comparison of your cost of goods to those of other Businesses (Franchise Agreement, Article 5).

e. Periodically advise you or offer guidance to you on other matters concerning the operation of your Business (Franchise Agreement, Articles 5 and 8).

f. Conduct quality control visits (both announced and unannounced), and also use a "secret shopper" program (Franchise Agreement, Articles 5 and 8).

g. At such time in the future as we deem appropriate, we will hold an annual conference at which new ideas and other matters will be discussed (Franchise Agreement, Article 7).

Optional Assistance

We may provide you with additional training and support on an as-needed basis and for the then-current fee. You may request additional support and the same will be given in our sole discretion. Any costs incurred by us in providing such additional services shall be paid by you.

Schedule for Opening

The typical length of time between the signing of the Franchise Agreement and the opening of a Business is approximately 5 to 7 months (Opening Period).

We will extend your Opening Period one time for a reasonable time in the event factors beyond your reasonable control prevent you from meeting the deadlines and you request an extension of time from

17

us at least 15 days before the end of the opening period. If after the passage of such reasonable time, the Franchisee has failed to open for business, Franchisor has the right to terminate this Agreement without any right to cure. The factors that affect the period required to open the Business may include the ability to obtain a lease, financing, building permits, zoning and local ordinances and licensing. Other factors include weather conditions and shortages and delays in obtaining equipment, fixtures and signs.

Advertising

Local Advertising

You will be required to spend a minimum of 2% of your monthly Gross Revenue for local advertising placement. We must first approve any advertising before it is placed in any medium, with the added requirement that such advertisement(s) be sent to us at least thirty (30) days before it is to be used. We will have 15 days within which to approve. If we do not deliver to you written notice in that time, the copy will be deemed to be approved.

You may advertise on the internet only through our internet portal.

National Advertising Fund and Regional and Cooperative Advertising

We do not now, but will, when we have 20 Businesses opened, collect 1% of the Gross Sales each month for advertising, concept development, collateral materials, and other items for the benefit of the System (National Advertising Fee). The National Advertising Fee will be due at the same time as your Royalties and as part of the EFT withdrawal. The National Advertising Fee will be placed in an interest bearing checking account, savings account, or any other account of our determination (Account). Any monies not used in any year will be carried to the next year. The Account will be administered by us at our sole discretion and may be used by us for all advertising expenditures reasonably intended to benefit the System, and for the payments to us of costs related to administering the Account such as reasonable salaries, administrative costs, travel expenses, and overhead. National Advertising Fees are used to promote the services sold by the franchises and are not used to sell additional franchises.

We make no guarantee to you or to any other franchisee that advertising expenditures from the Account will benefit you or any other franchisee directly or on a *pro rata* basis. We will assume no other direct or indirect liability or obligation to you with respect to collecting amounts due to the Account or with respect to maintaining, directing, or administering the Account.

Any company or Affiliate-owned Businesses will participate in any national or regional advertising programs in the same manner as the franchisees. Any fees not used in a calendar year will be rolled-over for use in the next or any subsequent year.

The National Advertising Fee will be used for the creation and placement of various advertising and promotional products. The media in which such advertising may be disseminated includes, but is not limited to, printed materials, posters, window clings, danglers in the Business, and/or the creation of television, internet, radio, and print on a local or regional basis. The advertising will be produced and placed by us or by a local, national, or international advertising agency.

Upon your prior written request, we will make available to you, no later than 120 days after the end of each calendar year, an annual unaudited financial statement for the Account.

18

We reserve the right, upon 30 days prior written notice to you, to allocate all or a portion of the National Advertising Fees to a regional advertising program (Regional Program) for the benefit of Businesses located within a particular region. We have the right to determine the composition of all geographic territories and market areas for the implementation of such a Regional Program and to require that you participate in it as and when it may be established. If the Regional Program is implemented on behalf of a particular region, we will only use contributions from franchisees within such region to the extent reasonably calculable by us. We will control and administer the Regional Program though we will permit franchisees within the region to reasonably suggest the manner of such expenditures. Upon your prior written request, we will make available to you, no later than 120 days after the end of each calendar year, the annual unaudited financial statement for the Regional Program account.

We may also establish an advertising cooperative (Advertising Cooperative) for a particular region to enable the cooperative to self-administer the Regional Program. If an Advertising Cooperative is established in your area, you must participate in it.

The Advertising Cooperative will be administered by the franchisees in the cooperative.

We have the right to change, dissolve, or merge any such cooperative. The cooperative will prepare unaudited financial statements and will deliver the same to use within 90 days of its year end. Each Regional Advertising Cooperative must adopt written governing documents. A copy of the governing documents of the Advertising Cooperative (if one has been established) for your region is available upon request.

As this is a new franchise, we have not collected any National Advertising Fees. As a result, we have not spent any money from the Fund. We do not have an advertising council that advises us.

Grand Opening

In addition to the advertising requirements described above, commencing no earlier than 60 days after the opening you will be required to spend $500 to advertise the grand opening of your Business. The grand opening plans advertising must be approved by us in the same manner as is your local advertising.

Computer Requirements

Your Business must have such computer and other equipment as we designate in the Manuals.

You will be required to purchase, lease, or license 1 desk-top computer of any make or model that must have the latest version of the Microsoft® operating system. It must have the following software installed and operational: i) the latest version of Microsoft Word and Excel; ii) the latest version of Internet Explorer®; and iii) the latest version of Quickbooks®.

You may already own a computer and software that meets these requirements.

The approximate cost of the computer hardware and software ranges from $500 to $1,000. This cost is included in the categories of "Computer Hardware and Software" in Item 7.

We may in the future offer a proprietary software or web based programs which may include accounting, word processing, and other features. There may be a fee for such programs.

You will be required to maintain the computer to keep it operational. You must maintain all software stored with all patches that may come from the manufacturer. The maintenance for hardware and software may occur at any time and as a result, there can be no estimate of the cost.

19

You are not required to maintain any hardware or software maintenance contracts.

We will require you to update all other computer hardware no more often than once every 5 years. We estimate this cost to be between $500 and $1,000. Computer software will be updated no more often than once every 3 years. The cost is estimated at between $100 and $1,000.

The computer in the Business must be attached to a high-speed internet access point. We will have the right to and will remotely access your computer to obtain information about your operations. This information may be used by us for any purpose and may include identification of your Business by name.

Manual and Table of Contents

We will lend you one copy of the Manual though it will always remain our property. It is part of the System and it contains our confidential, proprietary, and trade secret information. The Table of Contents of the Manual is found in Exhibit C to this Disclosure Document. The Manual contains approximately XXX pages.

Location Selection

A "Franchised Location" is the location for your Business that has been approved by us, and, if applicable, for which you have a lease that has been approved by us. You will lease your space from independent third parties.

If you do not already have a Franchised Location selected and approved before you sign the Franchise Agreement, you and we will designate, by addendum to the Franchise Agreement, a "Designated Area" within which to find a Franchised Location. A Designated Area is defined by geographic boundaries such as a perimeter defined by streets, landmarks, highways, or similar methods, or by political or mailing boundaries including neighborhoods, cities, counties, and zip codes. We reserve the right to change the method of identifying a Designated Area at any time.

The Designated Area gives you the exclusive right during the defined time period to find and develop your Business in that area.

You must locate a site for the Business in the Designated Area within 45 days after you sign the Franchise Agreement. We then have 30 days to approve or disapprove your site. If we do not approve your first proposed site, you will have an additional 45 days to find another site and submit it to us for approval. If you fail to meet the deadlines for the selection of a site or submit incomplete information regarding the site to us, we will allow you 15 days to cure the deficiency. If you fail to do so or we fail to reach an agreement as to a site, we have the right to terminate the Franchise Agreement, refund 40% of the IFF and retain the remainder of the IFF.

Our assistance in connection with the selection and approval of a location is limited to providing written criteria for a satisfactory Franchised Location, reviewing the information provided by you to determine whether the location fulfills the requisite criteria, and at our option, an on-site inspection if requested by you and at your cost. Using our Reasonable Business Judgment (Franchise Agreement Article 1), we will base our approval of your proposed site on a variety of factors including, but not limited to the various demographic characteristics of the site (including population density, income, and the like),

20

geographic, political, and physical boundaries, extent of competition, mix of residential and commercial, and whether the proposed site is urban, suburban, or rural.

Our employees and we have no special expertise in selecting sites. Any approval is intended only to indicate that the proposed site meets our minimum criteria based upon our general business experience.

Our approval of a location does not infer or guarantee the success or profitability in any manner.

After we approve the proposed Franchise Location you will have 30 days to negotiate a lease that must be submitted to us for approval. We will approve or disapprove the lease agreement within 15 days after receipt. We have the option to require that the lease: (i) be collaterally assigned to us by Collateral assignment of Lease agreement (Exhibit 4); or (ii) contain the following terms and conditions:

a. The landlord must agree that without its consent, the lease and your right, title, and interest under the lease may be assigned to us or our designee; and,

b. The landlord must provide written notice to us (at the same time it gives such notice to you) of any default by you under the lease. We must be given an additional 15 days after your period of cure has expired, to cure, at our sole option, any such default and, upon the curing of such default, we must be given the right to enter upon the leased premises and assume your rights under the lease as if the lease had been assigned by you to us.

You will operate your Business and use the Marks, the Proprietary Information, and the System only at the Franchised Location.

Our approval of any lease does not infer or guaranty the success or profitability of your business.

Once the site and the lease have been approved by us, the location will be your Franchised Location, and an Exclusive Territory will be identified by us, all of which will be identified in Exhibit 2 of the Franchise Agreement.

Maintenance and Renovations

You will be required to maintain your Business as needed to ensure a clean, safe, and attractive business. This may require you to purchase new equipment to replace worn-out equipment, and may require you to repaint or take other remedial action. This will be done as often as is necessary to maintain a safe, secure, and attractive Business. There can be no estimate of these costs as the maintenance will vary depending work that must be done.

You will be required to renovate the Business every 5 years in order to meet our then-current configuration (Renovation). The Renovation will also be required at the time that you are awarded Successor Franchise Rights, at each 5 year period during such Successor Franchise Rights term and after a transfer but before the new owner reopens the Franchised Location for business (with the understanding that if the renovations can be made while the Business is in operation, then the transferee will be permitted to make such changes while open). To the extent that this requires you to purchase goods that can be obtained only from our Affiliate or us, you will be required to make such purchases. Renovations may include changes to interior and exterior decor, furniture, fixtures, equipment, small wares, and changes to the system in order to conform to the then-current franchise system look and feel. We cannot estimate the cost of such renovation.

Training

We provide an initial training program to be conducted at our corporate headquarters (currently, in Denver, Colorado), or at an alternative location to be determined by us. The initial training program is offered by us as needed to meet the needs of our franchisees.

The initial training program is typically 5 business days in length, of which approximately 20 hours are classroom instruction and 20 hours are on-the-job training.

We reserve the right to waive a portion of any training program or to alter the training schedule, if in our sole discretion, we determine that you or your designated attendee has sufficient prior experience or training.

Up to 2 people may participate in any initial training program without additional fee. You (or if you are an entity, the "Principal Operator") and the "Designated Manager" must successfully complete the initial training program prior to the opening of your Business. The "Principal Operator" is the person designated by your business entity to operate the business and receive our training. The "Designated Manager" is the person besides you or your Principal Operator who is responsible for the day-to-day operations of the Business.

No tuition is charged for training. You must however, pay for all transportation, room, board, wages, and other living expenses which are incurred in connection with attendance at any training program.

Training will be conducted after the Franchise Agreement is signed but before you open for the first time.

We will also make the initial training program available to replacement or additional Designated Managers during the term of the Franchise Agreement. We reserve the right to charge a tuition or fee, commensurate with our then-current published prices, for such training, payable in advance (Item 6). You must pay for all travel, living expenses, and wages that are incurred by your personnel during attendance at the training program. The availability of the training program to such additional individuals will be subject to space considerations and prior commitments to new or other franchisees.

If you propose to sell or transfer the Business to a third party, part of our approval process will be the requirement that the transferee attend training and that he pay for the training at our then-current fee (Item 6).

Training consists of the following:

TRAINING PROGRAM

Subject	Hours of Classroom Training	Hours of On-the-Job Training	Location
What it takes to be a Successful Franchisee	5	0	The location of our then-current headquarters (currently Denver, Colorado), or other location that we designate.
Marketing and Sales to Customers	3	0	Same
Aardvark Care	7	15	Same

22

Subject	Hours of Classroom Training	Hours of On-the-Job Training	Location
Employee Care	3	0	Same
Retail Sales	2	5	Same
Total	**20**	**20**	

Mr. Ark, who is listed in Item 2, is the training instructor. He has had extensive experience in the day-to-day operation of our Affiliate's business. Our Affiliate's business is substantially similar to the Business being offered here. From time-to-time, persons who are active in the operations and administrative side of our business, as well as support staff, may assist with and/or provide training.

The initial training will include the following instructional materials: the confidential Operations Manual.

You may wish to get on-site training from us. This is optional and is not required for the operation of the business unless you feel it is necessary. We will charge our then-current fee (Item 6), plus all costs for travel, lodging, and food. This training can take place at any time.

If you request additional, extraordinary, or refresher courses or training, we may, at our option, charge our then-current per diem fee plus expenses (Item 6).

We may also offer additional training online or through web seminars (webinars). There may be a fee for such training. We will notify you of the training and the fee. Some of this training may be mandatory.

We will also provide such bulletins, brochures, manuals, and reports, if any, as may from time to time be published regarding plans, policies, developments, and activities. In addition we may provide such communication concerning new developments, techniques, and improvements in and to the System and the "Proprietary Information" (Item 14), as we feel may be relevant to the operation of the Business.

Annual Conference and Training Attendance

We do not now, but may, in the future, have an annual conference that, if held, will require attendance by all franchisees. You will be responsible for the payment of all expenses for travel, accommodations, food, and other expenses incurred. Though none is now required, we may in the future require an attendance fee that may be between $100 and $500. When it is known, you will be provided with the duration of such a meeting, as well as its location, the identities of those who will present information at the meeting, and the content of any seminars or information that will be delivered at that time. The annual conference will be held in a location to be determined by us.

In addition to the annual conference and though we do not now, we have the right, in the future to require you, and at least one of your principals or key employees to attend a local or regional training meeting one (1) time per year. All mandatory meetings will be offered without charge of a tuition or fee; however, you will be responsible for all travel and living expenses that are associated with attendance. Any additional local or regional meetings will last between one and two days and will be held at a location to be approved by us, and which will be within easy car or bus commuting distance. Any instructors at such

23

meetings will either be our principals, or other persons not yet identified by us, but whose identity and background will be disclosed to you before the meeting.

Item 12
TERRITORY

You will be assigned an "Exclusive Territory" at the time that the Franchised Location and the lease are approved, which will continue in force during the initial and any renewal term of the Franchise Agreement. It will be a geometric shape, the center of which is your Franchised Location and the radius of which is approximately 100 miles (more or less). The final perimeter will conform to physical, geographic, zip codes, political, and/or other boundaries and will be decided by us using our Reasonable Business Judgment (Franchise Agreement, Article 1).

We will not permit another franchisee, or company- or Affiliate-owned business to operate within your Exclusive Territory. Except as set forth below in the reservation of rights, we will not accept or solicit orders to provide services in your Exclusive Territory.

You may advertise the Business only within your Exclusive Territory, unless regional or cooperative advertising is implemented or unless you get our permission to advertise outside the Exclusive Territory. You can accept customers from anywhere, including another franchisee's territory, and other franchisees can accept customers from your Exclusive Territory.

All franchisees can advertise on the internet only through our web portal; except that we may grant you the right to separately advertise or promote your business on the internet only after you have first received our express written permission to do so. Our decision to grant or deny this right will be based upon our Reasonable Business Judgment.

You do receive rights to be awarded additional franchises (Franchise Agreement, Section 2.13). In order to qualify, you must:

i. Have been in operation for at least 12 months;
ii. Be in compliance with your Franchise Agreement at the time that you seek to purchase an additional site;
iii. Have received no notices of default from us during the years prior to the date that you apply for consideration of such a grant;
iv. Meet the then-current financial and business requirements that are applied to a new franchisee;
v. Demonstrate the business and financial ability to operate multiple Businesses;
vi. Have operated your current Business in such a manner that we, using our Reasonable Business Judgment, deem to be sufficient to warrant granting you an additional location; and,
vii. Using our then-current site criteria, have a location that will qualify as a Franchised Location; and,
vii. Be granted the right after we use our Reasonable Business Judgment.

If we grant you the right to an additional Franchise, you will sign the then-current franchise agreement and, if we deem it appropriate, you will attend additional training. Except as stated here, you have no other options, right of first refusal or similar contractual right to acquire additional Businesses.

The new franchise agreement may have terms significantly different than this franchise agreement, including a different IFF, royalty structure, advertising fee structure, and the like.

24

Continuation of the Exclusive Territory does not depend on any stated sales volume, market penetration, or other contingency. Your Exclusive Territory will continue in place until the end of your Initial Term. If you renew, we reserve the right to redefine the characteristics of your Exclusive Territory to meet our then-current standards.

Reservation of Rights

Our Affiliate and we reserve the right, among others, to:

a. Own, franchise, or operate businesses that are similar to your Business (and which use the Marks and the System) at any location outside of your Exclusive Territory, regardless of the proximity to your Exclusive Territory;

b. Use the Marks and the System to sell any products or services (which may be similar to those that you will sell) through any alternate channels of distribution within or outside of the Exclusive Territory. These alternate channels include, but are not limited to, retail locations (such as grocery stores or similar retail outlets), and other channels of distribution, such as television, mail order, catalog sales, wholesale to unrelated retail outlets, or over the internet. You cannot not use alternate channels of distribution without our express permission, which may be granted or denied for any reason or for no reason at all. You will not receive compensation for any such sales;

c. Use and license others to use, either within or outside of your Exclusive Territory or in alternate channels of distribution, other trademarks, trade names, service marks, logos, proprietary information, and methods of operation that are not the same as or confusingly similar to the Marks, in the operation of a business that offers goods, services, and related products and services that may be similar to, or different from, the Business;

d. Purchase, or be purchased by, or merge, or combine with any other business, including a business that competes directly with your Business, wherever located; and,

e. Acquire and convert to our system any businesses offering services and products similar to those offered by you, including such businesses operated by competitors or otherwise operated independently, or as part of, or in association with any other system or chain, whether franchised or corporately owned, and located outside of the Exclusive Territory.

Though we can use alternative channels of distribution within your Exclusive Territory to make sales of goods, items, and services associated with the System and the Marks, or associated with any other system or trademarks, service marks, trade names, logos, and the like, we have not done so as of the date of this disclosure document. We reserve the right to do so at any time.

Our Affiliate has established a business that is substantially similar to the one being offered here. It will never open a competing business in any portion of your Exclusive Territory.

Relocation

You may relocate your Business within your Exclusive Territory only if you first obtain our express written permission, which permission will be considered using our Reasonable Business Judgment.

25

If you are permitted to relocate, you must first have any location and its lease approved by us in the same manner as we are then approving locations and lease for new franchisees. You will pay us our then-current relocation fee. (Item 6). If the result of your relocation is that you encroach on the exclusive territory of another franchisee, you will not be permitted to relocate to that proposed site.

You must abide by all federal, state, and local government guidelines concerning your Business, its employees, and any independent contractor that you use.

Except as stated here, there is no exclusive right to any territory.

Item 13
TRADEMARKS

You receive the right to operate your Business under the Mark specified in the Manual and identified on the first page of this disclosure document. You may also use any other current or future Mark to operate your Business that we designate. By "Mark" we mean any trade name, trademark, service mark or logo used to identify your business.

On January 2, 2010 we filed for registration of the Mark with the United States Patent and Trademark Office which registration was granted as noted below:

Serial Number	Description of Mark	Principal or Supplemental Register of the USPTO	Filing date
1,234,567	**AARDVARKS ONLY**	Principal	January 2, 2010

We do not have federal registration for our principal trademark. Therefore, our trademark does not have the many legal benefits and rights as a federally registered trademark. If our right to use the trademark is challenged, you may have to change to alternative trademark, which may increase your expenses.

Presently, we know of no effective material determinations of the United States Patent and Trademark Office (USPTO), any trademark, trial and appeal board, any state trademark administrator, or of any federal or state court; or any pending infringement, opposition, or cancellation proceeding involving any of the Marks.

There are no currently effective agreements that significantly limit our rights to use or license the use of the Marks listed in this section in any manner material to the franchise. We know of no infringing uses or superior previous rights known to us that can materially affect your use of the Mark in this state or in any other state in which your business is to be located.

There is no pending federal or state court litigation regarding our use or ownership rights in any Marks.

You do not receive any rights to the Mark other than the nonexclusive right to use it in the operation of your Business. You must follow our rules when you use the Mark. You cannot use our name or the Mark (or any commercially similar derivation of the same) as part of a corporate name. You may not use any Mark in connection with the sale of any unauthorized products or services, or in any other manner that we do not authorize in writing. Any unauthorized use of the Mark by you is a breach of the

26

Franchise Agreement and an infringement of our rights in the Mark. You must not contest the validity or ownership of the Mark, including any Marks that we license to you after you sign the Franchise Agreement. You must not assist any other person in contesting the validity or ownership of the Marks.

We have the right to control any administrative proceedings or litigation involving a Mark licensed by us to you. If you learn of any claim against you for alleged infringement, unfair competition, or similar claims about the Marks, you must promptly notify us. We will take the action we deem necessary to defend you. We must indemnify you for any action against you by a third party based solely on alleged infringement, unfair competition, or similar claims about the Marks. We have no obligation to defend or indemnify you if the claim against you is related to your use of the Marks, or the System or Proprietary Information in violation of the Franchise Agreement.

We have the right to require you to modify or discontinue your use of any of the Marks. If we exercise this right, we will provide all franchisees with advance notice.

We have secured the following internet domain name: www._____.com. Other domain names may be added at our discretion.

In the event that the Franchisor, in its sole discretion, shall determine it necessary to modify or discontinue use of any proprietary Marks or to develop additional or substitute marks, you will, within a reasonable time after receipt of written notice of such a modification or discontinuation from us, take such action, at your sole expense, as may be necessary to comply with such modification, discontinuation, addition, or substitution.

If you learn that any third party who you believe is not authorized to use the Marks and is using them, or any variant of them, you must promptly notify us. We will determine whether or not we wish to take any action against the third party. We may commence or prosecute such action in our own name and may join you as a party to the action. You must cooperate with us in any way necessary in the event of such infringement. You will have no right to make any demand or to prosecute any claim against the alleged infringer. We will not pay any franchisee for exercising these rights.

Item 14
PATENTS, COPYRIGHTS, AND PROPRIETARY INFORMATION

We do not own any patents or copyright registrations that are material to the franchise.

We do claim common law copyrights and copyright protection in and on the System and all of the components of the System, including, but not limited to, the Marks, the content of the Manuals and related materials, training modules and techniques, our website, all advertisements in any medium, including the internet, and other promotional and written materials. Each and every component of the system is our proprietary, trade secret, and confidential information ("Proprietary Information," as more fully defined in the Franchise Agreement). Any component of the Proprietary Information can be used by you only as described in the Franchise Agreement. We know of no copyright infringement that could material affect your operation of your Business. Except as stated in Item 13, there are no agreements that limit your use of the System or any copyrighted materials.

We have the right to control any administrative proceedings or litigation involving the Proprietary Information. If you learn of any claim against you or us for an alleged infringement, unfair competition,

27

or similar claims relating to any component of the Proprietary Information, you must promptly notify us. We will take the action we deem necessary to defend you. We must indemnify you for any action against you by a third party based solely on alleged infringement, unfair competition, or similar claims. We have no obligation to defend or indemnify you if the claim against you is related to your use in violation of the Franchise Agreement.

If you learn of, or believe that any other person or entity is using any component of the Proprietary Information without our permission, you must immediately notify us in writing. We will take any action that we deem appropriate. We may commence or prosecute such action in our own name and may join you as a party to the action. You must cooperate with us in any way necessary in the event of such infringement. You will have no right to make any demand or to prosecute any claim against the alleged infringer. We will not pay any franchisee for exercising these rights.

In the event that the Franchisor, in its sole discretion, shall determine it necessary to modify or discontinue use of any portion of the Proprietary Information, or to develop additional or substitutes for that portion, you will, within a reasonable time after receipt of written notice of such a modification or discontinuation from us, take such action, at your sole expense, as may be necessary to comply with such modification, discontinuation, addition, or substitution.

You may never during the term of the Franchise Agreement, or at any time after the termination or expiration of the Franchise Agreement, reveal any component of the Proprietary Information to any person or entity, and you cannot use it for any other business. You may not copy any portion of the Proprietary Information unless we specifically authorize it in writing. All persons affiliated with you must sign a "Confidentiality and Non-Competition Agreement" which is attached to the Franchise Agreement as an exhibit.

In operating your Business, you will create a list of names and other identifying information of clients that have participated in your Business (Client List). You agree that the Client List was obtained through the use of the System, the Marks, and the Proprietary Information. As a result, the Client List is, and will remain, the sole and exclusive property of the Franchisor. At the termination of this Franchise Agreement for any reason, said list shall be delivered to us as part of our Proprietary Information and cannot be used by you in any manner or capacity.

Item 15
OBLIGATION TO PARTICIPATE IN THE
ACTUAL OPERATION OF THE FRANCHISE BUSINESS

Each Business must always be under the direct, full-time, day-to-day "on-premises" supervision of you, your Principal Operator, or your Designated Manager. Each such person must attend and satisfactorily complete our initial Management Training program before opening the Business. You must keep us informed at all times of the identity of your Principal Operator and/or your Designated Manager. If you must replace either person, the replacement must attend and satisfactorily complete our initial training program.

Individuals associated with your Business, including your owners (and members of their immediate families and households), officers, directors, partners, if you are a business entity, and your managers, executives, employees, and staff may be required to sign nondisclosure and non-competition agreements.

28

If your franchise is awarded to a business entity, or if you convert to a business entity (other than a sole proprietorship), then we reserve the right, using our Reasonable Business Judgment, to require the principals of your Business to sign the personal guaranty found at Exhibit 3 of the Franchise Agreement. To this end, the Franchisor reserves the right to review the operating documents of the Business prior to granting the franchise in order to determine who may be required to sign the guaranty.

Item 16
RESTRICTIONS ON WHAT THE FRANCHISEE MAY SELL

You must offer all of the items, goods, services, and products we specify. You may not sell any goods, services, or products that we have not authorized and you must discontinue offering the same upon receipt of notice from us. You may not use the Franchised Location for any other purpose than the operation of the Business and the sale of products approved by us. We may take action, including terminating your franchise, if you violate these restrictions. We may periodically change required or authorized services or products. There are no limits on our right to do so, and you commit to making these changes and they may require additional investment from you.

We may allow some franchisees to offer on a local basis certain items, goods, services, or products that are not otherwise authorized based on factors, including test marketing, your qualifications, and regional or local differences.

You may not market or solicit outside of your Exclusive Territory (except as described in Item 12), but you may provide services to any customer who enters your Business. Otherwise, we do not place restrictions on you with respect to who may be a customer of your Business.

Item 17
RENEWAL, TERMINATION, TRANSFER, AND DISPUTE RESOLUTION

This table lists important provisions of the franchise and related agreements. You should read these provisions in the agreements attached to this disclosure document.

THE FRANCHISE RELATIONSHIP

Provision	Section in Franchise or Other Agreement	Summary
a. Length of the Franchise Term	4	10 years
b. Renewal or extension of the term	4	2 additional consecutive 5-year terms (Successor Terms) if all obligations for Successor Franchise Rights are met.

29

Provision	Section in Franchise or Other Agreement	Summary
c. Requirements for franchisee to renew or extend	4	You must provide notice, you must have no outstanding material defaults or money owed, you must have not had more than 3 default notices, you may be required to renovate, and sign a general release, we must not have determined in our Reasonable Business Judgment not to renew, you must sign then current Agreement and pay renewal fee. You may be asked to sign a contract with materially different terms and conditions than your original contract, and the boundaries of the Exclusive Territory may change. The Royalties, advertising fees and other fees may be adjusted to conform with such fees then being charged to new franchisees.
d. Termination by franchisee	None	
e. Termination by franchisor without cause	None	
f . Termination by franchisor with cause	10	We can terminate only if you default. See g and h below
g. "Cause" defined –curable defaults	10	You have 30 days to cure: any defaults under the Franchise Agreement except for those described in (h) below
h. "Cause" defined – non-curable defaults	10	Non-curable defaults: bankruptcy, abandonment, offenses involving moral turpitude or which may affect the System, any felony, failure to pay fees (after 5 days notice), misuse of marks, disclosure of Systems, repeated breaches beyond 3 even if cured, repeated breaches beyond 2 during any successor term, even if cured, unapproved transfers, violation of law and failure to cure, material misrepresentation, violation of lease, understatement of 4% or more.
i. Franchisee's obligations on termination/non-renewal	11	Obligations include, deidentification (including removal of names, payments of all sums) payment of amounts due, cessation of use of trademarks and proprietary information, notification of non-affiliation, cease use of proprietary technology, and return of all proprietary information (also see r. below)

30

Provision	Section in Franchise or Other Agreement	Summary
j. Assignment of contract by franchisor	9	No restriction on franchisor's right to assign.
k. "Transfer" by franchisee – defined	9	Sale, assignment, gift pledge or mortgage or other disposition of any part of the Franchise Agreement, ownership of the franchisee or the Business.
l. Franchisor approval of transfer by franchisee	9	Transferee has background, financial resources, etc. We have 30 days right of first refusal; transferee pays for training (Item 6)
m. Conditions for franchisor approval of transfer	9	Must provide written notice of offer, must be in compliance; must pay fee; must not be in breach; new franchisee qualifies, you must have no outstanding defaults or money or reports owed, you must provide terms to us, new franchise must have signed current Franchise Agreement and have attended training, transfer fee paid, you must have signed release.
n. Franchisor's right of first refusal to acquire franchisee's business	9	30 days on same terms as bona fide offer
o. Franchisor's option to purchase your business	12	Our option upon termination or expiration of the Franchise Agreement to purchase a part or all of assets for fair market value before you offer to third party
p. Death or disability of franchisee	9	Franchise must be assigned by estate to approved transferee within 180 days
q. Non-competition covenants during the term of the franchise	15	No involvement in competing business.
r. Non-competition covenants after the Franchise is terminated or expires	15	No competing business for 2 years within 25 miles of your Franchised Location or within 25 miles of any other franchised location.
s. Modification of the Agreement	18	Only by both parties' written agreement, but Operation Manuals subject to change.

31

Provision	Section in Franchise or Other Agreement	Summary
t. Integration/merger clause	18	Only the terms of the Franchise Agreement and its attachments are binding (subject to state law). Any representations or promises outside of the disclosure document and Franchise Agreement may not be enforceable.
u. Dispute Resolution by arbitration or mediation	16	Except for certain claims, all disputes will be subject to arbitration (if the mandatory face-to-face meeting and mediation don't resolve issue).
v. Choice of forum	16	Meetings, mediation and arbitration to be conducted within 15 miles of our then-current headquarters.
w. Choice of Law	16	Subject to state law, the state law of our then-current headquarters

ITEM 18
PUBLIC FIGURES

Presently, we do not use any public figures to promote our franchise.

ITEM 19
FINANCIAL PERFORMANCE REPRESENTATIONS

The FTC's Franchise Rule permits a franchisor to provide information about the actual or potential financial performance of its franchise and/or franchisor-owned outlets if there is a reasonable basis for this information and if the information is included in the disclosure document. Financial performance information that is included in Item 19 may be given only if: 1) a franchisor provides the actual records of an existing outlet you are considering buying; or 2) a franchisor supplements the information provided in Item 19, for example, by providing information about possible performance at a particular location or under particular circumstances.

We do not make any representations about a franchisee's future financial performance or the past financial performance of company-owned or franchise outlets. We also do not authorize our employees or representatives to make any such representations either orally or in writing. If you are purchasing an existing outlet, however, we may provide you with the actual records of that outlet. If you receive any other financial performance information or projections of your future income, you should report it to the franchisor's management by contacting Noah's Ark at info@ _____.com, the Federal Trade Commission, and the appropriate state regulatory agencies.

ITEM 20
OUTLETS AND FRANCHISEE INFORMATION

Table No. 1
Systemwide Outlet Summary for the Year 2011*

Column 1 Outlet Type	Column 2 Year	Column 3 Outlets at the Start of the Year	Column 4 Outlets at the End of the Year	Column 5 Net Changes
Franchised	2011	0	0	0
Company Ownod	2011	1	1	0
Total Outlets		1	1	0

* For the year 2011, there was no Company-Owned Unit, but there was an Affiliate owned unit.

Table No. 2
Transfers of Outlets from Franchisees to New Owners
(Other than the Franchisor) for the Year 2011

Column 1 State	Column 2 Year	Column 3 Number of Transfers
None	2011	0
Total		0

Table No. 3
Status of Franchised Outlets for the Year 2011

Column 1 State	Column 2 Year	Column 3 Outlets at the start of the Year	Column 4 Outlets Opened	Column 5 Terminations	Column 6 Non-renewals	Column 7 Reacquired by Franchisor	Column 8 Ceased Operation– Other Reasons	Column 9 Outlets at End of the Year
None	2011	0	0	0	0	0	0	0
Total	2011	0	0	0	0	0	0	0

Table No. 4
Status of Company-Owned Units for the Year 2011*

Column 1 State	Column 2 Year	Column 3 Outlets at the Start of the Year	Column 4 Outlets Opened	Column 5 Outlets Reacquired from Franchisee	Column 6 Outlets Closed	Column 7 Outlets sold to Franchisee	Column 8 Outlets at End of the Year
Colorado	2011	1	0	0	0	0	1
Total	2011	1	0	0	0	0	1

*For the year 2011, there was no Company-Owned Unit, but there was an Affiliate owned unit.

Table No. 5
Projected Openings as of December 31, 2012

Column 1 State	Column 2 Franchise Agreements Signed but Outlet not Opened	Column 3 Projected new Franchise Outlets in the Next Fiscal Year	Column 4 Projected New Company-Owned Outlets in the Current Fiscal Year
Colorado	0	1	0
Totals	0	1	0

Exhibit D lists the names of all franchisees and the addresses and telephone numbers of their outlets as of the Effective Date of this Disclosure Document and the name, city, and state, and the current business telephone number (or, if unknown, the last known home telephone number) of every franchisee who had an outlet terminated, canceled, not renewed, or otherwise voluntarily or involuntarily ceased to do business under the Franchise Agreement during our most recently completed fiscal year, or who has not communicated with us within 10 weeks of the issuance date of this Franchise Disclosure Document.

If you buy this franchise, your contact information may be disclosed to other buyers when you enter or leave the franchise system.

In some instances, current or former franchisees sign provisions restricting their ability to speak openly about their experience with us. You may wish to speak with current and former franchisees, but be aware that all such franchisees will be able to communicate with you.

Exhibit E lists, to the extent known, the names, addresses, telephone numbers, e-mail address, and web address of each trademark-specific franchisee organization associated with the franchise system being offered that we have created, sponsored, or endorsed, and the independent franchisee organizations that have asked to be included in this disclosure document.

ITEM 21
FINANCIAL STATEMENTS

Attached as Exhibit G are our unaudited balance sheet and profit and loss statements for the period from inception through December 31, 2011. Prospective franchisees or sellers of franchises should be advised that no certified public accountant had audited these figures nor expressed his/her opinion with regard to the content or form. We have been in business for less than 3 years and cannot include all the financial statements required by law.

ITEM 22
CONTRACTS

Attached to this Disclosure Document are the following franchise-related contracts:

Exhibit B   Franchisee Agreement and all Exhibits

ITEM 23
RECEIPT

The Receipt is found at the end of this disclosure document as Exhibit H.

EXHIBIT A
STATE AGENCIES
Names and Addresses of State Regulatory Authorities
and Registered Agents in States

The following is a list of state administrators responsible for registration of these states. We may register in one or more of these states.

California

Commissioner of Corporations
One Sansome Street, Ste. 600
San Francisco, CA 94104

Commissioner of Corporations
320 W. 4th Street, Ste. 700
Los Angeles, CA 90013

Commissioner of Corporations
1515 K. Street, Ste. 200
Sacramento, CA 95814
(866) 275-2677 Toll Free

Connecticut

Connecticut Banking Commissioner
Department of Banking
Securities & Business Investments
  Division
260 Constitution Plaza
Hartford, CT 06103
(860) 240-8299

Florida

Division of Consumer Services
Attn: Business Opportunities
2005 Apalachee Pkwy
Tallahassee, FL 32399-6500

Hawaii

Commissioner of Securities
Department of Commerce &
  Consumer Affairs
335 Merchant St., Rm. 203
Honolulu, HI 96813
(808) 586-2722

Colorado

Colorado Attorney General
500 South Second St.
Springfield, CO 62706

Indiana

Indiana Secretary of State
Securities Division
302 West Washington St., Rm. E-111
Indianapolis, IN 46204

Kentucky

Office of the Attorney General
Consumer Protection Division
Attn: Business Opportunity
1024 Capital Center Dr.
Frankfort, KY 40601-8204

Maine

Department of Professional and Financial
Regulations
Bureau of Banking, Securities Division
121 Statehouse Station
Augusta, ME 04333

36

Maryland

Office of the Attorney General
Securities Division
200 St. Paul Pl.
Baltimore, MD 21202

Michigan

Department of the Attorney General
Consumer Protection Division, Franchise Unit
525 Ottawa Street
G. Mennen Williams Bldg., 6th Fl.
Lansing, MI 48909

Minnesota

Minnesota Department of Commerce
85 7th Place East, Ste. 500
St. Paul, MN 55101

Nebraska

Nebraska Department of Banking
and Finance
Commerce Court
1230 O Street, Ste. 400
Lincoln, NE 68509

New York

Bureau of Investor Protection and
Securities
New York State Department of Law
120 Broadway, 23rd Fl.
New York, NY 10271

North Carolina

Secretary of State
Securities Division
Old Revenue Complex
2 South Salisbury St.
Raleigh, NC 27601

North Dakota

North Dakota Securities Department
600 East Boulevard Ave.
State Capitol—5th Fl., Department 414
Bismarck, ND 58505-0510
(701) 328-4712

Rhode Island

Department of Business Regulation
John O. Pastore Complex
1511 Pontiac Ave.
Bldg. 69, First Fl.
Cranston, RI 02920

South Carolina

Office of the Secretary of State
1205 Pendleton St.
Edgar Brown Bldg, Ste. 525
Columbia, SC 29201

South Dakota

Department of Revenue and
Regulation
Division of Securities
445 East Capitol Ave.
Pierre, SD 57501

Texas

Office of the Secretary of State
Statutory Document Section
1019 Brazos St.
Austin, TX 78701

Utah

Utah Department of Commerce
Division of Consumer Protection
160 East Three Hundred South
P.O. Box 146704
Salt Lake City, UT 84114-6704

Virginia

State Corporation Commission
Division of Securities and Retail Franchising
Tyler Building, 9th Floor
1300 East Main St.
Richmond, VA 23219

Washington

Department of Financial Institutions
Securities Division
150 Israel Rd. SW
Olympia, WA 98501

Wisconsin

Division of Securities
Department of Financial Institutions
345 W. Washington Ave.
Madison, WI 53703

LIST OF STATE AGENTS FOR SERVICE OF PROCESS

The following state agencies are designated as our agent for service of process in accordance with the applicable state laws. We may register in one or more of these states.

California

Commissioner of Corporations
One Sansome St., Ste. 600
San Francisco, CA 94104

Commissioner of Corporations
320 W. 4th St., Ste. 700
Los Angeles, CA 90013

Commissioner of Corporations
1515 K St., Ste. 200
Sacramento, CA 95814
(866) 275-2677

Connecticut

Connecticut Banking Commissioner
Department of Banking
Securities & Business Investments
  Division
260 Constitution Plaza
Hartford, CT 06103
(860) 240-8299

Hawaii

Commissioner of Securities
Department of Commerce and
  Consumer Affairs Business
  Registration Division
Securities Compliance Branch
335 Merchant St., Rm. 203
Honolulu, HI 96813

Colorado

Colorado Attorney General
500 S. Second St.
Springfield, CO 62706

Indiana

Indiana Secretary of State
Securities Division
302 W. Washington St., Rm. E-111
Indianapolis, IN 46204

38

Maryland

Maryland Securities Commissioner
Office of Attorney General
Securities Division
200 St. Paul Place
Baltimore, MD 21202

Michigan

Michigan Department of Commerce
Corporations and Securities Bureau
P.O. Box 30054
6546 Mercantile Wy
Lansing, MI 48909

Minnesota

Minnesota Department of Commerce
85 7th Place East, Ste. 500
St. Paul, MI 55101

New York

Secretary of the State of New York
41 State St.
Albany, NY 12231

North Dakota

North Dakota Securities Department
State Capitol—5th Fl.
600 East Blvd.
Bismarck, ND 58505-0510

Rhode Island

Department of Business Regulation
John O. Pastore Complex
1511 Pontiac Ave.
Bldg. 69, First Fl.
Cranston, RI 02920

South Dakota

Department of Revenue and
  Regulation
Division of Securities
445 East Capitol Ave.
Pierre, SD 57501

Virginia

Clerk, State Corporation Commission
Tyler Building, 1st Fl.
1300 E. Main St.
Richmond, VA 23219

Washington

Director, Department of Financial
  Institutions
Securities Division
150 Israel Rd. SW.
Olympia, WA 98501

Wisconsin

Commissioner of Securities
345 W. Washington St., 4th Fl.
Madison, WI 53703

Our Registered Agent in Colorado is
Noah's Ark
123 First St.
Denver, CO 80000

EXHIBIT B
FRANCHISE AGREEMENT

[See Appendix B for a sample franchise agreement]

EXHIBIT C
[OPERATIONS MANUAL]
TABLE OF CONTENTS

[The franchisor would insert the table of contents from the operations manual for the business into this location]

EXHIBIT D
CURRENT FRANCHISEES and
FRANCHISEES WHO HAVE LEFT THE SYSTEM

If you buy this franchise, your contact information may be disclosed to other buyers when you leave the franchise system.

 None

EXHIBIT E
TRADEMARK-SPECIFIC FRANCHISEE ASSOCIATIONS AND
INDEPENDENT FRANCHISEE ASSOCIATIONS

None

EXHIBIT F
STATE-SPECIFIC ADDENDA

None

EXHIBIT G
FINANCIAL STATEMENTS

NOAH'S ARK FRANCHISING INC.
A Colorado corporation

AARDVARKS ONLY

123 First Street
Denver, CO 80000
(888) 555-1212

BALANCE SHEET
12/31/11Unaudited/Cash Basis

ASSETS

Current Assets

Cash on Hand	
Total Cash on Hand	$24,509.95
Total Current Assets	$24,509.95
Fixed Assets	
Franchise Development Project	$98,500.00
	$98,500.00

TOTAL ASSETS   **$123,009.95**

LIABILITIES AND EQUITY

Long-Term Liabilities	
Loan from Shareholders	$128,000.00
Total Long-Term Liabilities	$128,000.00
Retained Earnings	$(4,990.05)
Total Equity	$(4,990.05)

TOTAL LIABILITIES AND EQUITY   **$123,009.95**

EXHIBIT H
RECEIPT

RECEIPT
NOAH'S ARK FRANCHISING INC.

This disclosure document summarizes certain provisions of the franchise agreement and other information in plain English. Read this disclosure document and all agreements carefully. If Noah's Ark Franchising Inc. offers you a franchise, we must provide this disclosure document to you 14 calendar days before you sign a binding agreement or make a payment to us or an affiliate in connection with the proposed franchise sale.

If Noah's Ark Franchising Inc., does not deliver this disclosure document on time or if it contains a false or misleading statement, or a material omission, a violation of federal and state law may have occurred and should be reported to the Federal Trade Commission, Washington, DC, 20580 and to the appropriate state agency identified on Exhibit A.

SEE EXHIBIT A FOR OUR REGISTERED AGENTS AUTHORIZED TO RECEIVE SERVICE OF PROCESS.

Date of Issuance: _____

The Franchisor is Noah's Ark Franchising Inc., 123 First Street Denver, Colorado 80000 (888) 555-1212.

The franchise seller for this offering is _____, 123 First Street Denver, Colorado 80000 (888) 555-1212.

I have received these disclosure documents dated _____ that included the following Exhibits:

Exhibit A. List of State Agencies/Agents for Service of Process

Exhibit B. Franchise Agreement

Exhibit C. Table of Contents

Exhibit D. Current Franchisees and Franchisees that have left the System

Exhibit E. Trademark Specific Franchisee Associations and Independent Franchisee Associations

Exhibit F. State Specific Addenda

Exhibit G. Financial Statements

Exhibit H. Receipt

_____   _____
            Date   Prospective Franchisee

You should return 1 copy of the signed receipt by signing, dating and mailing to Noah's Ark Franchising Inc. at 123 First Street Denver, Colorado 80000 (888) 555-1212.

KEEP A COPY FOR YOUR RECORDS. This disclosure document is also available in PDF format. Noah's Ark at noah@_____.com.

RECEIPT
[Second copy provided to potential franchisee to keep for their records]

NOAH'S ARK FRANCHISING INC.

This disclosure document summarizes certain provisions of the franchise agreement and other information in plain English. Read this disclosure document and all agreements carefully. If Noah's Ark Franchising Inc. offers you a franchise, we must provide this disclosure document to you 14 calendar days before you sign a binding agreement or make a payment to us or an affiliate in connection with the proposed franchise sale.

If Noah's Ark Franchising Inc., does not deliver this disclosure document on time or if it contains a false or misleading statement, or a material omission, a violation of federal and state law may have occurred and should be reported to the Federal Trade Commission, Washington, DC, 20580 and to the appropriate state agency identified on Exhibit A.

SEE EXHIBIT A FOR OUR REGISTERED AGENTS AUTHORIZED TO RECEIVE SERVICE OF PROCESS.

Date of Issuance: _____

The Franchisor is Noah's Ark Franchising Inc., 123 First Street Denver, Colorado 80000 (888) 555-1212.

The franchise seller for this offering is _____, 123 First Street Denver, Colorado 80000 (888) 555-1212.

I have received these disclosure documents dated _____ that included the following Exhibits:

Exhibit A. List of State Agencies/Agents for Service of Process

Exhibit B. Franchise Agreement

Exhibit C. Table of Contents

Exhibit D. Current Franchisees and Franchisees that have left the System

Exhibit E. Trademark Specific Franchisee Associations and Independent Franchisee Associations

Exhibit F. State Specific Addenda

Exhibit G. Financial Statements

Exhibit H. Receipt

_____	_____
Date	Prospective Franchisee

You should return 1 copy of the signed receipt by signing, dating and mailing to Noah's Ark Franchising Inc. at 123 First Street Denver, Colorado 80000 (888) 555-1212.

KEEP A COPY FOR YOUR RECORDS. This disclosure document is also available in PDF format. Noah's Ark at noah@_____.com.

43

Franchise Agreement

T HE FOLLOWING DOCUMENT IS A SAMPLE SERVICE-BASED FRANCHISE agreement (where a unique service is sold). It is included in this Appendix B to illustrate typical terms and restrictions contained in franchise agreements. It was drafted pursuant to rules and laws in effect in 2012. It is provided as a reference resource. If you are contemplating a franchise venture, it is recommended that you consult with an attorney and have him or her review any franchise agreement before you execute the agreement.

As either a potential franchisor or a prospective franchisee, acquaint yourself with the evaluation pointers discussed in Chapter 2 and other portions of this book, and make your own evaluation of the sample franchise agreement.

As a franchisor, be aware of your franchisee's needs, because if the franchisee fails, so will you. You will want to supply all the support necessary to ensure the possibility of your franchisee's success.

NOAH'S ARK FRANCHISING INC.

AARDVARKS ONLY

FRANCHISE AGREEMENT

This Contract Is Subject to Arbitration

TABLE OF CONTENTS

2

4

EXHIBITS

5

NOAH'S ARK FRANCHISING INC.

FRANCHISE AGREEMENT

THIS FRANCHISE AGREEMENT ("Franchise Agreement" or "Agreement") is made this _____ day of _____, 20__ by and between Noah's Ark Franchising Inc., a Colorado corporation, hereinafter known as "Noah's Ark Franchising Inc.", "Franchisor", "we" or "us", or words of a similar nature, and _____ and _____, known individually or collectively as "Franchisee," "Franchisees", "you", "your", or words of a similar nature. You and we may sometimes be referred to in the singular as a "Party" or jointly as the "Parties."

RECITALS

WHEREAS, Franchisor has developed, operates, and owns the right to license a pet aardvark care service business that includes grooming and training, under our "Marks." Our Marks include our trademarks, service marks, trade names, logos, and other commercial symbols (including the Marks found on the first page of this Agreement);

    WHEREAS, the Marks are also associated with Franchisor's expertise and its unique, distinctive, comprehensive and uniform system ("System" as defined below) for the establishment and operation of the franchised businesses described in Article 1;

    WHEREAS, the System includes but is not limited to our: distinctive design of all of our proprietary products; trade dress; training methods; sales techniques and materials; signs; control systems, bookkeeping and accounting methods; décor and color schemes; uniform standards, specifications, and procedures for operations; quality control; training and ongoing operational assistance; advertising and promotional programs; and related benefits for use of all franchisees under the Marks, all of which may be changed, improved, and further developed by us from time to time;

    WHEREAS, Franchisor has established substantial goodwill and business value in its right to use, and in, the Marks, its expertise, and the System;

    WHEREAS, Franchisor and its Affiliate have developed, uses and permits the franchisees to use its confidential, trade secret and proprietary information ("Proprietary Information" as more fully set forth in Article 6) under the terms of this Agreement;

    WHEREAS, Franchisor continues to develop, use, and control the use of the Marks and each component of the System, to identify for the public the source of services and products marketed at the Business;

    WHEREAS, Franchisor has one affiliate Ark Pet Services Inc. (Affiliate). You may be required to purchase certain goods or services from the Affiliate;

    WHEREAS, Franchisee desires to enter into this Agreement for the right to use the Marks, the Proprietary Information, and the System for one of the Businesses (as specified in Exhibit 2) and understands and acknowledges the importance of maintaining the high standards of quality, cleanliness, appearance, and service when operating the Business;

    WHEREAS, for purposes of this Agreement, if you are a business entity, then the person designated by the business entity to operate the business and who has received our training is called the "Principal

6

Operator". The "Designated Manager" will be defined as the person, besides you (or your Principal Operator if you are a business entity), who is responsible for the day-to-day operations of the Business, has been trained by us, and who delivers our services directly to the customers;

NOW, THEREFORE, in consideration of the foregoing recitals and other good and valuable consideration, the receipt and sufficiency of which is hereby mutually acknowledged, the parties hereto, intending to be legally bound, do hereby agree as follows:

COVENANTS

ARTICLE 1
GRANT OF FRANCHISE LICENSE

1.1–Grant of Franchise

The Franchisor grants to the Franchisee, and the Franchisee accepts from the Franchisor, the non-exclusive right to use the System in connection with the establishment and operation of one "Business" as more fully described in Exhibit 2. This Franchise Agreement may be subject to the State Addendum found at Exhibit 8.

The Business will be based at the location described herein. The Franchisee agrees to use the Marks and the System as each may be changed, improved, and further developed by the Franchisor from time to time, only in accordance with the terms and conditions of this Agreement. The Franchisee shall complete the Statement of Ownership found at Exhibit 1.

1.2–Scope of Franchise Operations

The Franchisee shall at all times comply with the Franchisee's obligations hereunder and shall continuously use his/her best efforts to promote and operate the Business. The Franchisee shall utilize the Marks, the Proprietary Information, every component of the System (as appropriate for the Business selected), and the "Manuals" (which may be one or more manuals used to assist the Franchisee in the operation of the Business) to operate all aspects of the Business in accordance with the methods and systems developed and prescribed from time to time by the Franchisor. The Business shall offer all products and services that the Franchisor shall designate and shall be restricted from offering or selling any products and services not previously approved by the Franchisor in writing.

1.3–Reasonable Business Judgment

We will use our "Reasonable Business Judgment" in the exercise of our rights, obligations, and discretion, except where otherwise indicated. Use of our Reasonable Business Judgment will mean that our determination on a given matter will prevail even in cases where other alternatives are also reasonable so long as we are intending to benefit, or are acting in a way that could reasonably benefit any component of the System and/or the Marks, any one or more of the franchisees, or any other aspect of the franchise system. Such decisions may include, but will not be limited to, decisions which may: enhance and/or protect the Marks and the System; increase customer satisfaction; increase the use of the services all franchisees offer; and enhance matters which correspond with franchisee satisfaction. Franchisor will not be required to consider any franchisee's particular economic or other circumstances when exercising our Reasonable Business Judgment. Decisions made using our Reasonable Business Judgment will not affect all franchisees equally, with the result that some may be benefited while others are not.

As part of our Reasonable Business Judgment, and in order to respond timely to market conditions and the needs and wishes of customers to the Businesses, we reserve the right, in our sole and exclusive determination, to vary any standard of the System, the Marks, or the Manuals.

1.4–Reservation of Rights

We and our Affiliate reserve the right, among others, to:

a. Own, franchise, or operate businesses that are similar to your Business (and which use the Marks and the System) at any location outside of your Exclusive Territory, regardless of the proximity to your Exclusive Territory;

b. Use the Marks and the System to sell any products or services (which may be similar to those that you will sell) through any alternate channels of distribution within or outside of the Exclusive Territory. These alternate channels include, but are not limited to, retail locations (such as grocery stores or similar retail outlets), and other channels of distribution, such as television, mail order, catalog sales, wholesale to unrelated retail outlets, or over the internet. You cannot use alternate channels of distribution without our express permission, which may be granted or denied for any reason or for no reason at all. You will not receive compensation for any such sales;

c. Use and license others to use, either within or outside of your Exclusive Territory or in alternate channels of distribution, other trademarks, trade names, service marks, logos, proprietary information, and methods of operation that are not the same as or confusingly similar to the Marks, in the operation of a business that offers goods, services, and related products and services which may be similar to, or different from, the Business;

d. Purchase, or be purchased by, or merge, or combine with any other business, including a business that competes directly with your Business, wherever located; and,

e. Acquire and convert to our System any businesses offering services and products similar to those offered by you, including such businesses operated by competitors or otherwise operated independently, or as part of, or in association with any other system or chain, whether franchised or corporately owned, and located outside of the Exclusive Territory.

Though we can use alternative channels of distribution within your Exclusive Territory to make sales of goods, items, and services associated with the System and the Marks, or associated with any other system or trademarks, service marks, trade names, logos, and the like, we have not done so as of the date of this disclosure document. We reserve the right to do so at any time.

Our Affiliate has established a business that is substantially similar to the one being offered here. It will never open a competing business in any portion of your Exclusive Territory.

R

1.5–Other Covenants Relating to the Grant of this License

a. WE BOTH AGREE TO WAIVE THE RIGHT TO A JURY TRIAL, AND EXCEPT AS SET FORTH IN SECTION 16.8, THE RIGHT TO BE AWARDED EXEMPLARY, PUNITIVE, OR CONSEQUENTIAL DAMAGES IN ANY ACTION BROUGHT IN REFERENCE TO THE RELATIONSHIP BETWEEN YOU AND US.

b. **WE BOTH AGREE THAT EXCEPT AS SET FORTH IN SECTION 16.9, EACH OF US IS LIMITED TO BRINGING ANY LEGAL CLAIM AGAINST THE OTHER WITHIN ONE YEAR OF THE DATE THAT THE FACTS WHICH GIVE RISE TO THE CLAIM WERE DISCOVERED OR ONE YEAR FROM THE DATE THAT SUCH FACTS REASONABLY SHOULD HAVE BEEN DISCOVERED.**

c. **THIS FRANCHISE AGREEMENT DESCRIBES THE TERMS AND CONDITIONS ON WHICH WE CURRENTLY OFFER FRANCHISES TO NEW FRANCHISEES. WE MAY OFFER FRANCHISES UNDER DIFFERENT TERMS AND CONDITIONS IN ORDER TO ENHANCE, BUILD, AND PRESERVE THE SYSTEM.**

d. Franchisee covenants, represents, and warrants as follows and acknowledges that Franchisor is relying upon such covenants, representations, and warranties in making its decision to enter into this Agreement:

i. Franchisee acknowledges that he has received and has read this Franchise Agreement and all Exhibits attached hereto. Specifically, the Franchisee has been advised by us to seek out and use professional counsel of Franchisee's choosing in order to interpret any terms, covenants, or conditions of this Franchise Agreement and to obtain advice on the relationship overall. It is the Franchisee's sole and exclusive obligation to obtain such counsel, and Franchisor will not provide any legal, financial, or other counsel in reference to this Franchise Agreement.

ii. Franchisee has adequate funding to purchase and operate the Business and, as a result, is financially capable of undertaking the risks involved in the opening and operation of any business. Franchisee knows of no circumstances that would lead to litigation against him in the future.

iii. All statements made by Franchisee in writing in connection with its application for this Franchise were, to the best of its knowledge, true when made and continue to be true as of the date of this Agreement.

iv. Franchisee is not a party to any litigation or legal proceedings other than those that have been disclosed to Franchisor by Franchisee in writing.

v. Franchisee and its owners agree to comply with and/or to assist Franchisor to the fullest extent possible in Franchisor's efforts to comply with Anti-Terrorism Laws as defined below. As a result, the Franchisee and its owners certify, represent, and warrant that: A) none of their property or interests is subject to being "blocked" under any of the Anti-Terrorism Laws and that Franchisee and its owners are not otherwise in violation of any of the Anti-Terrorism Laws; B) none of them is listed in the Annex to Executive Order 13224; C) it will refrain from hiring (or, if already employed, will terminate the employment of) any individual who is listed in the Annex; D) it has no knowledge or information that, if generally known, would result in Franchisee, its owners, their employees, or anyone associated with Franchisee to be listed in the Annex to Executive Order 13224; E) it is solely responsible for ascertaining what actions it must take to comply with the Anti-Terrorism Laws, and Franchisee specifically acknowledges and agrees that its indemnification responsibilities set forth in this Agreement pertain to its obligations under this subparagraph; and F) any misrepresentation under this subparagraph or any violation of the Anti-Terrorism Laws by Franchisee, its owners, agents, and/or employees shall constitute grounds for immediate termination of this Agreement and any other agreement Franchisee has entered with Franchisor or any of Franchisor's affiliates (if any).

For purposes of this Franchise Agreement, "Anti-Terrorism Laws" means Executive Order 13224 issued by the President of the United States, the Terrorism Sanctions Regulations, and other regulations found at 31 CFR 515, 595, 597, and any laws which now pertain or which may in the future pertain to the matters of this subparagraph.

e. Franchisee (and each partner, member or shareholder if Franchisee is a partnership, limited liability business entity, or corporation) hereby represents that he or she has conducted an independent investigation of the Franchisor's business and System and recognizes that the business venture contemplated by this Agreement involves business risks and that its success will depend upon Franchisee's abilities as an independent businessperson. Franchisor expressly disclaims the making of, and Franchisee acknowledges that it has not received any warranty or guarantee, express or implied, as to the potential volume, profits or success of the business contemplated by this Agreement.

f. Except as provided in Item 19 to the franchise disclosure document (a copy of which you acknowledge receiving), we do not furnish or authorize our salespersons to furnish oral or written earnings claims information within this document concerning the actual sales, costs, income and or profits of a Business. Actual results will vary from unit to unit and we cannot estimate the results of any particular franchise.

g. If your franchise is awarded to a business entity, or if you convert to a business entity (other than a sole proprietorship), then we reserve the right, using our Reasonable Business Judgment to require the principals of the Business to sign the personal guarantee found at Exhibit 3 to this Franchise Agreement. To this end, the Franchisor reserves the right to review the operating documents of the Business prior to granting the franchise in order to determine who may be required to sign the guarantee.

h. At the present time, we do not receive rebates or any material benefits from our authorized and approved suppliers. We do reserve the right to receive rebates and material benefits at any time in the future. If we do receive revenue, we may or may not share it with the franchisees.

ARTICLE 2
OPENING PERIOD, EXCLUSIVE TERRITORY, DEVELOPMENT AND RELATED RIGHTS, AND OBLIGATIONS

2.1–Opening Period
The typical length of time between the signing of the Franchise Agreement and the opening of a Business is approximately 5 to 7 months (Opening Period).

10

We will extend your Opening Period one time for a reasonable time in the event factors beyond your reasonable control prevent you from meeting the deadlines and you request an extension of time from us at least 15 days before the end of the opening period. If after the passage of such reasonable time, the Franchisee has failed to open for business, Franchisor has the right to terminate this Agreement without any right to cure.

2.2–Franchised Location

A "Franchised Location" is the location for your Business that has been approved by us, and, if applicable, for which you have a lease that has been approved by us.

If you do not already have a Franchised Location selected and approved before you sign the Franchise Agreement, you and we will identify a "Designated Area" (Exhibit 1) within which to find a Franchised Location. A Designated Area is defined by geographic boundaries such as a perimeter defined by streets, landmarks, highways or similar methods, or by political or mailing boundaries including neighborhoods, cities, counties and zip codes. We reserve the right to change the method of identifying a Designated Area at any time.

The Designated Area gives you the exclusive right during the defined time period to find and develop your Business in that area.

Our assistance in connection with the selection and approval of a location is limited to providing written criteria for a satisfactory Franchised Location, reviewing the information provided by you to determine whether the location fulfills the requisite criteria, and at our option, an on-site inspection if requested by you and at your cost. Using our Reasonable Business Judgment, we base our approval of your proposed site on a variety of factors including, but not limited to the various demographic characteristics of the site (including population density, income, and the like), geographic, political and physical boundaries, extent of competition, mix of residential and commercial, and whether the proposed site is urban, suburban, or rural.

Our employees and we have no special expertise in selecting sites. Any approval is intended only to indicate that the proposed site meets our minimum criteria based upon our general business experience.

OUR APPROVAL OF A LOCATION DOES NOT INFER OR GUARANTEE THE SUCCESS OR PROFITABILITY IN ANY MANNER.

2.3–Approval of Lease

After we approve the proposed Franchise Location, you will have 30 days to negotiate a lease that must be submitted to us for approval. We will approve or disapprove the lease agreement within 15 days after receipt. We have the option to require that the lease: i) be collaterally assigned to us by Collateral Assignment of Lease agreement (Exhibit 4); or, ii) contain the following terms and conditions:

   a. The landlord must agree that without its consent, the lease and your right, title and interest under the lease may be assigned to us or our designee; and,

   b. The landlord must provide written notice to us (at the same time it gives such notice to you) of any default by you under the lease. We must be given an additional 15 days after your period

11

of cure has expired, to cure, at our sole option, any such default and, upon the curing of such default, we must be given the right to enter upon the leased premises and assume your rights under the lease as if the lease had been assigned by you to us.

You will operate your Business and use the Marks, the Proprietary Information, and the System only at the Franchised Location.

OUR APPROVAL OF ANY LEASE DOES NOT INFER OR GUARANTEE THE SUCCESS OR PROFITABILITY OF YOUR BUSINESS.

Once the site and the lease have been approved by us, the location will be your Franchised Location, and an Exclusive Territory will be identified by us, all of which will be identified in Exhibit 2 of this Franchise Agreement.

2.4–Exclusive Territory

You will be assigned an "Exclusive Territory" at the time that the Franchised Location and the lease are approved, which will continue in force during the initial and any renewal term of the Franchise Agreement. It will be a geometric shape, the center of which is your Franchised Location and the radius of which is approximately 100 miles (more or less). The final perimeter will conform to physical, geographic, zip codes, political, and/or other boundaries and will be decided by us using our Reasonable Business Judgment (Franchise Agreement, Article 1).

We will not permit another franchisee, or company- or Affiliate-owned business to operate within your Exclusive Territory. Except as set forth below in the reservation of rights, we will not accept or solicit orders to provide services in your Exclusive Territory.

You may advertise the Business only within your Exclusive Territory unless regional or cooperative advertising is implemented or unless you get our permission to advertise outside the Exclusive Territory. You can accept customers from anywhere including another franchisee's territory, and other franchisees can accept customers from your Exclusive Territory.

All franchisees can advertise on the internet only through our web portal; except that we may grant you the right to separately advertise or promote your business on the internet only after you have first received our express written permission to do so. Our decision to grant or deny this right will be based upon our Reasonable Business Judgment.

2.5–Permitting, Design, and Build Out

After this Agreement is signed, after the lease is signed, and when Exclusive Territory is defined, but before commencing the construction of the Business, the Franchisee, at its expense, shall comply with all of the following requirements:

a. We will supply you with generic plans for the design and build out of the interior and exterior structure. Franchisee will deliver the generic plans to a local architect and\or engineer who will conform the drawings to the Franchised Location. Franchisee shall submit the completed drawings to us for approval. We shall approve, disapprove, or comment on the plans within thirty (30) calendar days of the date that they are delivered. If we make comments, you shall revise the plans to conform to the comments within fifteen (15) days of delivery to you. If we

12

disapprove of the plans, we will provide comments. Thereafter, you will have thirty (30) days to revise the plans so that they can be approved by us;

b. Franchisee shall use a qualified general contractor or construction supervisor to oversee the construction of the Business and completion of all improvements, and Franchisee shall submit to Franchisor a statement identifying the general contractor or construction supervisor;

c. Franchisee shall obtain all licenses, permits and certifications required for lawful construction and operation of the Business including, without limitation, building, zoning, access, parking, driveway access, sign permits, and licenses, and shall certify in writing to Franchisor that all such permits, licenses, and certifications have been obtained. Franchisee shall obtain all health, safety, and other permits and licenses required for operation of the Business and shall certify that all such permits and licenses have been obtained prior to the Opening Date;

d. Franchisee shall cause such construction to be performed only in accordance with the site plan, and other plans and specifications approved by Franchisor and no changes will be made to the approved plans and specifications, or the design thereof, or any of the materials used therein, or to interior and exterior colors thereof, without the express written consent of Franchisor.

e. Franchisee will complete the interior and exterior with such furniture, Startup Kits, fixtures, workout and other equipment, signage, and the like so as to conform with our then-current look and equipment.

Should the Franchisee be unable to obtain all necessary permits and licenses during the stated period and extension time period or periods as a result of causes beyond the reasonable control of Franchisee (unless the requirement for the timely issuance of such permits and licenses is waived in writing by Franchisor), this Agreement may be terminated upon written notice from one party to the other without the necessity of further action or further documentation by either party. Franchisor will retain all fees that were paid to that date.

We may if requested by you, agreed upon by us, and at your cost send a representative to the site to ensure that construction is completed to our specifications. We will charge our then-current fee that will be found in the Operations Manual.

2.6–Computers, Software, and Other Equipment

The Business must have such computer and other equipment as Franchisor designates in the Manuals.

Franchisee will be required to purchase, lease, or license one (1) desk-top computer of any make or model that must have the latest version of the Microsoft® operating system. It must have the following software installed and operational: i) the latest version of Microsoft Word and Excel; ii) the latest version of Internet Explorer®; and iii) the latest version of QuickBooks®.

You may already own a computer and software that meets these requirements.

We may in the future offer a proprietary software or web-based programs that may include accounting, word processing and other features. There may be a fee for such programs.

You will be required to maintain the computer to keep it operational. You must maintain all software stored with all patches that may come from the manufacturer. The maintenance for hardware and software may occur at any time and as a result, there can be no estimate of the cost.

13

You are not required to maintain any hardware or software maintenance contracts.

We will require you to update all other computer hardware no more often than once every five (5) years.

The computer in the Business must be attached to a high-speed internet access point. We will have the right to, and will remotely access your computer to obtain information about your operations. This information may be used by us for any purpose and may include identification of your Business by name.

2.7–Purchase of Startup Kits

You must purchase the Startup Kit from our Affiliate or us. The content of the Startup Kit and the cost are more fully described in the Manuals. Any replacement inventory for the Startup Kit must be purchased from us or another approved vendor.

2.8–Other Furniture, Fixtures and Equipment

You will also be required to purchase all furniture, fixtures and equipment necessary to open and operate the Business. This list will be supplied to you in the manuals, as updated from time to time, and will include, but not be limited to: retail display kiosks or shelving, washing and grooming stations, tools including electric and manual grooming equipment, and similar items sufficient to provide the services offered. The list of required items will be delivered to you in the Manuals. You may be required to purchase additional or new equipment as the needs of the market place dictate. This will be communicated to you through amendments to the Manuals and may occur at any time.

2.9–Approval Process for Other Goods and Services

In some cases, you may wish to purchase a required good or service from a supplier that has not been previously approved by us. We will charge our then-current fee for this service. We do not maintain written criteria for approving suppliers and thus, these criteria are not available to you or your proposed supplier. To obtain our approval, you must submit such information as we may reasonably require in order to evaluate the prospective supplier. We will evaluate the submitted information and will provide written notice of our decision to you within 30 days. We may grant or deny approval for any reason or for no reason at all. Other than as stated here, we have no other process for approving suppliers.

Approval of alternative suppliers may be revoked by us if we determine in good faith that the goods or services they are supplying no longer meet the quality standards that are in effect at that time. We will notify you if we revoke our approval of any suppliers and you must immediately stop purchasing disapproved goods or services or purchases from a disapproved supplier.

2.10–Relocation

You may relocate your Business within your Exclusive Territory only if you first obtain our express written permission which permission will be considered using our Reasonable Business Judgment. If you are permitted to relocate, you must first have any location and its lease approved by us in the same manner as we are then approving locations for new franchisees. You will pay us our then-current

14

relocation fee that now is $5,000 (as provided in the Manuals). If the result of your relocation is that you encroach on the exclusive territory of another franchisee, you will not be permitted to relocate to that proposed site.

2.11–Maintenance and Renovation

You will be required to maintain your Business as needed to ensure a clean, safe and attractive business. This may require you to purchase new equipment to replace worn-out equipment, and may require you to repaint or take other remedial action. This will be done as often as is necessary to maintain a safe, secure and attractive Business. There can be no estimate of these costs, as the maintenance will vary depending work that must be done.

You will be required to renovate the Business every 5 years in order to meet our then-current configuration (Renovation). Renovation will also be required at the time that you are: awarded Successor Franchise Rights; at each 5 year period during such Successor Franchise Rights term; and, after a transfer but before the new owner reopens the Franchised Location for business (with the understanding that if the renovations can be made while the Business is in operation, then the transferee will be permitted to make such changes while open). To the extent that this requires you to purchase goods that can be obtained only from our Affiliates, or us you will be required to make such purchases. Renovations may include changes to interior and exterior decor, furniture, fixtures, equipment, small wares, and changes to the system in order to conform to the then-current franchise system look and feel. We cannot estimate the cost of such renovation.

2.12–Purchase of Additional Territory

You do receive rights to be awarded additional franchises. In order to qualify you must:

a. Have been in operation for at least 12 months;
b. Be in compliance with your Franchise Agreement at the time that you seek to purchase an additional site;
c. Have received no notices of default from us during the years prior to the date that you apply for consideration of such a grant;
d. Meet the then-current financial and business requirements that are applied to a new franchisee;
e. Demonstrate the business and financial ability to operate multiple Businesses;
f. Have operated your current Business in such a manner that we, using our Reasonable Business Judgment, deem to be sufficient to warrant granting you an additional location;
g. Using our then-current site criteria, have a location that will qualify as a Franchised Location; and
h. Be granted the right after we use our Reasonable Business Judgment.

If we grant you the right to an additional Business, you will sign the then-current franchise agreement and, if we deem it appropriate, you will attend additional training. **The new franchise agreement may have terms significantly different from this franchise agreement including a different IFF, royalty structure, advertising fee structure and the like.**

15

ARTICLE 3
FEES, ADVERTISING and REPORTING

3.1–Initial Franchise Fee

Your initial franchisee fee will be $15,000. This fee is non-refundable.

3.2–Gross Revenue–Definition

"Gross Revenue" means the total of all revenue and income from the sale of all products and services from all sources in connection with the Business whether or not sold at or from the "Franchised Location" (as that term is defined in Item 11) whether received in cash, in services in kind, from barter and/or exchange, on credit (whether or not payment is received) or otherwise. You may deduct from Gross Revenue all sales tax or similar taxes that by law, are chargeable to customers by any taxing authority. You may also deduct from Gross Revenue the amount of any documented refunds. All payments made to us including Royalties will be paid through an automatic electronic bank-to-bank transfer (EFT).

3.3–Royalty

You will pay a royalty of seven percent (7%) of the Gross Revenue on a monthly basis. (Royalty).

All Royalties are due on the third business day of the month following the month for which such Royalty is due.

3.4–Advertising and Advertising Fees

Local Advertising

You will be required to spend a minimum of 2 percent of your monthly Gross Revenue for local advertising placement. We must first approve any advertising before it is placed in any medium, with the added requirement that such advertisement(s) be sent to us at least thirty (30) days before it is to be used. We will have 15 days within which to approve. If we do not deliver to you written notice in that time, the copy will be deemed to be approved.

You may advertise on the internet only through our internet portal.

You may only advertise within your Exclusive Territory, though you can accept customers from anywhere including another franchisee's territory, and other franchisees can service customers from your Exclusive Territory.

National Advertising Fund and Regional and Cooperative Advertising

We do not now, but will, when we have 20 Businesses opened, collect 1 percent of the Gross Sales each month for advertising, concept development, collateral materials and other items for the benefit of the System (National Advertising Fee). The National Advertising Fee will be due at the same time as your Royalties and as part of the EFT withdrawal. The National Advertising Fee will be placed in an interest bearing checking account, savings account, or any other account of our determination (Account). Any monies not used in any year will be carried to the next year. The Account will be administered by us

16

at our sole discretion and may be used by us for all advertising expenditures reasonably intended to benefit the System, and for the payments to us of costs related to administering the Account such as reasonable salaries, administrative costs, travel expenses and overhead. National Advertising Fees are used to promote the services sold by the franchises and are not used to sell additional franchises.

We make no guarantee to you or to any other franchisee that advertising expenditures from the Account will benefit you or any other franchisee directly or on a pro rata basis. We will assume no other direct or indirect liability or obligation to you with respect to collecting amounts due to the Account or with respect to maintaining, directing or administering the Account.

Any company or Affiliate-owned Businesses will participate in any national or regional advertising programs in the same manner as the franchisees. Any fees not used in a calendar year will be rolled-over for use in the next or any subsequent year.

The National Advertising Fee will be used for the creation and placement of various advertising and promotional products. The media in which such advertising may be disseminated includes but is not limited to printed materials, posters, window clings, danglers in the Business, and/or the creation of television, internet, radio and print on a local or regional basis. The advertising will be produced and placed by us or by a local, national or international advertising agency.

Upon your prior written request, we will make available to you, no later than 120 days after the end of each calendar year, an annual unaudited financial statement for the Account.

We reserve the right, upon 30 days prior written notice to you, to allocate all or a portion of the National Advertising Fees to a regional advertising program (Regional Program) for the benefit of Businesses located within a particular region. We have the right to determine the composition of all geographic territories and market areas for the implementation of such a Regional Program and to require that you participate in it as and when it may be established. If the Regional Program is implemented on behalf of a particular region, we will only use contributions from franchisees within such region to the extent reasonably calculable by us. We will control and administer the Regional Program though we will permit franchisees within the region to reasonably suggest the manner of such expenditures. Upon your prior written request, we will make available to you, no later than 120 days after the end of each calendar year, the annual unaudited financial statement for the Regional Program account.

We may also establish an advertising cooperative (Advertising Cooperative) for a particular region to enable the cooperative to self-administer the Regional Program. If an Advertising Cooperative is established in your area, you must participate in it.

The Advertising Cooperative will be administered by the franchisees in the cooperative.

We have the right to change, dissolve, or merge any such cooperative. The cooperative will prepare unaudited financial statements and will deliver the same to use within 90 days of its year end. Each Regional Advertising Cooperative must adopt written governing documents. A copy of the governing documents of the Advertising Cooperative (if one has been established) for your region is available upon request.

We have the right to terminate the National Advertising Fund. We will not terminate the National Advertising Fund until all contributions and earnings have been used for advertising and promotional purposes or we have returned your pro rata share.

17

All advertising fees collected by us will be referred to collectively as the "Advertising Fees".

3.5–Grand Opening

In addition to the advertising requirements described above, commencing no earlier than 60 days after the opening you will be required to spend $500 to advertise the grand opening of your Business. The grand opening plans advertising must be approved by us in the same manner as is your local advertising.

3.6–Other Fees

We will create your own affiliated homepage that will be sponsored on our website, and you will pay us the $1,000.00 Technology Startup Fee. You will also pay the then-current monthly Technology Maintenance Fee as more fully described in the Manual.

Unless otherwise stated, all fees are payable in one lump sum, are due at the time you sign the Franchise Agreement, and are non-refundable under any circumstances.

There are not now, but in the future, there may be other fees that we may charge. All such fees will be disclosed in the Manuals, in updates, or in other communications to you.

We reserve the right to change or waive the fees mentioned above under special circumstances determined through our sole discretion.

3.7–Reporting

On a monthly basis and using the forms that we require and provide, you will deliver to us: a royalty report that accurately reflects all Gross Revenue generated during the preceding one-month period. This report must be received by us no later than the third business day of the month following the month for which it is due.

You will also deliver to us: a) profit and loss statements, balance sheets and trial balances prepared in accordance with generally accepted accounting principles, consistently applied, for each accounting period, to be received by Franchisor within fifteen (15) days after the expiration of each calendar quarter; b) a complete financial statement for your fiscal year, including, without limitation, both an income statement and balance sheet, which may be unaudited, together with such other information in such form as Franchisor may require; c) copies of all tax returns relating to sales at the Business to be received by Franchisor within ten (10) days of the end of the state sales tax reporting period; and, d) such other additional records, reports, information, and data as Franchisor may reasonably designate, in the forms, at the times and the places reasonably required by Franchisor, or as specified in the Manual or in writing. We have the right to change the required information that we may require and prior to requiring the same will provide you with reasonable written notice through a change to the Operations Manual.

The reports may be unaudited. All reports delivered by you will be signed and verified by you, or your principal financial or executive officer as being true and accurate.

Franchisee hereby grants us permission to release to Franchisee's landlord, lenders or prospective landlords or lenders, and to disclose in our franchise disclosure document, any financial and operational information relating to Franchisee and/or the Business.

18

3.8–Method of Payment

No later than 10 days prior to the opening of the Business, the Franchisee will execute an authorization agreement for the EFT from the Franchisee's bank account to the Franchisor's bank account. The EFT method will be used to collect Royalties, Advertising Fees, and any fees due under this Agreement. We have the right to change the method of collection at any time after reasonable notice is given to the Franchisee.

All Royalties, Advertising Fees and other fees due to us will be deposited into the Franchisee's operating account no later than 12:00 noon Mountain Time on third business day following the month for which the fees are due (Due Date). Franchisor will then sweep the operating account and deduct these fees.

In the event that the Franchisee fails to have sufficient funds in the account on the Due Date, or otherwise fails to pay any Royalties or other fees due under this Franchise Agreement, the Franchisee shall owe a $100.00 late fee which shall be due and payable for each day that the payment is late without other notice than this Agreement. This fee is in addition to all Royalties or other fees due. This will be automatically assessed and debited or paid along with the late debit or other such payment of Royalties. In addition, the Franchisor shall charge interest on any payments made after the Due Date at 1½ percent per month (Default Rate); except, the Late Fee will not exceed the maximum legal rate permitted by the law.

The Franchisee acknowledges that this subsection does not constitute the Franchisor's agreement to accept such payments after they are due or a commitment to extend credit to, or otherwise finance the operation of the Business. In no event shall the Franchisee be required to pay interest at a rate greater than the maximum interest rate permitted by applicable law. The collection of any late fee and the acceptance of any late payment will not diminish the Franchisor's right to any other remedies available under this Franchise Agreement.

3.9–Application of Payments

Notwithstanding any designation by the Franchisee as to the desired application of the payment, the Franchisor shall allocate any payments made by the Franchisee: first to any late fees and interest owed to us; then to any past due Royalties or other fees; then to any obligations that Franchisee has to any third party vendors that are paid by the Franchisor on your behalf; and then to the current Royalties and other fees owed to the Franchisor. The allocation set forth above shall not serve to postpone any payments that are due on any current or future due date.

We will also have the sole discretion to allocate in the same manner as stated in this subsection, any payments, or any credits from third party vendors that are delivered to the Franchisor on the Franchisee's behalf. To the extent necessary to carry out the intent of this subsection, the Franchisee hereby appoints the Franchisor as its attorney-in-fact, and grants his power of attorney for the sole purpose of allocating any such funds received. This power of attorney shall continue throughout the term of this Agreement, any extension thereof and if applicable, after the termination of this Agreement, but in the latter case, only to the extent that the Franchisee still owes money to the Franchisor from his operation of the franchise.

19

3.10–Record Keeping and Auditing

You agree to record all sales at the time of the sale in your computer or other sales recording system approved by us. You agree to retain all computer records, charge account records, sales slips, orders, return vouchers, sales tax reports, and all of your other business records and related background material, for at least seven (7) years following the end of the year in which the items were or should have been generated.

Our designated agents or we will have the right, at all reasonable times, to examine and copy the books, records, and tax returns of Franchisee and the Business. We will also have the right, at any time, to have an independent audit made of the books of the Business. If an inspection should reveal that any payments to Franchisor have been understated in any report then you will immediately pay to us the amount understated upon demand, in addition to interest on such amount from the date such amount was due until paid, at the Default Rate, calculated on a daily basis. If an inspection discloses an understatement of two percent (2%) or more in any payment to Franchisor, Franchisee shall pay the difference and shall reimburse us for any and all costs and expenses relating to the inspection (including, without limitation, travel, lodging and wage expenses and reasonable accounting and legal costs). At our discretion, Franchisee may also be required to submit audited financial statements prepared at your expense, by an independent auditor that we approve. If an inspection discloses an understatement in any payment to Franchisor of four percent (4%) or more, such act or omission may constitute grounds for termination of this Agreement. The foregoing remedies shall be in addition to any other remedies that we have pursuant to this Agreement and as provided at law and in equity.

ARTICLE 4
TERM AND SUCCESSOR FRANCHISE RIGHTS

4.1–Effective Date and Initial Term

This Agreement shall be effective on the date that it is fully executed by us (Effective Date). There is no agreement and this is not a contract between us until that date.

The initial term of this Franchise Agreement will be for ten (10) years from the Effective Date. (Initial Term).

The Initial Term will begin on the Effective Date. If we are required by law to give you notice before the termination or expiration of this Franchise Agreement, and if we fail to do so, this Franchise Agreement will remain in effect until we have given the required notice.

4.2–Successor Franchise Rights

At the end of the Initial Term, and for any Business, you will have the option, to extend the grant of these rights for two (2) additional 5-year terms (each being a "Successor Term"), by acquiring "Successor Franchise Rights." To be eligible, you must:

    a. Have complied with all provisions of this Agreement during the current term, including the timely payment of all amounts due to Franchisor. "Compliance" shall mean, at a minimum, that

20

the Franchisee has received no more than three (3) written notices from us of breach of this Agreement (each of which breach was timely cured is cure is available) during any 12 month period; and is current on all obligations under this Franchise Agreement at the time Franchisee applies for Successor Franchise Rights;

b. Agree to sign the then-current franchise agreement within thirty (30) calendar days of the date that it was received, **with the understanding that the terms of such an agreement (including the Royalty) may be significantly different then those found here.** Under the then-current franchise agreement, the Franchisee will not have any further Successor Franchise Rights. The signed franchise agreement will not be effective until the Franchisor finally signs it. It will not be a contract until that time;

c. Agree to sign the General Release, a copy of which is found at Exhibit 6. Notwithstanding the foregoing, to the extent that the law of the state in which the Business is located has determined that the requirement that a franchisee sign a General Release is unenforceable, then any such requirement shall be deemed to de deleted and the franchisee shall not be required to sign the same; or if signed then such General Release shall be deemed to be not enforceable. If however, the law of the state in which the Business is located permits the franchisee to sign such General Release, then the franchisee shall sign such a release as part of the transfer process found herein. The General Release will not release the Franchisor of any representations made in the franchise disclosure document; and,

d. Agree to pay the "Successor Franchise Fee" of fifty percent (50%) of the then-current IFF charged to new franchisees at the time.

Though the Franchisee may have met the above requirements, the Franchisor must consent pursuant to subparagraph 4.3 below. Until approved by the Franchisor, the Franchisee will be granted no Successor Franchise Rights.

If the Successor Franchise Rights are granted then the Successor Term will begin on the day following the end of the Initial Term or the preceding Successor Term.

If the Franchisee opts to extend its rights under this subsection, Franchisee must notify Franchisor of its intent by giving us written notice of such exercise no later than 180 days prior to the scheduled expiration of this Agreement. Successor Franchise Rights will become effective only after compliance with all of the terms of this Article 4 including obtaining Franchisor's consent.

4.3.–Conditions of Refusal

The Franchisor will not be obligated to grant the Franchisee Successor Franchise Rights if the Franchisee has:

a. i) Received a fourth written notice of breach of any combination of terms, covenants or conditions of this Agreement during any 12 month period even though each such breach may have been timely cured; or, ii) has received a third written notice of breach of any combination of terms, covenants or conditions of the franchise agreement in effect during any Successor Term even though each such breach may have been timely cured;

21

b. Failed to comply with any of the conditions necessary to obtain Successor Franchise Rights as described in subparagraph 4.2 above;

c. Is in breach of this Franchise Agreement at the time that you attempt to exercise your right to purchase Successor Franchise Rights, and even if such breach is timely cured; or,

d. We have determined in good faith and after using our Reasonable Business Judgment not to grant Successor Franchise Rights.

Upon occurrence of any of the events described just above, we will give you written notice at least sixty (60) days prior to the expiration of the Initial Term, and such notice shall set forth the reasons for such refusal to offer successor franchise rights.

4.4–Successor Franchise Renovation

In order to maintain a clean appearance, in order to meet the then-current decor requirements, and as a condition to granting Successor Franchise Rights, you must Renovate the Business as required by Article 2.

General maintenance of the Business is not considered to be a Renovation.

ARTICLE 5
MANUALS and SERVICES PROVIDED TO YOU BY US

5.1–Manuals

We will provide you one or more operations manuals, technical bulletins or other written materials (collectively referred to as the "Manuals") covering our standards, specifications and operating and marketing procedures to be used by you in operating the Business. You will comply with the Manuals as an essential aspect of your obligations under this Agreement. Your failure to comply substantially with the Manuals will be considered by us to be a breach of this Agreement. The Manuals will be updated from time to time and you must comply with any changes in every update within the time period provided in such updates.

You will only use the Marks, the System, and any Proprietary Information as specified in the Manuals. The Manuals are the sole property of the Franchisor and shall be used by you only during the term of this Agreement and in strict accordance with the terms and conditions of this Agreement.

5.2–Services Provided by Us Prior to Commencement of Operations

Except as stated below, the Franchisor is not required to provide you with any assistance.

Before you open your business, we will:

a. Assist you in selecting a Franchised Location by providing site selection criteria as described in Article 2 above.

b. Review your lease.

c. Once your Franchised Location is approved, we will designate your Exclusive Territory.

22

d. Furnish mandatory design specifications, layout criteria, and specifications for furniture, fixtures and equipment for the Business.

e. Furnish the Startup Kit.

f. Offer training as more specifically set forth in Article 7.

g. If requested by you and at your cost, we may agree to send a representative to the Business to ensure that improvements are completed to our specifications

h. At our option, the day before opening and for 2 days thereafter, we may send a representative to the Business to help with opening and initial operations.

i. Lend you one copy of the Operations Manual.

5.3–Services Offered by Us During the Operation

During the operation of your Business, we will provide the following services:

a. Modify, update or change the System including but not limited to the adoption and use of new or modified list of authorized and approved suppliers, trade names, trademarks, service marks, or copyrighted materials, new products, a new and evolving menu of services and new techniques.

b. Provide you with access to local advertising materials.

c. Help you coordinate your Grand Opening.

d. Provide feedback from the polling of your computers including a comparison of your cost of goods to those of other Businesses.

e. Periodically advise you or offer guidance to you on other matters concerning the operation of your Business.

f. Conduct quality control visits (both announced and unannounced), and also use a "secret shopper" program.

g. At such time in the future as we deem appropriate, we will hold an annual conference at which new ideas and other matters will be discussed.

Optional Assistance

We may provide you with additional training and support on an as-needed basis and for the then-current fee. You may request additional support and the same will be given in our sole discretion. Any costs incurred by us in providing such additional services shall be paid by you.

ARTICLE 6
PROPRIETARY INFORMATION, THE SYSTEM, COPYRIGHTS, AND MARKS

6.1.–Proprietary Information

Franchisee acknowledges that he will obtain from the Franchisor knowledge of proprietary matters, techniques, and business procedures that are necessary and essential to the operation of the Business, without which information Franchisee could not effectively and efficiently operate. Franchisee further acknowledges that such proprietary information was not known to Franchisee prior to execution of this Agreement and that the methods of operation used in the operation of the Business are unique and novel to the System.

As used herein, "Proprietary Information" will include, but not be limited to not only the above, but also:

a. Persons, corporations, or other entities which are, have been, or become franchisees or investors of the Franchisor;

b. Persons, corporations, or other entities which are, have been, or become customers of the Business;

c. The terms of and negotiations relating to past or current franchise agreements with respect to the System;

d. The operating procedures of the System, including without limitation: distinctive management; bookkeeping and accounting systems and procedures; advertising; promotional and marketing methods; personnel hiring and training procedures; the size, configuration, and interior and exterior decor; and, lists of vendors and suppliers;

e. The economic and financial characteristics of the System, including without limitation: pricing policies and schedules; profitability; earnings and losses; and capital and debt structures;

f. Any common law or statutory copyrighted materials and the protection afforded thereby;

g. The services and products offered to customers of the Business; and,

h. The Manuals, the Marks, the System, and every component of the System.

During the term of this Agreement and following the expiration or termination of this Agreement, Franchisee agrees not to divulge, directly or indirectly, any component of the Proprietary Information to any person or entity, without the prior written consent of Franchisor which consent will be granted or denied for any reason or for no reason at all. Nothing contained herein shall be construed so as to require Franchisor to divulge any secret processes, formulas, or the like.

You may disclose Proprietary Information only to such of your employees, agents and representatives as must have access to it in order to operate the Business. Franchisee shall obtain from each such employee, representative or agent, an agreement that such person shall not during the course of his employment, representation, or agency with Franchisee, or at any time thereafter, use, divulge, disclose or communicate, directly or indirectly, in any form or manner, to any person, firm or corporation, any of the Proprietary Information of Franchisor.

You acknowledge that any failure to comply with the requirements of this Article will cause Franchisor irreparable injury, and Franchisor shall be entitled to obtain specific performance of, or an injunction against any violation of, such requirements. To the fullest extent permitted by law, Franchisee waives any requirements for the posting of any bond(s) relating thereto. The foregoing remedies shall be in addition to any other legal or equitable remedies that Franchisor may have.

6.2.–Marks, Copyrights and the System

You receive the right to operate your Business under the Mark specified in the Manual and identified on the first page of this disclosure document. You may also use any other current or future Mark to operate your Business that we designate. By "Mark" we mean any trade name, trademark, service mark or logo used to identify your business.

On January 2, 2010 we filed for registration of the Mark with the United States Patent and Trademark Office which registration was granted as noted below:

24

Serial Number	Description of Mark	Principal or Supplemental Register of the USPTO	Filing date
1,234,567	**AARDVARKS ONLY**	Principal	January 2, 2010

We do not have federal registration for our principal trademark. Therefore, our trademark does not have many legal benefits and rights as a federally registered trademark. If our right to use the trademark is challenged, you may have to change to an alternative trademark, which may increase your expenses.

We also claim common law copyrights and copyright protection in and on all of the components of the System, including, but not limited to, the Marks, the content of the Manuals and related materials, training modules and techniques, our website, all advertisements in any medium, including the internet, and other promotional and written materials. Each and every component of the System is our proprietary, trade secret, and confidential information (Proprietary Information). Any component of the Proprietary Information can be used by you only as described in this Franchise Agreement.

You acknowledge that we own each component of the System. You acknowledge that we have valuable rights in and to the System and each component thereof is considered to be part of the Proprietary Information.

For purposes of this Franchise Agreement, your "Customer Lists" will refer to the name and contact information of all persons or entities that use your services, whether current or past. In consideration of the time and effort that we have put into the System and its goodwill, and for other good and valuable consideration, we retain ownership and control of your Customer List. You may not use the Customer List except in conjunction with the operation of the Business and must surrender the same upon the termination of this Franchise Agreement for any reason.

You, your Principal Operator, any Designated Manager, and any officers, directors, managers, members, the holder of any equitable interest in a business entity, agents, servants, employees, and all others in active concert or participation with you in the Business (Franchisee Parties), will never during the term of this Franchise Agreement, or at any time after the termination or expiration of this Franchise Agreement, reveal the Marks, or disclose any component of the System or the Proprietary Information to any person or entity nor use it for any other business.

We reserve the right to require each of the Franchisee Parties to sign a non-disclosure and non-competition agreement.

If your franchise is awarded to a business entity, or if you convert to a business entity (other than a sole proprietorship), then the principals of the business entity must sign the personal guarantee found at Exhibit 3. To this end, the Franchisor reserves the right to review the operating documents of the Business prior to granting the franchise (or at the time of a transfer or conversion to the business entity) in order to determine who may be required to sign the guarantee.

You will not copy any component of the Proprietary Information unless we specifically authorize it in writing, which authorization may be granted or denied for any reason or for no reason at all.

You acknowledge that you have not acquired and will not acquire in the future any right, title or

25

interest in any component of the Proprietary Information, the System or Marks except as permitted by this non-exclusive license.

You will not: a) directly or indirectly contest nor aid in contesting the validity of the ownership of the Marks, the System or the Proprietary Information; b) in any manner interfere with or attempt to prohibit our use of the Marks, or any component of the System or the Proprietary Information; or, c) interfere with the use of the Marks, the System or the Proprietary Information of our other franchisees.

6.3–Infringement

You will promptly notify us in writing of any possible infringement on the Marks, or any component of the Proprietary Information, or the use by others of any trademark, portion of the System, or any component of the Proprietary Information that may be the same as, or confusingly similar to that used by us.

You acknowledge that we shall have the right, in our sole discretion, to determine whether any action will be taken on account of any possible infringement or illegal use of the Marks, the System or the Proprietary Information. We may commence or prosecute such action in our own name and may join you as a party to the action if we determine it to be reasonably necessary for the continued protection and quality control of the Marks, and each component of the System. If you learn that any third party, whom you believe is not authorized to use the Marks, is using them, or any variant of them, you must promptly notify us. We will determine whether or not we wish to take any action against the third party. You will have no right to make any demand, or to prosecute any claim against the alleged infringer. We will not pay any franchisee for exercising these rights. You must cooperate with us in any way necessary in the event of such an infringement.

We have the right to control any administrative proceedings or litigation involving a Mark, or any component of the System or the Proprietary Information. If you learn of any claim against you for alleged infringement, unfair competition, or similar claims, you must promptly notify us. We will take the action we deem necessary to defend you. We must indemnify you for any action against you, by a third party, based solely on alleged infringement, unfair competition, or similar claims. We have no obligation to defend or indemnify you, if the claim against you related to your use of the Marks, or the System or Proprietary Information is in violation of this Franchise Agreement.

6.4–Business Name and Contact Information

You will not use the phrase "Noah's Ark", "Aardvarks Only", and/ or "Noah's Ark Aardvark Services" (or any commercially similar derivation of each such phrase) or any portion of the Marks in the legal name of your corporation, partnership or any other business entity used in conducting the business provided for in this Agreement. You also agree not to register or attempt to register a trade name using the any of the above phrase (or any commercially similar derivation of each such phrase) in your name, or that of any other person or business entity, without our prior written consent that may be withheld for any reason or for no reason at all. You may do business as " Corporation (or other business entity) doing business as Noah's Ark of _____ (city/county/state)" so long as this is only a "doing business as" or fictitious name and not part of the business entity name.

26

Except as permitted in the Manuals, you will not use any of the Marks as part of an electronic mail address or on any sites on the internet, nor shall you use or register any of the Marks as part of a domain name on the internet.

Franchisee understands and agrees that the telephone number(s), URLs, customer lists, and email addresses for the Business constitute a part of the System and are subject to the restrictions of this Agreement. Accordingly, Franchisee shall not change the telephone number(s) for the Business without prior notice and written approval by Franchisor. Franchisee shall advertise and publicize the telephone number(s) for the Business in the manner prescribed by Franchisor. You will sign the Collateral Assignment of Contact and Electronic Information found at Exhibit 5. Upon termination of this Agreement, all contact information shall be deemed the property of the Franchisor.

6.5–Modification and Discontinuation

In the event that the Franchisor, in its sole discretion, shall determine it necessary to modify or discontinue use of any Marks or any portion of the Proprietary Information or the System, or to develop additional or substitutes for any such component, you will, within a reasonable time after receipt of written notice of such a modification or discontinuation from us, take such action, at your sole expense, as may be necessary to comply with such modification, discontinuation, addition or substitution.

You have the right to use the Marks, the System, and the Proprietary Information only in the Exclusive Territory, and only for so long as you shall fully perform and comply with all of the conditions, terms and covenants of this Franchise Agreement, and our policies and procedures that we prescribe from time to time.

All other use of the Marks in advertising, in or outside of the Exclusive Territory, must be with our prior written approval as set forth in this Agreement and in the Manuals.

You further agree to execute any and all additional documents and assurances in connection with the Marks, the System, and any portion of the Proprietary Information as reasonably requested by us and agree to fully cooperate with us or any of our other franchisees or licensees in securing all necessary and required consents of any state agency or legal authority for the use of the Marks, any portion of the Proprietary Information, or any other components that are, or become a part of the System.

Any and all goodwill associated with the Marks, the Proprietary Information, and any portion of the System, including any goodwill that might be deemed to have arisen through your activities, shall inure directly and exclusively to our benefit, except as otherwise provided herein or by applicable law.

6.6.–No Use of Other Marks

No marks, logotypes, trade names, trademarks, or the like other than those specifically approved by us will be used by you in the identification, marketing, promotion or operation of the Business.

6.7–Protection of Marks, System and Proprietary Information

You agree to:

   a. Fully and strictly adhere to all security procedures prescribed by us for maintaining the secrecy of the Marks, each component of the System, and all of the Proprietary Information;

27

b. Disclose such information to your employees only to the extent necessary to make and market our products;

c. Refrain from using any component of the Marks, the System, or the Proprietary Information in any other business or in any manner not specifically authorized or approved by us in writing; and,

d. Exercise the highest degree of diligence and make every effort to maintain the absolute confidentiality of all such information during and after the term of the Franchise Agreement.

Franchisee, and any of its employees, will also refrain from conducting any activity at the Business or in connection therewith or take any action which is illegal or which could result in damage to or disparagement of the Marks, or which negatively impact the reputation and goodwill associated therewith. **Any breach of this covenant will result in immediate termination for which no cure is provided.**

6.8–Innovations by You

During the Initial Term or any Successor Term, you may create, design, or otherwise improve upon any portion of the System, the Marks, the Proprietary Information or the like (Innovation). Any such Innovation will be deemed to be the sole and exclusive property of the Franchisor and not Franchisee. Upon the creation of such Innovation, you will immediately notify the Franchisor in writing that will describe in detail, the nature of the Innovation. The Franchisor shall have the sole and exclusive right to approve or disapprove of any such Innovation for any reason or for no reason at all. If we approve of it, we may permit you to use the Innovation and may, in our sole and exclusive option, permit any one or more franchisees or company-owned stores to use any portion of the Innovation.

You agree that as between us, we will own the right, title and interest to the Innovation. You agree to take any action necessary to ensure that we obtain such right, title and interest, so long as such action costs you nothing.

We are not obligated to pay you for the Innovation, though we reserve the right to do so, without incurring the obligation to pay you or any other franchisee for any future Innovation.

ARTICLE 7
TRAINING

7.1–Initial Training

Franchisor provides an initial training program to be conducted in Denver, Colorado, or at an alternative location to be determined by us. The initial training program is offered by us as needed to meet the needs of our franchisees.

The initial training program is typically five (5) business days in length of which approximately 20 hours are classroom instruction and 20 hours are on-the-job training.

We reserve the right to waive a portion of the training program or alter the training schedule, if in our sole discretion, we determine that you or your designated attendee has sufficient prior experience or training.

Up to 2 people may participate in our initial training program without additional fee. You (or if you are an entity, your Principal Operator), and the Designated Manager must successfully complete

28

the initial training program prior to the opening of your Business. No tuition is charged for training. You must, however pay for all transportation, room, board, wages, and other living expenses which are incurred in connection with attendance at the training program. Each person must successfully complete the initial training program prior to the opening of your Business.

If you replace your Designated Manager or your Principal Operator, the replacement person must attend and complete our training program within 60 days of the hiring date. In our discretion, you may be charged our then-current training fee.

Your Business must be under the direct full-time day-to-day "on-premises" supervision of you (or, your Principal Operator, if you are a legal entity) or Designated Manager.

7.2–Additional Training, Seminars, and Other Education Development Programs

You may wish to get on-site training from us. This is optional and is not required for the operation of the business unless you feel it is necessary. We will charge our then-current fee, plus all costs for travel, lodging, and food. This training can take place at any time.

If you request additional, extraordinary, or refresher courses or training, we may, at our option, charge our then-current per diem fee plus expenses.

We may also offer additional training on-line or through web seminars (webinars). There may be a fee for such training. We will notify you of the training and the fee. Some of this training may be mandatory.

We will provide such bulletins, brochures, manuals and reports, if any, as may from time to time be published regarding plans, policies, developments, and activities. In addition, we may provide such communication concerning new developments, techniques, and improvements in and to the System and the Proprietary Information, as we feel may be relevant to the operation of the Business.

If you propose to sell or transfer the Business to a third party, part of our approval process will be the requirement that the transferee attend training and that he pay for the training at our then-current fee (Item 6).

In addition to the annual conference (described below), and though we do not now, we have the right, in the future to require you, and at least one of your principals or key employees to attend a local or regional training meeting one (1) time per year. All mandatory meetings will be offered without charge of a tuition or fee; however, you will be responsible for all travel and living expenses that are associated with attendance. Any additional local or regional meetings will last between 1 and 2 days and will be held at a location to be approved by us that will be within easy car or bus commuting distance. Any instructors at such meetings will either be our principals, or other persons not yet identified by us, but whose identity and background will be disclosed to you before the meeting.

7.3–Annual Conference

We do not now, but may, in the future, have an annual conference that, if held, will require attendance by all franchisees. You will be responsible for the payment of all expenses for travel, accommodations, food, and other expenses incurred. Though none is now required, we may in the future require an attendance fee. When it is known, you will be provided with the duration of such a meeting, as well as its location, the identities of those who will present information at the meeting, and the content of any seminars or information that will be delivered at that time. The annual conference will be held in a location to be determined by us.

7.4–Employees and Employee Training

Your employees are not our employees. You are exclusively responsible for the day-to-day performance of any and all employees including, but not be limited to: training of the employees; day-to-day management and oversight; employee discipline; hours worked; scheduling; the payment of taxes; purchasing any workers compensation or other insurance; and following all municipal, state, and federal rules, laws, and statutes pertaining to the employees.

ARTICLE 8
QUALITY CONTROL

In addition to all other obligations and representations of yours that are set forth in this Franchise Agreement, you also agree as follows:

8.1–System Compliance

You agree that the use of, and strict adherence to, all instructions concerning the Marks, System, the Manuals, and the Proprietary Information, and adherence to our standardized design and specifications for decor of the Business and uniformity of equipment, layouts, signs, and other incidents of the Business, are essential to the image and goodwill of the System.

You will use the System, Marks, Manuals, and Proprietary Information only for the operation of the Business and shall not use them in connection with any other line of business or any other activity.

Franchisee, and any of its employees, may not: a) conduct any business at the Business other than that authorized pursuant to this Agreement; or, b) conduct any activity at the Business that could result in damage to, or disparagements of the Marks, the System, or the reputation and goodwill of Franchisor.

You will maintain in sufficient supply, and use at all times only such products, goods, materials, and services specified by us, so as to permit the Business to operate at full capacity, and you will refrain from selling or offering for sale, any other products of any kind or character without first obtaining the express approval of Franchisor, which shall be granted or denied for any reason or no reason at all.

You will use and display the Marks at the Business in all capacities, including but not limited to; forms, business cards and stationery, paper and plastic products, and other supplies; or other items we may, in the future, designate.

You will purchase from our Affiliate, our authorized and approved suppliers, or us those products that carry our Marks.

You will comply with all other contracts that you enter into in reference to the operation of the Business with the understanding that your breach and failure to cure the breach of any material contract could result in the termination of this Agreement.

You will refrain from engaging in any trade practice or other activity or the sale of any product or literature from the Business, which we determine to be a deceptive trade practice, harmful to the

30

goodwill of the System or the Marks, or which may reflect unfavorably on the reputation of you, other franchisees, or us.

You will maintain the Business in a good, clean, and sanitary condition. You will maintain, repair or replace any item of decor (interior or exterior) and the furniture, fixtures and equipment as necessary in order to present a first class image to the public.

You may not alter, change, or modify the System in any way without our prior written consent and approval that we may grant or deny for any reason or for no reason at all.

You will participate in reasonable market research, testing, and product and service development programs.

You agree not to engage in any activity or practice that results or may reasonably be anticipated to result in any public criticism of the System or any part thereof.

You will accept cash, credit or debit cards, and if you accept checks, you will use a check verification system approved by us. You agree to use only the credit card processor approved by us for any of your credit card processing.

8.2–Compliance with Applicable Laws

You agree to comply with all applicable laws, ordinances, and regulations, or rulings of every nature whatsoever which in any way regulate or affect the operation of your Business. We have disclosed to you that the municipality, city, county or state in which you are operating may have special rules, regulations or laws that affect the operation of your Business. You and not we are responsible for determining the scope of such rules, regulations, or laws and you must adhere to the same to the fullest extent required by the law.

We have not made, and you have not relied on, any representation that no licenses, or only certain licenses, are necessary in connection with the operation of your Business.

You agree to obtain all building permits and inspections before you open your Business.

You agree to timely make all payments of taxes, employee withholding, and all similar assessments.

Your failure to comply with this subsection 8.2 will be a breach of this agreement for which no cure will be provided.

8.3–Inspections

You hereby consent to reasonable inspections and audits of the Business during normal business hours. As a result of such audits we may find matters that require immediate attention. In such an event, you will be required to make changes to the Business or any portion of your operation of the Business in order to comply.

You will permit our agents or us at any reasonable time, to remove from the Business samples of items without payment therefore, in amounts reasonably necessary for testing by an independent laboratory or us. The samples will be used to determine whether each meets our then-current standards and specifications. In addition to any other remedies it may have under this Agreement, we may require you to bear the cost of such testing if the supplier of the item has not previously been approved by us or if the sample fails to conform to our specifications.

31

You agree to cooperate and assist Franchisor with any customer or marketing research program that Franchisor may institute from time to time. Franchisee's cooperation and assistance shall include, but not be limited to, the distribution, display, and collection of customer comment cards, questionnaires, and similar items.

8.4–Approved Products, Product Purchases and Approval Method.

We and our Affiliates have the right (without incurring any liability) to consult with your suppliers about the status of your account with them and to advise your suppliers and others with whom you, we, our Affiliates, and other franchise owners deal, that you are in default under any agreement with our Affiliate or us (but only if we have notified you of such default).

You also agree that all furniture, fixtures, equipment, electronic equipment, and all other goods or services supplied by the Business shall comply with our standards and specifications. You must purchase the same from designated or approved sources and suppliers.

You agree to discontinue selling or offering for sale or using any products Franchisor may, in its absolute discretion, delete from its standards and specifications for any reason whatsoever or for no reason whatsoever.

8.5–Appearance and Customer Service

You will give prompt, courteous, and efficient service to your customers, and shall otherwise operate the Business in strict compliance with the System and the policies, practices, and procedures contained in the Manuals (or otherwise communicated to you in writing) so as to preserve, maintain, and enhance the reputation and goodwill of your Business and the System.

You will be required to have all personnel wear clean uniforms (conforming to such specifications as to color, design, etc. as Franchisor may designate, from time to time), while working at the Business, and to cause all employees to present a clean, neat appearance and render competent and courteous service to customers, as may be further detailed in the Manual.

You will hire a sufficient number of employees and maintain sufficient inventories as necessary to operate the Business at its maximum capacity.

You will have no jukeboxes, games of chance, video games, newspaper racks, children's rides, telephone booths, and cigarette, gum, candy, or other vending machines installed in or at the Business unless you first receive our express written approval.

You will issue and honor all gift certificates, coupons, and gift and loyalty cards and will administer customer loyalty and similar programs. You must participate in, and comply with the requirements of, our gift card and loyalty programs.

8.6–Timely Delivery of all Reports and Fees

You will timely deliver to us all reports and fees as required herein or in the Manuals.

8.7–Notification of Deficiencies

Should we notify you at any time of defects, deficiencies, or unsatisfactory conditions concerning the Business, you agree to immediately correct any such item or items, and in every event making such corrections within the time period for any cure that is granted by this Franchise Agreement or by the Manuals.

8.8–Compliance with all Terms of this Franchise Agreement

You agree to comply with all covenants and duties placed upon you by this Agreement and such compliance is deemed to part of this Article 8 though it may not be specifically enumerated herein.

8.9–Management

You, your Designated Manager or Principal Operator shall be required to devote his or her full time, attention and best efforts to the management and operation of the Business and the compliance with this Franchise Agreement.

8.10–Hours of Operation

Unless otherwise mutually agreed in writing, you must operate the Business during such hours and on such days as will be required by the Operations Manual. All days and hours of minimum required operation are subject to change at our discretion. You shall keep from participating in conflicting enterprises or any other activities, which would be detrimental to, or interfere with, the operations of the Business.

You understand and agree that the limited non-exclusive license granted to you herein is based on your commitment to the operation of the Business and your performance under this Franchise Agreement.

8.11–Modification and Pricing

We may reasonably change or modify the System, the Manuals and the Marks and you agree to accept, be bound by, use, implement and display any such changes to the System. You will make whatever expenditures are reasonably required to implement such changes or modifications. We shall have complete ownership and control of any changes, modifications, enhancements, or suggestions whether made by you or us.

We may, from time to time, advise you concerning suggested retail prices for goods and services. Franchisor and Franchisee agree that any list or schedules of prices furnished to Franchisee by Franchisor are suggested retail prices. Nothing contained herein shall be deemed a representation by Franchisor that the use of the Franchisor's suggested prices will in fact optimize profits. Franchisee may charge any price he deems appropriate for any good or service.

8.12–Disclosure

We can disclose in our disclosure documents or elsewhere any information concerning you or your Business, including your name, address, telephone number, financial, and other information.

8.13–Variances

We may approve exceptions to, or changes in, the uniform standards for you or other franchisees that we believe are necessary or desirable under particular circumstances. You have no right to object to such variances or to obtain the same variances for yourself.

ARTICLE 9
TRANSFERS

9.1–Sale or Assignment by Franchisor

This Franchise Agreement and all rights and obligations hereunder are fully assignable and transferable by us and if so assigned or transferred, shall be binding upon and inure to the benefit of our successors and assigns. We may be sold, or we may sell any portion of or all of our Marks, System and Proprietary Information, or other assets to a competitor or to any other entity. In addition, we may go public, may engage in a private or other placement of some or all of our securities, may merge, or acquire other entities or assets which may be competitive with the System, or not, we may be acquired by a competitive or other entity and/or may undertake any refinancing, leveraged buy-out or other transaction. You waive all claims, demands, and damages with respect to any transaction allowed under this section or otherwise. You will fully cooperate with any such proposal, merger, acquisition, conversion, sale, or financing.

9.2–Transfer by You

This Franchise Agreement is personal as to you, and is being entered into in reliance upon, and in consideration of, the qualifications and representations of you and, if you are a partnership, corporation, or limited liability company, your present partners, members or officers. Therefore, this Franchise Agreement, any of its rights or privileges, and/or any equitable, capital, voting, non-voting or other interest in the Franchisee if it be a corporation, partnership, or limited liability company, will be assigned, sold, transferred, or divided in any manner by you or anyone else only after you have obtained our express prior written approval.

In order to obtain such written approval, you will provide us with all documentation relating to the proposed transfer of the Franchise or the Business. Said approval will be based upon our Reasonable Business Judgment and will be conditioned as below described.

The term "Transfer" includes the voluntary, involuntary, direct or indirect assignment, sale, gift, or other disposition by you (or any of its owners) of any interest in: 1) this Franchise Agreement; 2) the ownership of the Franchisee; or 3) any assets of the Business (other than in the normal course of business).

An "assignment," "sale," "gift," or "other disposition" (all of which shall be referred to individually and jointly as an "Assignment") shall include: a transfer resulting from a: divorce insolvency, or corporate or partnership dissolution proceedings; by operation of law; or otherwise; or in the event of the death of a franchisee, transfer or disposition by will or under the laws of intestate succession; declaration of, or transfer in trust; and any other direct or indirect assignment, sale, gift, pledge, mortgage or the granting of any security interest encumbering the assets of the Business.

If a proposed transfer is only among existing shareholders, members of a limited liability business entity, or among existing partners of a partnership franchisee, or by an individual or partnership franchisee to a corporation or limited liability business entity owned by not less than fifty percent (50%) of the pre-existing franchisee or franchisees, there will be no transfer fee and we shall not be entitled to exercise our "Right of First Refusal" which is described below though we must receive sufficient proof that the control of the business entity remain as it was before such transfer.

34

Each stock certificate of a corporate franchisee, each certificate of a limited liability business entity franchisee, and any partnership or similar agreement, shall have endorsed upon its face that an assignment or transfer thereof is subject to the restrictions of this Agreement. You agree to provide us with a copy of each such certificate so that we can ensure compliance with this provision.

9.3–Conditions of Approval of any Transfer

In determining the acceptability of the proposed transferee or assignee (jointly or severally the "Proposed Transferee"), we will consider, among other things, our then-current standards for new franchisees, including the net worth, credit worthiness, background, training, personality, reputation and business experience of the Proposed Transferee, the terms and conditions of the proposed transfer, and any circumstances that would make the transfer contrary to our Reasonable Business Judgment or the best interests of the System.

We may meet with the Proposed Transferee and candidly discuss all matters relating to the Franchise Agreement and the Business. In no case will you or a Proposed Transferee rely on us to review or evaluate any proposed transfer. We will not be liable to you or the Proposed Transferee or any other person or entity relating to the transfer.

As a condition of any Transfer or Assignment otherwise permitted under this Franchise Agreement, you agree as follows:

a. To notify us of proposed Transfer or Assignment by sending a written notice to us and enclosing a copy of the written offer from the proposed purchaser, assignee or transferee;

b. To be in full compliance with this Franchise Agreement and not be in default hereunder at the time you request the transfer;

c. To have paid in full all accounts payable, Royalties, Advertising Fees, and other monetary obligations to our Affiliate or us;

d. To have timely submitted all required reports, financial statements and other documents;

e. To deliver to us the written document that comprises proposed Transfer or Assignment;

f. If approved, the Proposed Transferee must sign the then-current form of the franchise agreement and must fully renovate the Business to the then-current standards before he or she can reopen for business with the understanding that if the renovations can be made while the Business is in operation, then the transferee will be permitted to make such changes while open. The then-current form of franchise agreement may have terms that are significantly different from those found here.

g. The Proposed Transferee must attend training and will pay tuition (if any) that is then being charged to new franchisees. The transferee will also pay for his travel, room and board expenses for such training;

h. You or the Transferee must pay a transfer fee of 50 percent of the then-current IFF for the type of Business being Transferred or Assigned;

i. You and each of your owners must execute a General Release to us. A copy of the General Release is attached as Exhibit 6;

j. If required by the law of the state in which the transfer or assignment is to occur, the Proposed Transferee shall sign a document stating that it has received a copy of the franchise disclosure

35

documents at least fourteen (14) days (or for a greater or lesser period of time if required by the law of the state in which the transfer or assignment is taking place) prior to closing and that we have made no representations, promises or covenants concerning the past or future success of the franchise; and,

k. All restrictive covenants found in this Franchise Agreement including any post-term covenant not-to-compete, any indemnification covenants, confidentiality obligations, and the provisions relating to dispute resolution will survive any transfer and continue to be your obligation.

9.4–Invalidity of Transfers

Involuntary Transfers or Assignments by you, such as by legal process including bankruptcy, assignment for the benefit of creditors, assignment as security for any financial or non-financial matter or otherwise, are not permitted, are not binding on us, and are grounds for the termination of this Franchise Agreement without the right to cure. You agree that using this Franchise Agreement as security for a loan, or otherwise encumbering this Franchise Agreement, is prohibited unless we specifically consent to any such action in writing prior to the proposed transaction.

You agree not to grant a sub-franchise under this Franchise Agreement, nor to otherwise seek to license or permit others to use this Franchise, the Business, or any of the rights derived by you under this Franchise Agreement and any manner that violates the provisions herein.

Any attempt to transfer this Franchise Agreement in whole or in part, or any material portion of the property used by you in connection herewith without our express permission will be considered a breach of this Agreement and grounds for the termination of this Franchise Agreement.

9.5–Death or Incapacity

Upon the death or permanent disability of the Franchisee, (or the Principal Operator, or any other individual controlling the Franchisee entity), the executor, administrator, conservator, guardian, or other personal representative of such person shall transfer the Franchisee's interest in this Agreement and/or such interest in the Franchisee entity to an approved third party who may be the heirs or successors of the deceased or disabled individual. Such disposition (including, without limitation, transfer by operation of law, intestacy, bequest, or inheritance) shall be completed within a reasonable time, not to exceed 180 days from the date of death or permanent disability, and shall be subject to all terms and conditions applicable to transfers contained in this Article as though the Proposed Transferee were being introduced to us by the deceased or disabled Franchisee; provided, however, that for purposes of this section, there shall be no transfer fee charged by the Franchisor.

Failure to transfer the interest in this Agreement or such interest in the Franchisee entity within said period of time shall constitute a breach of this Agreement.

For the purposes hereof, the term "permanent disability" shall mean a mental or physical disability, impairment or condition that is reasonably expected to prevent or actually does prevent the Franchisee or the Principal Operator or other controlling individual from supervising the management and operation of the Business for a period of 120 days from the onset of such disability, impairment, or condition.

36

9.6–Right of First Refusal

In the event of a proposed Transfer or Assignment (including a Transfer or Assignment as a result of death or permanent disability) you agree the same is subject to our thirty (30) day right of first refusal to purchase such rights, interest or assets on the same terms and conditions as are contained in the written offer for the Transfer or Assignment (Right of First Refusal) provided, however, the following additional terms and conditions shall apply:

a. You will notify us of the proposed Transfer or Assignment by sending a written notice to us and enclosing a copy of the written offer from the proposed purchaser, assignee or transferee;

b. The 30-day right of first refusal period will run concurrently with the period in which the Franchisor has to accept or not accept the Transferee;

c. Such right of first refusal is effective for each proposed Transfer or Assignment, and any material change in the terms or conditions of the proposed Transfer or Assignment will be deemed a separate offer on which a new thirty (30) day right of first refusal shall be given to us;

d. If the consideration or manner of payment offered by a Transferee is such that we may not reasonably be required to furnish the same, then we may purchase the interest that is proposed to be sold for the reasonable cash equivalent. If the parties cannot agree within a reasonable time on the cash value of the consideration proposed to be paid by the Transferee, an independent appraiser shall be designated by the Franchisor, whose determination will be binding upon the parties. All expenses of the appraiser shall be paid for equally between the Franchisor and the Franchisee; and

e. If we choose not to exercise our right of first refusal, you will be free to complete the sale, transfer or assignment, subject to compliance with this Article 9. Our failure to reply to your notice of a proposed sale within the 30-day period is deemed a waiver of such right of first refusal.

9.7–Transfer After Retaking Possession

In some cases, you will make a Transfer or Assignment under this Article, but will agree to finance part of the consideration offered to you by the Transferee. In such an event, you may also agree that if the Transferee fails to perform under your financial arrangement that you will be able to retake possession of the Business. In such circumstances, and regardless of the fact that we may have approved of the original Transfer after reviewing the transfer documents (which may include an "asset purchase agreement," "stock purchase agreement," or similar document), if you retake possession of the Business, you will be permitted to operate it strictly on a temporary basis and as though you were the Designated Manager under the Transferee's franchise agreement. In such an event, you must apply to us within thirty (30) days of retaking possession, as a new Proposed Transferee. We will then have the right to evaluate granting you a new license in the same manner as we would a proposed Transferee. This evaluation will include a review of the situation using our Reasonable Business Judgment. We will also have the rights granted under subsection section 9.6.

IN SOME CASES, WE MAY NOT APPROVE OF YOU AS A TRANSFEREE, THE RESULT BEING THAT YOU WILL BE REQUIRED TO CLOSE THE BUSINESS. THERE IS NO GUARANTEE OF APPROVAL BY US.

37

ARTICLE 10
DEFAULT AND TERMINATION

10.1–Termination by Franchisor - Effective upon Notice

We have the right, at our option, to terminate this Franchise Agreement and all rights granted you hereunder, without affording you any opportunity to cure any default (subject to any state laws to the contrary, where such state law shall prevail), effective upon the mailing of our written notice, or if by overnight or hand delivery, then effective on the date of such delivery, or refusal by you to accept such delivery, upon the occurrence of any of the following events:

a. If you cease to operate the Business or otherwise abandon the Business for a period of fourteen (14) consecutive days, or any shorter period that indicates your intent to discontinue operation of the Business, unless and only to the extent that full operation of the Business is suspended or terminated due to acts of God, fire, flood, earthquake or other similar causes beyond the Franchisee's control and not related to the availability of funds to you;

b. If you become insolvent, as that term is commonly defined using generally accepted accounting principles, consistently applied; are adjudicated bankrupt; if any action is taken by you, or by others against you under any insolvency, bankruptcy or reorganization act; if you make an assignment for the benefit of creditors; or if a receiver is appointed. This provision may not be enforceable under federal bankruptcy law, 11 U.S.C. §§ 101 et seq.;

c. If any material judgment or award (or several judgments or awards which in the aggregate are material) is (are) obtained against you and remain(s) unsatisfied or of record for thirty (30) days or longer (unless a supersedes or other appeal bond has been filed); if execution is levied against the Business or any of the property used in the operation of the Business and is not discharged within five (5) days; or if the real or personal property of the Business or the business entity which operates the Franchisee shall be levied upon in accordance with the law of the state in which the Business is located;

d If you are convicted of, or plead no contest, to a crime (whether a misdemeanor or felony) involving moral turpitude; are convicted of, or plead no contest to, a felony of any nature; or are convicted of, or plead no contest to, any crime (whether a misdemeanor, or felony) or civil offense, and such pleas or convictions are reasonably likely, in the sole opinion of the Franchisor, to materially and unfavorably affect the System, Marks, Proprietary Information, or the goodwill or reputation thereof;

e. If you fail to pay any Royalties, Advertising Fees, or any other amounts due us, including any amounts which may be due as a result of any other agreements between you and us within five (5) days after receiving notice that such fees or amounts are overdue;

f. If you misuse or fail to follow our direction and guidelines concerning use of, and the confidentiality of, the Marks, the Manuals, or any component of the System or the Proprietary Information, and fail to correct the misuse or failure within 5 calendar days after notification from us. If your violation of this subparagraph is intentional, there will be no five-day right to cure, causing an immediate default, which may lead to immediate termination;

g. If you disclose to any unauthorized person any component of the System, the Marks, or the Proprietary Information;

h. If the Franchisee has: i) received a fourth written notice of breach of any combination of terms, covenants or conditions of this Agreement during the Initial Term even though each such breach may have been timely cured; or, ii) has received a third written notice of breach of any combination of terms, covenants or conditions of the franchise agreement then in force during any Successor Term even though each such breach may have been timely cured;

i. If you Transfer or Assign this Franchise Agreement, an interest in the Business, a substantial portion of the assets of the Business or the business which operates the Franchisee or otherwise violate the terms of Article 9 above;

j. If you violate any municipal, state or federal law which applies in any way to the Business or your operation under this Agreement (which such violations will include but not be limited to your failure to timely pay employees, or to fail to timely pay any tax which is due as a result of the operation of the Business);

k. If you make any material misrepresentations relating to the acquisition of your rights under this Franchise Agreement;

l. If you violate any covenant or condition of subparagraph 1.5.d.v above;

m. If you violate any term, covenant or condition of your lease for the real property, the result of which is that you lose your right to possession of the Franchised Location;

n. If an inspection of your records discloses an understatement of payments of four percent (4%) or more and you fail to cure the same within five (5) days of receipt of notice from us. Any subsequent violation of this subsection may result in immediate termination without any right to cure;

o. If you violate any other covenant or condition that contains its own cure provision and then fail to cure within the time period provided therein;

p. If you violate the terms, covenants or conditions of any other contract or agreement which is material to the operation of the Business (even if such agreement is not with us) and you fail to cure any such breach within the time permitted under such agreement the result of which is you being unable to operate the Business in accordance with the terms of this Agreement or that contract or agreement. In such an event, this Agreement will terminate at the same time as the other agreement terminates. You will provide us immediate notice in the event of the termination of such a material agreement.

q. If you engage in any activity, take any action, fail to take any action, fail to pay taxes, fail to pay employees, or otherwise, the consequence of which has an adverse effect on the System, the Proprietary Information or the Marks, or which otherwise disparages the System, the Proprietary Information or Marks or the goodwill associated therewith; or

r. If there is a violation of subparagraph 10.3 below.

10.2–Termination by Franchisor—Thirty Days Notice

We will have the right to terminate this Agreement (subject to any state laws to the contrary, in which case such state law shall prevail) effective upon thirty (30) days written notice to the Franchisee, if the

Franchisee breaches any other term, covenant, or condition of this Franchise Agreement and fails to cure the default during such thirty (30) day period.

After the passage of said period without cure, this Agreement will terminate without further notice to you.

Any of the itemized defaults under subparagraphs 10.1 or 10.2 will be known as an "Event of Default."

10.3–Cross Default

If Franchisee is a party to any other franchise agreements with us, or any contracts with our Affiliates, and if such agreement is breached and not timely cured within the time period permitted in such document with the result being that that franchise agreement or other agreement is terminated, then the Franchisor shall have the right to terminate this Agreement without affording you any additional right to cure.

10.4–Diligent Pursuit of Cure

If the breach is one for which cure is provided in subparagraph 10.2 above, then if you undertake the cure within five (5) days of the date that you receive our notice, and if you continue to pursue such cure in good faith but are unable to complete the cure within the time period provided in this Franchise Agreement, then you shall be given up to an additional ten (10) days after the end of the first cure period within which to complete such cure. If you fail to continually pursue the cure during this additional time period or are unable to complete such cure within this additional time period, then we have the right to terminate the Franchise Agreement without further notice to you.

Notwithstanding anything to the contrary herein, we have the right, in our sole discretion, to grant you an extended period of time to cure. In such an event, however, we will not be deemed to have waived our rights to later strictly enforce any right to cure, or to deny you the right to cure a future breach for which no cure is provided or to take such action as is allowed to us by this Franchise Agreement if you fail to cure during the extended period granted to you.

10.5–Termination at the End of the Initial Term

Unless it is terminated earlier, if you fail to elect to purchase Successor Franchise Rights, or if we decline to grant you Successor Franchise Rights, this Franchise Agreement will terminate at 12:00 midnight Mountain Time on the last day of the Initial Term.

If you elect to purchase Successor Franchise Rights, and we grant you this right, then termination shall be at 12:00 midnight Mountain Time on the last day of that Successor Term.

10.6–Our Rights to Damages

Upon your failure to cure any Event of Default within the time period specified above, or if no cure is provided, we may proceed to enforce any or all of the following non-exclusive remedies or any other remedy, claim, cause of action, award or damages allowed by law or equity, all without further written notice to you, with the understanding that the pursuit of any one remedy shall not be deemed an election or waiver by us to pursue additional remedies as all remedies are cumulative and are not exclusive:

40

a. Bring one or more actions for: lost profits as measured by the Royalties and other fees that would have been due and payable through the end of the then-current term had the Event of Default not occurred; plus penalties and interest as provided for in this Franchise Agreement; and for all other damages sustained by us because of your breach of this Franchise Agreement.

b. Accelerate the balance of any outstanding installment obligation due hereunder and bring an action for the entire accelerated balance.

c. Bring an action for temporary or permanent injunctions and orders of specific performance enforcing the provisions of this Franchise Agreement and otherwise stop you from engaging in actions prohibited hereby including, without limitation: i) improper use of the Marks, the System, or the Proprietary Information; ii) unauthorized assignment of the Franchise Agreement; iii) violation of any of the restrictive covenants; and, iv) your failure to meet or perform your obligations upon termination or expiration of this Franchise Agreement.

d. Terminate this Franchise Agreement and proceed to enforce our right to damages under this subsection with the understanding that the termination of the Franchise Agreement will not terminate our rights to all damages permitted herein, or in law, or equity. Such termination shall be effective upon delivery of a notice of termination to you without further action by us.

e. If you: operate the Business after a Transfer, Assignment, repurchase, termination, or expiration; or use any of the Marks or any component of the System or the Proprietary Information; or otherwise violate any restrictive covenant after the same, then, in addition to any remedies provided above, and in addition to any other remedies in law or equity (all of which shall be cumulative and shall not be deemed to be an election of remedies to the exclusion of other remedies), our remedies will include, but will not be limited to, recovery of the greater of: i) all profits earned by you in the operation of the business using our Marks or System after such Transfer, Assignment, repurchase, termination, or expiration; and/or ii) all Royalties, Advertising Fees, and other amounts which would have been due if such Transfer, Assignment, repurchase, termination, or expiration had not occurred; and/or iii) any other remedies available in law or equity.

f. Further, you agree that, in the event you continue to operate or subsequently begin to operate any other business, you will not use any reproduction, counterfeit, copy or colorable imitation of the Marks, either in connection with such other business or in the promotion thereof, which is likely to cause confusion, mistake or deception, or which is likely to dilute our exclusive rights in and to the Marks and the System, and further agree not to utilize any designation of origin or description or representation which falsely suggests or represents an association or connection with Franchisor.

10.7–Limitation of Right to Bring Action and Waiver of Punitive, Exemplary or Consequential Damages

EXCEPT AS SET FORTH IN SECTION 16.9, FRANCHISOR AND FRANCHISEE ARE LIMITED TO BRINGING ANY LEGAL CLAIM AGAINST THE OTHER WITHIN ONE YEAR OF THE DATE THAT THE FACTS THAT GIVE RISE TO THE CLAIM WERE DISCOVERED OR ONE YEAR FROM THE DATE THAT SUCH FACTS REASONABLY

SHOULD HAVE BEEN DISCOVERED AS MORE SPECIFICALLY SET FORTH IN SUBSECTION 16.9 BELOW.

BOTH FRANCHISOR AND FRANCHISEE AGREE TO WAIVE THE RIGHT TO A JURY TRIAL, AND EXCEPT AS SET FORTH IN SECTION 16.8, THE RIGHT TO BE AWARDED EXEMPLARY, PUNITIVE, OR CONSEQUENTIAL DAMAGES IN ANY ACTION BROUGHT IN REFERENCE TO THE RELATIONSHIP BETWEEN YOU AND US.

Initials as to both of the above paragraphs

_____
Initials of Franchisee

_____
Initials of Franchisee

_____
Initials of Franchisor

10.8–State or Federal Law Prevails

IF ANY MANDATORY PROVISIONS OF GOVERNING STATE LAW PROHIBIT TERMINATION OF THE FRANCHISE AGREEMENT AS DESCRIBED HEREIN, OR IF THE SAME OTHERWISE LIMIT FRANCHISOR'S RIGHTS TO TERMINATE BY IMPOSING DIFFERENT RIGHTS OR OBLIGATIONS AS ARE FOUND HEREIN, THEN SUCH MANDATORY PROVISIONS OF STATE LAW SHALL BE DEEMED INCORPORATED INTO THE AGREEMENT BY REFERENCE AND SHALL PREVAIL OVER ANY INCONSISTENT TERMS IN THE AGREEMENT. IF NO SUCH LAW EXISTS, OR IF SUCH LAW EXISTS BUT PERMITS THE FRANCHISEE TO AGREE TO ABIDE BY THE TERMINATION PROVISIONS AS SET FORTH HEREIN INSTEAD OF THAT STATE LAW, THEN THE FRANCHISEE AGREES THAT THE TERMS OF THIS AGREEMENT SHALL PREVAIL.

10.9–Payment of Fees is an Independent Covenant

You agree that you will not withhold payments of Royalties, Advertising Fees, regional advertising contributions, or any other amounts of money owed to us for any reason, even including a claim by you of the alleged nonperformance by us of any obligation hereunder. All such claims by you shall, if not otherwise resolved by us, be resolved as permitted in this Agreement. You agree that each covenant found herein is independent of any other covenant.

10.10–Action Against the Franchisor

Subject to the limitations of actions as found in subsection 10.7 and 16.9, which require you to take any action (which action will include providing the notice described in this subparagraph) before the expiration of the time limit found therein, prior to starting any arbitration against us or any of our officers, agents or employees, you agree to first give us or our officers, agents or employees, sixty (60) days prior written notice and an opportunity to cure any alleged act or omission within that time period. If such act or omission cannot be cured within such sixty (60) day period, and we, or our officers, agents or employees, are diligently continuing efforts to cure such alleged act or omission, you will give us, or our officers, agents or employees, such additional time as is reasonably necessary to cure which time shall not exceed an additional thirty (30) days. If we fail to complete such cure in a timely fashion, then you have such rights as are permitted by law.

ARTICLE 11
OBLIGATIONS OF FRANCHISEE UPON TERMINATION OR EXPIRATION

11.1–Obligations upon Termination or Expiration

Upon termination or expiration of this Franchise Agreement for any reason, you shall cease to be a licensed franchisee of Franchisor and shall:

a. Immediately pay for all product purchases, Royalties, Advertising Fees, and any other charges and fees owed or accrued to us;

b. Refrain from holding yourself out as a Franchisee and immediately cease to advertise or in any way use the System, the Marks, any Proprietary Information, any designs, logos, methods, procedures, processes, and other commercial property and symbols or promotional materials provided by or licensed to you by us or in any way connected with the Business;

c. Immediately take all necessary steps to disassociate yourself from the System and the Business, including, but not limited to, the removal of signs, destruction of letterhead, changing of telephone listings, telephone numbers, internet sites and web pages and the like and if requested by us, assign and transfer pre-existing telephone listings, telephone numbers and home web pages to us. In order to complete the latter, you agree that you will sign the agreement that is attached to this Franchise Agreement as Exhibit 5;

   If you fail or refuse to do so, the telephone company and other listing agencies may accept this Franchise Agreement as evidence of our exclusive rights in and to such telephone number(s) and listings and its authority to direct their transfer. You appoint us as your attorney-in-fact for the above transfers;

d. Take such action as shall be necessary to amend or cancel any assumed name, fictitious name or business name or equivalent registration which contains any trade name or mark of ours or in any way identifies you as being affiliated with the System, or if requested by us, assign and/or transfer same to us;

e. Immediately notify all suppliers, utilities, creditors and concerned others that you are no longer affiliated with us, the System or the Franchise, and provide proof to us of such notification. You covenant not to use any part of the System or any part of our trade secret or confidential or proprietary information or materials following the termination of this Franchise Agreement and not to identify any present or future business owned or operated by you as having been in any way associated with us or the System;

43

f. Within seven (7) calendar days, return to us by first class prepaid certified, return receipt requested, United States Mail, (including originals and any copies) all Manuals, all training, advertising and promotional aids, materials, and all other printed materials pertaining to the operation of the Business;

g. You will, at your expense, alter, modify, and change both the exterior and interior appearance of the former Business so that it will be easily distinguished from the standard or common appearance of other Businesses in the System and will cease using the signs, displays, advertisements, promotional materials, ingredient lists and the like that are unique or distinctive to the System;

h. Unless an earlier time is called for, in which case the earlier time prevails, furnish evidence satisfactory to us of compliance with this Article within sixty (60) calendar days after the termination, expiration or non-renewal of this Agreement;

i. Cease using or availing yourself of any of our software, hardware or other proprietary technology.

11.2–Additional Matters

Further, upon termination, expiration, or non-renewal of this Franchise Agreement for any reason:

a. No payment will be due to you from any source on account of any goodwill or other equity claimed by you as arising from your operation or ownership of the Business or this Franchise Agreement;

b. No fees, charges, Royalties, Advertising Fees, or other payments of any kind from you to us will be refundable in whole or in part; and,

c. You will have no equity or other continuing interest in this Franchise Agreement.

ARTICLE 12
FIRST RIGHT TO PURCHASE

Except as otherwise provided in Article 9 which shall prevail in the instance of a Transfer or Assignment, upon expiration or earlier termination of this Franchise Agreement, you hereby grant to us the right to acquire, in our sole discretion, all or any part of your inventory, equipment, signs, accessories and other personal property relating to the Business or the Franchise Agreement at the then-existing "Fair Market Value" (as below defined) of such item or items as of the date of expiration or termination of this Franchise Agreement.

"Fair Market Value" shall be deemed to be the value that a reasonable person who is under no duress or obligation would pay for the item that is being sold by a seller who is under no duress or obligation. If the parties do not agree to the Fair Market Value, it will be established by an independent appraisal. The appraisal shall be done at our expense by an appraiser selected by us but who is independent and disinterested in the outcome of any such valuation.

No goodwill shall be considered associated with the valuation of any item being sold under this Article.

We must exercise this option within thirty (30) days of such expiration or termination by giving written notice to you of our intent to exercise our option to purchase. Unless otherwise agreed by you, the purchase price as determined hereunder shall be paid in cash within the option period.

If we have not notified you of our election to exercise this option within the aforesaid thirty (30) day period, it shall be conclusively presumed that we have elected not to exercise our option and you are then free to sell or transfer such assets to any person or entity on such terms as you may so choose.

ARTICLE 13
RELATIONSHIP BETWEEN THE PARTIES

13.1–Independent Contractor

In all matters as between us, or between you and the public, you are an independent contractor. Nothing in this Franchise Agreement or in the franchise relationship constitutes a partnership, agency, joint venture or other arrangement between us.

Neither party is liable for the debts, liabilities, taxes, duties, obligations, defaults, compliance, intentional acts, wages, negligence, errors, or omissions of the other.

You are responsible for the management and control of the Business, and your compliance with this Franchise Agreement, including without limitation, its daily operations, managing and directing employees and salespersons, and paying all costs, taxes, employee wages, and all other expenses and liabilities incurred in the operation of your Business.

The parties agree not to hold themselves out by action or inaction, contrary to the foregoing.

None of your employees shall be deemed an employee of Franchisor and each employee shall be so notified. You and not we are responsible for any matter pertaining to your employees.

As used herein, "Franchisor" shall also mean Franchisor's predecessors, affiliates and Franchisor's officers, directors, shareholders, employees, agents or others with whose conduct Franchisor is chargeable.

Neither party shall act or have the authority to act as agent for the other and neither you nor we shall guarantee the obligations of the other or in any way become obligated for the debts or expenses of the other unless agreed to in writing.

13.2–No Fiduciary Relationship

It is understood and agreed between us that this Franchise Agreement does not establish a fiduciary relationship between us, and that nothing in this Franchise Agreement is intended to constitute either party an agent, legal representative, subsidiary, joint venture, partner, employee, or servant of the other for any purpose whatsoever.

13.3–Posting of Signs

You agree to post promptly and maintain any signs or notices specified by us or by applicable law indicating the status of the parties as described above.

13.4–Payment of Taxes

We will have no liability for the Franchisee's obligations to pay any taxes associated with the Franchisee's operation of the Business, including without limitation, any sales, use, service, occupation, excise, gross

45

receipts, income, property, withholding, employment, or other tax levied upon the Franchisee, the Franchisee's property, or the Business.

ARTICLE 14
INDEMNIFICATION

You agree to, and will indemnify, defend and hold harmless the Franchisor, its subsidiaries, parents and affiliates, and their respective shareholders, directors, officers, managers, members, employees, agents, successors and assignees (the "Indemnified Parties"), against, and to reimburse them for all "Claims" (as defined below), obligations, and damages, arising directly or indirectly out of: your operation of the Business; any matter pertaining to your employees; your use of the Marks, the System, and the Proprietary Information; or as a result of your performance or failure to perform under this Franchise Agreement.

For purposes of indemnification, "Claims" will mean any claim against the Franchisor or the Indemnified Parties, and shall include, and not be limited to any claim for: breach of contract; premises liability; employee-related matters; claims arising from: your operation of the Business; your performance under this Franchise Agreement; or, any other damages, causes of action, tort claims, or any other claim in law or equity against us which may arise as a result of your breach of any term, covenant or condition of this Franchise Agreement, your operation of the Business and/or your relationship to the public, to any governmental or quasi-governmental authority, your customers, and/or your employees.

Included in indemnification shall be the reimbursement or direct payment by you of any award, damage, consequential damages and costs reasonably incurred in the defense of any claim against the Indemnified Parties, including, without limitation, reasonable accountants', attorneys' and expert witness fees, costs of investigation and proof of facts, court costs, other litigation expenses, and travel and living expenses.

We have the absolute right to defend any such claim against us and shall have the right to have counsel of our own choosing, the reasonable cost of which shall be borne by the Franchisee.

This indemnity shall continue in full force and effect subsequent to and notwithstanding the expiration or termination of this Agreement and shall continue for any applicable limitation of actions statute.

ARTICLE 15
RESTRICTIVE COVENANTS

15.1–In-Term Covenant Not to Compete

You and we share a common interest in avoiding situations where persons or companies who are or have been franchisees within the System operate or otherwise become involved with a similar competing business either during or after the termination of this Agreement for any reason. In fact, the Franchisor would not have disclosed its System or the Proprietary Information, and would not have permitted the Franchisee to use the Marks if the Franchisee were then permitted to compete against the Franchisor or the system in a "Competing Business" (as that term is defined below).

46

Therefore, the Franchisee and each Franchisee Party will refrain from: owning; operating; leasing; franchising; consulting with; engaging in; having any interest in; assisting any person or entity engaged in for its own account; acting as an employee, consultant, partner, officer, director or shareholder of any other person, firm, entity, partnership or corporation engaged in any business that is a "Competitive Business", except with our prior written consent which consent may be granted or withheld for any reason or for no reason at all. For purposes of this Franchise Agreement a "Competing Business" will be a business that offers to its customers pet aardvark care services and products, including grooming, retail items, and aardvark training.

15.2–Post-Term Covenant Not to Compete

Upon termination or expiration of this Franchise Agreement for any reason, or upon the occurrence of any Transfer, Assignment, repurchase, or termination of your rights hereunder, and for a period of two (2) years thereafter, you agree that you and any of the Franchisee Parties, will refrain from: owning; operating; leasing; franchising; consulting with; engaging in; having any interest in; assisting any person or entity engaged in; or acting as an employee, consultant, partner, officer, director or shareholder of any other person, firm, entity, partnership or corporation that is engaged in any Competitive Business which is within twenty five (25) miles of the Franchised Location, and within twenty five (25) miles of any other franchisee, Franchisor- or Affiliate-owned Business.

15.3–No Disclosure

You and the Franchisee Parties further agree that during the term of this Franchise Agreement, during any Successor Franchise term, or at any other time after the termination of this Franchise Agreement (or any franchise agreement signed pursuant to the Successor Franchise term) for any reason, each will refrain from making any unauthorized disclosure or use of the Marks, any component of the System, or any portion of the Proprietary Information.

15.4–No Diversion

During the term of this Agreement, for a period of two (2) years following the expiration or termination of this Agreement for any reason, and in the area described in paragraph 15.2 above, Franchisee and the Franchisee Parties covenant they will not, either directly or indirectly, for themselves, or through, on behalf of, or in conjunction with any person or legal entity:

a. Divert or attempt to divert to any competitor of the Business (by direct or indirect inducement or otherwise) any business or customers of the Business.
b Do or perform, directly or indirectly, any other act injurious or prejudicial to the goodwill associated with the Marks, the System or both; and/or
c. Induce, directly or indirectly, any person who is at that time employed by Franchisor or by any other franchisee to leave his or her employment.

15.5–Survival

The foregoing restrictive covenants shall survive the termination or expiration of this Agreement and shall apply regardless of whether this Franchise Agreement was terminated by lapse of time, by default of either party or for any other reason.

15.6–Reasonable Restriction and Savings Clause

The covenants found in this Article are intended to be a reasonable restriction on Franchisee and the Franchisee Parties. The Franchisor, Franchisee and Franchisee Parties agree that the purpose of these restrictions is to protect the entire System from unfair competition and to protect the goodwill, and time and effort spent by Franchisor in the perfection of the Marks, the System, and the Proprietary Information. In fact, the Franchisor would not have shared such information with the Franchisee unless the Franchisee agreed to be bound by the terms of this Article 15.

The Franchisee and each Franchisee Party further agrees that he or she has skills of a general and specific nature and has other opportunities, or will have other opportunities to use such skills and that the enforcement of these covenants will not unduly deprive the Franchisee of the opportunity to earn a living.

For purposes of interpretation of the covenants found in this Article, every location of a Business, every month of time, each mile of distance, the definition of a "Competitive Business," or any other restriction, shall be subject to amendment. In the event an arbitrator or court of competent jurisdiction interprets a spatial, temporal or other limitation in any of the above restrictive covenants to be overly broad, then it shall adjust the offending limitation, in the most limited manner possible, so as to fashion a reasonably enforceable covenant which upholds the restrictive nature of this Article to the fullest extent of the law.

Notwithstanding anything herein to the contrary, the terms of the post-termination covenant not to compete will not apply to a case where the Franchisee owns five percent (5%) or less of a beneficial interest in the outstanding equity securities of any publicly-held corporation (as this term is generally defined by the Securities and Exchange Commission).

Franchisee expressly agrees that the existence of any claim it may have against Franchisor, whether or not arising from this Agreement, shall not constitute a defense to the enforcement by Franchisor of the covenants of this Article. Franchisee further agrees that Franchisor shall be entitled to set off against any amounts owed by Franchisor to Franchisee, any loss or damage to Franchisor resulting from Franchisee's breach of this Article.

15.7–Franchisor Is Entitled to Injunctive Relief

Franchisee acknowledges that any failure to comply with the requirements of this Article will cause Franchisor irreparable injury for which no adequate remedy at law may be available, and Franchisee hereby accordingly consents to the issuance by a court of competent jurisdiction of an injunction prohibiting any conduct by Franchisee in violation of the terms of this section, and waives any requirement for the

48

posting of any bond(s) relating thereto. Franchisor may further avail itself of any legal or equitable rights and remedies which it may have under the Agreement or otherwise.

ARTICLE 16
DISPUTE RESOLUTION

16.1–Resolution before Arbitration

You and we and both of us acting on behalf of our officers, directors, shareholders, members, managing members, and any holder of an equitable interest in any limited liability entity as well as our agents, servants, employees, and all others participating with us believe that it is important to resolve any disputes amicably, quickly, cost effectively and professionally and to return to business as soon as possible. We agree that the provisions of this Article support these mutual, practical business objectives and, therefore, agree as follows:

a. We each expressly waive all rights to any court proceeding, except as expressly provided below.

b. Any litigation, claim, dispute, suit, action, controversy, or proceeding of any type whatsoever including any claim for equitable relief and/or where you are acting as a "private attorney general," suing pursuant to a statutory claim or otherwise, between or involving us (and/or any affiliates of any party), on whatever theory and/or facts will be processed in the following manner:

    1. First, the parties agree to a face-to-face meeting held within 30 days after any party gives written notice to the other;

    2. Second, if the issues between the parties cannot be resolved within that time period then the disagreement shall be submitted to non-binding mediation before a neutral mediator from Judicial Arbitration and Mediation Service (JAMS) or its successor (or an organization designated by JAMS or its successor). If JAMS is unable or unwilling to conduct such proceeding(s), or is no longer in operation, and the parties to the dispute cannot agree on an appropriate organization or person to conduct such proceedings(s), then the mediation shall be heard by a single mediator from the American Arbitration Association.

        i. The parties shall agree upon the mediator. If the parties cannot agree upon the mediator then the senior most officer, director or manager of the association under which the mediation is to take place shall choose a neutral and disinterested mediator and such choice shall be final and binding upon the parties.

        ii. Any mediation will be conducted by a mediator experienced in franchising. Any party may be represented by counsel and may, with permission of the mediator, bring persons appropriate to the proceeding.

        iii.If the mediation does not resolve the matter, then the parties agree that the matter will be submitted to and finally be resolved by binding arbitration.

16.2–Resolution Under Arbitration

Arbitration will be held before, and in accordance with the arbitration rules of JAMS or its successor; provided that if such arbitration cannot be heard by this organization, then the arbitration will be conducted before and in accordance with the arbitration rules of JAMS or its successor (or an organization designated by JAMS or its successor). If JAMS is no longer in business or cannot conduct such proceeding(s), and the parties cannot agree on an appropriate alternative, then the arbitration shall be heard by a single arbitrator from the American Arbitration Association.

    a. The parties shall agree upon the single arbitrator. If the parties cannot agree upon the arbitrator then the senior most officer, director, or manager of the association under which the arbitration is to take place shall choose a neutral and disinterested arbitrator and such choice shall be final and binding upon the parties.

    b. The arbitrator must be experienced in franchising.

    c. Any party may be represented by counsel and may, with permission of the arbitrator, bring persons appropriate to the proceeding.

    d. The judgment of the arbitrator on any preliminary or final arbitration award will be final and binding, and may be entered in any court having jurisdiction.

    e. The arbitrator's award will be in writing. On request by any party to the arbitration, the arbitrator will provide a reasoned opinion with findings of fact and conclusions of law and the party so requesting will pay the arbitrator's fees and costs connected therewith.

    f. There will be no right to appeal the final award.

16.3–Confidentiality

The parties to any meeting/mediation/arbitration will sign confidentiality agreements, excepting only public disclosures and filings as are required by law.

16.4–Choice of Forum, Venue and Jurisdiction of Arbitration

Any meeting/mediation/arbitration will be conducted exclusively at a neutral location that is within 15 miles of the then-current location of our headquarters (currently Denver, Colorado); provided that if any court determines that this provision is unenforceable for any reason, mediation/arbitration (and any appeal) will be conducted at a location determined by the mediator/arbitrator.

The Arbitrator in any proceeding under this Article will apply all applicable laws and equity permitted under the laws of the state in which the headquarters of the Franchisor is then located.

Jurisdiction, venue, choice-of-forum, and applicable law will be that of the state in which our then-current headquarters is located, and at a location that is within 15 miles of our then-current headquarters.

The arbitrator will decide any factual, procedural, or legal questions relating in any way to the dispute between the parties including, but not limited to: any decision as to whether this Article, is applicable and enforceable as against the parties; subject matter; timeliness; scope; remedies; unconscionability; and any alleged fraud in the inducement.

The arbitrator may issue summary orders disposing of all or part of a claim and provide for temporary restraining orders, preliminary injunctions, injunctions, attachments, claim and delivery proceedings, temporary protective orders, receiverships, and other equitable and/or interim/final relief.

Each party consents to the enforcement of such orders, injunctions, etc. by any court having jurisdiction.

The arbitrator will have subpoena powers limited only by the laws of the state in which the main office of the Franchisor is located.

16.5–Discovery, other Procedural Matters, Fees, and Costs

The arbitrator will also have the right to make a determination as to any procedural matters as would a court of competent jurisdiction be permitted to make in the state in which the main office of the Franchisor is located.

The parties to the dispute will have the same discovery rights as are available in civil actions under the laws of the state in which the main office of the Franchisor is then located.

Each participant must submit or file any claim that would constitute a "compulsory counter-claim" (as defined by the applicable rule under the Federal Rules of Civil Procedure) within the same proceeding as the claim to which it relates. Any such compulsory counter-claim that is not submitted or filed in such proceeding will be forever barred.

All other procedural matters will be determined by applying the statutory, common laws, and rules of procedure that control a court of competent jurisdiction in which the main office of the Franchisor is then located.

In addition to any other remedy, the arbitrator will have the right to award the "Prevailing Party" his, her, or its costs, fees, reasonable attorneys fees, expert witness fees, and the like which that party expended in the preparation for and the prosecution of the case at arbitration.

For the purposes of this Franchise Agreement in general and this Article 16 specifically, the "Prevailing Party" shall be deemed to be that party which has obtained the greatest net judgment in terms of money or money equivalent. If money or money equivalent has not been awarded, then the Prevailing Party shall be that party which has prevailed on a majority of the material issues decided. The "net judgment" is determined by subtracting the smallest award of money or money equivalent from the largest award. If there is a mixed decision involving an award of money or money equivalent and equitable relief, the arbitrator shall award the above fees to the party that it deems has prevailed over the other party using reasonable business and arbitrator's judgment.

16.6–Disputes Not Subject to the Mediation/Arbitration Process

Claims or disputes relating primarily to the validity of the Marks and/or to any intellectual property licensed to you and/or the covenants not to compete shall be subject to court proceedings in a court of competent jurisdiction; except that the parties shall first attempt a face-to-face meeting and mediation in accordance with the above procedures before bringing such action. Notwithstanding the foregoing, only the portion of any claim or dispute relating primarily to the validity of the Marks and/or any intellectual property and/or the covenants not to compete licensed under this Agreement will be subject to court action.

16.7–The Intentions of the Parties

We mutually agree, have expressly had a meeting of the minds, and expressly intend that notwithstanding any contrary provisions of state or other law, and/or any statements in the mandated franchise disclosure document required by a state as a condition to registration or for some other purpose:

51

a. All issues and disputes relating to arbitrability of issues (including whether or not any particular claim, the limitation of damages, venue, choice of laws, shortened periods in which to bring claims, jurisdiction or the interpretation or enforcement of any of the dispute-resolution-related provisions of this Agreement) will be decided by the arbitrator;

b. All provisions of this Agreement (including the language of this Article) will be fully enforced, including, but not limited to, those relating to arbitration, waiver of jury trial, limitation of damages, venue, choice of laws and shortened periods in which to bring claims;

c. The parties intend to rely on federal pre-emption under the Federal Arbitration Act (9 U.S.C. § 1 et seq.) and, as a result, the provisions of this Agreement will be enforced according to its terms;

d. Except as expressly provided in this Franchise Agreement, each party knowingly waives all rights to a court trial and, instead, select arbitration as the sole means to resolve disputes understanding that arbitration may be less formal than a court or jury trial, may use different rules of procedure and evidence, that appeal is generally less available and that the fees and costs associated with mediation and/or arbitration may be substantially greater than in civil litigation;

e. The terms of this Agreement (including but not limited to this Article) will control with respect to any matters of choice of law; and,

f. Notwithstanding the fact that a party to this Franchise Agreement is or may become a party to a court action or special proceeding with a third party or otherwise, and whether or not such pending court action or special proceeding: i) may include issues of law, fact or otherwise arising out of the same transaction or series of related transactions as any arbitration between or involving the parties to this Agreement; ii) involves a possibility of conflicting rulings on common issues of law, fact or otherwise; and iii) such pending court action or special proceeding may involve a third party who cannot be compelled to arbitrate, the terms, covenants and conditions of this Franchise Agreement and any dispute between the parties to this Franchise Agreement will be enforced according to the terms found herein including the obligation to perform under this Article.

16.8–Mutual Waivers; Injunction Excepted

We each agree that each is choosing arbitration over resorting to litigation in court.

We each agree that each specifically recognize that each has the right to a trial by jury in a court and, being advised of the same, each hereby waives such right.

We each understand and agree that he, she, or it specifically agrees that any matters concerning the relationship between us shall be done on an individual basis and shall not be brought as a class action, or with multiple unrelated franchisees (whether as a result of attempted consolidation, joinder or otherwise).

It is agreed that the limitations of this subsection are prudent from a business standpoint because: a) the mediation and arbitration procedures contemplated by this Agreement function most effectively on an individual case basis; b) there are significant factors present in each individual Franchisee's situation which should be respected; and, c) class-wide or multiple plaintiff disputes do not foster quick, amicable, and economic dispute resolutions.

Notwithstanding the above provision for a face-to-face meeting, mediation and arbitration, we each shall have the right in the proper case to obtain injunctive relief from a court of competent jurisdiction. We each agree that the other may obtain such injunctive relief, after posting a bond or bonds totaling no more than $500; except as set forth in Sections 6.1 and 15.7 above, which require no posting of bonds. In event of the entry of such injunctive relief, the sole remedy of the enjoined party shall be to seek the dissolution of such injunctive relief, if warranted and after a hearing; provided, however, that all claims for damages by reason of the wrongful issuance of any such injunction are hereby expressly waived. Further, to the fullest extent possible, the parties shall hold the face-to-face meeting, the mediation, and arbitration, prior to or during the prosecution of the injunction.

Each party agrees that it has the right to seek damages that are in addition to the actual monetary loss that can be proven which would include, but not be limited to, such damages as consequential, exemplary, and punitive damages. Being advised of the same, we each waive such damages that may be in addition to any actual monetary damages suffered. This waiver does not affect, and will not limit in any manner, the damages that we can seek under the indemnification clause found above.

16.9– One Year Limitation of Action

Except for an alleged violation of the Marks (which may be brought at any time), no arbitration, action, or suit (whether by way of claim, counter-claim, cross-complaint, raised as an affirmative defense, offset or otherwise) between us will be permitted, whether for damages, rescission, injunctive, or any other legal and/or equitable relief, in respect of any alleged breach of this Franchise Agreement, or any other claim of any type, unless such party commences such arbitration proceeding, action or suit before the expiration of one (1) year from the date on which the facts giving rise to the cause of action comes to the attention of, or using reasonable diligence should have come to the attention of, such party. The one (1) year period will begin to run, and will not be tolled, merely because the claiming party was unaware of legal theories, statutes, regulations or case law upon which the claim might be based.

Notwithstanding the foregoing, if any federal or state law provides for a shorter limitation period than is described in this Article, then such shorter period will govern.

This subsection will not apply to issues of indemnification above and such actions under the indemnification covenant may be brought within the period provided by any limitation-of-action statute under the laws of the state in which the main office of the Franchisor is then located.

_____

Initials

_____

Initials

16.10–Survival of Obligations

Each provision of this Article 16, will be deemed to be self-executing and continue in full force and effect subsequent to and notwithstanding the expiration, termination, rescission or finding of unenforceability of this Agreement (or any part of it) for any reason.

53

ARTICLE 17
INSURANCE

17.1–Insurance is Required; Coverage

Prior to opening of the Business, you will purchase, and will maintain in full force and effect during the term of this Agreement and during any Successor Term, an insurance policy or policies protecting you and us, and the officers, directors, partners, and employees of both you and us against any loss, liability, personal injury, death, product and food liability, property damage, or expense whatsoever arising or occurring upon or in connection with the operation of the Business. Franchisor and its officers, directors, partners, and employees shall be named as an additional insured on all such policies.

Prior to the opening of the Business, and thereafter no later than two (2) business days of renewing of any such policy or policies, you shall deliver to us the actual policy or policies of insurance or endorsements issued by the insurer (and not the broker) evidencing the proper coverage with limits not less than those required hereunder.

All policies shall expressly provide that not less than thirty (30) days prior written notice shall be given to us in the event of material alteration to termination, non-renewal, or cancellation of the coverages evidenced by such policies.

You will obtain the following coverage:

a. Commercial General Liability Insurance, including coverage for products-completed operations, contractual liability, personal and advertising injury, product and food-service liability (to the extent that food services are offered), property, fire damage, earthquake, and similar loss all for the replacement value of the store all without co-insurance, and medical expenses, having a combined single limit for bodily injury of $2,000,000 per occurrence and $3,000,000 in the aggregate; plus,

b. Excess liability umbrella coverage for general liability coverage in an amount of not less than $1,000,000 per occurrence and 2,000,000 in the aggregate. All such coverages shall be on an occurrence basis and shall provide for waivers of subrogation; plus,

c. Employer's liability and worker's compensation Insurance, as required by state law in the state in which the Franchised Location is found; plus,

d. Business interruption insurance of not less than Fifty Thousand Dollars ($50,000.00) per month for loss of income and other expenses with a limit of not less than nine (9) months of coverage with the understanding that Royalties will be paid from any proceeds issued under such policy.

All such policy or policies shall be written by an insurance company rated A-minus or better, in Class 10 or higher, by Best Insurance Ratings Service and satisfactory to us in accordance with standards and specifications set forth in the Manuals or otherwise in writing, from time to time, and shall include, at a minimum (except as additional coverages and higher policy limits may be specified by us from time to time) the coverage found above.

17.2–No Limitations on Coverage

Your obligation to obtain and maintain, or cause to be obtained and maintained, the foregoing policy or policies in the amounts specified shall not be limited in any way by reason of any insurance which may be maintained by us, nor shall your performance of these obligations relieve you of liability under the indemnity provisions set forth herein.

17.3–Franchisor May Procure Insurance Coverage

Should you, for any reason, fail to procure or maintain the insurance required by this Agreement, as described from time to time by the Manuals or otherwise in writing, we shall have the right and authority (but no obligation) to procure such insurance and to charge the same to you which charges, together with a reasonable fee for our expenses in so acting, shall be immediately payable to us by you.

17.4–Destruction of Premises

In the event the building in which the Business is located is damaged or destroyed by fire or other casualty, and it can be repaired or reconstructed within 180 days, Franchisee shall commence the required repair or reconstruction as soon as is practicable and shall complete all required repair or reconstruction as soon as possible thereafter but in no event later than one hundred eighty (180) days from the date of such casualty. The minimum acceptable appearance for the restored building will be that which existed just prior to the casualty; however, every effort should be made to have the restored building include the then-current image, design, and specifications of new Business. If the building is substantially destroyed by fire or other casualty, and the repairs cannot be made within the 180 days, and if the landlord (or mortgagee if applicable) will permit the Franchisee to terminate the lease (or satisfy the mortgage without rebuilding), Franchisee may apply to us for the right to terminate the Agreement. If we agree to grant the termination, after using our good faith Reasonable Business Judgment, and upon payment to us of an amount equal to twenty five percent (25%) of all insurance proceeds available because of such casualty, this Agreement will terminate. Nothing herein will be deemed to be a guarantee that the Franchisor, or any landlord or mortgagee will permit any termination, and the grant of termination by one such entity will not guarantee the termination of this Agreement, a lease or mortgage by any other entity.

ARTICLE 18
MISCELLANEOUS

18.1–Entire Agreement–Merger

This Franchise Agreement, including all exhibits and addenda, contains the entire agreement between the parties and supersedes any and all prior oral, written, express or implied agreements concerning the subject matter hereof. All prior negotiations, understandings, agreements, oral or written, and representations are merged into this Franchise Agreement.

The Franchisee agrees and understands that Franchisor will not be liable or obligated for any oral representations or commitments made prior to the execution hereof or for claims of negligent or fraudulent misrepresentation based on any such oral representations or commitments.

We do not authorize and will not be bound by any representation of any nature other than those expressed in this Agreement. The Franchisee further acknowledges that no representations have been

55

made to Franchisee by us regarding projected sales volumes, market potential, revenue, profits of the Franchisee's Business, or operational assistance other than as stated in this Agreement or in any disclosure document provided by us to you or representatives.

Nothing in this Agreement or in any related agreement that you sign with us is intended to disclaim any representations in the franchise disclosure document.

18.2–Modification

This Agreement may only be modified in a written agreement that is signed by all parties to this Franchise Agreement.

You acknowledge however, that we may modify by amendment to the Manuals or by written notice to you, our standards, specifications and operating and marketing procedures including those set forth in the Manuals, any component of the System, the Marks, and any copyrighted or Proprietary Information, unilaterally, under any conditions and to the extent to which we, in our sole discretion, deem necessary to protect, promote or improve the Marks and the quality of the System in general. Once you are notified, you must make the change that is specified. All such changes will be effective when notice is received by you. We may also add and remove vendors at any time.

18.3–Delegation

From time to time, we shall have the right to and will delegate the performance of any portion or all of our obligations and duties hereunder to a third party who is approved by us to deliver such services and perform such duties, whether the same are agents of ours or independent contractors which we have contracted with to provide such services. The Franchisee agrees in advance to any such delegation by us of any portion or all of its obligations and duties hereunder.

18.4–Review of Agreement

You acknowledge that you had a copy of this Agreement in your possession for a period of time not less than fourteen (14) calendar days during which time you had the opportunity to submit same for professional review and advice by one or more professionals of the Franchisee's choosing prior to freely executing this Agreement.

18.5–No Waiver

No waiver of any condition or covenant contained in this Agreement or failure to exercise a right or remedy by either of us shall be considered to imply or constitute a further waiver by either of us of the same or any other condition, covenant, right or remedy.

18.6.–No Right to Set Off or Third Party Beneficiaries

You shall not be allowed to set off amounts owed to us for Royalties, Advertising Fees, or other amounts due hereunder, against any monies owed to you, nor shall you, in any event, withhold such amounts due to any alleged nonperformance by us hereunder, which right of set off is hereby expressly waived by you.

56

All obligations of the Franchisor under this Agreement are solely and exclusively for the benefit of the Franchisee, and no other party is entitled to rely on, enforce, benefit from, be deemed to be a third-party beneficiary, or otherwise obtain relief either directly or by subrogation.

18.7–Invalidity

If any provision of this Agreement is held invalid by any tribunal in a final decision from which no appeal is or can be taken, such provision shall be deemed modified to the least extent possible so as to eliminate the invalid element and, as so modified, such provision shall be deemed a part of this Agreement as though originally included. The remaining provisions of this Agreement shall not be affected by such modification.

18.8–Notices

Any and all notices required or permitted under this Agreement shall be in writing and shall be: personally delivered; mailed by certified or registered mail, return receipt requested; or by overnight delivery service, to the respective parties at the following addresses unless and until a different address has been designated by written notice to the other party:

Notices to Franchisor:

NOAH'S ARK FRANCHISING INC.

Noah's Ark Franchising Inc.
123 First Street
Denver, Colorado 80000

Notices to Franchisee

_____

Name of Franchisee Business Entity

_____

Name of Responsible Principal

_____

If an Individual, Name of Franchisee

_____

Address of Franchisee

_____

City, State, ZIP Code of Franchisee

Any notice by certified, registered or express mail, or overnight delivery service, shall be deemed to have been given at the earlier of the date and time of receipt or refusal of receipt or, three (3) days after being deposited in the United States mail. Any notice delivered by hand will be effective as of the date of the delivery.

18.9–Survival of Provisions and Independent Covenants

Any provisions that by their terms extend beyond termination or expiration of this Agreement shall continue in full force and effect subsequent to and notwithstanding the termination or expiration of this Agreement.

The Parties further agree that each covenant herein shall be construed to be independent of any other covenant or provision of this Agreement.

18.10–Force Majeure

Except for monetary obligations hereunder which are due regardless of the language of this section 18.10, or as otherwise specifically provided in this Franchise Agreement, if either Party shall be delayed or hindered in or prevented from the performance of any act required under this Agreement by reason of strikes, lock-outs, labor troubles, inability to procure materials, failure of power, restrictive governmental laws or regulations, riots, insurrection, war, or other causes beyond the reasonable control of the party required to perform such work or act under the terms of this Agreement through no fault of such party, then performance of such act shall be excused for the period of the delay, but in no event to exceed ninety (90) days from the date that performance was to be delivered.

18.11–Acknowledgment

BEFORE SIGNING THIS FRANCHISE AGREEMENT, THE FRANCHISEE SHOULD READ IT CAREFULLY WITH THE ASSISTANCE OF LEGAL COUNSEL. THE FRANCHISEE ACKNOWLEDGES THAT:

THE SUCCESS OF YOUR BUSINESS INVOLVES SUBSTANTIAL RISKS AND DEPENDS UPON THE FRANCHISEE'S ABILITY AS AN INDEPENDENT BUSINESS PERSON AND HIS OR HER ACTIVE PARTICIPATION IN THE DAILY AFFAIRS OF THE BUSINESS, AND

NO ASSURANCE OR WARRANTY, EXPRESS OR IMPLIED, HAS BEEN GIVEN AS TO THE POTENTIAL SUCCESS OF SUCH BUSINESS VENTURE OR THE EARNINGS LIKELY TO BE ACHIEVED, AND

NO STATEMENT, REPRESENTATION, OR OTHER ACT, EVENT, OR COMMUNICATION, EXCEPT AS SET FORTH IN THIS DOCUMENT, AND IN ANY OFFERING CIRCULAR SUPPLIED TO THE FRANCHISEE IS BINDING ON US IN CONNECTION WITH THE SUBJECT MATTER OF THIS AGREEMENT.

Further, the Franchisee shall review and sign the "Closing Acknowledgment" that is attached as Exhibit 7 to this Franchise Agreement.

18.12–Recitals and Convenience

The Recitals are made part of this Franchise Agreement. The headings are for the convenience only of the reader and are not intended to be inclusive or exclusive of any term, covenant, or condition.

18.13–State Addendum

In some cases, this Franchise Agreement may be amended by a state addendum. Please see Exhibit 8 for an addendum for your state.

Signature Page Follows

IN WITNESS WHEREOF, the parties have executed this Agreement as of the date first above set forth.

FRANCHISOR   FRANCHISEE

NOAH'S ARK FRANCHISING INC.   _____

by: _____   by:_____

print name: _____   print name: _____

its: _____Managing Member_____   its: _____

                                    INDIVIDUAL FRANCHISEES

                                    _____
                                                Individually

                                    _____
                                                Print name

                                    _____
                                                Individually

                                    _____
                                                Print name

EXHIBIT 1
STATEMENT OF OWNERSHIP

Franchisee: _____

Trade Name (if different from above): _____

Form of Ownership
(Check One)

_____Individual	_____Partnership	_____Corporation	_____Limited Liability Business Entity

If a partnership, provide name and address of each partner showing percentage owned, whether active in management or not, and indicate the state in which the partnership was formed.

If a limited liability business entity, provide the name and address of each equity-interest holder (Members and Managing Members), show the percentage owned, and indicate the state in which and the date the limited liability business entity was formed.

If a corporation, give the state and date of incorporation, the names and addresses of each officer and director, and list the names and addresses of every shareholder showing what percentage of stock is owned by each.

_____

_____

_____

Franchisee acknowledges that this Statement of Ownership applies to the Business authorized under this Franchise Agreement.

Use additional sheets if necessary. Any and all changes to the above information must be reported to the Franchisor in writing.

FRANCHISOR	**FRANCHISEE**

NOAH'S ARK FRANCHISING INC. _____

by: _____ by:_____

print name: _____ print name: _____

its: _____Managing Member_____ its: _____

INDIVIDUAL FRANCHISEES

_____

Individually

_____

Print name

_____

Individually

_____

Print name

EXHIBIT 2
SPECIFIED BUSINESS TYPE, DESIGNATED AREA, FRANCHISED LOCATION, and EXCLUSIVE TERRITORY

The Designated Area shall be:

_____

_____

_____

_____

_____

The Franchised Location is:

_____

_____

_____

_____

The Exclusive Territory is:

_____

_____

_____

_____

_____

<u>**EXHIBIT 3**</u>
GUARANTEE

GUARANTEE OF FRANCHISEE'S OBLIGATIONS

This Guarantee of Franchisee's Obligations (Guarantee) is entered into this _____ day of _____, 20___ by and between, Noah's Ark Franchising Inc., (Franchisor), _____ (Franchisee) and _____, whose address is _____ and _____, whose address is _____ (herein jointly and severally known as Guarantor(s)).

RECITALS

WHEREAS,   Franchisee signed a franchise agreement with Franchisor on the ____ day of _____, 20__ (Franchise Agreement);

WHEREAS, as an inducement to the Franchisor for granting the Franchise Agreement the Guarantor(s) agreed to fully guarantee the performance of Franchisee under the Franchise Agreement;

NOW, THEREFORE, for and in consideration of the mutual covenants found herein and for other good and valuable consideration, which consideration is deemed to be adequate by all parties, each of the undersigned hereby personally and unconditionally agree to the following:

COVENANTS

1. Guarantor(s) guarantee to Franchisor and its successors and assigns, for the term of the Franchise Agreement, and thereafter as provided in the Agreement, including any amendments thereto or renewals thereof, that the Franchisee shall timely pay any amount required by the Franchise Agreement, and shall perform each and every undertaking, agreement and covenant set forth in the Franchise Agreement and any addenda or Exhibits attached thereto as each may be amended or renewed.

2. Guarantor(s) further agrees to be personally bound by each and every term of the Franchise Agreement, as amended or renewed, and agree to be personally liable for the breach of, and if permitted, the cure, of each and every breach of any term, covenant, or condition of the Franchise Agreement.

3. As part of the inducement given to Franchisor by the Guarantor(s) to permit the Franchisee to enter into the Franchise Agreement, the Guarantor(s) further agree to waive the following:

    a. Acceptance and notice of acceptance of the foregoing undertaking;

    b. Notice of demand for payment of any indebtedness or notice of any nonperformance of any obligations hereby guaranteed;

    c. Protest and notice of default with respect to the indebtedness or nonperformance of any obligations hereby guaranteed;

    d. Any right Guarantor may have to require that any action be first brought against Franchisee or any other person or entity as a condition of liability; and

    e. Any and all other notices and legal or equitable defenses to which Guarantor may be entitled.

63

4. Guarantor(s) further consent and agree that:

    a. Guarantor(s) direct and immediate liability under this guarantee shall be joint and several;

    b. Guarantor(s) shall render any payment or performance required under the Franchise Agreement upon demand of Franchisor if Franchisee fails or refuses punctually to do so;

    c. Guarantor(s) performance shall not be contingent or conditioned upon pursuit of any remedies against Franchisee or any other person;

    d. Guarantor(s) liability shall not be diminished, relieved or otherwise affected by any extension of time, credit or other indulgence (including without limitation the acceptance of any partial payment or performance, or the compromise or release of any claims), which Franchisor may from time to time grant to Franchisee or to any other person, none of which shall in any way modify or amend this Guarantee, which shall be continuing and irrevocable during the term of the Franchise Agreement, including renewals thereof;

IN WITNESS WHEREOF, each of the undersigned has affixed his, her, or its signature as of the date first found above.

_____

Individually

_____

Print name

_____

Individually

_____

Print name

STATE OF _____)

)ss.

COUNTY OF _____)

64

The above Guarantee was acknowledged before me this ___ day of _____, 20__, by _____ as the _____ of Noah's Ark Franchising Inc.

_____
Notary Public

My Commission expires on: _____

STATE OF _____)
)ss.
COUNTY OF _____)

EXHIBIT 4
COLLATERAL ASSIGNMENT OF LEASE AGREEMENT

NOAH'S ARK FRANCHISING INC.
COLLATERAL ASSIGNMENT OF LEASE AGREEMENT

THIS COLLATERAL ASSIGNMENT OF LEASE AGREEMENT (Assignment) is made this _____ day of
_____, 20__, by and between Noah's Ark Franchising Inc. (Franchisor) and _____
(Franchisee) and _____ (Landlord), involving the franchised business (Business)
located at _____ (Franchised Location).

RECITALS

WHEREAS, on _____, 20____, Franchisee and Landlord entered into a Lease Agreement
(hereinafter called "Lease"), a fully executed copy of which is attached hereto as Exhibit A, pursuant
to the terms of which Franchisee leased Franchised Location from Landlord to operate the Business
thereon.

WHEREAS, on _____, 20____, Franchisor and Franchisee executed a Franchise
Agreement pursuant to the terms of which Franchisee obtained a franchise from Franchisor to operate
a Business at the Franchised Location.

WHEREAS, Franchisor, Franchisee, and Landlord desire to enter into this Agreement to define the
rights of Franchisor in and to the Franchise Location and to protect the interests of Franchisor in the
continued operation of the Business at the Franchised Location during the entire term of the Lease, and
any and all renewals and extensions thereof, and Landlord desires to consent to this assignment on the
terms and conditions set forth herein.

NOW, THEREFORE, IT IS AGREED:

1. Franchisee hereby assigns, transfers, and conveys to Franchisor all of Franchisee's right, title, and
   interest in and to the Lease; however, this assignment is for collateral purposes and shall become
   effective only upon Franchisor's exercise of the option granted to Franchisor in Paragraph 3
   herein subsequent to the occurrence of any of the following events:

   a. If Franchisee shall be in default in the performance of any of the terms of the Lease, unless
      such default is cured within the period required in the Lease or within thirty (30) days follow-
      ing the written demand given Franchisor, whichever is sooner.
   b. If Franchisee shall be in default in the performance of any of the terms of the Franchise Agree-
      ment, or upon the occurrence of any acts that would result in termination of the Franchise
      Agreement as specified in the Franchise Agreement.
   c. If Franchisee shall have failed or elected not to exercise an option to renew or extend the
      Lease within the time specified in the Lease for such renewal or extension, after having been
      directed in writing by Franchisor to do so. Upon failure of Franchisee to so elect to extend
      or renew the Lease as aforesaid, Franchisee hereby irrevocably appoints Franchisor as its true

66

and lawful attorney-in-fact to exercise such extension or renewal options in the name, place and stead of Franchisee for the sole purpose of effecting such extension or renewal.

   d. Upon Franchisee's sale of: a substantial portion of its assets of the business the result of which will make the operation of the business by Franchisee in the normal course impractical or impossible; the transfer or sale of 20 percent or more of the capital stock, Memberships, or other equity or capital interest in any Franchisee business entity; or any other transfer, sale, or disposition the result of which is to divest the Franchisee of direction or control over the franchise.

   e. If Franchisee fails to exercise an option to renew the Franchise Agreement.

   Except as specified herein, Franchisor shall have no liability or obligation of any kind whatsoever arising in connection with this agreement or the Lease unless Franchisor shall take possession of the Franchise Location pursuant to the terms hereof and shall expressly agree in writing to assume the obligations of Franchisee thereunder.

2. Landlord hereby consents to this Assignment, which consent shall remain in effect during the entire term of the Lease and any and all renewals or extensions thereof, and agrees that the Lease shall not be amended, modified, assigned, extended, surrendered, terminated or renewed, nor shall the Franchise Location be sublet by Franchisee, without the prior written consent of Franchisor. Landlord agrees to provide Franchisor with copies of any notice of Franchisee's default.

3. Landlord further agrees that it will provide written notice to us (at the same time it gives such notice to the Tenant) of any default by you under the Lease. Such notice must be provide us with an additional thirty (30) days after your period of cure has run within which to cure, at our sole option, any such default and, upon the curing of such default, we must be given the right to enter upon the leased premises and assume your rights under the lease as if the lease had been assigned by you to us.

4. Franchisor may exercise the option granted herein, and thereby make this assignment unconditional, by giving written notice to Franchisee and Landlord of its exercise of said option in the manner specified in Paragraph 7 hereof and by thereafter delivering to Landlord, within ten (10) business days after Landlord requests the same, a written assumption of the obligations of the Lease.

   Franchisor shall have the right, concurrently with, or subsequent to Franchisor's exercise of the option granted herein, to assign and transfer its rights under this Agreement to a new Franchisee selected by Franchisor to operate the Business, with prior written consent of Landlord, which shall not be unreasonably withheld, provided that such new Franchisee shall have a credit rating and a net worth adequate for the operation of the Business. In such event, such new Franchisee shall obtain the assignment of the Lease and shall assume the obligations of the Lease in place and instead of Franchisor and Franchisor shall be released from liability under the Lease from and after the date such new Franchisee assumes the Lease.

5. Upon the exercise of the option granted to Franchisor herein, Franchisee shall no longer be entitled to the use or occupancy of the Franchise Location; all of the Franchisee's prior rights in and to the Lease will have been, in all respects, assigned to Franchisor, or its assignee; and Franchisee shall immediately vacate the Franchise Location. If Franchisee shall fail or refuse to

take any of these actions, Franchisor shall have the right to expel Franchisee from the Franchise Location and to enter the Franchise Location and take possession of the Franchise Location; all without being deemed to have elected any remedies to the exclusion of any other remedies.

6. Franchisee hereby agrees to indemnify and hold Landlord and Franchisor harmless from and against any and all loss, costs, expenses (including attorneys fees), damages, claims and liabilities, however caused, resulting directly or indirectly from, arising from, or pertaining to the exercise by Franchisor and/or Landlord of the rights and remedies granted under this Agreement.

7. The remedies granted pursuant to this Agreement are cumulative and in addition to and not in substitution of any or all other remedies available under the Franchise Agreement, any other contracts by and between Franchisor and Franchise, or at law or in equity to Franchisor; and Franchisee agrees that the Franchisor's exercise of the option granted herein shall not divest it of any other rights or remedies it may have.

8. All notices, requests, demands, payments, consents, and other communications hereunder shall be transmitted in writing and shall be deemed to have been duly given three (3) days after being sent by registered or certified United States mail, postage prepaid, to addresses supplied by each party from time to time.

   Any party may change its address by giving written notice of such change of address to the other parties. Mailed notices shall be deemed communicated within three (3) days from the time of mailing if mailed as provided in this Agreement.

9. Miscellaneous
   a. Franchisee and Landlord recognize the unique value and secondary meaning attached to Noah's Ark Franchising Inc., its trademark, trade names, service marks, insignia and logo designs, and the Franchise Location displaying same, and agrees that any non-compliance with the terms of this Agreement will cause irreparable damage to Franchisor and its Franchisees. Franchisee and Landlord therefore agree that in the event of any non-compliance with the terms of this Agreement, Franchisor shall be entitled to seek injunctive relief from any court of competent jurisdiction in addition to any other remedies prescribed by law.
   b. The parties agree to execute such other documents and perform such further acts, as may be necessary or desirable to carry out the purposes of this Agreement.
   c. This Agreement shall be binding upon and inure to the benefit of the parties, their heirs, successors, and assigns.
   d. This Agreement represents the entire understanding between the parties as to the subject matter herein, and supersedes all other negotiations, agreements, representations, and covenants, oral or written, only in reference thereto. This Agreement may only be modified in writing.
   e. Failure by any party to enforce any rights under this Agreement shall not be construed as a waiver of such rights. Any waiver, including waiver of default, in any one instance shall not constitute a continuing waiver or a waiver in any other instance.
   f. As used herein, reference to one gender shall include the other and neuter genders; the singular shall include the plural, and the plural, the singular.

g. This Agreement shall not be binding on Franchisor unless and until it shall have been accepted and signed by an authorized officer of Franchisor.

h. If any Party commences an action against any other Party arising out of or in connection with this Agreement, the "Prevailing Party" shall be entitled to have and receive from the other party its reasonable attorneys fees and costs of suit. For the purposes of this Agreement, the "Prevailing Party" shall be deemed that Party that has prevailed on a majority of the material issues brought before the court (or which has received the greatest monetary award or judgment).

i. This Agreement (but not the Franchise Agreement) shall be governed by and construed in accordance with the internal laws of the state in which the real property is located.

j. Any provision of this Agreement that may be determined by competent authority to be prohibited or unenforceable in that jurisdiction shall, as to that jurisdiction only, be ineffective to the extent of the prohibition of unenforceability without invalidating the remaining provisions of this Agreement. Any prohibition against or unenforceability of any provisions of this Agreement in any jurisdiction, including the state whose laws govern this Agreement, shall not invalidate the provision or render it unenforceable in any other jurisdiction.

To the extent permitted by applicable law, Franchisee and Landlord waive any provision of law that renders any provision of this Agreement prohibited or unenforceable in any respect.

Done as of the date first found above.

FRANCHISOR   **FRANCHISEE**

NOAH'S ARK FRANCHISING INC.   _____

by: _____   by: _____

print name: _____   print name: _____

its: _____Managing Member_____   its: _____

                                          INDIVIDUAL FRANCHISEES

                                          _____
                                                                    Individually

                                          _____
                                                                    Print name

                                          _____
                                                                    Individually

                                          _____
                                                                    Print name

69

EXHIBIT A
LEASE

Copy of lease should be inserted here as "Exhibit A."

70

EXHIBIT 5
COLLATERAL ASSIGNMENT OF CONTACT AND
ELECTRONIC INFORMATION

Collateral Assignment of Contact and Electronic Information

This Collateral Assignment of Contact and Electronic Information (Agreement) is made this _____ day of _____, 20____, by and between Noah's Ark Franchising Inc. (Franchisor) and _____ _____ (Franchisee).

RECITALS

WHEREAS, on _____, 20____, Franchisor and Franchisee executed a "Franchise Agreement" pursuant to the terms of which Franchisee obtained a franchise from Franchisor to operate a Business at the Franchised Location.

WHEREAS, as part of the Franchise Agreement, the Franchisee agreed that upon termination of the Franchise Agreement, that the Franchisor would have the right, title and interest in and to all contact and electronic information relating to the Franchisee's Business;

WHEREAS, in order to ensure that the Franchisor will have such rights, the parties have agreed to enter into this Agreement;

WHEREAS, any capitalized term not defined herein will have the meaning set forth in the Franchise Agreement;

NOW THEREFORE, for and in consideration of the covenants found in the Franchise Agreement and for other good and valuable consideration the adequacy of which is admitted by all parties hereto, it is agreed as follows:

COVENANTS

1. Franchisee acknowledges that, as between Franchisee and Noah's Ark Franchising Inc., the Franchisor has the sole rights to and interest in all telephone, telecopy or facsimile machine numbers, directory listings, URLs, web page identifiers, email addresses, social network addresses (including Twitter and Face Book) that are associated with any Mark.

2. Franchisee authorizes Franchisor, and hereby appoints Franchisor and any of its officers as Franchisee's attorney-in-fact, to direct the telephone company, all telephone directory publishers, any electronic transfer agency, any URL or webpage host, and any other electronic business, company, transfer agent, host, webmaster, and the like to transfer to the Franchisor all telephone, facsimile machine numbers, and directory listings, and all electronic listings, web pages, social network pages or identities (including twitter and Face Book), URLs, email addresses and the like that relate to the Franchised Business. Should Franchisee fail or refuse to do so, any party named herein may accept such direction under this Agreement as conclusive of Franchisor's exclusive rights in and to such information, site, URL, electronic media, telephone numbers, directory listings and the like and Franchisor's authority to direct their transfer.

71

3. This Agreement is only effective at such time as the Franchise Agreement is terminated for any reason and then only if the Franchisee fails or refuses to make the necessary assignments as contemplated by this Agreement.

4. The Recitals are incorporated into this Agreement by this reference.

In Witness Whereof, the parties hereto have executed and delivered this Agreement as of the day and year first written above.

FRANCHISOR   **FRANCHISEE**

NOAH'S ARK FRANCHISING INC.   _____

by: _____   by:_____

print name: _____   print name: _____

its: _____Managing Member_____   its: _____

INDIVIDUAL FRANCHISEES

_____

Individually

_____

Print name

_____

Individually

_____

Print name

EXHIBIT 6
GENERAL RELEASE

GENERAL RELEASE

This General Release (Release) is made this ____ day of _____, 20__, by and between Noah's Ark Franchising Inc., (Franchisor), _____ (Franchisee) and the Franchisee on behalf of the Franchisee Parties.

RECITALS

WHEREAS, Franchisor and Franchisee entered into that certain franchise agreement dated _____ (Franchise Agreement);

WHEREAS, pursuant to the Agreement, Franchisee was permitted to open and operate a Franchised Location at _____ (hereinafter the "Business");

WHEREAS, Franchisee desires to have the Franchisor _____

_____

WHEREAS, as a material inducement to the Franchisor approving the same and taking such action, the Franchisee has agreed to provide this Release;

WHEREAS, all capitalized terms not defined herein shall have the meaning set forth in the Franchise Agreement;

NOW, THEREFORE, for and in consideration of the mutual covenants found herein, for that consideration stated below, and for other good and valuable consideration the adequacy of which is admitted by all parties hereto, it is agreed as follows:

COVENANTS

1. The Recitals are incorporated herein by this reference.
2. Franchisee for and on behalf of itself, himself or herself, its officers, directors, shareholders, and employees, and on behalf of any parent corporation or subsidiary, business entity, successor, assignee and their officers, directors, shareholders and employees, and the Franchisee Parties, for itself, himself, or herself, and on behalf of itself, its officers, directors, shareholders, and employees, and on behalf of any parent corporation or subsidiary, business entity, successor, assignee and their officers, directors, shareholders, and employees and for and in consideration of: the Franchisor granting to the Franchisee the right to do the following; _____ _____; and for other good and valuable consideration all of which is deemed adequate by all parties hereto, does (or do) hereby release, forever forgive and discharge Franchisor, its officers, directors, shareholders and employees, from any: equitable or legal claim; cause of action; complaint; direct, indirect or consequential damages; judgment; award; injury, or any other right or action (Claim) which relates in any way to: i) the delivery of the Franchise Disclosure Document (FDD) to Franchisee; ii) the performance or failure of performance of Franchisor under the Franchise Agreement up to and including the date of this Release; and iii) the performance or the failure to perform of Franchisor under any other

73

agreement, covenant or document by and between the parties from the beginning of time to the date of this Release.

3. The Release shall be interpreted in accordance with the laws of the state in which the offices of the Franchisor are found as of the date that this Release was signed and shall be enforceable in accordance with the requirements found in the applicable sections of the Agreement which are incorporated herein as if fully set forth.

4. Franchisee and the Franchisee Parties each deliver this Release with the intent that Franchisor rely upon the same. The Franchisor and the Franchisee Parties each expressly states that the grant by the Franchisor to the Franchisee of the right described in paragraph 1 above, was made in contemplation of not only known damages and the consequences thereof, but also in contemplation of the possibility that the Franchisee and/or the Franchisee Parties may or will sustain future damages presently unknown to them but which accrued on or before the date of this Release.

5. If any mandatory provisions of the governing state law limit or prohibit the use of this Release, or which in any manner impose different rights or obligations as are found herein, then such mandatory provisions of state law shall be deemed incorporated in the Franchise Agreement and this Release by reference, and shall prevail over any inconsistent terms in this Release. If no such law exists, or if such law exists but permits the Franchisee to agree to abide by the terms of this Release, then the Franchisee shall agree to abide by the terms of this Release. Nothing in this Release or in any related agreement that you sign with us is intended to disclaim any representations in the franchise disclosure document.

6. The Franchisee and the Franchisee Parties fully realize that each may have sustained unknown and unforeseen losses, costs, expenses, damages, liabilities, claims and business losses, and the consequences thereof, which may be at this time, heretofore and hereafter unknown, unrecognized and not contemplated by them. By executing this Release, the Franchisee and the Franchisee Parties fully intend to release the Franchisor from any and all liability for any and all such unknown and unforeseen losses, expenses, damages, costs, liabilities, business losses, and the consequences thereof, not known, recognized nor contemplated at any time by them up to the date of this Release.

7. Each Party expressly assumes: i) any and all risks that the facts and law may be, or become, different from the facts and law as known to, or believed to be by them as of the date of this Release; and, ii) the risk that the settlement underlying the execution of this Release was made on the basis of mistakes or mistake, mutual or unilateral, and forever waive any right to assert that this Release was the result of a mistake of any kind, waiving all claims based upon the doctrine of mistake.

8 Notwithstanding anything herein to the contrary, nothing in this Release or in any related agreement that you sign with us is intended to disclaim any representations in the franchise disclosure document.

DONE AS OF THE DATE FIRST FOUND ABOVE.

74

FRANCHISOR	**FRANCHISEE**

NOAH'S ARK FRANCHISING INC.   _____

by: _____   by: _____

print name: _____   print name: _____

its: _____ Managing Member _____   its: _____

INDIVIDUAL FRANCHISEES

_____

Individually

_____

Print name

_____

Individually

_____

Print name

75

<u>**EXHIBIT 7**</u>
CLOSING ACKNOWLEDGMENT

Franchisee Name: _____

Franchisee Address:_____

Telephone:_____

Today's Date: _____

A.–General Questions

1. I had a face-to-face meeting with a franchise marketing representative.
   ❑ Yes   ❑ No

   If yes, the date of said meeting was: _____

2. The date which I received the Franchise Disclosure Document (FDD) from Franchisor. _____

   _____

3. The earliest date on which I signed the Franchise Agreement or any other binding document (not including the Receipt). _____

   _____

4. The earliest date on which I delivered cash, check, or consideration to the franchise marketing representative or any other person. _____

   _____

5. Did you initiate negotiations about the Franchise Agreement with the Franchisor? ❑ Yes   ❑ No

   If yes, what was that date? _____

   _____

B.–Representations

PLEASE RESPOND TO EACH PARAGRAPH. IN RESPONDING, PLEASE STATE WHETHER THE STATEMENT IS TRUE OR FALSE AND PROVIDE ANY OTHER INFORMATION THAT IS IMPORTANT TO YOU

76

1. I had an opportunity to review the FDD and other agreements attached to the disclosure document and understand the terms, conditions, and obligations of these agreements.
   ❑ **True**   ❑ **False**

   _____   _____

                                                              initials

2. I had an opportunity to seek professional advice regarding the FDD, the Franchise Agreement, and all matters concerning the purchase of my franchise.
   ❑ **True**   ❑ **False**

   _____   _____

                                                              initials

3. Except as specifically written in the Franchise Agreement, no promises, agreements, contracts, commitments, representations, understandings, "side deals," or otherwise have been made to or with me with respect to any matter, including, but not limited to, any representations or promises regarding advertising (television or otherwise), marketing, site location, operational assistance or other services.
   ❑ **True**   ❑ **False**

   _____   _____

                                                              initials

4. Even if promises, agreements, contracts, commitments, representations, understandings, "side deals," or otherwise have been made to or with me with respect to any matter, including, but not limited to, any representations or promises regarding advertising (television or otherwise), marketing, site location, operational assistance or other services, I have not relied in any way on any such promises, agreements, contracts, commitments, representations, understanding or "side deals" when making my decision to purchase this franchise.
   ❑ **True**   ❑ **False**

   _____   _____

                                                              initials

5. No oral, written, or visual claim or representation, promise, agreement, contract, commitment, representation, understanding, or otherwise which contradicted or was inconsistent with the disclosure document or the Franchise Agreement was made to me.
   ❑ **True**   ❑ **False**

   _____   _____

                                                              initials

6. Even if an oral written or visual claim or representation, promise, agreement, contract, commitment, representation, understanding, or otherwise which contradicted or was inconsistent with

77

the disclosure document or the Franchise Agreement was made to me, I have not relied in any way on any such matter that contradicts or is inconsistent with the disclosure document when making the decision to purchase this franchise.

❏ **True** ❏ **False**

_____   _____

initials

7. Except as specifically stated in Item 19 of the disclosure document, no oral, written, visual, or other claim or representations were made which stated or suggested any sales, income, expense, profits, cash flow, tax effects, or otherwise was made to me by any person or entity representing the Franchisor; or if made, I did not rely on the same when making my decision to purchase this franchise.

❏ **True** ❏ **False**

_____   _____

initials

8. I have made my own independent determination that I have adequate working capital to develop, open, and operate my Business.

❏ **True** ❏ **False**

_____   _____

initials

9. I understand that my investment in the franchise contains substantial business risks and that there is no guarantee that it will be profitable.

❏ **True** ❏ **False**

_____   _____

initials

10. I acknowledge that the success of my franchise depends in large part upon my ability as an independent businessperson and my active participation in the day-to-day operation of the business.

❏ **True** ❏ **False**

_____   _____

initials

C.–Statements of the Franchisor

THE PARAGRAPHS BELOW ARE POLICIES OF THE FRANCHISOR. IF ANY IS UNTRUE OR IS CONTRADICTED BY YOUR EXPERIENCE, PLEASE PROVIDE AN EXPLANATION.

1. The Franchisor <u>does not permit</u> any employee, salesperson, officer, director, or other individual to make or endorse any representations, warranties, projections, or disclosures of any type relat-

78

ing to the financial success of the franchise business and, except as specifically stated in item 19, or by you at the line below, no information as to sales, income, expenses, profits, cash flows, tax consequences, or otherwise have been given to the Franchisee. If any such representations have been made to you by any person in the Franchisor's employ, please state so below and immediately inform the President of the Franchisor.

❏ **None were made**

_____   _____

                                                                                                            initials

2. The Franchisor <u>does not permit</u> any employee, salesperson, officer, director, or other individual working with it to project any results that a franchisee can expect in the operation of this franchise business. If any such representations have been made to you by any person, please state so below and immediately inform the President of the Franchisor.

❏ **None were made**

_____   _____

                                                                                                            initials

3. The Franchisor <u>does not permit</u> any promises, agreements, contracts, commitments, representations, understandings, "side deals", variations or changes in, or supplements to the franchise agreement except by means of a written addendum thereto signed by the franchisee and the president of the Franchisor. If any such deals or changes have been made or promised, please state so below and immediately inform the President of the Franchisor.

❏ **None were made**

_____   _____

                                                                                                            initials

I have completed this Closing Acknowledgment and have disclosed any information that is contrary to any printed statement or have provided any other information that I deem to be important.

Done this _____ day of _____, 20___

FRANCHISOR

NOAH'S ARK FRANCHISING INC.

by: _____

print name: _____

its: <u>Managing Member</u>

FRANCHISEE

_____

by:_____

print name: _____

its: _____

INDIVIDUAL FRANCHISEES

_____

Individually

_____

Print name

_____

Individually

_____

Print name

EXHIBIT 8
STATE SPECIFIC ADDENDUM

(State specific addenda will go here)

81

Background Questionnaire for Franchise Disclosure Document

AS A FRANCHISOR, YOU WILL BE REQUIRED—EITHER BY FEDERAL OR state laws—to prepare and use a franchise disclosure document when offering a franchise for sale. This disclosure document incorporates certain required information concerning such items as:

- ▶ The description of your business to be franchised;
- ▶ Your business's litigation and bankruptcy history;
- ▶ Your background and that of your principals as franchisors; and
- ▶ The extent of the support you plan to give your franchisees.

To help you gather this information and other important facts and figures for your disclosure document, complete the background questionnaire in this appendix. When you have filled out this questionnaire, you will not only have learned more about you and your business, you also will have helped facilitate the disclosure document process. By saving time on this critical information gathering, you could even possibly reduce your attorney fees for preparing the first draft of your disclosure document.

When answering the questions, be sure to attach additional sheets if needed. Questions 1–17 should cover only the last 10 years.

1. a. Franchisor's name, principal business address (home office in the United States), and telephone number (if a franchise corporation is to be formed, insert the name of the proposed new corporation; the business address cannot be a post office): _____

    _____

    _____

    b. Name, principal business address, and telephone number of international home office: ____

    _____

    _____

2. If the franchisor had a predecessor, i.e., a person from whom the franchisor acquired, during the past 10 years, or will acquire—directly or indirectly—the major portion of the franchisor's assets, give the name, address, and telephone number of the predecessor. _____

    _____

3. If the proposed franchisor has an affiliate—defined as a corporation or entity other than a natural person—controlled by, controlling, or under common control with the franchisor that is offering franchises in any line of business or is providing products or services to the franchisee of the franchisor, give the name, address, and telephone number. _____

    _____

4. The name under which the franchisor does or intends to do business: _____

    _____

5. The name, address, and telephone number of person who will be listed as agent for service of process: _____

    _____

6. State of incorporation or business organization and the type of business organization (corporation, partnership, sole proprietorship): _____

    _____

7. a. Does the franchisor operate a business of the type being franchised? _____
    ❑ Yes ❑ No
    If yes, give a brief description of the location and type of business:

    _____

    _____

    b. Does or has the franchisor sold or granted franchises?
      ❑ Yes ❑ No
    If yes, please describe when, where, and to whom: _____

_____

_____

8. List the franchisor's other business activities: _____

_____

_____

9. Please give a brief description of the business to be conducted by the franchisees:

_____

_____

10. Describe briefly the general market for the product or service to be offered by the franchisee. Is it a relatively new product or service, or is the market fairly saturated? Will the goods or services be seasonal, or offered primarily to a certain group of purchasers? _____

_____

_____

11. Are there any regulations specific to the industry in which your franchise business will operate? (Include any special licenses or legal restriction on operations set by statutes.) _____

_____

_____

12. Give a brief description of the competition that your franchisees will face:

_____

_____

13. Give the prior business experience of the franchisor, including: 1) the length of time the franchisor has conducted a business of the type to be operated by the franchisee; and 2) the length of time the franchisor has offered franchises for the same type of business as that to be operated by the franchisee and in which states the franchises were offered. _____

_____

_____

14. Describe whether the franchisor has offered franchises in any other lines of business, including:

   a. A description of each other line of business: _____

_____

_____

b. The number of franchises sold in each other line of business: _____

_____

_____

c. The length of time the franchisor has offered each other franchise: _____

_____

_____

15. Briefly describe the business experience of any predecessor and/or affiliate of the franchisor, including: 1) the length of time each predecessor or affiliate has conducted a business of the type to be operated by the franchisee; and 2) the length of time each predecessor and affiliate has offered franchises for the same type of business as that to be operated by the franchisee. _

_____

_____

16. Describe whether or not each predecessor and affiliate offered franchises in another line of business and, if so, include:

a. The description of each other line of business: _____

_____

_____

b. The number of franchises sold in each other line of business: _____

_____

_____

c. The length of time each predecessor and affiliate offered each other franchise: _____

_____

17. List by name and position all of the directors of the corporation, or general partners of the partnership, or trustees of the trust, and include each person's principal occupation and employers during the past five years, with the beginning date and departure date for each job so designated, as well as the location of the job.

Director, General Partner, Trustee (strike inapplicable words): _____

_____

_____

Director, General Partner, Trustee (strike inapplicable words): _____

_____

_____

Director, General Partner, Trustee (strike inapplicable words): _____

_____

_____

Director, General Partner, Trustee (strike inapplicable words): _____

_____

_____

18. List by name and present position the principal officers and other executives who will have management responsibility relating to the franchises offered by this disclosure document. (Include jobs for the last five years, with beginning and departure dates.)

Chief executive officer: _____

_____

_____

Chief operating officer: _____

_____

_____

President: _____

_____

_____

Treasurer or chief financial officer: _____

_____

_____

Franchise marketing officer: _____

_____

_____

Franchise training officer: _____

_____

_____

Franchise operations officer: _____

_____

_____

Director: _____

_____

_____

Director: _____

_____

_____

Director: _____

_____

_____

Other employees or consultants having management responsibilities:

_____

_____

19. Does the franchisor have a franchise broker, i.e., an independent firm that specializes in selling franchises? ❑ Yes ❑ No

    If yes, please briefly state the names, addresses, and telephone numbers of the franchise broker's directors, principal officers, and executives with management responsibilities to market or service the franchisor, including their beginning and departure dates of employment for the past five years:

    _____

    _____

20. State whether or not the franchisor, its predecessor, a person identified in Item 2, or an affiliate operating franchises under the franchisor's principal trademark has been involved in any of the following: _____

    a. Please state whether or not there is an administrative, criminal, or material civil action pending against that person(s), entity, or entities alleging a violation of a franchise, antitrust, or securities law, fraud, unfair or deceptive practices, or comparable allegations. In addition, include actions other than ordinary routine litigation incidental to the business that are significant in the context of the number of franchisees and the size, nature, or financial condition of the franchise system or its business operations. ❑ Yes ❑ No

       If yes, disclose the names of the parties and the forum, nature, and current status of pending action: _____

_____

_____

b. Please state whether or not such person(s), entity, or entities have, during the 10-year period immediately before the date of this questionnaire, been convicted of a felony or pleaded *nolo contendere* to a felony charge, or been held liable in a civil action by final judgment, or been the subject of a material action involving a violation of franchise, antitrust or securities law, fraud, unfair deceptive practices, or comparable allegations. ❏ Yes ❏ No

If yes, disclose the names of the parties and the forum and date of conviction or the date the judgment was entered, penalty or damages assessed, and/or terms of the settlement, including the name of the court and the number of the action: _____

_____

_____

c. Please state whether or not the above-named person(s), entity, or entities are subject to a currently effective injunctive or restrictive order or decree relating to the franchise or under a federal, state, or Canadian franchise, securities, antitrust, trade regulation, or trade practice law resulting from a concluded or pending action or proceeding brought by a public agency. _____ ❏ Yes ❏ No

If yes, disclose the names of the person, the public agency and court, a summary of the allegations found by the agency or court and the date, nature, terms, and conditions of the order or decree: _____

_____

_____

(Note: For the purposes of the aforementioned, "franchisor" includes the franchisor, its predecessors, persons identified in Item 2, and affiliates offering franchises under the franchisor's principal trademarks. The definition of an "action" includes any complaints, cross-claims, counterclaims, or third-party claims in a judicial proceeding and their equivalent in administrative action or arbitration proceeding. The franchisor may disclose its counterclaims. Please omit actions that were dismissed by final judgment without liability of injury of an adverse order against the franchisor. The definition of "material" is an action or an aggregate of actions that a reasonable prospective franchisee would consider important in making a decision about the franchise business. It should also be noted that settlement of action does not diminish its materiality if the franchisor agrees to pay material consideration or agrees to be bound by obligations that are materially adverse to the franchisor's interest. Also note that "held liable" includes a finding by final judgment in judicial binding arbitration or administrative proceeding that the franchisor, as a result of claims or counterclaims, must pay money or other consideration, must reduce an indebtedness by the amount of the award, cannot enforce its rights, or must take action adverse to its interest. Give the title of each action, and state the case numbers or citations along with the filing date, the opposing party's name, and the opposing party's relationship with the franchisor. "Relationship" includes competitor, supplier, lessor, franchisee, former franchisee, or class of franchisees. You should also summarize the relief sought or obtained. "Conviction" involves the title of the action and state citation in parentheses with the title underlined. Include the name of the person convicted or held liable and state the crime or violation and date of conviction as well as disclose any sentence or penalty.)

21. Please state whether the franchisor, its affiliates, predecessor, officers, or general partner during the 10-year period immediately before the date of this questionnaire:

   a. Filed as a debtor (or had filed against it) a petition to start an action under the U.S. Bankruptcy Code? ❑ Yes ❑ No

   b. Obtained a discharge of its debts under the Bankruptcy Code?

   ❑ Yes ❑ No

   c. Was a principal officer of a company or a general partner in a partnership that either filed as a debtor (or had filed against it) a petition to start an action under the U.S. Bankruptcy Code or obtained a discharge of its debts under the Bankruptcy Code within one year after the officer or general partner of the franchisor held the position in the company or partnership? ❑ Yes ❑ No

   If yes, disclose the name of the person or company that was the debtor under Bankruptcy Code, date of the action, and the material facts, including the name of the party that filed or had filed against it. If the debtor was an affiliate of the franchisor, state the relationship. If the debtor in the bankruptcy proceeding is unaffiliated with the franchisor, state the name, address, and principal business of the bankrupt company: _____

   _____

   _____

   _____

   d. Did the entity referred to in subparagraph c) file bankruptcy or reorganization under the bankruptcy law? ❑ Yes ❑ No

   If so, identify the date of original filing, the bankruptcy court, the case name and number, the date the debtor obtained a discharge in bankruptcy (including a discharge under Chapter 7), and confirmation of any plans of reorganization under Chapters 11 and 13 of the Bankruptcy Code:

   _____

   _____

_____

_____

(Note: Cases, actions, or other proceedings under the laws of foreign nations relating to bankruptcy proceedings should be included in answers where responses are required.)

22 a. State what you think would be the initial franchise fee (includes all fees and payments for services or goods received from the franchisor before the business opens) and how you arrived

at this figure: _____

_____

_____

b. State whether or not the initial franchise fee includes all fees and payments, whether payable in a lump sum or installments before the franchisee's business opens. If no, please describe fees not included: _____

_____

_____

c. Is the initial franchise fee uniform? ❑ Yes ❑ No

If no, disclose the formula or range of initial fees paid in the previous fiscal year, if any, before the application date and the factors that determined the amount of these initial fees: _____

_____

_____

d. If the initial franchise fee is payable in installments, disclose the installment payment terms in this portion of the questionnaire as well as in the following portion, which is dedicated to information regarding Item 10 of the disclosure document, i.e., the financial arrangements. _____

_____

_____

23. Other Fees:

Name of Fee	Amount	Due Date	Remarks[1]
Royalty			
Advertising Fund			
Cooperative Advertising			
Local Advertising			

Name of Fee	Amount	Due Date	Remarks[1]
Additional Promotional Fees			
Initial Training			
Additional Training			
Transfer Fee			
Renewal Fee			
Audit Fee			

[1]Be sure to indicate, in the Remarks column, answers to each of the following questions:

Is the fee imposed and collected by franchisor?

Is the fee non-refundable?

At what point in time does interest begin?

Are the fees collected by the franchisor? If no, indicate those that are and those that are not and who collects the ones that are not collected by the franchisor.

Are all of the fees listed in the above chart non-refundable? If no, which fees are refundable?

Will the franchisor-owned outlets (company-owned office) have voting power on any fees imposed by cooperatives? If yes, disclose a range for the fee.

(Note: When listing fees, as in the above chart, please remember that fees are royalty, lease negotiation, construction and remodeling, additional training, advertising, additional assistance, audit and accounting, inventory, transfer, and renewal fees. These are fees that are paid either to you as franchisor or your affiliate or fees that you or an affiliate collect in whole or part on behalf of the third party.)

24. Initial Investment: Disclose the following the expenditures, including high and low estimates where appropriate, to the best of your ability. For each expenditure applicable to your franchise operation, include the amount or estimated amount, method of payment, when payment is due, and to whom payment is to be made:

Non-refundable initial franchise fee: _____

_____

Area development option fee: _____

_____

Leasehold improvements: _____

_____

Equipment, furnishings, and fixtures: _____

_____

Signage: _____

_____

Blueprints, plans, permits: _____

_____

Rent: _____

_____

Initial inventory and operating supplies: _____

_____

Security deposits: _____

_____

Insurance: _____

_____

Initial advertising and promotions: _____

_____

Miscellaneous (travel and living expenses while training, permits, organizational expenses, etc.):

_____

Additional funds necessary to commence or continue operation for three months: _____

_____

Other expenses: _____

_____

Now, add up all of the expenses listed above: _____

Total estimated expenses = $_____ to $_____

(Note: If a specific amount is not ascertainable, use a low/high estimated range based on your current experience. If a building is involved, describe the probable location of the building— such as a strip shopping mall, downtown, or rural—when filling out the chart pertaining to real estate and improvement. If you or an affiliate finance a part of the initial investment, state the expenditures that you will finance, the required down payment, the annual percentage interest rate and rate factors, and the estimated loan repayments. Please make descriptions brief. Also, remember to answer this question again when referring to Item 10 of the disclosure document regarding financing.)

25. Disclose any obligations you wish to impose on the franchisee to purchase or lease from you or your designee or from suppliers approved by you as franchisor or under your specifications: _

_____

_____

For each obligation, disclose:

a. The required goods, services, supplies, fixtures, equipment, inventory, computer hardware or software, or real estate relating to establishing or operating the franchise business: ___

_____

_____

b. The manner in which you issue and modify specifications or grants and revoke approval for suppliers: _____

_____

_____

c. Whether and for what categories of goods and services you as franchisor or your affiliates are approved suppliers or the only approved suppliers:

_____

_____

d. Whether you as the franchisor or your affiliates will or may derive revenue or other material consideration as a result of required purchases or leases from you or your designee or your approved supplier and, if so, the precise basis: _____

_____

_____

e. If you require such purchases by the franchisee from you, your designee, or your approved supplier, estimate the proportion of these required purchases and leases to all purchases and leases by the franchisee of goods and services in establishing and operating a franchise business. In other words, if you require the franchisee to purchase $100 worth of equipment from you and the franchisee will purchase and lease other goods and services from other sources for $1,000, your estimated percentage proportion would be 10 percent (100 divided by 1,000): _____ percent.

26. Is there or will there be a purchasing or distribution cooperative? ❏ Yes ❏ No

If yes, please describe: _____

_____

(Note: Do not include goods and services provided as part of the franchise without a separate charge, for example, a fee for initial training when the cost is included in the franchise fee. Do not include fees disclosed in your previous responses.)

27. Will you require the franchisee to follow specifications and standards? ❏ Yes ❏ No

If yes, please describe what the standards will apply to such items as procedures, construction, premises, software, hardware, or uniforms, and also how you would formulate and modify these specifications: _____

_____

_____

28. Disclose whether your specification standards are issued by you to franchisees, subfranchisors, or approved suppliers, and how and when they are updated: _____

_____

_____

29. Describe how your suppliers are evaluated and approved or disapproved by you: _____

_____

_____

30. Will your criteria for suppliers be available to the franchisees? ❑ Yes ❑ No

31. State the fees, if any, that a franchisee must pay you and the procedures he or she must follow to secure your approval of his or her suppliers as well as how your approval would be removed:

_____

32. State the time period that it will take you to approve or disapprove a supplier: _____

_____

_____

33. Does a designated supplier make payments to you as franchisor because of transactions with your franchisees? ❑ Yes ❑ No

    If yes, disclose the basis for the payment and specify a percentage or flat amount that supplier will pay to you: _____

_____

    (Note: When answering this question, please remember that purchases of similar goods or services by you at a lower price than available to your resale to the franchisee is a payment to you when you pass on the goods or services at a higher price to your franchisee.)

34. Do you negotiate purchase arrangements with suppliers, including price terms for the benefit of franchisees? ❑ Yes ❑ No

35. Do you provide material benefits (for example, renew or granting additional franchises) to a franchisee based on a franchisee's use of designated or approved sources? ❑ Yes ❑ No

    If yes, please describe: _____

_____

_____

36. The following items A–Y include obligations that many franchisors impose upon franchisees. Please state after each obligation whether or not you desire at this time to impose such an obligation on your franchisees.

   a. Site selection and acquisition/lease: ❏ Yes ❏ No

   b. Pre-opening purchases/lease: ❏ Yes ❏ No

   c. Site development and other pre-opening requirements: ❏ Yes ❏ No

   d. Initial and ongoing training: ❏ Yes ❏ No

   e. Opening obligations: ❏ Yes ❏ No

   f. Fees (including royalty, advertising, transfer, renewal): ❏ Yes ❏ No

   g. Compliance with standards and policies/operating manual: ❏ Yes ❏ No

   h. Trademarks and proprietary information obligations: ❏ Yes ❏ No

   i. Restrictions on products and services offered: ❏ Yes ❏ No

   j. Warranty and other consumer service requirements: ❏ Yes ❏ No

   k. Territorial development and sales quota: ❏ Yes ❏ No

   l. Ongoing products and service purchases: ❏ Yes ❏ No

   m. Maintenance, appearance, and remodeling requirements: ❏ Yes ❏ No

   n. Insurance requirements: ❏ Yes ❏ No

   o. Advertising requirements: ❏ Yes ❏ No

   p. Indemnification: ❏ Yes ❏ No

   q. Owner's participation/management staffing: ❏ Yes ❏ No

   r. Records and reports: ❏ Yes ❏ No

   s. Inspections and audits: ❏ Yes ❏ No

   t. Transfers: ❏ Yes ❏ No

   u. Renewals: ❏ Yes ❏ No

   v. Post-termination obligations: ❏ Yes ❏ No

   w. Non-competition covenants: ❏ Yes ❏ No

   x. Dispute resolution, such as arbitration with FAM or the American Arbitration Association: ❏ Yes ❏ No

y. Others: ❏ Yes ❏ No

If yes, describe other obligations you will impose upon your franchisees:

_____

_____

(Note: These obligations will be listed in the disclosure document and cross- referenced to the sections in the disclosure document and franchise agreement.)

37. Financing: Do you intend to finance your franchisee, including its initial franchise fee or its monetary requirements for equipment, etc.? (Remember: financing includes leasing and install-ment contracts. Payments due you within 90 days on an open account need not be disclosed.) ❏ Yes ❏ No

If yes, describe the written arrangements between you, your affiliate, and any lender for the lender to offer financing to the franchisee. Any arrangement by which you, as franchisor, or your affiliate receive a benefit from a lender for franchisee financing is an "indirect offer of financing," since any benefit received from a lender is indirect financing, and it must be dis-closed. (For example, if you as franchisor guarantee a note, lease, or obligation of a franchisee, it is an "indirect offer of financing.") _____

_____

_____

If you intend to offer financing to franchisees, please complete a summary of financing available that includes each item that can be financed and for each item: amount financed, down pay-ment, term, APR, monthly payment, prepay penalty (if any), security required, and any other significant terms of the financing: _____

_____

_____

_____

_____

38. Franchisor's Obligations: Please describe your obligations you intend at this time to include in your agreement in assisting your client prior to opening:

Prior to Opening: The following is a list of some obligations you may impose on yourself, if you choose, and that will require a brief description:

a. Will you locate a site for the franchised business and negotiate the purchase or lease of this site for the franchisee? ❏ Yes ❏ No

If yes, will you own the premises and lease it to the franchisee? ❏ Yes ❏ No

b. Will you conform the premises to local ordinances and building codes and obtain the required permits? ❑ Yes ❑ No

c. Will you construct, remodel, or decorate the premises for the franchised business? ❑ Yes ❑ No

d Will you purchase or lease equipment, signs, fixtures, opening inventory, and supplies for the franchisee? ❑ Yes ❑ No

If yes, will you provide these items directly? ❑ Yes ❑ No

If no, will you merely provide the names of approved suppliers? ❑ Yes ❑ No

Do you have written specifications for these items? ❑ Yes ❑ No

Do you deliver or install these items? ❑ Yes ❑ No

e. Do you hire and train employees for the franchisee? ❑ Yes ❑ No

f. List any other obligations you wish to impose on yourself prior to the franchisee's opening:

_____

_____

After Opening: The following is a list of questions about your obligations during the operation of the franchised business that you may feel should be in your agreement.

a. Do you offer products or services to the franchisee to offer to its customers during the term of the agreement? ❑ Yes ❑ No

b. Do you hire and train employees of the franchisee during the term of the agreement? ❑ Yes ❑ No

c. Do you make improvements and developments in the franchised business during the term of the agreement? ❑ Yes ❑ No

d. Do you do pricing during the term of the agreement? ❑ Yes ❑ No

e. Do you do administrative, bookkeeping, accounting, and inventory control procedures during the term of the agreement? ❑ Yes ❑ No

f. Do you handle or troubleshoot operating problems encountered by the franchisee during the term of the agreement? ❑ Yes ❑ No

g. Do you desire an advertising program that will feature the product or service offered by your franchisee? ❑ Yes ❑ No

If yes, provide the information elicited in the following 10 sections.

1. In which media do you intend to disseminate the advertising (for example, print, radio, or television)? _____

   _____

2. Is the coverage of the media local, regional, or national in scope? _____

   _____

3. What is the source of the advertising (e.g., in-house advertising department, a national or regional advertising agency)? _____

   _____

4. Under what conditions you will permit the franchisees to use their own advertising material? _____

   _____

5. If there is an advertising council composed of franchisees that advises you on advertising policies, indicate:

   a. How members of the council are selected;

   b. Whether the council serves in an advisory capacity only or has operational or decision-making power;

   c. Whether you as franchisor have the power to form, change, or dissolve the advertising council.

   _____

6. If, during the term of the agreement you feel the franchisee must participate in a local or regional advertising cooperative, indicate

   a. How the area or membership of the cooperative is defined:

   _____

   b. How the franchisee's contribution to the cooperative is calculated:

   _____

   c. Who is responsible for administration of the cooperative (e.g., franchisor, franchisees, advertising agency):

   _____

   d. Whether cooperatives must operate from written governing documents and whether the documents are available for review by the franchisee:

e. Whether cooperatives must prepare annual or periodic financial statements and whether the statements are available for review by the franchisee:

_____

f. Whether the franchisor has the power to require cooperatives to be formed, changed, dissolved, or merged:

_____

7. If applicable, for each advertising fund not described in above subpart (6), indicate:

a. Who contributes to each fund (e.g., franchisees, franchisor-owned units, outside vendors, or suppliers): _____

_____

b. Whether the franchisor-owned units must contribute to the fund and, if so, whether it is on the same basis as franchisees: _____

_____

c. How much the franchisee must contribute to the advertising fund(s) and whether other franchisees are required to contribute at a different rate (it is not necessary to disclose the specific rates): _____

_____

d. Who administers the fund(s): _____

_____

e. Whether the fund is audited and when, and whether financial statements of the fund are available for review by the franchisee: _____

_____

f. If you already have a fund, please provide the following for the most recently concluded fiscal year: a) the percentage spent on production: _____ percent; b) the percentage spent on media: _____ percent; c) the percentage spent on administrative expenses: _____ percent; and d) the percentage spent on other (define: _____: _____ percent; _____: _____ percent). Your total should equal 100 percent.

g. Whether you or an affiliate receives payment for providing goods or services to an advertising fund. ❑ Yes ❑ No

If yes, describe: _____

_____

8. Will you as franchisor be obligated to spend any amount on advertising in the area or territory where the franchisee is located? ❑ Yes ❑ No

If yes, describe: _____

_____

_____

9. If all advertising fees are not spent in the fiscal year in which they accrue, explain how you will use the remaining amounts: _____

_____

_____

Will the franchisees receive a periodic accounting of how advertising fees are spent? ❏ Yes ❏ No

If yes, how frequent is the accounting? _____

_____

_____

10. Disclose the percentage of advertising funds, if any, used for advertising that is principally a solicitation for the sale of franchises:

_____

_____

39. If your franchise agreement will require the franchisee to buy or use an electronic cash register or computer system, provide a general description of the systems in nontechnical language. Include in your description an identification of each hardware component and software program by brand, type, and principal functions and whether or not it is your proprietary property or that of an affiliate or a third party: _____

_____

_____

40. Do you, an affiliate, or a third party have a contractual obligation to provide ongoing maintenance, repair, upgrades, or updates to the hardware and software sold to your franchisee?

❏ Yes ❏ No

41. Disclose the current annual cost of any optional or required maintenance and support contracts, upgrades, and updates:

_____

42. If the hardware component or software program is the proprietary property of a third party and no compatible equivalent is available, identify the third party by name, business address, and telephone number: _____

_____

_____

43. If the hardware component or software program is not proprietary, identify compatible equivalent components or programs that perform the same functions and indicate whether you as franchisor have approved them: _____

_____

44. State whether the franchisee has any contractual obligation to upgrade or update any hardware component or software program during the term of the franchise and, if so, whether there are any contractual limitations on the frequency and cost of the obligation: _____

_____

45. For each electronic cash register system or software program, describe how it will be used in the franchisee's business and the types of business information or data that will be collected and generated: _____

_____

46. State whether you, as the franchisor, will have independent access to the information and data set forth above and, if so, whether there are any contractual limitations on the franchisor's right to access the information and data: _____

_____

47. Attach a copy of the table of contents of your operating manual, which will be provided to the franchisee as of the franchisor's last fiscal year end or a more recent date. Please indicate the number of pages devoted to each subject listed in the table of contents and the total number of pages in the manual as of this date.

(Note: An alternative disclosure can be accomplished if the prospective franchisee is allowed to view the manual before the purchase of the franchise.)

FRANCHISOR'S METHODS FOR SELECTING THE LOCATION OF THE FRANCHISEE'S BUSINESS

48. Do you select the site or approve an area within which the franchisee selects a site? ❑ Yes ❑ No

    If yes, describe: _____

    _____

49. Describe how and whether you must approve a franchisee's selected site: _____

    _____

50. List the factors that you as franchisor consider in selecting or approving sites (for example, general location and neighborhood, traffic patterns, parking, size, physical characteristics of existing buildings, and lease terms): _____

_____

_____

_____

51. Define the time limit for you as franchisor to locate or to approve or disapprove the site:

Describe the consequences if the franchisor and franchisee cannot agree on a site:

52. Indicate the typical length of time (a range is permissible) between the signing of the franchise agreement or the first payment of consideration for the franchise and the opening of the franchisee's business:

53. Describe any factors that may affect the time period of opening, such as a delay in obtaining a lease, financing or building permits, zoning and local ordinances, weather conditions, shortages, or delays in the installation of equipment, fixtures, and signs:

TRAINING PROGRAM OF THE FRANCHISOR

54. Describe the location, duration, and general outline of the training program:

55. How often will the training program be conducted after the pre-opening training program and who is required to attend?

56. List the names and experience of your instructors, in number of years and subjects:

57. List charges to be made to the franchisee and indicate who must pay travel and living expenses of the enrollees in the training program:

58. For all non-mandatory training programs, if available, state the percentage of new franchisees who enrolled in these non-mandatory training programs during the preceding 12 months:

_____

59. State whether or not any additional training programs and/or refresher courses are required.

❑ Yes ❑ No

If yes, please describe: _____

_____

_____

TERRITORY

60. Describe any exclusive territory granted to the franchisee and how its boundaries were determined—by population, zip code, or other method:

_____

_____

61. Have you established or will you establish any franchisee who may use your trademark in another franchisee's territory? ❑ Yes ❑ No

If yes, explain: _____

_____

62. Have you established or may you establish a company-owned outlet or other channels of distribution using your name in a franchisee's territory? ❑ Yes ❑ No

If yes, explain: _____

_____

63. Describe the minimum area granted to the franchisee and how it is determined—by specific miles, specific population, or any other means: _____

_____

_____

64. Will the franchise be granted for a specific location or a location to be approved by the franchisor? ❑ Yes ❑ No

65. State the conditions under which you will approve the relocation of the franchised business or the establishment of additional franchised outlets: _____

_____

66. Describe restrictions on you as a franchisor regarding operating company-owned stores or granting franchised outlets for a similar or competitive business within the defined area:

_____

_____

(Note: It is not a good policy to allow any company-owned stores or franchised outlets for a similar or competitive business within a franchisee's territory.)

67. Will you restrict franchisees from soliciting or accepting orders outside of the defined territories? ❏ Yes ❏ No

If yes, describe these restrictions: _____

_____

68. Describe any restrictions on you as franchisor from soliciting or accepting orders inside the franchisee's defined territory: _____

_____

69. State any compensation that you as franchisor may pay to a franchisee for soliciting or accepting orders inside the franchisee's defined territory, if any: _____

_____

70. Describe the franchisee's options, rights of first refusal, or similar rights to acquire additional franchises within his or her territory or contiguous territories: _____

_____

TRADEMARKS

71. Describe your principal trademarks, which means the primary trademarks, service marks, names, logos, and symbols to be used by the franchisee to identify the franchised business:

_____

72. State the date and identification number of each trademark registration or registration application with the United States Patent and Trademark Office: _____

_____

73. Have you filed all required affidavits? ❏ Yes ❏ No

74. Has any registration been renewed? ❏ Yes ❏ No

75. State whether the principal marks are registered on the Principal or Supplemental Register of the U.S. Patent and Trademark Office: _____

_____

76. State whether or not an "Intent to Use" application or an application based on actual use has been filed with the U.S. Patent and Trademark Office. If so, list the trademark in question and the serial number of the application: _____

    _____

77. Disclose any currently effective material determinations of the Patent and Trademark Office, the Trademark Trial and Appeal Board, the trademark administrator of your state, or any court; pending infringement, opposition, or cancellation; and pending material litigation involving the principal trademarks, including the name of the principal trademarks, a brief summary of such opposition, and the current status: _____

    _____

    _____

78. Describe any litigation affecting your trademarks if it could significantly affect the ownership or use of the trademarks: _____

    _____

    _____

79. Disclose any agreements currently in effect that significantly limit the rights of you as franchisor to use or license other franchisees to use the trademark in a manner material to the franchise:

    _____

    _____

    _____

80. State whether you as franchisor will protect the franchisee's right to use the trademarks and protect the franchisee against claims or infringements or unfair competition arising out of your use of them. ❏ Yes ❏ No

    If no, indicate what, if any, protection will be given to the franchisee: _____

    _____

81. Do you wish to have the franchisee obligated to notify you in case of any claims? ❏ Yes ❏ No

82. Do you want the franchise agreement to require you as franchisor to take affirmative action when notified of these uses or claims? ❏ Yes ❏ No

83. Do you want to have the right to control administrative proceedings or litigation?
    ❏ Yes ❏ No

84. Do you wish to include a clause that would require the franchisee to modify or discontinue use of the trademark as a result of a proceeding or settlement or any other obstacles that you encounter? ❏ Yes ❏ No

85. Do you know of any superior prior right or any infringing use that could materially affect the franchisee's use of the principal trademarks in this state or in the state in which the franchised business is to be located? ❑ Yes ❑ No

   If yes, describe. _____

   _____

PATENTS, COPYRIGHTS, AND PROPRIETARY INFORMATION

86. If you as franchisor own any rights in patents or copyrights that are material to the franchise, describe these patents and copyrights and their relationship to the franchise. Include their duration and whether you as franchisor can and intend to renew the copyrights. If you are claiming proprietary rights in confidential information or trade secrets, describe their general subject matter and the terms and conditions for use by the franchisee: _____

   _____

   _____

87. If you have any patents, give the patent number, issue date, and title for each patent. If you have any patent applications pending, give the serial number, filing date, and title for each application: _____

   _____

   _____

88. If you know of any infringements or any actions affecting any patent or copyright, describe:

   _____

   _____

   _____

OBLIGATION TO PARTICIPATE IN THE ACTUAL OPERATION
OF THE FRANCHISE BUSINESS

89. Will you require personal, on-premises supervision? ❑ Yes ❑ No

   If not, will you recommend on-site supervision by the franchisee? ❑ Yes ❑ No

90. State any limitations on whom the franchisee can hire as an on-premises supervisor: _____

   _____

91. Will the on-premises supervisor be required to successfully complete your training program? ❑ Yes ❑ No

92. If the franchisee is a business entity, state the amount of equity interest that the on-premises supervisor must have in the franchise, if any: _____ percent.

93. Do you wish to require the franchisee to place restrictions on its manager, including maintaining trade secrets, non-competition, etc.? ❏ Yes ❏ No

    If yes, describe: _____

    _____

RESTRICTIONS ON WHAT THE FRANCHISEE MAY SELL

94. Do you want the franchisee to be obligated to sell only goods and services that you approve? ❏ Yes ❏ No

95. Do you want the franchisee to sell only goods and services that you authorize? ❏ Yes ❏ No

96. Do you want to retain the right to change the types of authorized goods and services? ❏ Yes ❏ No

    If so, are there any limits on your right to make such changes? ❏ Yes ❏ No

    If so, what are they? _____

    _____

97. Do you wish the franchisee to be restricted regarding customers? ❏ Yes ❏ No

    If yes, describe the restrictions: _____

    _____

RENEWAL, TERMINATION, TRANSFER, AND DISPUTE RESOLUTION

98. The following are areas that require answers, if you can provide them at this time:

    a. Desired length of term of the franchise agreement: _____

    b. Renewal or extension of the term: _____

    c. Do you wish requirements for franchisee to renew or extend? ❏ Yes ❏ No

    d. Will you allow the franchisee to terminate other than with good cause? ❏ Yes ❏ No

    e. Do you want provisions by which you can terminate without cause? ❏ Yes ❏ No

    f. Do you want provisions by which you can terminate the agreement with cause? ❏ Yes ❏ No

    g. Do you want obligations on the franchisee on termination or non-renewal? ❏ Yes ❏ No

    h. Do you want the right to assign the agreement? ❏ Yes ❏ No

    i. Do you want a transfer fee in the event the franchisee desires to transfer? ❏ Yes ❏ No

If yes, what fee do you think is reasonable? $_____

j. Do you want approval of any transfer of the franchisee? ❑ Yes ❑ No

k. Do you want a right of first refusal to acquire the franchise business upon any transfer? ❑ Yes ❑ No

l. Do you want a general option to purchase the franchise business at any time? ❑ Yes ❑ No

m. Do you want a non-compete covenant during the term of the franchise? ❑ Yes ❑ No

n. Do you want a non-compete covenant after the franchise is terminated or expires? ❑ Yes ❑ No

If yes, indicate the miles, the restrictions, and the years the non-compete covenant would be in effect: _____

_____

o. Do you desire an arbitration clause? ❑ Yes ❑ No

p. Do you desire a mediation clause? ❑ Yes ❑ No

q. Do you want to specify a state in which any legal action should be brought? ❑ Yes ❑ No

If so, name the state: _____

r. Do you want the law of your state to apply? ❑ Yes ❑ No

If so, name the state: _____

Note: Your answers to the questions in part 98 will be placed in a table, summarized, and cross-referenced to the franchise agreement.

PUBLIC FIGURES

99. Will you be using a public figure to promote the franchise, i.e., a person whose name or physical appearance is generally known to the public in the geographic area where the franchisor will be located? ❑ Yes ❑ No

If yes, please disclose the name, compensation to be paid, the person's position and duties in your business structure, and the amount of his or her investment, if any, in your franchise:

_____

FINANCIAL PERFORMANCE REPRESENTATIONS

100. Do you intend to make representations regarding financial performance to your franchisees? ❑ Yes ❑ No

If so, describe such claims and the reasonable basis in writing that can be presented to the authorities as evidence that these earnings claims have a reasonable basis: _____

_____

_____

OUTLETS AND FRANCHISEE INFORMATION

101. Do you have any franchises at this time? ❏ Yes ❏ No

    If so, describe them: _____

    _____

    _____

102. Do you have any of your own outlets at this time? ❏ Yes ❏ No

    If so, list them, including name, address, telephone number, and years in business:

    _____

    _____

103. If you have any franchisees, provide a complete list including names, addresses, and telephone numbers: _____

    _____

    _____

    _____

    _____

104. Estimate the number of franchises to be sold throughout the United States during the one-year period after the close of the franchisor's most recent fiscal year: _____

    _____

105. If any franchises have closed, cancelled, not renewed, been reacquired, or otherwise ceased to do business, list each of them with the name and last known address and telephone number of every franchisee: _____

    _____

    _____

    _____

    _____

106. Summarize the status of franchise centers and company-owned outlets for the last three fiscal years. For each year, list all franchise openings, transfers, cancellations or terminations, non-renewals, and the total number of franchises centers operating at year end. For each franchise center listed, provide the state in which the franchise center operations. For each year, also list all company-owned centers opened during the year, closed during the year, and operating at year end and the state for each center. _____

Year: 20__

_____

_____

_____

_____

Year: 20__

_____

_____

_____

_____

Year: 20__

_____

_____

_____

_____

FINANCIAL STATEMENTS

107. You will be required to provide financial statements audited by an independent certified public accountant. The audited financials should include the balance sheet of the franchise corporation for the last two fiscal years before the application date or, if less than two years, the actual time that your franchise entity has been in business. In addition, you must include a Statement of Operations of stockholders' equity and of cash flow for each of the franchisor's last three fiscal years or, if less than three fiscal years, the time it has been in business. If the most recent balance sheet and statement of operations date from more than 90 days before the application date, then you must also submit an unaudited balance sheet and a Statement of Operations as of the date within 90 days of the application date.

CONTRACTS

108. List all agreements in addition to the franchise agreement that attorney will need to prepare such as any leases, options, and purchase agreements that are separate from the franchise agreement but that you will require your franchisee to use: _____

_____

_____

_____

_____

_____

_____

_____

_____

_____

The undersigned has prepared the responses to this questionnaire and compiled the above material on behalf of the franchisor and declares that, to the best of his or her knowledge, they are true and correct.

_____
Signature

_____
Title

_____
Date

Your disclosure document cannot be drafted until your attorney knows the above information. Please attach additional sheets as needed.

Background Information for Franchise Agreement

A s you franchise your business, keep in mind that the more carefully you choose your franchisees, the less your agreement will need onerous "weeding out" provisions, such as minimum annual sales quotas, nonexclusive sales territories, short-term franchise agreements, and new contractual provisions upon transfer or renewal.

This questionnaire was designed to help you, as a franchisor, retain just enough control to ensure quality and consistency in the way each franchisee offers your services or products while not economically strangling the franchisee's ability to make a reasonable profit.

Pay particular attention to establishing initial franchise and royalty fees that are fair and operable. Consider each franchised location as if it were a company-owned location with the franchisee paying the bills. Never sell a franchise to a person that you would not hire for life as a manager of your company-owned operation.

After considering these ideas, you can properly frame a franchise agreement that will be workable for both parties, allowing you to achieve greater success through your franchisees than if your agreement were heavily weighted in your favor.

Attach additional sheets, if needed, for each question.

Franchisor: Person to contact about this questionnaire:

Name: _____   Name: _____

Address: _____   Address: _____

City/State/Zip: _____   City/State/Zip:_____

Telephone:_____   Telephone:_____

SERVICE MARKS

Indicate the service marks or trademarks used, as well as their registration dates and registration numbers with the United States Patent and Trademark Office and/or state trademark authorities:

_____

Will you defend a franchise that is sued for using your service mark or trademark by a third party claiming your trademark or service mark is an infringement of its service mark or trademark?
❑ Yes ❑ No

TERRITORY

Will each franchised territory be exclusive, meaning no other franchise or company units will be located in a territory? ❑ Yes ❑ No

Describe how your territorial boundaries will be determined (for example, zip code, county, population, number of businesses): _____

_____

_____

_____

DEFINITION OF FRANCHISE BUSINESS

Give a brief description of the type of business that will be franchised: _____

_____

_____

_____

_____

_____

INTERNAL FRANCHISEE IDENTIFICATION

Set forth any type of prefix or suffix you, as the franchisor, may require to identify each franchisee in your internal records (for example: "McDonald's of Oakland" or "McDonald's #6"):

_____

_____

FRANCHISOR TRAINING

Initial Training Prior to Opening

Locations	Number of Trainers	Number of Working Days	Hours per Day

Training at Time of Franchise Opening (Grand Opening)

Locations	Number of Trainers	Number of Working Days	Hours per Day

What additional training will be available to the franchisee throughout the term of the agreement? _

_____

Will such training will be mandatory? ❑ Yes ❑ No

OTHER FRANCHISOR ASSISTANCE

Describe any other assistance the franchisor will provide the franchisee. _____

_____

Prior to the Opening

Site selection: _____

_____

Market-area survey: _____

_____

Inventory supplies: _____

_____

Equipment: _____

_____

Financial assistance: _____

_____

Hiring of personnel: _____

_____

Local business licenses: _____

_____

Public relations: _____

_____

Other: _____

_____

AFTER THE OPENING

Purchasing assistance: _____

_____

Accounting services: _____

_____

Product updates: _____

_____

Procedure improvements: _____

_____

Public relations: _____

_____

Inspections: _____

_____

Other: _____

_____

FRANCHISEE FEE

Indicate the amount of the initial franchise fee you, as the franchisor, feel you can charge a franchisee.
$ _____

How did you arrive at this fee? _____

_____

Terms of payment of the initial franchise fee:

Down payment $ _____ Balance payment $ _____

Monthly Royalty

Percent of gross receipts you expect to receive as a royalty each month: _____ percent

List reasons for estimating this percentage: _____

_____

_____

Would any minimums be desired? Amount of these minimums: $ _____

(Consideration can also be given to reducing a monthly royalty upon the attainment of a certain amount of gross receipts per month or deferring all or part of the royalty for an initial specified period of time.)

PROMOTION AND ADVERTISEMENTS

Percent of gross receipts or other formula that you desire in establishing a general advertising fee fund:
_____ percent

List reasons for arriving at this percentage: _____

_____

_____

_____

What amount must the franchisee spend on local advertising?

Percentage of gross sales: _____ percent or a minimum: $ _____

Must the franchisee enter into cooperative advertising with fellow franchisees? ❑ Yes ❑ No

Explain any limits upon such advertising expenditures: _____

_____

_____

OPERATIONS MANUAL

Will a confidential operations manual be provided to the franchisee? ❑ Yes ❑ No

Describe the areas covered: _____

_____

_____

Day-to-day operations: _____

_____

_____

Marketing: _____

_____

_____

Purchasing: _____

_____

_____

Advertising: _____

_____

_____

Accounting procedures: _____

_____

_____

Hiring of employees: _____

_____

_____

Training of staff: _____

_____

_____

Public relations: _____

_____

_____

Other: _____

_____

_____

FRANCHISE OPERATION

Is the franchisee allowed to sell products or render services other than those designated by the franchisor? ❑ Yes ❑ No

If so, what are the restrictions on the products or services that the franchisee can sell or render?

_____

_____

Amount of supervisory time that a franchisee or approved manager must render for actual on-premises operation of the franchise: _____ hours per week _____ weeks per year

INSURANCE

Most franchisors desire public liability insurance in amounts of $1,000,000 combined single limits for bodily injury and property damage.

Is this satisfactory to your insurance agent for the type of franchise business in question? ❑ Yes ❑ No

Is a fidelity bond insurance requirement of $50,000 necessary and satisfactory? ❑ Yes ❑ No

If not, list the desired policy limits: _____

_____

NON-COMPETITION PROVISIONS

What non-competition restrictions do you desire, if any, including distance from existing franchisees and number of years in which competition is prohibited? _____

_____

_____

OFFICE MANAGEMENT PERSONNEL

Are you agreeable to absentee management? ❏ Yes ❏ No

Do you wish to require that all franchisees' managers and personnel be trained by your personnel?

❏ Yes ❏ No

Do you wish to require that any assignee of the franchise who purchases the business also be trained by you? ❏ Yes ❏ No

TERM AND TRANSFERS

Do you desire to have the franchise agreement last for an infinite amount of time, with the only contingency being that any transfer to third parties, heirs, or relatives be made with the approval of the franchisor as to financial ability and suitability? ❏ Yes ❏ No

If not, do you desire a length of franchise term in number of years, such as 10, 20, or 30? State your suggested term and renewal terms, if any: _____

Do you want a transfer fee payable to the franchisor when a franchisee sells his or her business and transfers it to another party with your approval? ❏ Yes ❏ No

If yes, what transfer fee amount would you like? $ _____

What renewal fee amount? $ _____

FRANCHISEE'S INITIAL INVESTMENT

As best you can, provide the projected amount a franchisee would have to pay to start up a franchise of yours, in each of the following categories:

CATEGORY	AMOUNT
Leasehold improvements	$ _____
Equipment	$ _____
Decor	$ _____
Furnishings	$ _____
Signs	$ _____
Rent* (first and last months)	$ _____
Cash registers	$ _____
Uniforms	$ _____
Opening inventory for three months	$ _____
Working capital necessary to commence or continue operation for one month	$ _____

DEPOSITS

Rental	$ _____
Telephone	$ _____
Electricity	$ _____
Insurance	$ _____
Auto	$ _____
Errors and omissions	$ _____
Fidelity bond	$ _____
Liability	$ _____
Other	
_____	$ _____
_____	$ _____
TOTAL	$ _____

*Average square footage of your franchise premises buildings is _____ sq. ft.

OBLIGATION OF FRANCHISEE TO PURCHASE FROM FRANCHISOR
OR FROM FRANCHISOR'S DESIGNATED SUPPLIER

Describe any obligations of the franchisee to purchase goods or services from you or from your designated supplier. (If the franchisee is required to purchase from a designated supplier, also give the name and address of the supplier, the reason for requiring the purchase from a designated supplier, and a brief description of what must be purchased.) _____

_____

_____

If the franchisee is obligated to purchase goods or services from you or from your designated supplier, will you receive any profit or revenue from such sales? ❑ Yes ❑ No

If such purchases are required, what percent of the franchisee's total requirements of that service or product will constitute purchases from you or your designated supplier? _____ percent

FINANCING ARRANGEMENT

Will you take back promissory notes or carry some paper from the franchisee? ❑ Yes ❑ No

If so, please describe: _____

_____

Franchise Bible

Will you assist the franchisee in securing financing from independent third parties? ❑ Yes ❑ No

If yes, please explain: _____

_____

SERVICES THE FRANCHISOR MAY PROVIDE

Describe any services you may provide although not legally obligated to do so under the franchise agreement. _____

Periodic visits by representatives: _____

_____

Telephone consultation (describe limits on hours of such): _____

_____

Suggested advertising: _____

_____

Other advisory services: _____

_____

PATENTS AND COPYRIGHTS

Describe any patents or copyrights you may offer to the franchisee: _____

_____

_____

PUBLIC FIGURES

Will you provide public figures in promotion of the franchise? ❑ Yes ❑ No

If yes, please explain, providing the names of the public figures, basic arrangement with the public figures, including compensation, duration of the agreement, and general description of the services of the public figure to the franchisee.

Public Figure	Compensation	Duration	Services

ACTUAL AVERAGE, PROJECTED, OR FORECASTED FRANCHISE SALES, PROFITS, OR EARNINGS

Do you wish to provide average, projected, or forecasted franchise sales to potential franchisees? ❏ Yes ❏ No

(If so, your projections must be based on figures, data, and information that is documented and may need to be submitted to the state officials so that the appropriate state agency can determine the feasibility of your forecast.)

If yes, provide a written substantiation showing that such projections will be valid for your franchisees operating in other locations: _____

_____

_____

PROVISION FOR LEGAL FEES

Reasonable Attorney Fee to Prevailing Party

In some states, it is permissible to insert a clause to the effect that if there is a dispute and the matter is brought to arbitration or trial, the prevailing party would be entitled to reasonable attorney fees. This clause on its face seems desirable. However, the downside of the clause is that it may encourage franchisees to bring action since they feel that they will win and that the franchisor will have to pay their attorney fees. In some cases, an attorney may take the franchisee's lawsuit on a contingency basis, figuring that if he or she wins, the franchisor will pay his or her fees. In addition, the courts do not always award all of the attorney fees to the prevailing party. In some cases, the court will order payment of an amount less than the actual amount billed, on the grounds that this is what the courts feel is reasonable, not what the attorney charged.

As a franchisor, do you wish to have a clause inserted which would provide that the prevailing party in any law action or arbitration would have a right to an award for reasonable attorney fees? ❏ Yes ❏ No

ARBITRATION

More and more franchisors are utilizing arbitration to resolve problems between franchisees and franchisors. Arbitration allows the parties to pick knowledgeable arbitrators; this is far less costly and takes considerably less time. An arbitration award cannot be appealed, for all practical purposes, but it can eliminate many of the costly preliminary procedures, such as depositions, interrogatories, motions, etc. Some franchisors prefer not to include arbitration clauses, because they feel that if the franchisee were to go to court, he or she would eventually run out of money because of high court costs and attorney fees for court appearances. However, by the same token, if the franchisor were to have any appreciable number of lawsuits, he or she would also run out of money.

The disadvantage of an arbitration clause is that it is not appealable. However, as a practical matter, appeals are extremely expensive and time-consuming, and only the more financially endowed franchisee can make use of this procedure. In addition, in the majority of appeals, the original decision is upheld.

Do you want to have an arbitration clause in your agreement with your franchisees? ❏ Yes ❏ No

MAXIMUM MULTIPLE FRANCHISE LOCATIONS FOR ONE FRANCHISEE

If a franchisee has the right to purchase more than one franchise, what total number of franchise locations will you allow a franchisee to open in one area? _____

(Some businesses, such as fine restaurants, require almost all of the time and attention of the franchisee and, therefore, allowing additional locations could cause the franchisee to fail. Take this into consideration when answering this question.)

Considerations: _____

_____

OTHER DESIRED CLAUSES

List your thoughts regarding additional clauses that are of particular importance to you and the business you are franchising: _____

_____

_____

_____

The undersigned has prepared the responses to this questionnaire and compiled the above material on behalf of the franchisor.

_____

Date

_____

Signature of party answering questionnaire

_____

Printed or typed name and title of party answering questionnaire

State Franchise Information Guidelines

A LTHOUGH ALL FRANCHISES ARE SUBJECT TO THE FTC REGULATIONS, many states have additional laws governing franchises and similar business opportunities. The information contained in this appendix is a compilation of the available data from those states that have franchise registration laws or business opportunity statutes, or both. Included under each state heading, where applicable, is information on:

- ▶ State franchise and business opportunity statutes;
- ▶ Laws affecting franchise transfers, renewals, and terminations;
- ▶ State franchise law enforcement offices; and
- ▶ State advertising filings and review procedures.

The last two pages of this appendix consist of charts containing information on fees charged by states with franchise registration and business opportunity statutes.

State Guidelines

Use these guidelines only as an initial reference resource. As a prospective franchisor or franchisee, you should consult your own state regarding its laws, especially to request updated instructions and forms for filing a uniform franchise offering circular. Registration states have personnel, usually attorneys, who examine each offering circular submitted.

Remember: Any failure on the part of the franchisor in using, preparing, or filing the required circular could result in censure or penalties. Use this section of the book so you are knowledgeable when you talk to your attorney.

Alabama

Alabama has enacted a Deceptive Trade Practices Act that makes it unlawful to make certain misrepresentations in any franchise, distributorship, and seller-assisted marketing plan. ALA. CODE Section 8-19-1.

Arkansas

Arkansas has a franchise relationship act known as the Franchise Practices Act that doesn't require registration or disclosure, but prohibits termination or nonrenewal of franchisees without good cause and protects franchisees from the wrongful acts of franchisors in the misuse of advertising fees. ARK. STAT. Section 70-807 and ANN. Section 4-72-201 through 4-72-210.

California

California has a Franchise Investment Act, which requires full disclosure and registration by the franchisor. CAL. CORP. CODE Section 31000 to 31516. It should be noted that California has a Seller Assisted Marketing Plan Act, which covers certain types of marketing that are akin to franchising. CAL. CIVIL CODE Section 1812-200 to 1812-221. California's Franchise Relations Act became effective January 1, 1981, and pertains to termination with good cause and prior 180-day notification if the franchisor does not intend to renew a contract. The act further provides for compensation for franchises that have not been renewed but are intended for conversion to company-owned outlets. CAL.BUS. & PROF. CODE Section 20000-20043. Brochures and ads must be submitted in duplicate and avoid any statements regarding success, safe investments, unlikelihood of default, or earnings not supported by Item 19 in the disclosure document. The ad must be filed with the Department of Corporations at least three business days prior to publishing the ad.

Connecticut

Connecticut has a Business Opportunity Investment Act that requires registration and disclosure by any person who is engaged in the business of selling or offering for sale a business opportunity. CONN. GEN. STAT. Title 36, Ch. 662a, Section 36b-60 through 36b-80. Connecticut also has a Franchise Termination Act that requires good cause for nonrenewal or termination of franchises. CONN. GEN. STAT. Section 42-133e through 42-133g.

Delaware

Delaware has a Franchise Security Law that is a franchisee-franchisor relationship statute requiring good cause for terminations and nonrenewals of franchises. DEL. CODE ANN. Title 6, Section 2551 through 2556.

Florida

Florida's Business Opportunity Act provides for filing, full disclosure, and securing an advertising number. Under certain conditions, an exception from filing can be secured. Certain misrepresentations are prohibited. FLA. STAT. 1995, Ch. 817, Section 559.8 to 559.815, effective Oct. 1, 1998. The Florida Franchise Misrepresentation Act pertains to misrepresentation by franchisors. FLA. STAT. Section 817.416.

Georgia

Georgia has a Business Opportunity Statute pertaining to fraudulent and deceptive practices in the sale of business opportunities. A disclosure must be provided in multilevel distributions. GA. CODE ANN. Section 10-1-410 through 10-1-417.

Hawaii

Hawaii has a Franchise Investment Law pertaining to filing an application and disclosure. HAW. REV. STAT. Section 482E.1 through 482E.5. Hawaii also has a Franchise Rights and Prohibitions Act regarding prohibited actions and good cause requirements for non-renewals and terminations and an antidiscrimination provision in regard to charges made for royalties, goods, services, equipment, rentals, and advertising services unless made at different times and in different circumstances. HAW. REV. STAT. Section 482E. Hawaii does not review advertising.

Illinois

Illinois has a Franchise Disclosure Act that regulates full disclosure, registration, good cause termination, and nonrenewal provisions. ILL. COMP. STATS. 1992, Ch. 815, Section 705/19 through 705/44. Illinois has a Business Opportunity Sales Law of 1995. Illinois Laws of 1995, Public Act 89-209; ILL. COMP. STATS. 1996, Ch. 815, Section 60215-1 to 60215-135. (See also Illinois [815 IL CS 705/20].) Illinois does not require a franchisor to amend its registration when a negotiated change is made unless it is a material change and will be applied in subsequent sales of franchises.

Indiana

Indiana has a Registration Disclosure Statute in addition to a Deceptive Franchise Practices Act (IND. CODE 23-2-217) affecting good cause on nonrenewals and 90-day termination notices. IND. CODE 23-2-2.5-1 to 51. See Business Opportunity Transaction, IND. CODE, Title 24, Art. 5, Ch. 8, Section 1-21 (Par. # 5138.19). Section 23-2-2.5-25 requires advertising copy to be filed with the commission at least five business days prior to first publication.

Iowa

Iowa has two franchise acts: the 1992 Act applies to agreements prior to July 1, 2000 (1992 Act) and the 2000 Act applies to agreements after July 1, 2000 (Section 537 A.10), covering transfers, encroachments, good-cause terminations, good-cause nonrenewals, and a duty of good faith performance. IOWA CODE (2003), Title XIII, Section 523B and 523B 13 and 523H, Section 523H.1 through 523 H.17.

Kentucky

Kentucky has a Business Opportunity Disclosure Act calling for registration of nonexempt offerings. KY. REV. STAT. Section 367.801 et seq. and 367.990.

Louisiana

Louisiana has a Business Opportunity Law that does not provide for filing, but a surety bond is required in certain instances. LA. REV. STAT. Section 51:1801 through 51:1804.

Maine

Maine has a Business Opportunity Act that includes registration of nonexempt offerings and disclosure requirements pertaining to the sale of any business opportunity. ME. REV. STAT. ANN. Chapter 69-B, Section 4691 and Chapters 542 and 597 (Sections 4696-4697).

Maryland

Maryland has a Franchise Registration and Disclosure Law regulating franchises. MD. CODE ANN. Bus. Reg. Section 14-201 et seq. to 14-233. Maryland also has an Equity Participation Investment Program Act, passed for the purpose of encouraging and developing franchises in Maryland, and the Maryland Fair Distributorship Act (1993), regarding cancellation or nonrenewal notices, repurchases, and arbitration between a grantor and a distributor. ANN. CODE of Maryland, Title 14, Section 14-101 through 14-129, Section 14-201 through 14-233, Article of Commercial Law, Title 11, Section 11-1301 through 11-1306.

Michigan

Michigan has a Franchise Investment Law that includes good cause for termination and renewal provision laws and repurchase requirements for nonrenewals. MICH. COMP. LAWS Section 445.1527(c). It also has a Business Opportunity Act requiring a notice filing (MICH. COMP. LAWS Section 445.901 through 445.922) and a Void and Unenforceable Provisions Law (MICH. COMP. LAWS Section 445.1527). See MICH. COMP. LAWS Section 445.1525.

Minnesota

Minnesota has a Franchise Registration and Full Disclosure Act that also covers business opportunities in addition to a Pyramid and Unfair Practice Act and requires good cause for terminations and 90 days' prior written notice with a 60-day cure period for nonrenewals. MINN. STAT. Section 80C.01 et seq. to 80C.22. It has an antidiscrimination provision and ads must be filed five business days prior to the first publication.

Mississippi

Mississippi's Franchise Termination Statute also includes provisions regarding profit projections and misrepresenting earnings. Take special notice of the Repurchase of Inventory from Retailers upon Termination of Contract Statute and required 90-day written nonrenewal and termination notices. MISS. CODE ANN. Section 75-24-51 to 75-24-61.

Missouri

Missouri's statute prohibits termination without notice, requires a nonrenewal written 90-day notice, and includes a Pyramid Sales Statute. MO. REV. STAT. Section 407.400 through 407.410, 407.420.

Nebraska

Nebraska's Franchise Practice Act has provisions regarding 60 days' prior written notice and good cause for non-renewals and terminations. NEB. REV. STAT. Section 87-401 through 87-410. In addition, it has a Business Practice Act that is, in essence, a seller-assisted marketing plans act. NEB. REV. STAT. Section 59-1701 through 59-1761.

New Hampshire

New Hampshire has a Distributor Disclosure Act. N.H. REV. STAT. ANN. Section 339-C1 through 339-C9 and Section 358-E1 through 358-E6.

New Jersey

New Jersey has a Franchise Practice Act requiring 60 days prior written notice and good cause for terminations, cancellations, and nonrenewals. N.J. REV. STAT. Section 56:10-1 through 56:10-12.

New York

New York's Franchise Registration and Disclosure Statute became effective January 1, 1981, N.Y. GEN. BUS. LAW Section 680 through 695, Laws of 1989 Ch. 61 approved effective April 1, 1989. Franchisors are free to negotiate with prospective franchisees.

North Carolina

North Carolina's Business Opportunities Disclosure Law requires filing two copies of the disclosure statement that are nonexempt offerings with the secretary of state. N.C. GEN. STAT. Section 66.94 to 66-100.

North Dakota

North Dakota's Franchise Investment Law governs registration, full disclosure, termination, and renewal of provisions. N.D. CENT. CODE ANN. Section 51.19.01 through Section 51.19.17.

Ohio

Ohio has a non-filing Business Opportunity Act requiring a disclosure be provided to prospective purchasers. OHIO REV. CODE Section 13340.01 through 1334.15 and 1334.99.

Oklahoma

Oklahoma's Business Opportunity Sales Act requires registration of nonexempt offerings. OKLA. STAT. Section 71-4-801 through 828.

Oregon

Oregon's Franchise Transactions Statute requires full disclosure but does not require registration. OR. REV. STAT. Section 650.005 through 650.085. It also has a little FTC Act prohibiting certain misrepresentation actions. OR. REV. STAT. Section 646.605. No advertising filing is required.

Rhode Island

Rhode Island's Franchise Distributor Investment Regulation Act requires the franchisor to fully disclose and register. R.I. GEN. LAWS Section 19-28-1 through 19-28.1-34. Franchisors can negotiate changes with prospective franchisees and ads must be filed three business days prior to first publication.

South Carolina

South Carolina's Business Opportunity Sales Act requires filing a disclosure with the secretary of state. S.C. CODE Section 39-57-10 to 39-57-80.

South Dakota

South Dakota's Franchises for Brand-Name Goods and Services Law requires registration and full disclosure. S.D. CODIFIED LAWS ANN. Section 37-5A-1 through 37-5A-87. Its Business Opportunity Statute requires filing of business opportunities. S.D. CODIFIED LAWS ANN. Section 37-25A-1 through 37-25A-54.

Texas

Texas has a Business Opportunity Act requiring registration unless the offering is exempt as a franchise offering and a notice of exemption is filed with the secretary of state. TEX. BUS. & COM. CODE, Title 4, Ch. 41, Section 41.001 through 41.303. (See Section 97.21.)

Utah

Utah has a Business Opportunity Disclosure Act in which it refers to "assisted marketing plans" and requires filing of nonexempt offerings. A notice of claim for exception can be filed with a fee. UTAH CODE ANN. Section 13-15-1 through 13-15-6.

Virginia

Virginia has a Retail Franchise Act that requires disclosure and registration (VA. CODE Section 13.1-557 through 13.1-574) and a Business Opportunity Law that does not require registration (VA. CODE Section 59.1-262 through 59.1-269). It also has a statute requiring good cause for cancellation (VA. CODE Section 13.1-564) and it gives the franchisee the right to negotiate changes.

Washington

Washington has a Franchise Investment Protection Act, which requires full disclosure and registration (WASH. REV. CODE Section 19.100.10 through 19.100.940), as well as provisions regarding renewal with buyout compensation and good cause termination (WASH. REV. CODE Section 19.100.180 and 19.100.190). It also has a Business Opportunity Fraud Act requiring registration (WASH. REV. CODE Section 19.110.010 through 19.100.930).

Washington, DC

D.C. Franchising Act, D.C. CODE ANN. Section 29-1201, requires good cause for terminations, cancellations, failure to renew, or failure to consent to a transfer with a required 60-day cure period. D.C. has an antidiscrimination provision and franchisors can renegotiate if initiated by the franchisees.

Wisconsin

Wisconsin's Franchise Investment Law requires annual registration by notification on a prescribed form and full disclosure. WIS. STAT. Section 553.01 through 553.78. Its Fair Dealership Law requires "good cause" in order to terminate or fail to renew. WIS. STAT. Section 135.01 to 135.07.

United States

The Federal Trade Commission (FTC) has a general disclosure act covering franchises (Rule 436.1, which was the subject of "Amended Rule" release January 2, 2007, sometimes referred to as "New FTC Rule"). No registration is required (16 C.F.R. Part 436).

Note: All states are subject to the FTC Act whether or not they have franchise or business opportunity statutes. The FTC does not require registration of the FTC disclosure. A copy of the FTC requirements for the content of a disclosure document is in Appendix G.

Filing Fees of Franchise Registration States

State	Initial Filing	Renewal	Post-Effective Amendment	Exemption Notice	Exemption Notice Renewal
California	$675	$450	$50	$450	$150
Hawaii	$250	$250	N/A	$250	N/A
Illinois	$500	$100	$25/$100	N/A	N/A
Indiana	$500	$250	$50	$250	N/A
Maryland	$500	$250	$100	$250	$0
Michigan	$250	$0	$0		
Minnesota	$400	$200	$100	N/A	N/A
New York	$750	$150	$150	$0	$0
North Dakota	$250	$100	$50	$100	$50
Oregon	(No registration but statute dictates type of disclosure document and contracts to be used)				
Rhode Island	$600	$300	$120	$360	$0
South Dakota	$250	$150	$100	N/A	N/A
Virginia	$500	$250 + $50 if changes made	$100	$100	N/A
Washington	$600	$100	$100	$100	N/A
Wisconsin	$400	$0	$200	$200	$0

Business Opportunity Registration Fees

State	Reg. Fee	Renewal Fee	Amendment Fee	Exemption
Alabama	No registration			
California	$100	$100	$30	
Connecticut	$400	$100	$0	
Florida	$300	$300	$50	$100
Georgia	No registration			
Indiana	$50	$10	$10	
Iowa	$500	$250	$0	$100
Kentucky	$0	$0	$0	
Louisiana	$0	$0	$0	
Maine	$25	$10	$0	
Maryland	$250	$100	$50	
Michigan	$0	$0	$0	
Minnesota	See General Franchise Law Fee			
Nebraska	$100	$50	$50	$100
New Hampshire	$0	$0	$0	
North Carolina	$10			
Ohio	$0	$0	$0	
Oklahoma	$250	$150	$0	
South Carolina	$100	$0	$0	
South Dakota	$100	$50	$0	
Texas	$195	$25	$25	$25
Utah	$0	$0	$0	
Virginia	$0	$0	$0	
Washington	$200	$125	$30	

Directory of State and Federal Agencies

L ISTED HERE ARE THE NAMES, ADDRESSES, AND TELEPHONE NUMBERS of state and federal agency personnel responsible for franchising disclosure/registration laws and selected business opportunity laws. Entries for Alberta and the Federal Trade Commission appear at the end of the list, along with the membership roster of the NASAA Franchise and Business Opportunities Committee.

California

Department of Corporations
Los Angeles
320 W. 4th St. Ste. 750
Los Angeles, CA 90013-2344
(213) 576-7500
Toll free: (866) 275-2677
www.corp.ca.gov

Sacramento

1515 K St., Ste. 200
Sacramento, CA 95814-4052
(916) 455-7205
Toll free: (866) 275-2677

San Diego

1350 Front St., Rm. 2034
San Diego, CA 92101-3697
(619) 525-4233
Toll free: (866) 275-2677

San Francisco

One Sansome St., Ste. 600
San Francisco, CA 94105-4428
(415) 972-8565
Toll free: (866) 275-2677

Connecticut

Connecticut Banking Commissioner
Department of Banking
Securities & Shop Investments Division
260 Constitution Plz.
Hartford, CT 06103-1800
(860) 240-8299
Toll free: (800) 832-7255
www.ct.gov/dob/

Florida

Department of Agriculture and Consumer
Services
Division of Consumer Services
2005 Apalachee Pkwy
Tallahassee, FL 32399
(850) 410-3800
Toll free: (800) 435-7352
www.800helpfla.com

Hawaii

Commissioner of Securities
Department of Commerce and Consumer Affairs
King Kalakaua Bldg
335 Merchant St., Rm. 205
Honolulu, HI 96813
(808) 586-2744
www.hawaii.gov/dcca/sec

Illinois

Illinois Attorney General
500 S. Second St.
Springfield, IL 62706
(217) 782-1090
www.illinoisattorneygeneral.gov

Indiana

Secretary of State
Securities Division
302 W. Washington St., Rm. E-111
Indianapolis, IN 46204

(317) 232-6681
www.in.gov/sos/business/index.htm

Iowa

Iowa Insurance Division
Iowa Securities Bureau
330 Maple St.
Des Moines, IA 50319-0065
(515) 281-5705
Toll free: (877) 955-1212
www.iid.state.ia.us/securities

Kentucky

Office of the Attorney General
Consumer Protection Division
Attn: Shop Opportunity
Capitol Ste. 118
700 Capitol Ave.
Frankfort, KY 40601-3499
(502) 696 5389
Toll free: (888) 432-9257
www.Ag.ky.gov/civil/consumerprotection/

Maine

Department of Professional and Financial
Regulations
Bureau of Banking
Securities Division
121 State House Sta.
Augusta, ME 04333
(207) 624-8551
Toll free: (877) 624-8551
www.investors.maine.gov/

Maryland

Maryland Division of Securities
200 St. Paul Pl., 20th Fl.
Baltimore, MD 21202
(410) 576-6360
Toll free: (888) 743-0073
www.oag.state.md.us/securities/

Michigan

Department of Attorney General
Consumer Protection Division,
Franchise Unit
525 Ottawa St.
G. Mennen Williams Bldg, 1st Fl.
Lansing, MI 48909
(517) 373-7117
www.michigan.gov/ag

Minnesota

Minnesota Department of Commerce
Market Assurance Division
85 E. 7th Place, Ste. 500
St. Paul, MN 55101-2198
(651) 296-4026 www.sos.state.mn.us

Nebraska

Department of Banking and Finance
Commerce Court Ste. 400
1230 O St.
Lincoln, NE 68509-5006
(402) 471-2171
www.ndbf.ne.gov

New York

Bureau of Investor Protection and
Securities
New York State Department of Law
120 Broadway, 23rd Fl.
New York, NY 10271
(212) 416-8236
www.ag.ny.gov/burea/investor-
protection-bureau

North Carolina

Secretary of State
Securities Division
Old Revenue Complex
2 S. Salisbury St.
Raleigh, NC 27601-2903

(919) 733-3924
www.secretary.state.nc.us/sec

North Dakota

Office of Securities Commissioner
State Capitol – 5th Fl.
600 E. Blvd.
Bismarck, ND 58505-0510
(701) 328-2946
Toll free: (800) 297-5124
www.ndsecurities.com

Oregon

Department of Consumer and Business
Services
Division of Finance and Corporate
Securities
350 Winter St. NE, Rm. 410
Salem, OR 97301-3881
(503) 378-4140
www.cbs.state.or.us/external/dfcs/
securities.html

Rhode Island

Department of Banking and Business
Administration
John O. Pastore Complex
1511 Pontiac Ave.
Building 69, First Fl.
Cranston, RI 02920
(401) 462-9500
www.dbr.ri.gov

South Carolina

Office of Secretary of State
1205 Pendleton St.
Edgar Brown Bldg., Ste. 525
Columbia, SC 29201
(803) 734-2170
www.scsos.com

South Dakota

Department of Labor and Regulation
Division of Securities
445 E. Capitol Ave.
Pierre, SD 57501-3185
(605) 773-4823
http://dlr.sd.gov/securities/

Texas

Office of Secretary of State
Registrations Unit
P.O. Box 13350
James Earl Rudder Office Building
1019 Brazos Street, 5th Floor
Austin, Texas 78701
512) 463-5705.
www.sos.state.tx.us

Utah

Utah Department of Commerce
Division of Consumer Protection
160 E. 300 S.
P.O. Box 146704
Salt Lake City, UT 84114-6704
(801) 530-6601
Toll free: (800) 721-SAFE
consumerprotection.utah.gov/

Virginia

State Corporation Commission
Division of Securities and Retail Franchising
Tyler Building, 9th Fl.
1300 E. Main St.
Richmond, VA 23219
(804) 371-9051
Toll free: (800) 552-7945
www.scc.virginia.gov/srf/

Washington

Department of Financial Institutions
Securities Division

P.O. Box 9033
150 Israel Rd. SW
Tumwater, WA 98501
(360) 902-8760
www.dfi.wa.gov/sd/

Wisconsin

Department of Financial Institutions
Division of Securities 4th Fl.
P.O. Box 1768
Madison, WI 53701-1768
(608) 266-8557www.wdfi.org/fi/securities

Federal Trade Commission

Bureau of Consumer Protection
Division of Marketing Practices
600 Pennsylvania Ave. NW
Washington, DC 20580
(202) 326-3128
www.ftc.gov/bcp/bcpmp.shtm

Canada

Alberta

Government of Alberta
Consumer Programs
3B Commerce Plc.
10155 102 St.
Edmonton, AB T5J-4L4
(780) 422-8166
www.servicealberta.ca/consumer_info.cfm

Ontario

Ministry of Government Services
8th Fl., Ferguson Block
77 Wellesley St. W.
Toronto, Ontario M7A 1N3
(416) 326-8881
www.mgs.gov.on.ca/en/index.html

Amended FTC Rule Regarding Contents of a Disclosure Document

T HE FOLLOWING IS THE AMENDED FEDERAL TRADE COMMISSION guidelines that set forth the requirements for what must be included in a franchise disclosure document. For examples of the tables and charts required by the FTC rule, refer to the sample disclosure document in Appendix A.

CODE OF FEDERAL REGULATIONS › TITLE 16 › CHAPTER I › SUBCHAPTER D › PART 436 ›

Subpart C
§ 436.3 Cover Page

Begin the disclosure document with a cover page, in the order and form as follows:

(a) The title "FRANCHISE DISCLOSURE DOCUMENT" in capital letters and bold type.
(b) The franchisor's name, type of business organization, principal business address, telephone number, and, if applicable, email address and primary home page address.
(c) A sample of the primary business trademark that the franchisee will use in its business.

(d) A brief description of the franchised business.

(e) The following statements:

(1) The total investment necessary to begin operation of a [franchise system name] franchise is [the total amount of Item 7 (§ 436.5(g))]. This includes [the total amount in Item 5 (§ 436.5(e))] that must be paid to the franchisor or affiliate.

(2) This disclosure document summarizes certain provisions of your franchise agreement and other information in plain English. Read this disclosure document and all accompanying agreements carefully. You must receive this disclosure document at least 14 calendar-days before you sign a binding agreement with, or make any payment to, the franchisor or an affiliate in connection with the proposed franchise sale. [The following sentence in bold type] **Note, however, that no governmental agency has verified the information contained in this document**.

(3) The terms of your contract will govern your franchise relationship. Don't rely on the disclosure document alone to understand your contract. Read all of your contract carefully. Show your contract and this disclosure document to an advisor, like a lawyer or an accountant.

(4) Buying a franchise is a complex investment. The information in this disclosure document can help you make up your mind. More information on franchising, such as "A Consumer's Guide to Buying a Franchise," which can help you understand how to use this disclosure document, is available from the Federal Trade Commission. You can contact the FTC at 1-877-FTC-HELP1-877-FTC-HELP or by writing to the FTC at 600 Pennsylvania Avenue, NW., Washington, DC 20580. You can also visit the FTC's home page at www.ftc.gov for additional information. Call your state agency or visit your public library for other sources of information on franchising.

(5) There may also be laws on franchising in your state. Ask your state agencies about them.

(6) [The issuance date].

(f) A franchisor may include the following statement between the statements set out at paragraphs (e)(2) and (3) of this section: "You may wish to receive your disclosure document in another format that is more convenient for you. To discuss the availability of disclosures in different formats, contact [name or office] at [address] and [telephone number]."

(g) Franchisors may include additional disclosures on the cover page, on a separate cover page, or addendum to comply with state pre-sale disclosure laws.

§ 436.4 Table of Contents

Include the following table of contents. State the page where each disclosure Item begins. List all exhibits by letter, as shown in the following example.

Table of Contents

1. The Franchisor and any Parents, Predecessors, and Affiliates
2. Business Experience

3. Litigation
4. Bankruptcy
5. Initial Fees
6. Other Fees
7. Estimated Initial Investment
8. Restrictions on Sources of Products and Services
9. Franchisee's Obligations
10. Financing
11. Franchisor's Assistance, Advertising, Computer Systems, and Training
12. Territory
13. Trademarks
14. Patents, Copyrights, and Proprietary Information
15. Obligation to Participate in the Actual Operation of the Franchise Business
16. Restrictions on What the Franchisee May Sell
17. Renewal, Termination, Transfer, and Dispute Resolution
18. Public Figures
19. Financial Performance Representations
20. Outlets and Franchisee Information
21. Financial Statements
22. Contracts
23. Receipts
    Exhibits

A. FRANCHISE AGREEMENT

§ 436.5 Disclosure Items

(a) *Item 1: The Franchisor, and any Parents, Predecessors, and Affiliates.*
Disclose:

(1) The name and principal business address of the franchisor; any parents; and any affiliates that offer franchises in any line of business or provide products or services to the franchisees of the franchisor.

(2) The name and principal business address of any predecessors during the 10-year period immediately before the close of the franchisor's most recent fiscal year.

(3) The name that the franchisor uses and any names it intends to use to conduct business.

(4) The identity and principal business address of the franchisor's agent for service of process.

(5) The type of business organization used by the franchisor (for example, corporation, partnership) and the state in which it was organized.

(6) The following information about the franchisor's business and the franchises offered:

(i) Whether the franchisor operates businesses of the type being franchised.

(ii) The franchisor's other business activities.

(iii) The business the franchisee will conduct.

(iv) The general market for the product or service the franchisee will offer. In describing the general market, consider factors such as whether the market is developed or developing, whether the goods will be sold primarily to a certain group, and whether sales are seasonal.

(v) In general terms, any laws or regulations specific to the industry in which the franchise business operates.

(vi) A general description of the competition.

(7) The prior business experience of the franchisor; any predecessors listed in § 436.5(a)(2) of this part; and any affiliates that offer franchises in any line of business or provide products or services to the franchisees of the franchisor, including:

(i) The length of time each has conducted the type of business the franchisee will operate.

(ii) The length of time each has offered franchises providing the type of business the franchisee will operate.

(iii) Whether each has offered franchises in other lines of business. If so, include:

(A) A description of each other line of business.
(B) The number of franchises sold in each other line of business.
(C) The length of time each has offered franchises in each other line of business.

(b) *Item 2: Business Experience.* Disclose by name and position the franchisor's directors, trustees, general partners, principal officers, and any other individuals who will have management responsibility relating to the sale or operation of franchises offered by this document. For each person listed in this section, state his or her principal positions and employers during the past five years, including each position's starting date, ending date, and location.

(c) *Item 3: Litigation.*

(1) Disclose whether the franchisor; a predecessor; a parent or affiliate who induces franchise sales by promising to back the franchisor financially or otherwise guarantees the franchisor's performance; an affiliate who offers franchises under the franchisor's principal trademark; and any person identified in § 436.5(b) of this part:

(i) Has pending against that person:

(A) An administrative, criminal, or material civil action alleging a violation of a franchise, antitrust, or securities law, or alleging fraud, unfair or deceptive practices, or comparable allegations.

(B) Civil actions, other than ordinary routine litigation incidental to the business, which are material in the context of the number of franchisees and the size, nature, or financial condition of the franchise system or its business operations.

(ii) Was a party to any material civil action involving the franchise relationship in the last fiscal year. For purposes of this section, "franchise relationship" means contractual obligations between the franchisor and franchisee directly relating to the operation of the franchised business (such as royalty payment and training obligations). It does not include actions involving suppliers or other third parties, or indemnification for tort liability.

(iii) Has in the 10-year period immediately before the disclosure document's issuance date:

(A) Been convicted of or pleaded nolo contendere to a felony charge.

(B) Been held liable in a civil action involving an alleged violation of a franchise, antitrust, or securities law, or involving allegations of fraud, unfair or deceptive practices, or comparable allegations. "Held liable" means that, as a result of claims or counterclaims, the person must pay money or other consideration, must reduce an indebtedness by the amount of an award, cannot enforce its rights, or must take action adverse to its interests.

(2) Disclose whether the franchisor; a predecessor; a parent or affiliate who guarantees the franchisor's performance; an affiliate who has offered or sold franchises in any line of business within the last 10 years; or any other person identified in § 436.5(b) of this part is subject to a currently effective injunctive or restrictive order or decree resulting from a pending or concluded action brought by a public agency and relating to the franchise or to a Federal, State, or Canadian franchise, securities, antitrust, trade regulation, or trade practice law.

(3) For each action identified in paragraphs (c)(1) and (2) of this section, state the title, case number or citation, the initial filing date, the names of the parties, the forum, and the relationship of the opposing party to the franchisor (for example, competitor, supplier, lessor, franchisee, former franchisee, or class of franchisees). Except as provided in paragraph (c)(4) of this section, summarize the legal and factual nature of each claim in the action, the relief sought or obtained, and any conclusions of law or fact.[1] In addition, state:

(i) For pending actions, the status of the action.

(ii) For prior actions, the date when the judgment was entered and any damages or settlement terms.[2]

(iii) For injunctive or restrictive orders, the nature, terms, and conditions of the order or decree.

(iv) For convictions or pleas, the crime or violation, the date of conviction, and the sentence or penalty imposed.

(4) For any other franchisor-initiated suit identified in paragraph (c)(1)(ii) of this section, the franchisor may comply with the requirements of paragraphs (c)(3)(i) through (iv) of this

---

[1] Franchisors may include a summary opinion of counsel concerning any action if counsel consent to use the summary opinion and the full opinion is attached to the disclosure document.

[2] If a settlement agreement must be disclosed in this Item, all material settlement terms must be disclosed, whether or not the agreement is confidential. However, franchisors need not disclose the terms of confidential settlements entered into before commencing franchise sales. Further, any franchisor who has historically used only the Franchise Rule format, or who is new to franchising, need not disclose confidential settlements entered prior to the effective date of this rule.

section by listing individual suits under one common heading that will serve as the case summary (for example, "royalty collection suits").

(d) *Item 4: Bankruptcy.*

(1) Disclose whether the franchisor; any parent; predecessor; affiliate; officer, or general partner of the franchisor, or any other individual who will have management responsibility relating to the sale or operation of franchises offered by this document, has, during the 10-year period immediately before the date of this disclosure document:

    (i) Filed as debtor (or had filed against it) a petition under the United States Bankruptcy Code ("Bankruptcy Code").

    (ii) Obtained a discharge of its debts under the Bankruptcy Code.

    (iii) Been a principal officer of a company or a general partner in a partnership that either filed as a debtor (or had filed against it) a petition under the Bankruptcy Code, or that obtained a discharge of its debts under the Bankruptcy Code while, or within one year after, the officer or general partner held the position in the company.

(2) For each bankruptcy, state:

    (i) The current name, address, and principal place of business of the debtor.

    (ii) Whether the debtor is the franchisor. If not, state the relationship of the debtor to the franchisor (for example, affiliate, officer).

    (iii) The date of the original filing and the material facts, including the bankruptcy court, and the case name and number. If applicable, state the debtor's discharge date, including discharges under Chapter 7 and confirmation of any plans of reorganization under Chapters 11 and 13 of the Bankruptcy Code.

(3) Disclose cases, actions, and other proceedings under the laws of foreign nations relating to bankruptcy.

(e) *Item 5: Initial Fees.* Disclose the initial fees and any conditions under which these fees are refundable. If the initial fees are not uniform, disclose the range or formula used to calculate the initial fees paid in the fiscal year before the issuance date and the factors that determined the amount. For this section, "initial fees" means all fees and payments, or commitments to pay, for services or goods received from the franchisor or any affiliate before the franchisee's business opens, whether payable in lump sum or installments. Disclose installment payment terms in this section or in § 436.5(j) of this part.

(f) *Item 6: Other Fees.* Disclose, in the following tabular form, all other fees that the franchisee must pay to the franchisor or its affiliates, or that the franchisor or its affiliates impose or collect in whole or in part for a third party. State the title "OTHER FEES" in capital letters using bold type. Include any formula used to compute the fees.[3]

---

[3] If fees may increase, disclose the formula that determines the increase or the maximum amount of the increase. For example, a percentage of gross sales is acceptable if the franchisor defines the term "gross sales."

Item 6 Table			
OTHER FEES			
Column 1 Type of Fee	Column 2 Amount	Column 3 Due Date	Column 4 Remarks

(1) In column 1, list the type of fee (for example, royalties, and fees for lease negotiations, construction, remodeling, additional training or assistance, advertising, advertising cooperatives, purchasing cooperatives, audits, accounting, inventory, transfers, and renewals).

(2) In column 2, state the amount of the fee.

(3) In column 3, state the due date for each fee.

(4) In column 4, include remarks, definitions, or caveats that elaborate on the information in the table. If remarks are long, franchisors may use footnotes instead of the remarks column. If applicable, include the following information in the remarks column or in a footnote:

   (i) Whether the fees are payable only to the franchisor.

   (ii) Whether the fees are imposed and collected by the franchisor.

   (iii) Whether the fees are non-refundable or describe the circumstances when the fees are refundable.

   (iv) Whether the fees are uniformly imposed.

   (v) The voting power of franchisor-owned outlets on any fees imposed by cooperatives. If franchisor-owned outlets have controlling voting power, disclose the maximum and minimum fees that may be imposed.

(g) *Item 7: Estimated Initial Investment.* Disclose, in the following tabular form, the franchisee's estimated initial investment. State the title "YOUR ESTIMATED INITIAL INVESTMENT" in capital letters using bold type. Franchisors may include additional expenditure tables to show expenditure variations caused by differences such as in site location and premises size.

Item 7 Table:				
YOUR ESTIMATED INITIAL INVESTMENT				
Column 1 Type of Expenditure	Column 2 Amount	Column 3 Method of Payment	Column 4 When Due	Column 5 To Whom Payment Is to be Made
Total				

(1) In column 1:

    (i) List each type of expense, beginning with pre-opening expenses. Include the following expenses, if applicable. Use footnotes to include remarks, definitions, or caveats that elaborate on the information in the Table.

        (A) The initial franchise fee.

        (B) Training expenses.

        (C) Real property, whether purchased or leased.

        (D) Equipment, fixtures, other fixed assets, construction, remodeling, leasehold improvements, and decorating costs, whether purchased or leased.

        (E) Inventory to begin operating.

        (F) Security deposits, utility deposits, business licenses, and other prepaid expenses.

    (ii) List separately and by name any other specific required payments (for example, additional training, travel, or advertising expenses) that the franchisee must make to begin operations.

    (iii) Include a category titled "Additional funds – [initial period]" for any other required expenses the franchisee will incur before operations begin and during the initial period of operations. State the initial period. A reasonable initial period is at least three months or a reasonable period for the industry. Describe in general terms the factors, basis, and experience that the franchisor considered or relied upon in formulating the amount required for additional funds.

(2) In column 2, state the amount of the payment. If the amount is unknown, use a low-high range based on the franchisor's current experience. If real property costs cannot be estimated in a low-high range, describe the approximate size of the property and building and the probable location of the building (for example, strip shopping center, mall, downtown, rural, or highway).

(3) In column 3, state the method of payment.

(4) In column 4, state the due date.

(5) In column 5, state to whom payment will be made.

(6) Total the initial investment, incorporating ranges of fees, if used.

(7) In a footnote, state:

    (i) Whether each payment is non-refundable, or describe the circumstances when each payment is refundable.

    (ii) If the franchisor or an affiliate finances part of the initial investment, the amount that it will finance, the required down payment, the annual interest rate, rate factors, and the estimated loan repayments. Franchisors may refer to § 436.5(j) of this part for additional details.

(h) *Item 8: Restrictions on Sources of Products and Services.* Disclose the franchisee's obligations to purchase or lease goods, services, supplies, fixtures, equipment, inventory, computer hardware and software, real estate, or comparable items related to establishing or operating the franchised business either from the franchisor, its designee, or suppliers approved by the franchisor, or under the franchisor's specifications. Include obligations to purchase imposed by the franchisor's written agreement or by the franchisor's practice.[4] For each applicable obligation, state:

(1) The good or service required to be purchased or leased.

(2) Whether the franchisor or its affiliates are approved suppliers or the only approved suppliers of that good or service.

(3) Any supplier in which an officer of the franchisor owns an interest.

(4) How the franchisor grants and revokes approval of alternative suppliers, including:

    (i)   Whether the franchisor's criteria for approving suppliers are available to franchisees.

    (ii) Whether the franchisor permits franchisees to contract with alternative suppliers who meet the franchisor's criteria.

    (iii) Any fees and procedures to secure approval to purchase from alternative suppliers.

    (iv) The time period in which the franchisee will be notified of approval or disapproval.

    (v) How approvals are revoked.

(5) Whether the franchisor issues specifications and standards to franchisees, subfranchisees, or approved suppliers. If so, describe how the franchisor issues and modifies specifications.

(6) Whether the franchisor or its affiliates will or may derive revenue or other material consideration from required purchases or leases by franchisees. If so, describe the precise basis by which the franchisor or its affiliates will or may derive that consideration by stating:

    (i)   The franchisor's total revenue.[5]

    (ii) The franchisor's revenues from all required purchases and leases of products and services.

    (iii) The percentage of the franchisor's total revenues that are from required purchases or leases.

    (iv) If the franchisor's affiliates also sell or lease products or services to franchisees, the affiliates' revenues from those sales or leases.

(7) The estimated proportion of these required purchases and leases by the franchisee to all purchases and leases by the franchisee of goods and services in establishing and operating the franchised businesses.

(8) If a designated supplier will make payments to the franchisor from franchisee purchases, disclose the basis for the payment (for example, specify a percentage or a flat amount). For

---

[4] Franchisors may include the reason for the requirement. Franchisors need not disclose in this Item the purchase or lease of goods or services provided as part of the franchise without a separate charge (such as initial training, if the cost is included in the franchise fee). Describe such fees in Item 5 of this section. Do not disclose fees already described in § 436.5(f) of this part.

[5] Take figures from the franchisor's most recent annual audited financial statement required in § 436.5(u) of this part. If audited statements are not yet required, or if the entity deriving the income is an affiliate, disclose the sources of information used in computing revenues.

purposes of this disclosure, a "payment" includes the sale of similar goods or services to the franchisor at a lower price than to franchisees.

(9) The existence of purchasing or distribution cooperatives.

(10) Whether the franchisor negotiates purchase arrangements with suppliers, including price terms, for the benefit of franchisees.

(11) Whether the franchisor provides material benefits (for example, renewal or granting additional franchises) to a franchisee based on a franchisee's purchase of particular products or services or use of particular suppliers.

(i) *Item 9: Franchisee's Obligations*. Disclose, in the following tabular form, a list of the franchisee's principal obligations. State the title "FRANCHISEE'S OBLIGATIONS" in capital letters using bold type. Cross-reference each listed obligation with any applicable section of the franchise or other agreement and with the relevant disclosure document provision. If a particular obligation is not applicable, state "Not Applicable." Include additional obligations, as warranted.

Item 9 Table		
FRANCHISEE'S OBLIGATIONS		
This table lists your principal obligations under the franchise and other agreements. It will help you find more detailed information about your obligations in these agreements and in other items of this disclosure document.		
Obligation	**Section in Agreement**	**Disclosure Document Item**
a. Site selection and acquisition/lease		
b. Pre-opening purchase/leases		
c. Site development and other pre-opening requirements		
d. Initial and ongoing training		
e. Opening		
f. Fees		
g. Compliance with standards and policies/operating manual		
h. Trademarks and proprietary information		
i. Restrictions on products/services offered		
j. Warranty and customer service requirements		
k. Territorial development and sales quotas		
l. Ongoing product/service purchases		

Obligation	Section in Agreement	Disclosure Document Item
m. Maintenance, appearance, and remodeling requirements		
n. Insurance		
o. Advertising		
p. Indemnification		
q. Owner's participation/management/ staffing		
r. Records and reports		
s. Inspections and audits		
t. Transfer		
u. Renewal		
v. Post-termination obligations		
w. Non-competition covenants		
x. Dispute resolution		
y. Other (describe)		

(j) *Item 10: Financing.*

(1) Disclose the terms of each financing arrangement, including leases and installment contracts, that the franchisor, its agent, or affiliates offer directly or indirectly to the franchisee.[6] The franchisor may summarize the terms of each financing arrangement in tabular form, using footnotes to provide additional information. For a sample Item 10 table, see Appendix A of this part. For each financing arrangement, state:

(i) What the financing covers (for example, the initial franchise fee, site acquisition, construction or remodeling, initial or replacement equipment or fixtures, opening or ongoing inventory or supplies, or other continuing expenses).[7]

(ii) The identity of each lender providing financing and their relationship to the franchisor (for example, affiliate).

(iii) The amount of financing offered or, if the amount depends on an actual cost that may vary, the percentage of the cost that will be financed.

---

[6] Indirect offers of financing include a written arrangement between a franchisor or its affiliate and a lender, for the lender to offer financing to a franchisee; an arrangement in which a franchisor or its affiliate receives a benefit from a lender in exchange for financing a franchise purchase; and a franchisor's guarantee of a note, lease, or other obligation of the franchisee.

[7] Include sample copies of the financing documents as an exhibit to § 436.5(v) of this part. Cite the section and name of the document containing the financing terms and conditions.

(iv) The rate of interest, plus finance charges, expressed on an annual basis. If the rate of interest, plus finance charges, expressed on an annual basis, may differ depending on when the financing is issued, state what that rate was on a specified recent date.

(v) The number of payments or the period of repayment.

(vi) The nature of any security interest required by the lender.

(vii) Whether a person other than the franchisee must personally guarantee the debt.

(viii) Whether the debt can be prepaid and the nature of any prepayment penalty.

(ix) The franchisee's potential liabilities upon default, including any:

(A) Accelerated obligation to pay the entire amount due;

(B) Obligations to pay court costs and attorney's fees incurred in collecting the debt;

(C) Termination of the franchise; and

(D) Liabilities from cross defaults such as those resulting directly from non-payment, or indirectly from the loss of business property.

(x) Other material financing terms.

(2) Disclose whether the loan agreement requires franchisees to waive defenses or other legal rights (for example, confession of judgment), or bars franchisees from asserting a defense against the lender, the lender's assignee or the franchisor. If so, describe the relevant provisions.

(3) Disclose whether the franchisor's practice or intent is to sell, assign, or discount to a third party all or part of the financing arrangement. If so, state:

(i) The assignment terms, including whether the franchisor will remain primarily obligated to provide the financed goods or services; and

(ii) That the franchisee may lose all its defenses against the lender as a result of the sale or assignment.

(4) Disclose whether the franchisor or an affiliate receives any consideration for placing financing with the lender. If such payments exist:

(i) Disclose the amount or the method of determining the payment; and

(ii) Identify the source of the payment and the relationship of the source to the franchisor or its affiliates.

(k) *Item 11: Franchisor's Assistance, Advertising, Computer Systems, and Training.* Disclose the franchisor's principal assistance and related obligations of both the franchisor and franchisee as follows. For each obligation, cite the section number of the franchise agreement imposing the obligation. Begin by stating the following sentence in bold type: "Except as listed below, [the franchisor] is not required to provide you with any assistance."

(1) Disclose the franchisor's pre-opening obligations to the franchisee, including any assistance in:

(i) Locating a site and negotiating the purchase or lease of the site. If such assistance is provided, state:

    (A) Whether the franchisor generally owns the premises and leases it to the franchisee.

    (B) Whether the franchisor selects the site or approves an area in which the franchisee selects a site. If so, state further whether and how the franchisor must approve a franchisee-selected site.

    (C) The factors that the franchisor considers in selecting or approving sites (for example, general location and neighborhood, traffic patterns, parking, size, physical characteristics of existing buildings, and lease terms).

    (D) The time limit for the franchisor to locate or approve or disapprove the site and the consequences if the franchisor and franchisee cannot agree on a site.

(ii) Conforming the premises to local ordinances and building codes and obtaining any required permits.

(iii) Constructing, remodeling, or decorating the premises.

(iv) Hiring and training employees.

(v) Providing for necessary equipment, signs, fixtures, opening inventory, and supplies. If any such assistance is provided, state:

    (A) Whether the franchisor provides these items directly or only provides the names of approved suppliers.

    (B) Whether the franchisor provides written specifications for these items.

    (C) Whether the franchisor delivers or installs these items.

(2) Disclose the typical length of time between the earlier of the signing of the franchise agreement or the first payment of consideration for the franchise and the opening of the franchisee's business. Describe the factors that may affect the time period, such as ability to obtain a lease, financing or building permits, zoning and local ordinances, weather conditions, shortages, or delayed installation of equipment, fixtures, and signs.

(3) Disclose the franchisor's obligations to the franchisee during the operation of the franchise, including any assistance in:

(i) Developing products or services the franchisee will offer to its customers.

(ii) Hiring and training employees.

(iii) Improving and developing the franchised business.

(iv) Establishing prices.

(v) Establishing and using administrative, bookkeeping, accounting, and inventory control procedures.

(vi) Resolving operating problems encountered by the franchisee.

(4) Describe the advertising program for the franchise system, including the following:

(i) The franchisor's obligation to conduct advertising, including:

    (A) The media the franchisor may use.

    (B) Whether media coverage is local, regional, or national.

(C) The source of the advertising (for example, an in-house advertising department or a national or regional advertising agency).

(D) Whether the franchisor must spend any amount on advertising in the area or territory where the franchisee is located.

(ii) The circumstances when the franchisor will permit franchisees to use their own advertising material.

(iii) Whether there is an advertising council composed of franchisees that advises the franchisor on advertising policies. If so, disclose:

(A) How members of the council are selected.

(B) Whether the council serves in an advisory capacity only or has operational or decision-making power.

(C Whether the franchisor has the power to form, change, or dissolve the advertising council.

(iv) Whether the franchisee must participate in a local or regional advertising cooperative. If so, state:

(A) How the area or membership of the cooperative is defined.

(B) How much the franchisee must contribute to the fund and whether other franchisees must contribute a different amount or at a different rate.

(C Whether the franchisor-owned outlets must contribute to the fund and, if so, whether those contributions are on the same basis as those for franchisees.

(D) Who is responsible for administering the cooperative (for example, franchisor, franchisees, or advertising agency).

(E) Whether cooperatives must operate from written governing documents and whether the documents are available for the franchisee to review.

(F) Whether cooperatives must prepare annual or periodic financial statements and whether the statements are available for review by the franchisee.

(G) Whether the franchisor has the power to require cooperatives to be formed, changed, dissolved, or merged.

(v) Whether the franchisee must participate in any other advertising fund. If so, state:

(A) Who contributes to the fund.

(B) How much the franchisee must contribute to the fund and whether other franchisees must contribute a different amount or at a different rate.

(C) Whether the franchisor-owned outlets must contribute to the fund and, if so, whether it is on the same basis as franchisees.

(D) Who administers the fund.

(E) Whether the fund is audited and when it is audited.

(F) Whether financial statements of the fund are available for review by the franchisee.

(G) How the funds were used in the most recently concluded fiscal year, including the percentages spent on production, media placement, administrative expenses, and a description of any other use.

(vi) If not all advertising funds are spent in the fiscal year in which they accrue, how the franchisor uses the remaining amount, including whether franchisees receive a periodic accounting of how advertising fees are spent.

(vii) The percentage of advertising funds, if any, that the franchisor uses principally to solicit new franchise sales.

(5) Disclose whether the franchisor requires the franchisee to buy or use electronic cash registers or computer systems. If so, describe the systems generally in non-technical language, including the types of data to be generated or stored in these systems, and state the following:

(i) The cost of purchasing or leasing the systems.

(ii) Any obligation of the franchisor, any affiliate, or third party to provide ongoing maintenance, repairs, upgrades, or updates.

(iii) Any obligations of the franchisee to upgrade or update any system during the term of the franchise, and, if so, any contractual limitations on the frequency and cost of the obligation.

(iv) The annual cost of any optional or required maintenance, updating, upgrading, or support contracts.

(v) Whether the franchisor will have independent access to the information that will be generated or stored in any electronic cash register or computer system. If so, describe the information that the franchisor may access and whether there are any contractual limitations on the franchisor's right to access the information.

(6) Disclose the table of contents of the franchisor's operating manual provided to franchisees as of the franchisor's last fiscal year-end or a more recent date. State the number of pages devoted to each subject and the total number of pages in the manual as of this date. This disclosure may be omitted if the franchisor offers the prospective franchisee the opportunity to view the manual before buying the franchise.

(7) Disclose the franchisor's training program as of the franchisor's last fiscal year-end or a more recent date.

(i) Describe the training program in the following tabular form. Title the table "TRAINING PROGRAM" in capital letters and bold type.

Item 11 Table			
TRAINING PROGRAM			
Column 1 Subject	Column 2 Hours of Classroom Training	Column 3 Hours of on-the-Job Training	Column 4 Location

(A) In column 1, state the subjects taught.

(B) In column 2, state the hours of classroom training for each subject.

(C) In column 3, state the hours of on-the-job training for each subject.

(D) In column 4, state the location of the training for each subject.

(ii) State further:

(A) How often training classes are held and the nature of the location or facility where training is held (for example, company, home, office, franchisor-owned store).

(B) The nature of instructional materials and the instructor's experience, including the instructor's length of experience in the field and with the franchisor. State only experience relevant to the subject taught and the franchisor's operations.

(C) Any charges franchisees must pay for training and who must pay travel and living expenses of the training program enrollees.

(D) Who may and who must attend training. State whether the franchisee or other persons must complete the program to the franchisor's satisfaction. If successful completion is required, state how long after signing the agreement or before opening the business the training must be completed. If training is not mandatory, state the percentage of new franchisees that enrolled in the training program during the preceding 12 months.

(E) Whether additional training programs or refresher courses are required.

(l) *Item 12: Territory.*
Disclose:

(1) Whether the franchise is for a specific location or a location to be approved by the franchisor.

(2) Any minimum territory granted to the franchisee (for example, a specific radius, a distance sufficient to encompass a specified population, or another specific designation).

(3) The conditions under which the franchisor will approve the relocation of the franchised business or the franchisee's establishment of additional franchised outlets.

(4) Franchisee options, rights of first refusal, or similar rights to acquire additional franchises.

(5) Whether the franchisor grants an exclusive territory.

(i) If the franchisor does not grant an exclusive territory, state: "You will not receive an exclusive territory. You may face competition from other franchisees, from outlets that we own, or from other channels of distribution or competitive brands that we control."

(ii) If the franchisor grants an exclusive territory, disclose:

(A) Whether continuation of territorial exclusivity depends on achieving a certain sales volume, market penetration, or other contingency, and the circumstances when the franchisee's territory may be altered. Describe any sales or other conditions. State the franchisor's rights if the franchisee fails to meet the requirements.

(B) Any other circumstances that permit the franchisor to modify the franchisee's territorial rights (for example, a population increase in the territory giving the franchisor the right to grant an additional franchise in the area) and the effect of such modifications on the franchisee's rights.

(6) For all territories (exclusive and non-exclusive):

(i) Any restrictions on the franchisor from soliciting or accepting orders from consumers inside the franchisee's territory, including:

(A) Whether the franchisor or an affiliate has used or reserves the right to use other channels of distribution, such as the Internet, catalog sales, telemarketing, or other direct marketing sales, to make sales within the franchisee's territory using the franchisor's principal trademarks.

(B) Whether the franchisor or an affiliate has used or reserves the right to use other channels of distribution, such as the Internet, catalog sales, telemarketing, or other direct marketing, to make sales within the franchisee's territory of products or services under trademarks different from the ones the franchisee will use under the franchise agreement.

(C) Any compensation that the franchisor must pay for soliciting or accepting orders from inside the franchisee's territory.

(ii) Any restrictions on the franchisee from soliciting or accepting orders from consumers outside of his or her territory, including whether the franchisee has the right to use other channels of distribution, such as the Internet, catalog sales, telemarketing, or other direct marketing, to make sales outside of his or her territory.

(iii) If the franchisor or an affiliate operates, franchises, or has plans to operate or franchise a business under a different trademark and that business sells or will sell goods or services similar to those the franchisee will offer, describe:

(A) The similar goods and services.

(B) The different trademark.

(C) Whether outlets will be franchisor owned or operated.

(D) Whether the franchisor or its franchisees who use the different trademark will solicit or accept orders within the franchisee's territory.

(E) The timetable for the plan.

(F) How the franchisor will resolve conflicts between the franchisor and franchisees and between the franchisees of each system regarding territory, customers, and franchisor support.

(G) The principal business address of the franchisor's similar operating business. If it is the same as the franchisor's principal business address stated in § 436.5(a) of this part, disclose whether the franchisor maintains (or plans to maintain) physically separate offices and training facilities for the similar competing business.

(m) *Item 13: Trademarks.*

(1) Disclose each principal trademark to be licensed to the franchisee. For this Item, "principal trademark" means the primary trademarks, service marks, names, logos, and commercial

symbols the franchisee will use to identify the franchised business. It may not include every trademark the franchisor owns.

(2) Disclose whether each principal trademark is registered with the United States Patent and Trademark Office. If so, state:

- (i) The date and identification number of each trademark registration.
- (ii) Whether the franchisor has filed all required affidavits.
- (iii) Whether any registration has been renewed.
- (iv) Whether the principal trademarks are registered on the Principal or Supplemental Register of the United States Patent and Trademark Office.

(3) If the principal trademark is not registered with the United States Patent and Trademark Office, state whether the franchisor has filed any trademark application, including any "intent to use" application or an application based on actual use. If so, state the date and identification number of the application.

(4) If the trademark is not registered on the Principal Register of the United States Patent and Trademark Office, state: "We do not have a federal registration for our principal trademark. Therefore, our trademark does not have many legal benefits and rights as a federally registered trademark. If our right to use the trademark is challenged, you may have to change to an alternative trademark, which may increase your expenses."

(5) Disclose any currently effective material determinations of the United States Patent and Trademark Office, the Trademark Trial and Appeal Board, or any state trademark administrator or court; and any pending infringement, opposition, or cancellation proceeding. Include infringement, opposition, or cancellation proceedings in which the franchisor unsuccessfully sought to prevent registration of a trademark in order to protect a trademark licensed by the franchisor. Describe how the determination affects the ownership, use, or licensing of the trademark.

(6) Disclose any pending material federal or state court litigation regarding the franchisor's use or ownership rights in a trademark. For each pending action, disclose:[8]

- (i) The forum and case number.
- (ii) The nature of claims made opposing the franchisor's use of the trademark or by the franchisor opposing another person's use of the trademark.
- (iii) Any effective court or administrative agency ruling in the matter.

(7) Disclose any currently effective agreements that significantly limit the franchisor's rights to use or license the use of trademarks listed in this section in a manner material to the franchise. For each agreement, disclose:

- (i) The manner and extent of the limitation or grant.

---

[8] The franchisor may include an attorney's opinion relative to the merits of litigation or of an action if the attorney issuing the opinion consents to its use. The text of the disclosure may include a summary of the opinion if the full opinion is attached and the attorney issuing the opinion consents to the use of the summary.

(ii) The extent to which the agreement may affect the franchisee.

(iii) The agreement's duration.

(iv) The parties to the agreement.

(v) The circumstances when the agreement may be canceled or modified.

(vi) All other material terms.

(8) Disclose:

(i) Whether the franchisor must protect the franchisee's right to use the principal trademarks listed in this section, and must protect the franchisee against claims of infringement or unfair competition arising out of the franchisee's use of the trademarks.

(ii) The franchisee's obligation to notify the franchisor of the use of, or claims of rights to, a trademark identical to or confusingly similar to a trademark licensed to the franchisee.

(iii) Whether the franchise agreement requires the franchisor to take affirmative action when notified of these uses or claims.

(iv) Whether the franchisor or franchisee has the right to control any administrative proceedings or litigation involving a trademark licensed by the franchisor to the franchisee.

(v) Whether the franchise agreement requires the franchisor to participate in the franchisee's defense and/or indemnify the franchisee for expenses or damages if the franchisee is a party to an administrative or judicial proceeding involving a trademark licensed by the franchisor to the franchisee, or if the proceeding is resolved unfavorably to the franchisee.

(vi) The franchisee's rights under the franchise agreement if the franchisor requires the franchisee to modify or discontinue using a trademark.

(9) Disclose whether the franchisor knows of either superior prior rights or infringing uses that could materially affect the franchisee's use of the principal trademarks in the state where the franchised business will be located. For each use of a principal trademark that the franchisor believes is an infringement that could materially affect the franchisee's use of a trademark, disclose:

(i) The nature of the infringement.

(ii) The locations where the infringement is occurring.

(iii) The length of time of the infringement (to the extent known).

(iv) Any action taken or anticipated by the franchisor.

(n) *Item 14: Patents, Copyrights, and Proprietary Information.*

(1) Disclose whether the franchisor owns rights in, or licenses to, patents or copyrights that are material to the franchise. Also, disclose whether the franchisor has any pending patent applications that are material to the franchise. If so, state:

(i) The nature of the patent, patent application, or copyright and its relationship to the franchise.

(ii) For each patent:

(A) The duration of the patent.

(B) The type of patent (for example, mechanical, process, or design).

(C) The patent number, issuance date, and title.

(iii) For each patent application:

(A) The type of patent application (for example, mechanical, process, or design).

(B) The serial number, filing date, and title.

(iv) For each copyright:

(A) The duration of the copyright.

(B) The registration number and date.

(C) Whether the franchisor can and intends to renew the copyright.

(2) Describe any current material determination of the United States Patent and Trademark Office, the United States Copyright Office, or a court regarding the patent or copyright. Include the forum and matter number. Describe how the determination affects the franchised business.

(3) State the forum, case number, claims asserted, issues involved, and effective determinations for any material proceeding pending in the United States Patent and Trademark Office or any court.[9]

(4) If an agreement limits the use of the patent, patent application, or copyright, state the parties to and duration of the agreement, the extent to which the agreement may affect the franchisee, and other material terms of the agreement.

(5) Disclose the franchisor's obligation to protect the patent, patent application, or copyright; and to defend the franchisee against claims arising from the franchisee's use of patented or copyrighted items, including:

(i) Whether the franchisor's obligation is contingent upon the franchisee notifying the franchisor of any infringement claims or whether the franchisee's notification is discretionary.

(ii) Whether the franchise agreement requires the franchisor to take affirmative action when notified of infringement.

(iii) Who has the right to control any litigation.

(iv) Whether the franchisor must participate in the defense of a franchisee or indemnify the franchisee for expenses or damages in a proceeding involving a patent, patent application, or copyright licensed to the franchisee.

(v) Whether the franchisor's obligation is contingent upon the franchisee modifying or discontinuing the use of the subject matter covered by the patent or copyright.

(vi) The franchisee's rights under the franchise agreement if the franchisor requires the franchisee to modify or discontinue using the subject matter covered by the patent or copyright.

---

[9] If counsel consents, the franchisor may include a counsel's opinion or a summary of the opinion if the full opinion is attached.

(6) If the franchisor knows of any patent or copyright infringement that could materially affect the franchisee, disclose:

   (i)   The nature of the infringement.
   (ii) The locations where the infringement is occurring.
   (iii) The length of time of the infringement (to the extent known).
   (iv) Any action taken or anticipated by the franchisor.

(7) If the franchisor claims proprietary rights in other confidential information or trade secrets, describe in general terms the proprietary information communicated to the franchisee and the terms for use by the franchisee. The franchisor need only describe the general nature of the proprietary information, such as whether a formula or recipe is considered to be a trade secret.

(o)   *Item 15: Obligation to Participate in the Actual Operation of the Franchise Business.*

(1) Disclose the franchisee's obligation to participate personally in the direct operation of the franchisee's business and whether the franchisor recommends participation. Include obligations arising from any written agreement or from the franchisor's practice.

(2) If personal "on-premises" supervision is not required, disclose the following:

   (i)   If the franchisee is an individual, whether the franchisor recommends on-premises supervision by the franchisee.
   (ii) Limits on whom the franchisee can hire as an on-premises supervisor.
   (iii) Whether an on-premises supervisor must successfully complete the franchisor's training program.
   (iv) If the franchisee is a business entity, the amount of equity interest, if any, that the on-premises supervisor must have in the franchisee's business.

(3) Disclose any restrictions that the franchisee must place on its manager (for example, maintain trade secrets, covenants not to compete).

(p) *Item 16: Restrictions on What the Franchisee May Sell.* Disclose any franchisor-imposed restrictions or conditions on the goods or services that the franchisee may sell or that limit access to customers, including:

(1) Any obligation on the franchisee to sell only goods or services approved by the franchisor.
(2) Any obligation on the franchisee to sell all goods or services authorized by the franchisor.
(3) Whether the franchisor has the right to change the types of authorized goods or services and whether there are limits on the franchisor's right to make changes.

(q) *Item 17: Renewal, Termination, Transfer, and Dispute Resolution.* Disclose, in the following tabular form, a table that cross-references each enumerated franchise relationship item with the applicable provision in the franchise or related agreement. Title the table "THE FRANCHISE RELATIONSHIP" in capital letters and bold type.

(1) Describe briefly each contractual provision. If a particular item is not applicable, state "Not Applicable."

(2) If the agreement is silent about one of the listed provisions, but the franchisor unilaterally offers to provide certain benefits or protections to franchisees as a matter of policy, use a footnote to describe the policy and state whether the policy is subject to change.

(3) In the summary column for Item 17(c), state what the term "renewal" means for your franchise system, including, if applicable, a statement that franchisees may be asked to sign a contract with materially different terms and conditions than their original contract.

Item 17 Table THE FRANCHISE RELATIONSHIP This table lists certain important provisions of the franchise and related agreements. You should read these provisions in the agreements attached to this disclosure document.		
Provision	**Section in Franchise or Other Agreement**	**Summary**
a. Length of the franchise term		
b. Renewal or extension of the term		
c. Requirements for franchisee to renew or extend		
d. Termination by franchisee		
e. Termination by franchisor without cause		
f. Termination by franchisor with cause		
g. "Cause" defined–curable defaults		
h. "Cause" defined–non-curable defaults		
i. Franchisee's obligations on termination on-renewal		
j. Assignment of contract by franchisor		
k. "Transfer" by franchisee–defined		
l. Franchisor approval of transfer by franchisee		
m. Conditions for franchisor approval of transfer		
n. Franchisor's right of first refusal to acquire franchisee's business		
o. Franchisor's option to purchase franchisee's business		
p. Death or disability of franchisee		

Provision	Section in Franchise or Other Agreement	Summary
q. Non-competition covenants during the term of the franchise		
r. Non-competition covenants after the franchise is terminated or expires		
s. Modification of the agreement		
t. Integration/merger clause		
u. Dispute resolution by arbitration or mediation		
v. Choice of forum		
w. Choice of law		

(r) *Item 18: Public Figures.*

Disclose:

(1) Any compensation or other benefit given or promised to a public figure arising from either the use of the public figure in the franchise name or symbol, or the public figure's endorsement or recommendation of the franchise to prospective franchisees.

(2) The extent to which the public figure is involved in the management or control of the franchisor. Describe the public figure's position and duties in the franchisor's business structure.

(3) The public figure's total investment in the franchisor, including the amount the public figure contributed in services performed or to be performed. State the type of investment (for example, common stock, promissory note).

(4) For purposes of this section, a public figure means a person whose name or physical appearance is generally known to the public in the geographic area where the franchise will be located.

(s) *Item 19: Financial Performance Representations.*

(1) Begin by stating the following:

The FTC's Franchise Rule permits a franchisor to provide information about the actual or potential financial performance of its franchised and/or franchisor-owned outlets, if there is a reasonable basis for the information, and if the information is included in the disclosure document. Financial performance information that differs from that included in Item 19 may be given only if: (1) a franchisor provides the actual records of an existing outlet you are considering buying; or (2) a franchisor supplements the information provided in this Item 19, for example, by providing information about possible performance at a particular location or under particular circumstances.

(2) If a franchisor does not provide any financial performance representation in Item 19, also state:

We do not make any representations about a franchisee's future financial performance or the past financial performance of company-owned or franchised outlets. We also do not authorize our employees or representatives to make any such representations either orally or in writing. If you are purchasing an existing outlet, however, we may provide you with the actual records of that outlet. If you receive any other financial performance information or projections of your future income, you should report it to the franchisor's management by contacting [name, address, and telephone number], the Federal Trade Commission, and the appropriate state regulatory agencies.

(3) If the franchisor makes any financial performance representation to prospective franchisees, the franchisor must have a reasonable basis and written substantiation for the representation at the time the representation is made and must state the representation in the Item 19 disclosure. The franchisor must also disclose the following:

(i) Whether the representation is an historic financial performance representation about the franchise system's existing outlets, or a subset of those outlets, or is a forecast of the prospective franchisee's future financial performance.

(ii) If the representation relates to past performance of the franchise system's existing outlets, the material bases for the representation, including:

(A) Whether the representation relates to the performance of all of the franchise system's existing outlets or only to a subset of outlets that share a particular set of characteristics (for example, geographic location, type of location (such as free standing vs. shopping center), degree of competition, length of time the outlets have operated, services or goods sold, services supplied by the franchisor, and whether the outlets are franchised or franchisor-owned or operated).

(B) The dates when the reported level of financial performance was achieved.

(C) The total number of outlets that existed in the relevant period and, if different, the number of outlets that had the described characteristics.

(D) The number of outlets with the described characteristics whose actual financial performance data were used in arriving at the representation.

(E) Of those outlets whose data were used in arriving at the representation, the number and percent that actually attained or surpassed the stated results.

(F) Characteristics of the included outlets, such as those characteristics noted in paragraph (3)(ii)(A) of this section, that may differ materially from those of the outlet that may be offered to a prospective franchisee.

(iii) If the representation is a forecast of future financial performance, state the material bases and assumptions on which the projection is based. The material assumptions underlying a forecast include significant factors upon which a franchisee's future results are expected to depend. These factors include, for example, economic or market conditions that are basic to a franchisee's operation, and encompass matters affecting, among other things, a franchisee's sales, the cost of goods or services sold, and operating expenses.

(iv) A clear and conspicuous admonition that a new franchisee's individual financial results may differ from the result stated in the financial performance representation.

(v) A statement that written substantiation for the financial performance representation will be made available to the prospective franchisee upon reasonable request.

(4) If a franchisor wishes to disclose only the actual operating results for a specific outlet being offered for sale, it need not comply with this section, provided the information is given only to potential purchasers of that outlet.

(5) If a franchisor furnishes financial performance information according to this section, the franchisor may deliver to a prospective franchisee a supplemental financial performance representation about a particular location or variation, apart from the disclosure document. The supplemental representation must:

(i) Be in writing.

(ii) Explain the departure from the financial performance representation in the disclosure document.

(iii) Be prepared in accordance with the requirements of paragraph (s)(3)(i)-(iv) of this section.

(iv) Be furnished to the prospective franchisee.

(t) *Item 20: Outlets and Franchisee Information.*

(1) Disclose, in the following tabular form, the total number of franchised and company-owned outlets for each of the franchisor's last three fiscal years. For purposes of this section, "outlet" includes outlets of a type substantially similar to that offered to the prospective franchisee. A sample Item 20(1) Table is attached as Appendix B to this part.

Item 20 Table No. 1 Systemwide Outlet Summary For years [ ]				
Column 1 Outlet Type	Column 2 Year	Column 3 Outlets at the Start of the Year	Column 4 Outlets at the End of the Year	Column 5 Net Change
Franchised	2004			
	2005			
	2006			
Company-Owned	2004			
	2005			
	2006			
Total Outlets	2004			
	2005			
	2006			

(i) In column 1, include three outlet categories titled "franchised," "company-owned, and "total outlets."

(ii) In column 2, state the last three fiscal years.

(iii) In column 3, state the total number of each type of outlet operating at the beginning of each fiscal year.

(iv) In column 4, state the total number of each type of outlet operating at the end of each fiscal year.

(v) In column 5, state the net change, and indicate whether the change is positive or negative, for each type of outlet during each fiscal year.

(2) Disclose, in the following tabular form, the number of franchised and company-owned outlets and changes in the number and ownership of outlets located in each state during each of the last three fiscal years. Except as noted, each change in ownership shall be reported only once in the following tables. If multiple events occurred in the process of transferring ownership of an outlet, report the event that occurred last in time. If a single outlet changed ownership two or more times during the same fiscal year, use footnotes to describe the types of changes involved and the order in which the changes occurred.

(i) Disclose, in the following tabular form, the total number of franchised outlets transferred in each state during each of the franchisor's last three fiscal years. For purposes of this section, "transfer" means the acquisition of a controlling interest in a franchised outlet, during its term, by a person other than the franchisor or an affiliate. A sample Item 20(2) Table is attached as Appendix C to this part.

Item 20 Table No. 2		
Transfers of Outlets from Franchisees to New Owners (other than the Franchisor)		
For years [ ]		
Column 1 **State**	**Column 2** **Year**	**Column 3** **Number of Transfers**
	2004	
	2005	
	2006	
	2004	
	2005	
	2006	
Totals	2004	
	2005	
	2006	

(A) In column 1, list each state with one or more franchised outlets.

(B) In column 2, state the last three fiscal years.

(C) In column 3, state the total number of completed transfers in each state during each fiscal year.

(ii) Disclose, in the following tabular form, the status of franchisee-owned outlets located in each state for each of the franchisor's last three fiscal years. A sample Item 20(3) Table is attached as Appendix D to this part.

Item 20 Table No. 3 Status of Franchised Outlets For years [ ]				
Column 1 State	Column 2 Year	Column 3 Outlets at Start of the Year	Column 4 Outlets Opened	Column 5 Terminations
	2004			
	2005			
	2006			
	2004			
	2005			
	2006			
Totals	2004			
	2005			
	2006			

Item 20 Table No. 3 Status of Franchised Outlets For years [ ]				
Column 1 State	Column 6 Non-Renewals	Column 7 Reacquired by Franchisor	Column 8 Ceased Operations—Other Reasons	Column 9 Outlets at End of the Year
Totals				

(A) In column 1, list each state with one or more franchised outlets.

(B) In column 2, state the last three fiscal years.

(C) In column 3, state the total number of franchised outlets in each state at the start of each fiscal year.

(D) In column 4, state the total number of franchised outlets opened in each state during each fiscal year. Include both new outlets and existing company-owned outlets that a franchisee purchased from the franchisor. (Also report the number of existing company-owned outlets that are sold to a franchisee in Column 7 of Table 4).

(E) In column 5, state the total number of franchised outlets that were terminated in each state during each fiscal year. For purposes of this section, "termination" means the franchisor's termination of a franchise agreement prior to the end of its term and without providing any consideration to the franchisee (whether by payment or forgiveness or assumption of debt).

(F) In column 6, state the total number of non-renewals in each state during each fiscal year. For purposes of this section, "non-renewal" occurs when the franchise agreement for a franchised outlet is not renewed at the end of its term.

(G) In column 7, state the total number of franchised outlets reacquired by the franchisor in each state during each fiscal year. For purposes of this section, a "reacquisition" means the franchisor's acquisition for consideration (whether by payment or forgiveness or assumption of debt) of a franchised outlet during its term. (Also report franchised outlets reacquired by the franchisor in column 5 of Table 4).

(H) In column 8, state the total number of outlets in each state not operating as one of the franchisor's outlets at the end of each fiscal year for reasons other than termination, non-renewal, or reacquisition by the franchisor.

(I) In column 9, state the total number of franchised outlets in each state at the end of the fiscal year.

(iii) Disclose, in the following tabular form, the status of company-owned outlets located in each state for each of the franchisor's last three fiscal years. A sample Item 20(4) Table is attached as Appendix E to this part.

				Item 20 Table No. 4 Status of Company-Owned Outlets For years [ ]			
Column 1 State	Column 2 Year	Column 3 Outlets at Start of the Year	Column 4 Outlets Opened	Column 5 Outlets Reacquired from Franchisee	Column 6 Outlets Closed	Column 7 Outlets Sold to Franchisee	Column 8 Outlets at End of the Year
	2004						
	2005						
	2006						
	2004						
	2005						
	2006						
Totals	2004						
	2005						
	2006						

(A) In column 1, list each state with one or more company-owned outlets.

(B) In column 2, state the last three fiscal years.

(C) In column 3, state the total number of company-owned outlets in each state at the start of the fiscal year.

(D) In column 4, state the total number of company-owned outlets opened in each state during each fiscal year.

(E) In column 5, state the total number of franchised outlets reacquired from franchisees in each state during each fiscal year.

(F) In column 6, state the total number of company-owned outlets closed in each state during each fiscal year. Include both actual closures and instances when an outlet ceases to operate under the franchisor's trademark.

(G) In column 7, state the total number of company-owned outlets sold to franchisees in each state during each fiscal year.

(H) In column 8, state the total number of company-owned outlets operating in each state at the end of each fiscal year.

(3) Disclose, in the following tabular form, projected new franchised and company-owned outlets. A sample Item 20(5) Table is attached as Appendix F to this part.

Item 20 Table No. 5			
Projected Openings As Of [Last Day of Last Fiscal Year]			
Column 1 State	Column 2 Franchise Agreements Signed but Outlet Not Opened	Column 3 Projected New Franchised Outlet in the Next Fiscal Year	Column 4 Projected New Company-Owned Outlet in the Next Fiscal Year
Total			

(i) In column 1, list each state where one or more franchised or company-owned outlets are located or are projected to be located.

(ii) In column 2, state the total number of franchise agreements that had been signed for new outlets to be located in each state as of the end of the previous fiscal year where the outlet had not yet opened.

(iii) In column 3, state the total number of new franchised outlets in each state projected to be opened during the next fiscal year.

(iv) In column 4, state the total number of new company-owned outlets in each state that are projected to be opened during the next fiscal year.

(4) Disclose the names of all current franchisees and the address and telephone number of each of their outlets. Alternatively, disclose this information for all franchised outlets in the state, but if these franchised outlets total fewer than 100, disclose this information for franchised

outlets from contiguous states and then the next closest states until at least 100 franchised outlets are listed.

(5) Disclose the name, city and state, and current business telephone number, or if unknown, the last known home telephone number of every franchisee who had an outlet terminated, canceled, not renewed, or otherwise voluntarily or involuntarily ceased to do business under the franchise agreement during the most recently completed fiscal year or who has not communicated with the franchisor within 10 weeks of the disclosure document issuance date.[10] State in immediate conjunction with this information: "If you buy this franchise, your contact information may be disclosed to other buyers when you leave the franchise system."

(6) If a franchisor is selling a previously owned franchised outlet now under its control, disclose the following additional information for that outlet for the last five fiscal years. This information may be attached as an addendum to a disclosure document, or, if disclosure has already been made, then in a supplement to the previously furnished disclosure document.

(i) The name, city and state, current business telephone number, or if unknown, last known home telephone number of each previous owner of the outlet;

(ii) The time period when each previous owner controlled the outlet;

(iii) The reason for each previous change in ownership (for example, termination, non-renewal, voluntary transfer, ceased operations); and

(iv) The time period(s) when the franchisor retained control of the outlet (for example, after termination, non-renewal, or reacquisition).

(7) Disclose whether franchisees signed confidentiality clauses during the last three fiscal years. If so, state the following: "In some instances, current and former franchisees sign provisions restricting their ability to speak openly about their experience with [name of franchise system]. You may wish to speak with current and former franchisees, but be aware that not all such franchisees will be able to communicate with you." Franchisors may also disclose the number and percentage of current and former franchisees who during each of the last three fiscal years signed agreements that include confidentiality clauses and may disclose the circumstances under which such clauses were signed.

(8) Disclose, to the extent known, the name, address, telephone number, email address, and Web address (to the extent known) of each trademark-specific franchisee organization associated with the franchise system being offered, if such organization:

(i) Has been created, sponsored, or endorsed by the franchisor. If so, state the relationship between the organization and the franchisor (for example, the organization was created by the franchisor, sponsored by the franchisor, or endorsed by the franchisor).

(ii) Is incorporated or otherwise organized under state law and asks the franchisor to be included in the franchisor's disclosure document during the next fiscal year. Such

---

[10] Franchisors may substitute alternative contact information at the request of the former franchisee, such as a home address, post office address, or a personal or business email address.

organizations must renew their request on an annual basis by submitting a request no later than 60 days after the close of the franchisor's fiscal year. The franchisor has no obligation to verify the organization's continued existence at the end of each fiscal year. Franchisors may also include the following statement: "The following independent franchisee organizations have asked to be included in this disclosure document."

(u) *Item 21: Financial Statements.*

(1) Include the following financial statements prepared according to United States generally accepted accounting principles, as revised by any future United States government mandated accounting principles, or as permitted by the Securities and Exchange Commission. Except as provided in paragraph (u)(2) of this section, these financial statements must be audited by an independent certified public accountant using generally accepted United States auditing standards. Present the required financial statements in a tabular form that compares at least two fiscal years.

   (i) The franchisor's balance sheet for the previous two fiscal year-ends before the disclosure document issuance date.

   (ii) Statements of operations, stockholders equity, and cash flows for each of the franchisor's previous three fiscal years.

   (iii) Instead of the financial disclosures required by paragraphs (u)(1)(i) and (ii) of this section, the franchisor may include financial statements of any of its affiliates if the affiliate's financial statements satisfy paragraphs (u)(1)(i) and (ii) of this section and the affiliate absolutely and unconditionally guarantees to assume the duties and obligations of the franchisor under the franchise agreement. The affiliate's guarantee must cover all of the franchisor's obligations to the franchisee, but need not extend to third parties. If this alternative is used, attach a copy of the guarantee to the disclosure document.

   (iv) When a franchisor owns a direct or beneficial controlling financial interest in a subsidiary, its financial statements should reflect the financial condition of the franchisor and its subsidiary.

   (v) Include separate financial statements for the franchisor and any subfranchisor, as well as for any parent that commits to perform post-sale obligations for the franchisor or guarantees the franchisor's obligations. Attach a copy of any guarantee to the disclosure document.

(2) A startup franchise system that does not yet have audited financial statements may phase-in the use of audited financial statements by providing, at a minimum, the following statements at the indicated times:

(i) The franchisor' first partial or full fiscal year selling franchises.	An unaudited opening balance sheet.
(ii) The franchisor' second fiscal year selling franchises.	Audited balance sheet opinion as of the end of the first partial or full fiscal year selling franchises.
(iii) The franchisor' third and subsequent fiscal years selling franchises.	All required financial statements for the previous fiscal year, plus any previously disclosed audited statements that still must be disclosed according to paragraphs (u)(1)(i) and (ii) of this section.

(iv) Startup franchisors may phase-in the disclosure of audited financial statements, provided the franchisor:

(A) Prepares audited financial statements as soon as practicable.

(B) Prepares unaudited statements in a format that conforms as closely as possible to audited statements.

(C) Includes one or more years of unaudited financial statements or clearly and conspicuously discloses in this section that the franchisor has not been in business for three years or more, and cannot include all financial statements required in paragraphs (u)(1)(i) and (ii) of this section.

(v) *Item 22: Contracts.* Attach a copy of all proposed agreements regarding the franchise offering, including the franchise agreement and any lease, options, and purchase agreements.

(w) *Item 23: Receipts.* Include two copies of the following detachable acknowledgment of receipt in the following form as the last pages of the disclosure document:

(1) State the following:

Receipt

This disclosure document summarizes certain provisions of the franchise agreement and other information in plain language. Read this disclosure document and all agreements carefully.

If [name of franchisor] offers you a franchise, it must provide this disclosure document to you 14 calendar-days before you sign a binding agreement with, or make a payment to, the franchisor or an affiliate in connection with the proposed franchise sale.

If [name of franchisor] does not deliver this disclosure document on time or if it contains a false or misleading statement, or a material omission, a violation of federal law and state law may have occurred and should be reported to the Federal Trade Commission, Washington, D.C. 20580 and [state agency].

(2) Disclose the name, principal business address, and telephone number of each franchise seller offering the franchise.

(3) State the issuance date.

(4) If not disclosed in paragraph (a) of this section, state the name and address of the franchisor's registered agent authorized to receive service of process.

(5) State the following:

I received a disclosure document dated _____ that included the following Exhibits:

(6) List the title(s) of all attached Exhibits.

(7) Provide space for the prospective franchisee's signature and date.

(8) Franchisors may include any specific instructions for returning the receipt (for example, street address, email address, facsimile telephone number).

Subpart D—Instructions

§ 436.6 Instructions for Preparing Disclosure Documents

(a) It is an unfair or deceptive act or practice in violation of Section 5 of the FTC Act for any franchisor to fail to include the information and follow the instructions for preparing disclosure documents set forth in Subpart C (basic disclosure requirements) and Subpart D (updating requirements) of part 436. The Commission will enforce this provision according to the standards of liability under Sections 5, 13(b), and 19 of the FTC Act.

(b) Disclose all required information clearly, legibly, and concisely in a single document using plain English. The disclosures must be in a form that permits each prospective franchisee to store, download, print, or otherwise maintain the document for future reference.

(c) Respond fully to each disclosure Item. If a disclosure Item is not applicable, respond negatively, including a reference to the type of information required to be disclosed by the Item. Precede each disclosure Item with the appropriate heading.

(d) Do not include any materials or information other than those required or permitted by part 436 or by state law not preempted by part 436. For the sole purpose of enhancing the prospective franchisee's ability to maneuver through an electronic version of a disclosure document, the franchisor may include scroll bars, internal links, and search features. All other features (e.g., multimedia tools such as audio, video, animation, pop-up screens, or links to external information) are prohibited.

(e) Franchisors may prepare multi-state disclosure documents by including non-preempted, state-specific information in the text of the disclosure document or in Exhibits attached to the disclosure document.

(f) Subfranchisors shall disclose the required information about the franchisor, and, to the extent applicable, the same information concerning the subfranchisor.

(g) Before furnishing a disclosure document, the franchisor shall advise the prospective franchisee of the formats in which the disclosure document is made available, any prerequisites for obtaining the disclosure document in a particular format, and any conditions necessary for reviewing the disclosure document in a particular format.

(h) Franchisors shall retain, and make available to the Commission upon request, a sample copy of each materially different version of their disclosure documents for three years after the close of the fiscal year when it was last used.

(i) For each completed franchise sale, franchisors shall retain a copy of the signed receipt for at least three years.

§ 436.7 Instructions for Updating Disclosures

(a) All information in the disclosure document shall be current as of the close of the franchisor's most recent fiscal year. After the close of the fiscal year, the franchisor shall, within 120 days, prepare a revised disclosure document, after which a franchise seller may distribute only the revised document and no other disclosure document.

(b) The franchisor shall, within a reasonable time after the close of each quarter of the fiscal year, prepare revisions to be attached to the disclosure document to reflect any material change to the disclosures included, or required to be included, in the disclosure document. Each prospective franchisee shall receive the disclosure document and the quarterly revisions for the most recent period available at the time of disclosure.

(c) If applicable, the annual update shall include the franchisor's first quarterly update, either by incorporating the quarterly update information into the disclosure document itself, or through an addendum.

(d) When furnishing a disclosure document, the franchise seller shall notify the prospective franchisee of any material changes that the seller knows or should have known occurred in the information contained in any financial performance representation made in Item 19 (section 436.5(s)).

(e) Information that must be audited pursuant to § 436.5(u) of this part need not be audited for quarterly revisions; provided, however, that the franchisor states in immediate conjunction with the information that such information was not audited.

SUBPART E—EXEMPTIONS

§ 436.8 Exemptions

(a) The provisions of part 436 shall not apply if the franchisor can establish any of the following:

(1) The total of the required payments, or commitments to make a required payment, to the franchisor or an affiliate that are made any time from before to within six months after commencing operation of the franchisee's business is less than $500.

(2) The franchise relationship is a fractional franchise.

(3) The franchise relationship is a leased department.

(4) The franchise relationship is covered by the Petroleum Marketing Practices Act, 15 U.S.C. 2801

(5)

    (i) The franchisee's initial investment, excluding any financing received from the franchisor or an affiliate and excluding the cost of unimproved land, totals at least $1 million and the prospective franchisee signs an acknowledgment verifying the grounds for the exemption. The acknowledgment shall state: "The franchise sale is for more than $1 million—

excluding the cost of unimproved land and any financing received from the franchisor or an affiliate—and thus is exempted from the Federal Trade Commission's Franchise Rule disclosure requirements, pursuant to 16 CFR 436.8(a)(5)(i)"; or

(ii) The franchisee (or its parent or any affiliates) is an entity that has been in business for at least five years and has a net worth of at least $5 million.

(6) One or more purchasers of at least a 50% ownership interest in the franchise: within 60 days of the sale, has been, for at least two years, an officer, director, general partner, individual with management responsibility for the offer and sale of the franchisor's franchises or the administrator of the franchised network; or within 60 days of the sale, has been, for at least two years, an owner of at least a 25% interest in the franchisor.

(7) There is no written document that describes any material term or aspect of the relationship or arrangement.

(a) The large franchise exemption applies only if at least one individual prospective franchisee in an investor-group qualifies for the exemption by investing at the threshold level stated in this section.

(b) For purposes of the exemptions set forth in this section, the Commission shall adjust the size of the monetary thresholds every fourth year based upon the Consumer Price Index. For purposes of this section, "Consumer Price Index" means the Consumer Price Index for all urban consumers published by the Department of Labor.

SUBPART F—PROHIBITIONS

§ 436.9 Additional Prohibitions

It is an unfair or deceptive act or practice in violation of Section 5 of the Federal Trade Commission Act for any franchise seller covered by part 436 to:

(a) Make any claim or representation, orally, visually, or in writing, that contradicts the information required to be disclosed by this part.

(b) Misrepresent that any person:

(1) Purchased a franchise from the franchisor or operated a franchise of the type offered by the franchisor.

(2) Can provide an independent and reliable report about the franchise or the experiences of any current or former franchisees.

(c) Disseminate any financial performance representations to prospective franchisees unless the franchisor has a reasonable basis and written substantiation for the representation at the time the representation is made, and the representation is included in Item 19 (§ 436.5(s)) of the franchisor's disclosure document. In conjunction with any such financial performance representation, the franchise seller shall also:

(1) Disclose the information required by §§ 436.5(s)(3)(ii)(B) and (E) of this part if the representation relates to the past performance of the franchisor's outlets.

(2) Include a clear and conspicuous admonition that a new franchisee's individual financial results may differ from the result stated in the financial performance representation.

(d) Fail to make available to prospective franchisees, and to the Commission upon reasonable request, written substantiation for any financial performance representations made in Item 19 (§ 436.5(s)).

(e) Fail to furnish a copy of the franchisor's disclosure document to a prospective franchisee earlier in the sales process than required under § 436.2 of this part, upon reasonable request.

(f) Fail to furnish a copy of the franchisor's most recent disclosure document and any quarterly updates to a prospective franchisee, upon reasonable request, before the prospective franchisee signs a franchise agreement.

(g) Present for signing a franchise agreement in which the terms and conditions differ materially from those presented as an attachment to the disclosure document, unless the franchise seller informed the prospective franchisee of the differences at least seven days before execution of the franchise agreement.

(h) Disclaim or require a prospective franchisee to waive reliance on any representation made in the disclosure document or in its exhibits or amendments. Provided, however, that this provision is not intended to prevent a prospective franchisee from voluntarily waiving specific contract terms and conditions set forth in his or her disclosure document during the course of franchise sale negotiations.

(i) Fail to return any funds or deposits in accordance with any conditions disclosed in the franchisor's disclosure document, franchise agreement, or any related document.

SUBPART G—OTHER PROVISIONS

§ 436.10 Other Laws and Rules

(a) The Commission does not approve or express any opinion on the legality of any matter a franchisor may be required to disclose by part 436. Further, franchisors may have additional obligations to impart material information to prospective franchisees outside of the disclosure document under Section 5 of the Federal Trade Commission Act. The Commission intends to enforce all applicable statutes and rules.

(b) The FTC does not intend to preempt the franchise practices laws of any state or local government, except to the extent of any inconsistency with part 436. A law is not inconsistent with part 436 if it affords prospective franchisees equal or greater protection, such as registration of disclosure documents or more extensive disclosures.

§ 436.11 Severability

If any provision of this part is stayed or held invalid, the remainder will stay in force.

Franchise Resources

Franchise Attorney

Michael Katz

Corporon and Katz Attorneys at
Law

Michael@businesslawyer.com

www.businesslawyer.com

(888) 287-6777

(303) 790-4103

Franchise Developer and Consultant

Rick Grossmann

Enspiren Inc.

rgrossman@enspiren.com

www.enspiren.com

(303) 378-2221

Franchise Education

Franchise U

Info@FranchiseU.com

www.FranchiseU.com

Franchise Owner Coach

Brian Destarac

Cobalt Business Solutions

brian@cobaltbusiness.com

www.cobaltbusiness.com

(888) 444-0088

International Franchise Association

www.franchise.org

1501 K St., N.W., Ste. 350

Washington, DC 20005

Phone: (202) 628-8000

Fax: (202) 628-0812

Small Business Administration (SBA) Franchise Registry

www.franchiseregistry.com

franchiseregistry@frandata.com

(800) 485-9570

Entrepreneur.com

Find franchise opportunities and small business franchises for sale. Includes franchising costs, fees, training, and rankings information online. http://www.entrepreneur.com/

Entrepreneur's Franchise 500

Annual ranking of America's top franchise opportunities http://www.entrepreneur.com/franchise500/index.html

Entrepreneur Magazine Franchise-Focused Issues

JANUARY—FRANCHISE 500®

Each January, Entrepreneur offers the world's most comprehensive listing of franchises in the Franchise 500®

FEBRUARY—FASTEST-GROWING FRANCHISES

These franchises put the pedal to the metal and are looking to smash records with their full-throttle growth.

MARCH—TOP NEW FRANCHISES

Entrepreneur names the top new franchises

APRIL—TOP FOOD FRANCHISES/MULTI-UNIT FRANCHISES

This feature lists the top food franchises and it's a good resource guide for current and upcoming franchisees that are interested in multi-unit franchises.

About the Authors

Erwin James Keup

Erwin ("Erv") Keup graduated from Marquette University with a B.S. degree in business administration in 1953 and received his law degree from Marquette Law School in 1958 after serving in the United States Army. He held corporate law department positions with Miller Brewing Company in Milwaukee, Wisconsin, Glidden Paint Company in Huron, Ohio, and Snelling and Snelling, a personnel agency franchisor located at that time in Philadelphia, Pennsylvania. He then established a private law practice in Newport Beach, California, and helped hundreds of franchisors expand their businesses. During his 51 years in practice, he specialized in franchise law, franchise consulting, and general corporate and business law. He was a member of the American and California Bar Associations. He was admitted to the Supreme Court of Ohio and California and was a former member of the Wisconsin Bar Association. He was also a member of the American Bar Association's Forum on Franchising, served as an arbitrator and mediator in franchise disputes, and conducted seminars on franchising and franchise law. In addition to *Franchise Bible*, he authored the *Mail Order Legal Guide* and numerous business articles on franchising.

Erv was a talented and conscientious attorney and a caring family man, who assiduously guided and assisted his clients, and his children and grandchildren, no matter what obstacles or resistance he faced. He lived his life with great passion, knowing what mattered most, and offered his insight to all who were willing to open their ears, hearts, and minds. On October 16, 2011, Erv passed away peacefully at his home in Costa Mesa, California, after a brief battle with cancer. He is survived by his wife, Mary; his eight children, Chris, Ellen, Craig, Kenny, Maricay, Karen, Elaine, and Peter; and his seventeen grandchildren.

Peter Erwin Keup

Peter Keup is Erv's youngest child. Peter graduated from the University of San Diego with a degree in business economics in 1992 and with a law degree from the University of California Hastings College of the Law in 1995. Peter has extensive experience as an attorney in both private and public practice, including working as a United States District Court law clerk and as in-house counsel at the Los Angeles Unified School District, which is the second largest school district in the nation. Peter currently works for the firm of Boykin & Davis in Columbia, South Carolina, and is an adjunct professor in the School of Education at the University of South Carolina, teaching graduate school education law courses. He is married to Jennifer Keup and they have two sons, Aidan and Shane.

Index